P9-DDA-075

DISMANTLING CANADA

DISMANTLING CANADA

Stephen Harper's New Conservative Agenda

BROOKE JEFFREY

with liberal good wishes

Brooke Jeffrey

McGill-Queen's University Press
Montreal & Kingston • London • Ithaca

ISBN 978-0-7735-4481-9 (cloth)
ISBN 978-0-7735-8250-7 (ePDF)
ISBN 978-0-7735-8251-4 (ePUB)

Legal deposit first quarter 2015
Bibliothèque nationale du Québec

Printed in Canada on acid-free paper that is 100% ancient forest free (100% post-consumer recycled), processed chlorine free

McGill-Queen's University Press acknowledges the support of the Canada Council for the Arts for our publishing program. We also acknowledge the financial support of the Government of Canada through the Canada Book Fund for our publishing activities.

Library and Archives Canada Cataloguing in Publication

Jeffrey, Brooke, author
Dismantling Canada: Stephen Harper's new conservative agenda / Brooke Jeffrey.

Includes bibliographical references and index.
Issued in print and electronic formats.
ISBN 978-0-7735-4481-9 (bound). – ISBN 978-0-7735-8250-7 (ePDF). – ISBN 978-0-7735-8251-4 (ePUB)

1. Harper, Stephen, 1959–. 2. Conservative Party of Canada. 3. Conservatism – Canada. 4. Canada – Politics and government – 2006–. I. Title.

FC640.J44 2015 971.07'3 C2014-907580-4
C2014-907581-2

This book was typeset by Interscript in 10.5/13 Sabon.

For Bill and Yvonne

Contents

Acknowledgments

Over the past two years while I was working on this book, many individuals provided valuable background information and assistance in locating sources. Others were most helpful in suggesting additional avenues of exploration. Several of them, including a number of former parliamentarians and bureaucrats, graciously agreed to lengthy interviews. However, virtually all of them declined to be identified, either in the manuscript or in the acknowledgments, a singularly revealing indicator of the climate of fear permeating the federal government and official Ottawa under the Harper administration. But as many of them noted, after nine years in power there is now so much material available on the public record that their own contributions, while useful to me, merely serve to reinforce what is becoming widely apparent. Nevertheless, I am grateful to them for taking the time to assist me along the way, and trust they will recognize themselves and their contributions in this text.

As always, I am also grateful for the support and encouragement I have received from colleagues and students at Concordia University, as well as the thoughtful and insightful comments on earlier drafts provided by several reviewers. They not only forced me to refine and occasionally clarify or expand on my initial arguments, but saved me from a number of minor, but potentially embarrassing, mistakes.

This book would never have seen the light of day without the gentle prodding of Jacqueline Mason, my very supportive editor at McGill-Queen's University Press, who successfully convinced me to undertake this project in the first place, despite my initial reluctance to take on yet another multi-year commitment. I am also grateful to my very efficient and long-suffering copy editor, Patricia Kennedy, and to Ryan Van Huijstee, managing editor at MQUP, for shepherding the final draft through to publication in record time.

Finally, a huge debt of gratitude is owed to my endlessly supportive husband, whose technological expertise saved the day more than once, and to family and friends who were forced to endure regular progress reports. My thanks to all for their patience and understanding.

DISMANTLING CANADA

Introduction

I think the country has unlimited potential. That's why I think it would be so exciting to realize that potential.

Stephen Harper, when asked by a reporter
"Do you love this country?"
29 November 2005

A new approach can draw in new people. Many traditional Liberal voters, especially from key ethnic and immigrant communities, will be attracted to a party with strong traditional views of values and family. This is similar to the phenomenon of the Reagan Democrats in the United States, who were so important in the development of the conservative coalition there.

Stephen Harper, 2003

Stephen Harper is a man of many firsts, each more impressive than the last. In 2003 he became the first leader of the merged Reform/Alliance Party and the venerable Progressive Conservative Party, a merger which only a few years earlier would have been unthinkable. In 2006 he became the first prime minister to represent the new Conservative Party of Canada, a victory which would have been inconceivable less than six years earlier. In fact, when the Liberals secured their third successive majority victory in 2000, political scientist Bruce Doern wrote, "Jean Chrétien stands astride the political scene without much effective opposition at the federal level."[1]

The magnitude of Harper's accomplishment is reinforced by the speed with which it was achieved. In 2002 he managed to come back from the political wilderness to take over the struggling Alliance Party from Stockwell Day. The following year he orchestrated a hostile takeover of the Progressive Conservative Party. These actions alone speak volumes about Harper's determination, strategic skills, and ability to outmanoeuvre opponents, attributes which have been outlined in detail by former advisers and colleagues.[2] Then, after a closely fought battle in the 2004 federal election, which reduced the previously unbeatable Liberals to a slim minority under the hapless Paul Martin, Harper required less than two years to turn his long-held dream of a Canada governed by a right-wing conservative party into a reality.

But Harper was not in power simply to implement specific right-wing policies, or to eliminate some long-resented Liberal programs, although these were certainly important short-term objectives. He was a man with a mission. He made this crystal clear in his 2011 victory speech, when he became the first Canadian political leader to declare that his long-term objectives included nothing less than the destruction of his political opposition, the despised Liberal Party of Canada, and the remaking of the political culture of the country he was about to govern, a country he could not say he loved.

Harper made considerable progress in implementing his short-term objectives, despite five years of minority government. This fact was underlined by Conservative pundit Tim Powers at a conference in the fall of 2010. Powers told participants that Harper no longer believed it was essential to obtain a parliamentary majority to accomplish much of his agenda. In a revealing comment, which spoke to Harper's single-minded focus and unprecedented control of the levers of power, Powers attributed the prime minister's confidence to the fact that he had already implemented a great deal of his agenda through non-legislative means, bypassing parliament.

Nevertheless, Harper was intent on achieving a majority and, in the May 2011 election, he succeeded. Moreover, he did it by becoming the first prime minister to form a majority government without the support of the province of Quebec, and without significant representation from the major urban centres of Canada, two extraordinary developments that would have far-reaching consequences.

Since then, Harper has wasted little time implementing the legislative side of his agenda, introducing sweeping reforms in several major policy areas, while maintaining an iron grip on virtually all aspects of governance. With the next federal election not scheduled until October 2015, the potential for the Harper Conservatives to effect even greater change is undeniable.

There can be little doubt that, if Stephen Harper is successful in implementing his agenda, he will have fundamentally changed the country. Indeed, the change that he envisages is nothing short of revolutionary. In virtually every policy field his objectives – and his very definition of what constitutes the issues of the day that require his government's attention – fly in the face of more than a century of successive policy direction by Liberal and Progressive Conservative governments. In this regard, it is important to note that Mr Harper has been almost as critical of his Progressive Conservative predecessors as of the Liberal Party, and that many Progressive Conservative politicians, such as former prime minister Joe Clark have actively resisted and even disowned Harper's new party.

Many people in Canada and around the world have wondered how it was possible for someone whose views are so far removed from the mainstream to be elected, never mind to form a majority government. And how has it been possible for him to remain in power for more than eight years with so little visible opposition outside parliament? Have Canadians, and perhaps Canada itself, changed so dramatically? Has our political culture actually shifted to the right, as some people have speculated? Have Canadians become less liberal-minded, and indeed more conservative, in the face of contemporary issues and challenges? Is the new Conservative Party well on its way to becoming the natural governing party?

This book attempts to answer some of the fundamental questions raised by the Harper Conservatives' remarkable success. First and foremost, it explains *why* they are so determined to change the very nature of the country, and *how* have they managed to win power and implement so much of their agenda so quickly. It examines *what* actual policy changes they have made so far, and whether these changes are likely to be permanent. Finally, it outlines their efforts to achieve their long-term objective of replacing the Liberal Party as he natural governing party, and evaluates their prospects for success.

It begins by exploring the underlying philosophy that motivates Harper's drive to remake Canada, namely, a new brand of conservatism that combines economic, social, and moral conservative values. Stephen Harper's philosophical approach to government is unique in the Canadian context. It rejects outright the liberal thinking that has dominated Canadian politics for so long. Nor is his party simply an updated version of the Progressive Conservatives. He does not share their Tory roots either, despite his relentless campaign to convince Canadians that his party is the unbroken continuation of the progressive Tory tradition of Sir John A. Macdonald. Indeed, both of the mainstream political parties that have formed national governments in Canada – the Liberals and the Progressive Conservatives – have shared a commitment to the underlying values and principles of modern liberalism, such as individual rights, equality of opportunity, tolerance of diversity, and a belief in the potential role of the state as a force for good.

The Canada Stephen Harper found so unappetizing is one that epitomized a liberal culture, albeit one that was shaped by its unique set of founding characteristics. As a result, Canada's political culture was not only liberal, but leaned further to the "left" than most European conceptions of liberalism (to say nothing of those of the United States), influenced as it was by the influx of both British Tory and eastern European socialist strands of political thought that came with the immigrants arriving during its formative years. The result has been a deep-seated commitment to the collective well-being, and an emphasis on fair and equitable treatment of all citizens across regional, linguistic, and cultural divides. In concrete terms, this has led to the development of the various programs of the welfare state, equalization, and the Charter of Rights and Freedoms, all of which are viewed by the vast majority of Canadians as important elements of national identity. It has also led to the withdrawal of the state from areas of personal morality, and at the same time to a significant role for the state in levelling the economic playing field.

While there have always been genuine differences between the Progressive Conservatives and the Liberals, the two major national parties that have formed a federal government in the past, and they may disagree on the appropriate means to achieve some of these objectives, or on the details of specific policy initiatives, there has also been a long-standing consensus on these underlying values, one that has fixed the parameters of acceptable political debate in Canada. Nowhere have these parameters been more clearly defined than in the case of medicare, where, for example, Progressive Conservative leader Brian Mulroney took great pains during the 1984 election campaign to declare that this program was "a sacred trust." Similar examples can be found in Progressive Conservative support for bilingualism (which led PC leader Robert Stanfield to refuse to sign the nomination papers of anti-French activist Leonard Jones) and PC leader Joe Clark's support for the Charter of Rights and Freedoms and legalization of same-sex marriage.

Instead, Harper's conservatism is inspired by Margaret Thatcher and Ronald Reagan (and by earlier conservative philosophers, such as Hobbes and Burke), and is much further to the "right" than anything seen in Canada before the emergence of the Reform Party, of which he was a founding member.[3] As a result, this new conservatism is almost diametrically opposed to the modern liberal values underpinning Canadian politics. For these conservatives, individual freedom trumps the role of government in the economy and society. The programs of the welfare state are viewed not as a public good but as unacceptable entitlements that detract from personal responsibility, while measures to ensure consumer safety or environmental protection are viewed as unacceptable intrusions into the marketplace, which should be left to police itself. Indeed, for them the ideal role of the state is as minimalist as possible, the so-called "nightwatchman" model. At the same time, since these conservatives prioritize values such as authority, loyalty, and justice over liberal values of compassion, tolerance, or compromise, they are prepared to utilize the power of the state to impose order, exact retribution, and take rigidly moral stands at home and abroad. Harper himself has made it clear that he sees modern liberalism as a form of "moral nihilism," which fails to take any moral stands at all, and consequently represents a serious threat to the traditional family and conventional society.[4]

This new conservatism is accompanied by an unswerving belief in the rightness of its views. Opposing views are therefore seen not merely as different, but wrong. This, too, is a trait shared with Margaret Thatcher in the UK and the New Right Republicans in the US. The Harper Conservatives' refusal to compromise, often described as taking "principled" policy positions, is equally unfamiliar to Canadians, and to a Canadian political culture that has also traditionally valued moderation and compromise in its governments, whatever their political stripe.

This leads logically back to the question of how someone with such different views could succeed in capturing enough of the popular vote to win three successive elections, albeit two of them minorities. Many analysts have pointed to the nature of Canada's first-past-the-post electoral system, which allowed Harper to win a majority with only 39 per cent of the popular vote, and to the ever-decreasing level of voter participation, which disadvantages the Liberals, because their supporters are most likely to stay home. Others, such as political scientists Jon Pammett and Lawrence LeDuc, have drawn attention to the cyclical nature of Canadian politics over time, in which lengthy and predominantly Liberal "dynasties" have been interspersed with brief, primarily Progressive Conservative, "interludes."[5] They conclude that a dynasty's demise frequently is brought about by scandal and accusations of corruption or incompetence, a development that becomes increasingly likely the longer the dynasty is in power. Put another way, it is often more accurate to say that governments are defeated, rather than that their opponents are elected.

Certainly a case can be made that these factors play a part in explaining the Harper Conservatives' victories. Their timing, for example, was fortuitous, coming together as a united right-wing political party at the precise moment when the Chrétien/Martin dynasty was on the brink of collapse under the self-inflicted burden of the Adscam scandal and the Gomery Commission. Moreover, as Pammett and LeDuc also outline, there have been at least four major yardsticks on which Canadians typically evaluate political parties during election campaigns, regardless of policy platform details: leadership, administrative competence, commitment to social policy, and ability to manage national unity. Once again, Harper could hardly have timed his arrival better, as the Liberals under a succession of incompetent leaders, from Martin to Dion and Ignatieff, led Canadians to conclude that Harper by comparison was the most effective leader and his party the most competent, by default.[6] In this sense, then, Harper's Conservatives can be seen to have enjoyed electoral success *in spite of* their underlying conservative values – which they tried hard to keep in check in any event – rather than *because* of them. And they know it. Hence Stephen Harper's remarkable statement on the eve of the 2006 election: that Canadians could safely trust him with a majority because the bureaucracy, the Senate, and the Supreme Court were all filled with Liberal appointees who would ensure he could not impose his hidden agenda.

However these various factors do not adequately explain the electoral success of the Harper Conservatives. The very fact that they were unable to obtain even 40 per cent of the popular vote, after three tries, speaks volumes about the skepticism of the electorate towards this new breed of conservative. (Hence the importance of the "hidden agenda" theme raised by the Liberals and New Democrats in all three federal elections.) The question remains, then, as to how the Harper Conservatives were able to overcome the mistrust and profound concern of a sufficient number of voters about their underlying values and beliefs.

As this book outlines, there are several reasons. To begin with, Harper worked diligently to move his party's *image* towards the political centre, downplaying the extremist viewpoints expressed by previous leaders, such as Preston Manning and Stockwell Day (even if they were views he shared), all the while claiming to be the new incarnation of the Progressive Conservative Party, and thereby retaining many loyal Tory voters and reassuring substantial numbers of those Canadians who were undecided but anxious about his "hidden agenda." But it was his intimate knowledge of the tactics of key right-wing Republicans, and his ability to adapt them so successfully to the Canadian context, that were crucial to his electoral success. Like his Republican counterparts, Harper was always well aware of his party's underdog status, and knew he would have to employ a variety of unprecedented strategies in order to overcome this disadvantage. As a result, he is the first Canadian political leader to focus on building a narrow, targeted coalition of voters sufficient to achieve electoral success, while simply ignoring large segments of the population that he knew he could not win over to his cause. Subsequently, as prime minister, he has been the first to devote so much political attention and financial resources to retaining that coalition, often at the expense of the national interest or the public good.

Similarly, in order to convert his minority to a majority, and to implement as much of his agenda as possible, as quickly as possible, he has religiously followed the example of the Republicans' New Right strategists in shutting down public opposition to his plans, and finding new ways to communicate his own message to the public. Less than a decade ago, few Canadians would have believed that a federal government that shunned the national media, marginalized and even attacked various elements of civil society, and repeatedly ignored the public warnings of experts, provincial premiers, and opinion leaders, would be able to dominate the political scene as quickly or as completely as the Harper Conservatives.

Here, too, Harper has broken new ground. His government's suppression of dissent, iron-fisted control over information, disregard for parliamentary procedure and judicial rulings, and determination to ignore scientific evidence, contradict virtually all established norms of political behaviour in this country. With little or no access to accurate information or informed policy debate, the public has been successfully misled or kept in the dark on many of his most controversial policy initiatives, demonstrating the extent to which a determined government can execute policy by stealth.

Meanwhile, Harper's adoption of the New Right's innovative strategy of the "permanent campaign" has resulted in unprecedented expenditures of public and party money for self-promotion and advertising propaganda in support of his agenda. More importantly, he has used the tools of power to establish other groundbreaking precedents, which arguably have gone some distance towards "Harperizing" Canadians' views of his party and its hold on power.[7] And, in spite of initial setbacks, he has successfully eliminated much public financing for his political opponents, while maintaining an unprecedented private-sector fundraising machine of his own.

Yet another important consideration in understanding both the motivation and the apparent success of the Harper Conservatives is the inherent dichotomy between philosophy and pragmatism which confronts them on an almost daily basis. As Harper's former mentor, University of Calgary professor Tom Flanagan, frequently noted, despite the Conservatives' achievement of majority government, Canada's political culture remained inherently liberal. As a result, Harper agreed that much of the real conservative agenda could only be accomplished slowly and incrementally if the Conservatives were to avoid political disaster. But he also recognized that a pragmatic realism was necessary, even if it amounted to adopting a liberal measure (such as stimulus spending), or avoiding a conservative one (such as abortion), in order to stay in power. Quite simply, living to fight another day, while actively attempting to change the liberal political culture that forces them to be pragmatic, is an underlying imperative of Harper's agenda, and its importance should never be underestimated.

Moreover it is this inherent conflict between conservative ideology and pragmatic politics that explains many of the Harper Conservatives' most perplexing and unexpected policy decisions and outright policy reversals. As the second half of this book reveals, such conflicts have taken place in virtually every policy field. For example, Stephen Harper had not been in power six months when he astonished observers by introducing a resolution in the House of Commons recognizing Quebec as a nation, pragmatically seizing an opportunity to undercut his Liberal opponents and simultaneously strengthen his standing with Quebec nationalists, whom he coveted as part of his coalition. That the motion contradicted his longstanding opposition to special status for Quebec, as demonstrated in his earlier vigorous rejection of the Meech Lake and Charlottetown accords, did not deter him in the slightest from taking advantage of this opportunity. Likewise, having repeatedly rejected any form of government intervention to provide economic stimulus in the face of the 2008 global recession, Harper suddenly reversed himself when it appeared his re-election was in peril, and his government subsequently allocated billions of dollars for stimulus measures through their Economic Action Plan budgets. Then, having run up a significant deficit as a result of the tax cuts and stimulus spending, Harper's government embarked upon a draconian series of cuts to government programs and personnel, all the while committing some $45 billion to the purchase of F-35 fighter jets and spending more than $30 million to commemorate the obscure War of 1812.

Throughout these "necessary" deviations in the name of political expediency, however, Harper has never lost sight of his objectives or his agenda. Having explored the why and the how of his stunning rise to power, the book will examine *what* Stephen Harper and his new Conservative Party have actually accomplished. Without question, his determination to reduce the size and impact of the federal government, to restore order and respect for family values, to eliminate much of the welfare state, and to take a principled stand internationally against evil empires, has been made manifest not just in the rhetoric of Harper and his ministers, but in countless policy measures introduced by his government. And, as he made perfectly clear in his comments at the party's November 2013 convention in Calgary, he "couldn't care less" what his opponents and critics think. To paraphrase his idol Margaret Thatcher, it would seem that "the gentleman is not for turning."

Still, after nearly eight years in power, Stephen Harper remains a mystery to most Canadians. Considered by many to be austere, secretive, and even anti-social, as well as ruthless and hyperpartisan, he is neither loved nor admired, despite receiving consistently high approval ratings for competence and leadership. More surprising, perhaps, is the fact that many Canadians are still unfamiliar with some of the measures he has put in place to implement his agenda, to say nothing of their ignorance of the long-term consequences of those measures. While jobs, health care, the environment, and the growing gap between rich and poor are repeatedly identified as their greatest concerns, Harper's government has consistently focused on the military, law and order, immigration, and tax cuts. Likewise, Canadians continue to support government intervention to protect the environment and reduce the impact of climate change, while almost all of the Conservatives' actions have been diametrically opposed. Yet these contrary and out-of-step views have not cost the Harper government much political capital, as their three successive electoral victories, including their 2011 majority win, attest.

While the failure of the opposition parties to present credible alternatives is obviously important, a large part of the explanation lies in the success of Harper's tactics of information control and suppression. This success is highlighted by the fact that, some two years after his government had revoked Canada's signature on the Kyoto Accord, more than 60 per cent of Canadians were unaware of that move, just as they remained in the dark about so many of the changes his government has made to the administration of justice, the delivery of health care, and the provision of social services. At the same time, Harper's efforts to communicate his own message also appear to have borne fruit. Polls have shown that many Canadians now believe his government's rhetoric that medicare and the Canada Pension Plan are unaffordable. As a July 2014 study demonstrated, Canadians also grossly overestimate the importance of the oil sands to the national economy, leading many to conclude the projects are a necessary evil, despite the fact they would prefer to see their federal government pursue more environmentally friendly renewable energy policies.[8]

Nevertheless there appears to be a vague, but growing, popular consensus that Canada is "moving in the wrong direction," and that the Conservatives may be part of the problem rather than the solution. A steady string of political scandals in 2013 have damaged the prime minister's personal credibility in the crucial area of accountability, an issue on which he built his initial victory and which ironically may prove to be his Achilles heel. Perhaps most significantly, polls consistently demonstrate that Canadian public opinion since

2006 has not shifted appreciably on any of the key factors affecting the entrenched liberal political culture. If anything, Canadians appear to be more liberal now than they were when the Harper Conservatives took power.

By the next federal election, scheduled for October 2015, the Conservatives will have been in power for more than nine years, and may well face an electorate tired of conflict and deception. And unlike Brian Mulroney, who was once widely admired but whose party nevertheless crashed and burned after ten years, Stephen Harper has never been popular and has much less far to fall. Meanwhile the Liberal Party of Canada, under new leader Justin Trudeau, has demonstrated that the party's brand is still strong. Public-opinion polls throughout 2013 and 2014 showed a steady upward trend for the party, and several placed the Liberals in first place. After his wins in two significant Ontario by-elections in June 2014, pollster Nik Nanos concluded that Trudeau "has a real shot" at becoming the next prime minister. Still, both Trudeau and his party remain untested in an election campaign, and many observers have stressed the importance of Harper's continued high ratings for competence, to say nothing of his well-honed debating skills and tendency to go for the jugular.

Regardless of the outcome of the next election, however, the most important question for Canadians may be whether the changes which Harper is able to make during his time in power are either significant or permanent. Certainly if the party's downward slide in support continues, Stephen Harper may be not only the first, but the last, of the new Conservatives to hold power, as the party comes to terms with its failures and reconstitutes itself in the more familiar and philosophically acceptable Tory brand of the Progressive Conservatives.

PART ONE

Taking Control

1

Right Thinking

Your country, and particularly your conservative movement, is a light and an inspiration to people in this country and across the world.

Stephen Harper, Speech to the American Council for National Policy, 1997

We can create a country built on solid conservative values … a country the Liberals wouldn't even recognize, the kind of country I want to lead.

Stephen Harper, Speech to the Civitas Society, 2003

If Reform has done anything, it has taught conservative voters that they do not have to be content with Toryism, that they can have their own party, that such a party can elect MPs and that it can influence the political agenda in Ottawa.

Stephen Harper, 1996

In the spring of 2013, when newly minted Liberal leader Justin Trudeau was asked to comment on the Boston Marathon bombings, he offered a comprehensive response. First he expressed sympathy for the victims and survivors. Then he went on to support police efforts to locate the perpetrators. Finally he mused about the eventual need to consider the root causes of such home-grown violence.

Prime Minister Stephen Harper was quick to mock Trudeau as unrealistic and dangerously weak. Only days after Conservative attack ads began denigrating the Liberal leader, Harper described Trudeau's concern with the root causes of terrorism as the typical muddled thinking of a bleeding-heart liberal. Speaking to reporters in London, England, where he was attending the funeral of former British prime minister Margaret Thatcher, Mr Harper volunteered his views to a surprised press corps – which had not asked about Trudeau's comments. He then accused Trudeau of trying to "rationalize or make excuses" for those responsible. The right response, he said, was to "condemn it categorically, and to the extent you can deal with the perpetrators you deal with them as harshly as possible."[1]

After seven years in power, virtually no one was surprised by Harper's hyperpartisan take on Trudeau. What *did* surprise most Canadians was Harper's subsequent statement in the House of Commons about Trudeau's alleged soft-on-terrorism approach. Now is not the time, he said, to "commit sociology." Commit sociology? What did the prime minister mean by this strange and unexpected turn of phrase, one that outraged sociologists, puzzled ordinary Canadians, and delighted political cartoonists?

This was hardly the first time that Harper or one of his ministers had said or done something unexpected. Certainly no one anticipated Industry Minister Tony Clement's June 2010 announcement that Statistics Canada's long-form census would be eliminated. Nor did anyone expect that Harper's government would so consistently ignore expert opinion and facts that the Conservatives would become widely known as "anti-science." And no one ever thought bureaucrats and opposition politicians would be talking seriously about the need for a federal government to *return to evidence-based decision-making.*

Canadians were equally surprised by the sudden announcements that the term "royal" would be reinstated for the armed forces, and that millions of dollars would be dedicated to promoting the War of 1812. Although many were amused, almost everyone wondered about Harper's motives. Surely the word "royal" would inflame tensions in Quebec? And, with his government hoping to forge closer ties with the United States, this enthusiasm for highlighting a bygone conflict with the Americans seemed all the more quixotic.

Then there was Public Safety Minister Vic Toews's sudden announcement that his department would be eliminating the positions of all non-Christian chaplains in federal prisons, shortly after the prime minister announced the creation of a new post of Ambassador of Religious Freedom in the Department of Foreign Affairs. Both moves were controversial, but it was the apparent contradiction in policy terms that left observers shaking their heads. So did Foreign Affairs Minister John Baird's surprising recommendation that Canada withdraw from an obscure UN anti-drought convention – putting this country offside with all 195 member states – a recommendation that perplexed international officials as well as Canadians.

Similarly Harper had repeatedly promised to "respect" provincial rights as part of his vaunted "open federalism" agenda. How, then, to explain Finance Minister Jim Flaherty's attacks on the McGuinty government in Ontario and the Charest government in Quebec over their fiscal policies or Flaherty's refusal to consult with premiers before tabling an unprecedented take-it-or-leave-it health-care deal? And, having courted Quebec voters aggressively in two successive elections, who would have expected Harper to support Justice Minister Rob Nicholson's vow to destroy the gun-registry records for that province, despite vigorous opposition from the provincial government?

There have been many other occasions when even veteran observers of the Harper government have been nonplussed by policy announcements that seem to have no discernible rationale, or take a direction that seems diametrically opposed to the formal Conservative policy agenda spelled out in platforms and prime ministerial statements. Some of these incidents have been dismissed as mere whims or unintentional gaffes, but almost all have been described as isolated exceptions rather than a logical outcome of Conservative thinking.

However, a closer look at the philosophical underpinnings of the new Conservative Party and its leader, Stephen Harper, sheds a different light on these unexplained policy anomalies. The underlying values and beliefs of Harper and his colleagues reveal a more coherent conservative policy agenda than might otherwise have been apparent, but also one that is far more radical than Canadians have seen before. The philosophy of the new Conservative Party has been heavily influenced by the thinking of two very right-wing conservative leaders of the 1980s, Margaret Thatcher and Ronald Reagan, who challenged the liberal consensus of their day. As a result, Harper's new conservative philosophy not only rejects the liberalism that has dominated Canadian politics, but breaks with the traditional Tory brand of conservatism that he considers to be simply a pale imitation of that liberalism.

In addition, a closer look at the new Conservatives' philosophical outlook demonstrates that it is not only *what* these right-wing conservatives believe that is important, but *how attached they are* to their beliefs. The rigidity of their policy positions can be traced back to a firm (and unprecedented) conviction in the rightness of their beliefs. This certainty is what leads them to see opposing policy positions as not simply different – and therefore worthy of consideration and debate – but wrong, and hence easily dismissed. As a result, neither compromise nor conciliation are acceptable or even possible.

Seen in this light, their willingness to ignore expert opinion and evidence can be understood not so much as an ostrich-like refusal to accept reality (although there is certainly an element of this) but rather as a tendency to view the facts as *irrelevant*. Thus the phrase "not letting the facts get in the way of their opinions" is literally correct in describing the new Conservatives' approach to governing. And this, too, is a clear break with tradition. Unlike Canadian politicians of all political stripes in the past, these conservatives believe it should be values, not facts, which drive public policy. Coupled with the actual content of their values and beliefs, many of which are well outside the traditional parameters of public debate in Canada, this attitude set the stage for significant conflict and many unexpected policy twists as soon as the new Conservative Party took office in 2006.

Stephen Harper is indeed a very right-wing conservative, and the consistency of his ideological thinking over more than two decades is remarkable,[2] equalled perhaps only by that of his primary ideological foe, Pierre Trudeau. But an in-depth analysis of his thinking also reveals the deep-rooted conflict between his new conservative ideology and his pragmatism, a conflict resulting from the gap between his conservative values and those of the liberal mainstream in Canada. This conflict has resulted in many unexpected and often contradictory positions such as those outlined above. Quite simply, Harper will do whatever he deems necessary to remain in power, viewing such policy reversals as short-term but necessary setbacks in order to fight another day.

Finally, such an analysis also helps to explain the motivation for Mr Harper's single-minded determination to eliminate his political opposition in the Liberal Party. His actions are driven by his overarching ambition to replace the liberalism that has dominated Canadian political thinking with his own brand of conservativism. It follows that the Liberal Party – which embodies that liberalism – is not a worthy opponent, but the enemy.

It is important to recognize the underlying tenets of the liberalism that Stephen Harper so despises, in order to understand just how different the philosophical perspective he brings to the political landscape in Canada really is. It is this perspective which drives his government's agenda, and explains his motives.

CANADIAN LIBERALISM AND THE LIBERAL CONSENSUS

As Stephen Harper knows only too well, liberalism has been the dominant political philosophy in Canada, and in fact it has dominated thinking in western democracies for nearly two hundred years. Yet it is a philosophy that he has categorically rejected, and that he once described in its modern incarnation as verging on "moral nihilism."

At the heart of liberalism's philosophical approach is the concept of *individual liberty*, and the primacy of the individual over the state or community. This means first of all that freedom of speech, assembly, and religion must be guaranteed as rights of citizenship. In institutional terms, liberalism created the concept of charters or declarations of rights, and democratic principles, such as the separation of church and state, representative government, and an independent judiciary. These principles were designed to ensure the legitimacy of the state, and also to limit its powers. Above all, there was a requirement that a constitution form the basis for the structure and operation of the state. This "constitutionalism" required a formal legal framework (written laws, conventions, and common law), an *acceptance of the constitution as the supreme law, and compliance with the constitution by rulers and their laws.*[3]

In addition, liberalism's belief in the equality of individuals has meant that tolerance of diversity and state support for pluralism are fundamental. In a liberal democracy the state must tolerate dissent and protect the rights of the minority while respecting the will of the majority. It must also treat all citizens in a fair and impartial fashion. In addition to this protection of individuals *from* the state, modern liberalism also holds that individuals may need help from the state to reach their full potential, which is viewed as the ultimate objective of society. Thus equality of opportunity is another fundamental principle of modern liberalism, and requires government to act as a force for good, levelling the playing field against the inherent inequities of the marketplace and the disadvantages of a hierarchical society. In practical terms, this has resulted in the creation of the modern welfare state, the regulation of financial sectors and industries, and the creation of state enterprises where the private sector cannot or will not compete.

Canadian liberalism incorporated all of these principles, but it also developed some unique characteristics. For example, liberal programs such as bilingualism and multiculturalism were introduced to support diversity, reflecting the unique nature of our demographics, while concepts such as equalization evolved to support equality of opportunity in light of the distinct geographic realities of the country. These and other unique aspects of Canadian liberalism are commonly seen to have resulted from our formative experiences. Historically Canada has been viewed as a "fragment" society in which early immigrants from Europe brought with them fragments of political thought from their homelands.[4] Hence fragments of British Tory and French or eastern European collectivist political culture are seen to have influenced the evolution of Canadian liberalism. In particular, it is important to stress the British Tory strand brought to Canada by United Empire Loyalists, which formed the basis of the Progressive Conservative Party, and which emphasized the role of the state in protecting citizens. Canadian liberalism has actually been reinforced by this Tory perspective, and citizens "feel strongly that the state is responsible for its citizens and is obligated to provide for their well-being."[5] As professors David Bell and Lorne Tepperman note, in their book *The Roots of Disunity*, this Canadian brand of liberalism quickly became entrenched in the Canadian psyche, having "the full force of the state, church, media, and educational system behind it."[6]

Other liberal democracies also embodied these principles and institutions, and their mainstream political parties shared these underlying values and beliefs, differing primarily in the ways and means to implement some of their objectives. But although there was an overwhelming consensus on these values and principles, there was inevitably a minority who did not share these views. And, just as the industrial revolution of the nineteenth century caused a major upheaval in political thought concerning the role of the state, so the economic turmoil of the late-twentieth-century post-industrial era, characterized by globalization and dramatic technological innovation, produced another opportunity for alternative viewpoints to be heard. It was during this period of economic and social upheaval that a small group of right-wing conservatives emerged to challenge the liberal consensus.

This context is important, since much of Stephen Harper's underlying philosophy stems directly from the theories about government put forward by key political actors during this period, who became his most important role models. The first is Margaret Thatcher, whose funeral Harper attended personally in 2013. The second is Ronald Reagan, the man whose election as president of the United States led to the so-called Reagan Revolution in American party politics and paved the way for the New Right Republicans Harper has also long admired – and many of whom he knows personally. Much of Harper's thinking has been shaped by these two conservative politicians and their successors. In setting himself the task of dismantling the liberal consensus in Canada, therefore, Harper has looked to both of his role models for inspiration. They were the ground-breaking leaders of the new conservative movement, and their thinking is evident in much of his government's actions and agenda since taking power.

RIGHT THINKING: THATCHER BREAKS THE LIBERAL CONSENSUS

In the post-war era, the British welfare state was considered among the most advanced in Europe, and state intervention in the economy, through direct ownership and regulation, was highly developed as well.[7] Like Canada, the major political parties in Britain shared a commitment to the underlying principles of the welfare state and differed primarily with respect to the degree or method of implementation of various policies designed to further this broadly accepted liberal framework.[8] That the first major crack in the liberal consensus would appear in Britain was therefore not something that many had expected.

However by the mid-1970s Britain's economy was badly battered by a number of destabilizing forces, including a global recession and the collapse of its industrial and manufacturing base. By 1975, the lengthy post-war growth that Britain had enjoyed came to a shuddering halt. This led to growing public unrest, caused by the combination of high unemployment, rampant inflation, and labour strife, and exacerbated by the failure of successive Labour governments to rein in the unions, increase economic efficiency, or even present a compelling leader to defend liberalism. In this vacuum a young

Conservative politician emerged to challenge the liberal consensus. Margaret Thatcher, who would go on to become one of Britain's best-known and longest-serving prime ministers, was about to champion the new conservative agenda.

An unobtrusive junior cabinet minister in the traditional Conservative government of Edward Heath, Thatcher emerged from Heath's shadow to challenge him for the leadership in 1975. Her subsequent victory was described by one former colleague as primarily due to the fact that she was not Edward Heath, and "very much an outsider." It was this appeal of a new face, not her philosophical positions, that led to her victory. No one anticipated she would shift the party so far to the right, or the messianic zeal with which she would pursue her objectives. As the moderate majority in the Conservative Party watched with increasing anxiety, Thatcher published an aggressive manifesto entitled *Right Thinking*, the bible that guided her actions throughout her time in office. By now Thatcher was an ardent disciple of right-wing dissident economist Friedrich Hayek, who viewed almost all state intervention in either the economy or society as unacceptable. Impatient with the discussion at a Conservative policy conference, she once produced a copy of one of his books from her handbag and declared, "*This* is what we believe." Her manifesto "was a revolutionary tract that rejected almost all of the traditional liberal economic and social doctrine … and proposed in its place a minimalist approach to government."[9] Or, as Labour leader James Callaghan warned, "It broke the consensus."

Thatcher herself was clear about her desire to undo the liberal consensus. For her, tolerance of diversity was offensive, and liberals were "in the process of abandoning all beliefs, principles, and values."[10] Her conservatism combined the laissez-faire economic thinking of Adam Smith, stressing the unfettered marketplace, with an emphasis on authority, tradition, and individual *responsibility* rather than rights and freedoms. "Conservatives are not egalitarians," her document declared. Thatcher herself also famously stated, "There is no such thing as society."[11] Instead, there were only individual voters, taxpayers, and shareholders, and she believed they should depend on themselves, not the state.

Thatcher was ruthless in her determination to achieve her agenda in spite of what she perceived to be the irksome constraints of parliamentary democracy and liberal institutions. Conservative MP Julian Critchley summed up the Iron Lady's attitude by stating "she cannot see an institution without hitting it with her handbag." A cabinet colleague added "While she has not yet 'handbagged' traditional cabinet government beyond recognition, she has nonetheless flouted much of its spirit and given its conventions the greatest hammering since the epoch of Lloyd George."[12] Her leadership opponent, Michael Heseltine, went further, stating she "is not averse to the exercise of prime ministerial power right up to its constitutional limits," and often went beyond those limits in pursuit of her objectives.[13]

Her manifesto dismissed the rationale for the welfare state, arguing "we must do more to help people to help themselves, and families to look after their own. We must also encourage the voluntary movement and self-help groups working in partnership with the statutory services."[14] In practice, this led to a concerted attack on the programs of the welfare state, including public housing, social assistance, education, and the vaunted national health care system. Taken together, these measures led to a dramatic decline in social cohesion in Britain that lasted long after Thatcher had departed the political stage.[15]

Thatcher's economic mission was to shrink government and free the marketplace. As she explained in a BBC interview in 1983, "What I am desperately trying to do is create one nation, with everyone being a man of property or having the opportunity to be a man of property." To that end she introduced widespread privatization of state enterprises, notably in the transportation sector, deregulated industries, and waged war on labour unions. Meanwhile Thatcher's tough-on-crime agenda saw Britain substantially increase expenditures on law enforcement. Her hard line on Northern Ireland included increased military interventions and resulted in the death of ten prisoners on hunger strikes. She also adopted an aggressive foreign policy, which championed opposition to communism and supported renewed British military might, when she engaged her country in the Falklands War with Argentina.

Over time it became clear that there were negative consequences to many of her major changes. Her determination to drastically reduce the size of government had not produced results. When she left office, government expenditures were actually up, and so were unemployment and inflation. The transportation sector was in chaos. And, rather than the "one Britain" that she had hoped to create, there was not only an increased gap between rich and poor, but a yawning regional divide between an affluent south and an impoverished north, a gap which remains to this day.

Thatcher's authoritarian manner eventually led to the undoing of the woman her own party referred to behind her back as "The Great She Elephant" and "She Who Must Be Obeyed." But long before the many failings of the Thatcher revolution had become obvious, she had inspired like-minded politicians in many western democracies, including a young Stephen Harper and his future colleagues John Baird and Tony Clement. As Clement told reporters on learning of her passing, "In the 1970s conservatism was a poor, pale imitation of liberalism. Why would anyone vote for it? And here was a woman who said 'No, we stand for something very different.'" John Baird described her role as "groundbreaking," and "not merely for what she accomplished in the UK, but what she accomplished in the world by inspiration."[16] Harper himself was effusive in his praise. In a special press release marking her death, he declared, "With the passing of Baroness Thatcher, the world has lost a giant among leaders ... While many in positions of power are defined by the times in which they govern, Margaret Thatcher had that rarest of abilities to herself personify and define the age in which she served. Indeed, with the success of her economic policies, she defined contemporary conservatism itself."

Certainly "Thatcherism" became a major force in the 1980s and early 1990s, inspiring the careers of Helmut Kohl, Brian Mulroney, and Ronald Reagan, and a second generation of conservative politicians, including Stephen Harper.[17] And it was Ronald Reagan who provided Stephen Harper with additional support for his conservative views, and inspiration about the ways in which those views could be successfully communicated.

THE REAGAN REVOLUTION AND NEW RIGHT CONSERVATISM

Margaret Thatcher captured one of the two mainstream parties that had frequently formed a government in Britain. Ronald Reagan took over a Republican Party that was always the underdog, and repositioned it philosophically, so that it would be capable of winning again. This was a more difficult task, not only because the Democrats were traditionally the dominant party, but because in 1980 the

Republicans were at an additional disadvantage after Richard Nixon's departure in disgrace.

Like Thatcher, Reagan was considered an outsider by the party elites. Nor did those elites expect Reagan to take such a hard right turn once he obtained the presidential nomination. Republicans most often had been successful when they closed the philosophical gap with the Democrats, not when it was widened. Yet this was precisely the course that Reagan pursued.

Economic policy was Reagan's principal concern, as it had been Thatcher's. In fact, his words echoed hers uncannily. "What I want to see above all," he told one reporter, "is that this remains a country where someone can always get rich."[18] To that end he adopted a laissez-faire economic policy that stunned the moderates in his own party. As his economic adviser, Milton Friedman, (the originator of the now-discredited "trickle-down" theory), once explained, "Reaganomics" had "four simple principles: lower marginal tax rates, less regulation, restrained government spending, and noninflationary monetary policy."[19] Reagan cut taxes (especially for the rich), deregulated much of the economy, and waged war on labour unions (a move epitomized by his landmark decision to fire eleven thousand striking air-traffic controllers). He insisted that a return to fiscal balance was not only possible but essential, and that cutting government programs was the best way to do it.

Reagan also emphasized social policies based on individual responsibility and decried any role for the state. Firmly opposed to affirmative action, social assistance, gun control, and even, albeit indirectly, desegregation, Reagan championed a social agenda that favoured capital punishment and opposed abortion. Meanwhile, in foreign policy, his condemnation of the "Evil Empire" of communism and his championing of patriotism and renewed American military might – in the aftermath of the Americans' humiliating withdrawal from Vietnam and Jimmy Carter's equally humiliating failed Iran-hostage rescue – were cornerstones of his agenda.

Through a combination of brilliant communication techniques and a strategy of targeting specific segments of the population and regions of the country, Reagan succeeded in turning the Republicans' fortunes around. He was given two terms in office, to the consternation of traditional Republicans as well as Democrats[20] – and despite growing evidence that his economic policies were a disaster.

Some Americans did indeed become fabulously rich as a result of Reagan's policies. The *Forbes* 400 richest Americans saw their fortunes triple. However there was overwhelming evidence that the rising tide had not lifted all boats. While the net worth of the wealthiest Americans increased by a stunning 3 per cent in less than eight years, the middle class shrank and the number of homeless increased dramatically. Meanwhile, in the transportation sector, widespread deregulation resulted in decreased safety and lack of service while failing to cut costs for consumers.[21] Elsewhere it led to the financial- and banking-sector woes epitomized by the Michael Milken junk-bond scandal and arguably paved the way for the 2008 mortgage crisis.

Perhaps most importantly, Reagan's commitment to fiscal prudence had been a sham. He had financed his tax cuts and huge increase in defence spending by allowing the federal debt to balloon. One New Right supporter joked that at least this meant the Democrats would have no money to spend on more liberal programs once they returned to power, but this was in fact no accident. Another prominent Reagan adviser, Grover Norquist, a well-known proponent of small government, had specifically recommended hobbling the federal government by decreasing its revenue, for example by cutting taxes. Norquist's motto, "starve the beast," became a rallying cry for the New Right that followed in Reagan's footsteps,[22] while Norquist himself went on to champion the cause through his stewardship of Americans for Tax Reform.

Reagan's successor, George Bush Sr, a traditional moderate Republican who had once described Reagan's economic conservatism as "voodoo economics," paid the price for this legacy. He was limited to one term in office when Democrat Bill Clinton defined the 1992 election issue as "the economy, stupid." With the Republicans out of office, a group of conservatives even more radical than Reagan, who referred to themselves as the New Right, emerged within the party. Although Reagan had cut taxes, eliminated several federal agencies, scaled back affirmative-action programs, and appointed a raft of conservative judges to the Supreme Court, the New Right's principal critique of his time in office was that he had not gone nearly far enough.[23]

Throughout much of the 1990s, the public face of this increasingly powerful group of party dissidents was Newt Gingrich, a congressman from Georgia who served at one point as Minority Leader and then as Speaker of the House. Gingrich generated renewed interest in the party through a platform entitled "Contract with America," which played to the social and moral aspects of the new conservatism. Specifically, it assembled a broad coalition of right-wing special-interest groups and Christian evangelicals. From Reagan's limited use of groups opposed to gun control and abortion, the New Right expanded their reach to include organizations opposed to gay rights, feminism, stem-cell research, reproductive technologies, public television, and immigration, as well as groups in favour of such measures as the death penalty, home schooling, and state funding for religious education. These new coalition partners shaped the content of the Contract, parts of which – as many experts noted – were not only extreme but unworkable, while others were patently unconstitutional.

But the results were gratifying. With Clinton's first year in office marred by numerous scandals and moral issues, including his failed attempt to implement a campaign promise regarding gays in the military ("don't ask, don't tell"), the moral conservatism of the New Right proved politically advantageous. The Republicans regained control of the House of Representatives in 1994, in what Gingrich described as "the most shatteringly one-sided Republican victory since 1946." It was more than that. As Washington journalist Elizabeth Drew perceptively concluded:

> This was a whole new phenomenon in American politics. The Republicans won the House in 1994, after 40 years of Democratic control, and they wanted to hold onto it, not simply because they wanted two more years of power, and not simply because they wanted to pass certain kinds of bills, but because they saw it as the long-term way to continue to dictate and shape the political agenda. They're after a long-term goal, which is called realignment, in other words a shift in the pre-dominance of one political party over another in American politics. They want to get a conservative hegemony over American politics.[24]

Their success had far-reaching political consequences. Indeed, the New Right's decision to embrace moral conservatism led to the most significant change in the political party system in the US in fifty years, a crucial change given its implications for Canada and the philosophy of the Harper Conservatives. First and foremost, it divided the

Republican Party between moderates and extremists, whose social and moral conservatism eventually led them to form a breakaway sect, the Tea Party. Secondly, it marked the end of an era of brokerage politics, when bipartisan cooperation and compromise were possible. Instead, the stage was set for protracted paralysis in Congress and severe limitations on presidential power. It culminated – despite Barack Obama's initial efforts to achieve cross-partisan agreement – in the "fiscal cliff" drama of January 2013 and the subsequent string of budget crises caused by the implacable opposition of the Tea Party Republicans.

MORAL CONSERVATISM AND THE CLOSING OF THE CONSERVATIVE MIND

As several analysts have outlined, a primary reason for this aggressive new political mindset is the philosophical underpinnings of the New Right Republicans, whose moral certainty has produced unprecedented partisan sniping and negative election campaigns. Indeed, the rigidity of the evangelical Christian doctrine, and the depth of commitment of its supporters, is reflected in the thinking of the Reverend Jerry Falwell, an ardent Reagan supporter who coined the term "the Moral Majority." In many respects this thinking is the antithesis of liberalism, since it rejects dissenting opinions as wrong, while liberalism celebrates dissent as a key element of civil liberty in democracies. The irreconcilable nature of this cleavage was originally captured by the bumper stickers sported by Democrats that proclaimed "The moral majority is neither." (More recently it was evident in the pronouncements of renegade Tea Party spokespersons, who ignored all the evidence to the contrary and insisted that Mitt Romney's loss to Barack Obama in 2012 was caused by his failure to stick with the philosophical hard line, rather than by their failure to attract large segments of the population, including women, black, and Hispanic voters.)

As political psychologist Jonathan Haidt has pointed out, the values and beliefs prioritized by conservatives and liberals are significantly different. In his seminal work, *The Righteous Mind*, Haidt identifies six categories of values. Liberals give strong precedence to what he terms the *care/harm* and *liberty/oppression* values, and show fairly strong concern for *fairness/cheating*. But they are largely indifferent to, or even dismissive of, the categories of *loyalty/betrayal*, *authority/subversion,* and *sanctity/degradation.* Meanwhile social and moral conservatives attach equal importance to all six categories. In addition there is a yawning gap between the two groups in terms of the primary objective they assign to society and government. In the case of liberals it is "to care for victims of oppression." In the case of moral conservatives, it is "to preserve those institutions and traditions that sustain a moral community."[25]

While some of the conclusions Haidt draws from his findings have been criticized, including how liberal politicians should respond to this unprecedented rigidity in their political opponents, there has been little or no disagreement about these findings themselves. For politicians, the differences are crucial. They do not merely produce two different sets of priorities, but diametrically opposed solutions to the same policy issues. Hence liberal affirmative-action policies, welfare programs, human-rights legislation, and foreign aid are vehemently opposed by moral conservatives, who do not want to merely modify or amend them but eliminate them entirely.

In Canada, this righteous moral perspective is deeply embedded in the new Conservative Party. Their extremely rigid and confrontational viewpoint was perfectly represented by Rondo Thomas, the Conservative Party candidate in Ajax–Pickering in Ontario in the 2006 election, when he stated: "There is going to be a clash of morality views between those who believe in righteousness and those who believe in immorality and when we collide there is going to be conflict ... It doesn't matter what the media says, it doesn't matter what bureaucrats say, the facts don't count. We are going to win this conflict."[26]

Although Thomas was unsuccessful, many of his like-minded counterparts were elected. Several of Harper's cabinet stalwarts, such as Jim Flaherty, Tony Clement, and John Baird had been ministers in the Ontario government of Mike Harris, well-known for its uncompromising attitude.[27] It is these new conservatives' divergence with liberals on underlying values and beliefs that helps to explain their resistance to issues such as climate change and environmental protection, as well as their punitive approach on matters such as immigration and criminal justice. Unlike liberals, they place great emphasis on punishment and retribution. Consequently, scientific evidence, for example about rates of recidivism or rehabilitation, is simply irrelevant. Indeed, the entire academic field of study known as sociology, and its subfield of criminology, is anathema to this group's thinking. As Canadian scholar Joseph Heath has noted, this explains perfectly the hostile reaction of Stephen Harper to any suggestion that he "commit sociology" in the face of terrorism. "Hostility to expertise in all of its forms is the closest thing that Canadian neoconservatives have to a unifying ideology," Heath claimed somewhat facetiously. "Criminologists, however, rankle them just a little bit more than others because their expertise happens to touch on an area that many conservatives feel so strongly about."[28]

This moral certainty and refusal to compromise has been demonstrated repeatedly by various members of Harper's cabinet, and was memorably captured by Harper himself in a Conservative Party convention speech delivered in late 2013, when his government was under siege because of the mushrooming Senate expenses scandal. Refusing to apologize, Harper went on the offensive. He listed past accomplishments and outlined his upcoming agenda, telling delegates he "couldn't care less" what his opponents thought of that agenda. This statement – remarkable for any Canadian politician, let alone a sitting prime minister – produced the longest standing ovation of the evening.

THE INFLUENCE OF THE NEW RIGHT ON HARPER'S CONSERVATISM

It is difficult to overestimate the influence that Ronald Reagan and the New Right Republicans' views have had on the thinking of Canada's new conservatives. Both Harper and Preston Manning know Newt Gingrich personally. While Manning was Reform Party leader and Harper was his research director, he often met with Gingrich. During his ill-fated run for the GOP leadership in 2012, Gingrich delivered a major speech in which he actually singled out Harper as a "real conservative" and very "pro-American."

In addition, Harper has studied the economists that influenced Thatcher and Reagan, such as Hayek and Friedman, and his Master's degree at the University of Calgary praised their economic theories. While studying there, he also came under the influence of conservative thinkers such as Tom Flanagan and Ted Morton, American-born-and-educated scholars who were instrumental in the development of the so-called Calgary School. Among other things, the school's members have supported an almost libertarian approach to the economy and the role of the government, rejected the welfare state, and questioned the legitimacy of the Charter of Rights.[29]

Virtually all of Harper's cabinet and caucus share his admiration for his American role models. A classic example of this thinking can be found in a speech by Diane Finley as minister of Human Resources and Skills Development, the department responsible for virtually all the social programs of the welfare state. In a talk filled with references to "the limits of government intervention" and "the importance of individual initiative," Ms Finley approvingly cited Ronald Reagan's claim that "the nine most terrifying words in the English language are 'I'm from the government and I'm here to help.'" She then went on to announce that her department would begin seeking offers from the corporate sector to help finance social programs, because "we can't fund every single solitary service that people want ... it's time to shift gears."[30]

Similarly, the new Conservatives share the Republicans' overarching ambition to change the very nature of their society. In his June 2003 speech to the secretive right-wing Civitas Society, where he outlined his philosophical approach in detail, Harper told his audience, "We can create a country built on solid conservative values ... a country the Liberals wouldn't even recognize, the kind of country I want to lead."

However a key difference between the Harper Conservatives and their Republican counterparts appears to be Harper's ability to put aside even deeply held philosophical preferences and take a pragmatic approach to politics when absolutely necessary. Although he has never lost sight of his ultimate objectives, he has demonstrated that he can accept what he views as merely temporary setbacks in order to fight another day, even when those "setbacks" appear to the outside world to be policy contradictions of clear-cut and significant proportions. An evangelical Christian, he has nevertheless become a master of tactical compromise, choosing his moments to advance certain elements of the social and moral conservative agenda while insisting that others remain dormant. His peremptory treatment of two backbench MPs who tried to resurrect the abortion issue in early 2013 exemplified this determination to avoid issues where he feels he cannot win. As Canadian philosopher Christian Nadeau has pointed out, there is method in his madness:

> The Conservatives want to ensure that their ideas and values become dominant and omnipresent. They would prefer to accomplish their goals quickly, but they also want to ensure that their government will have a lasting impact, so they are prepared

> to be patient. As pragmatists rather than dreamers, they have a clear idea of what they want and what they can accomplish during a few years in power.[31]

Equally important in the Canadian context, Harper has been acutely conscious of the fact that he must not go too far in offending supporters of the traditional Progressive Conservative Party if he is to forge a winning coalition and break the liberal consensus. This was an especially challenging task, since, as we have seen, the new conservatism of Stephen Harper rejects the Tory strand found in the Progressive Conservative Party as being merely a pale imitation of liberalism.

THE NEW CONSERVATIVES VERSUS THE TORIES

Unlike Progressive Conservative prime ministers before him, Stephen Harper's origins lie in the defunct Reform and Canadian Alliance parties. When those parties merged with the remaining fragments of the decimated Progressive Conservative party, he became the first leader of the new Conservative Party and, ultimately, that party's first prime minister. This unique path to power is significant for many reasons, but most importantly for the unprecedented philosophical perspective Mr Harper has brought to national politics.

As discussed, Progressive Conservatives historically shared many of the underlying values and beliefs of the Liberals, due primarily to their origins in the British Tory tradition.[32] The new Conservative Party philosophy does not share those values. Harper, who disagreed with Reform leader Preston Manning on so many issues, nevertheless once wrote that "if Reform has done anything, it has taught conservative voters that they do not have to be content with Toryism, that they can have their own party, that such a party can elect MPs, and that it can influence the political agenda in Ottawa."[33]

Despite the media's tendency to conflate the two, and to use the term "Tory" to refer to the new Conservative Party, these new conservatives have little in common with traditional Tories like Robert Stanfield, Joe Clark, Hugh Segal, or Bill Davis. They do not support the welfare state or social justice, affirmative action, official bilingualism, or multiculturalism policies, and see almost no role for the state in the lives of its citizens. As Stephen Harper told the American National Policy Council, when he predicted that a merger would soon take place between his old Reform/Alliance Party and the Progressive Conservatives, "one party is going to win out ... And Reform is not going to lose that contest in the long term."[34]

The extent of the difference between the old and new conservative philosophies can be seen in the reaction of Progressive Conservative elites to the "merger" of their party with the Reform/Alliance Party in 2003. Former Progressive Conservative prime minister Joe Clark refused to be associated with the new party and even declared that he would vote for the Martin Liberals as the lesser of two evils. "I'm that concerned with the imprint of Stephen Harper," Clark declared, "Not only what he has stood for in the past ... but the way he has led this party. This is not my party. This is something entirely new." Clark made it clear he would not consider becoming the interim leader of the merged group. "I don't believe that the Harper party can get away with the masquerade that it is the Progressive Conservative Party," he declared.[35]

Clark's views were echoed by his former intergovernmental affairs minister, Senator Lowell Murray, who insisted on retaining his designation as a Progressive Conservative in the Senate, as did well-known PC election organizer Norm Atkins and several others appointed under the Tory banner. At the time, Murray declared the new party was "fundamentally different," and "incompatible" with Progressive Conservative values.

Several former cabinet ministers under Brian Mulroney, including Indian affairs minister David Crombie, also declined to be identified with Harper's new Conservative Party. Other Progressive Conservative MPs, such as John Herron and Scott Brison, actually joined the Liberal Party and ran under that banner in the next federal election.

Perhaps the most damming critique came from a self-described Red Tory, Senator Hugh Segal, a former Stanfield and Mulroney adviser. In his book *Beyond Greed: A Traditional Conservative Confronts Neo-Conservative Excess*, Segal specifically set out to differentiate what he referred to as "traditional" conservatives from "neo-conservatives," a term he used to described the views of Conservative Party members. To do so he built on a statement in his earlier memoir, *No Surrender*, in which he declared, "Progressive Conservatives cannot embrace the nihilistic defeatism that masquerades as a neo-conservative polemic in support of individual freedom and disengagement."[36]

Harper in the past has been as critical of the Tories as they have been of him. In fact, Harper's negative view of Canada's Tories is reminiscent of Margaret Thatcher's contempt for the moderate "wets" or "high Tories" in her own party. In his 1997 speech to the American Council for National Policy, for example, Harper disparaged the PC party as an "oxymoron." Its members, he claimed, were only slightly conservative on economic matters and very liberal on social matters. To support this claim, he noted that the party was "officially in favour of the entrenchment of our universal, collectivized health care system and multicultural policies in the constitution of this country," and "officially" in favour of gun control, gay rights, and abortion on demand, all of which he and his audience rejected.

Not surprisingly, given these views, Harper was also very disdainful of the last PC prime minister, Brian Mulroney, whom he saw as epitomizing this Tory thinking. Mulroney's basic support for the welfare state, evidenced by his mere tinkering at the margins over funding, his huge deficits, his introduction of the GST and increased overall government spending, his moderate views on criminal justice and foreign aid, and his outright support for the United Nations and international efforts to limit climate change, were anathema to Harper. The final straw was Mulroney's obsession with the constitution, a futile exercise that Harper believed was unnecessary, because most of his desired changes were "administrative in nature" and "simply require a federal government that is willing to act."[37]

Mulroney was not a social conservative; nor were his cabinet ministers or the majority of his caucus. This meant that many issues which the Reform/Alliance members saw as important were not even being considered by the Mulroney government, let alone receiving priority treatment. For right-wing conservatives in Canada it was clear that Mulroney, despite some pretence of being an economic conservative, did not go nearly far enough.

A recent examination of Canadian and American conservatives by political scientist James Farney reinforces the differences between the old Progressive Conservatives and the new Conservative Party, and stresses the importance of social and moral conservatism in the new conservatism.[38] Farney outlines three categories of conservative. His "traditional" conservatives had their origins in the British Tory tradition, valued order and good governance above even individual liberties, and were economic mercantilists, but socially progressive, believing government had a responsibility to its citizens.

This was the predominant conservative strain in Canada for most of our history. From John A. Macdonald through to Robert Stanfield and Joe Clark, this Tory strain of conservative thought was made manifest in their early introduction of tariffs and subsidies, in their desire to retain ties to Great Britain and the monarchy (for example in the flag debate and in their opposition to metrification and armed forces unification), and their support for the welfare state. In modern times, these views have been epitomized in the Progressive Conservative Party.

Farney's "laissez-faire" category of economic conservatism translates quite well into the PC Party under Brian Mulroney, with his stated preference for minimal state intervention in the economy and emphasis on privatization, deregulation, and reliance on free-market forces. Although he failed to deliver on this agenda in many respects, his privatization of much state enterprise and introduction of a free trade agreement with the United States were classic examples of this approach. During this time the Progressive Conservative Party increasingly consisted of a mix of traditional Tories and new economic conservatives. As academics William Christian and Colin Campbell note, this obliged the party to carry out a delicate balancing act between its belief in "collectivism and privilege" and its support for "individualism and freedom."[39] Nevertheless, the strong Tory commitment to socially progressive policies continued, as evidenced for example by Mulroney's initiatives to end apartheid in South Africa and promote sustainable development through the UN.

It is the third category, the "social conservatives," that is of greatest interest and utility in explaining the evolution of the new Conservative Party philosophy and the much more extreme ideological perspective of Mr Harper. Indeed, with the election of the Harper Conservatives in 2006, social conservatives had not only found a home in a Canadian political party, they had arrived on the governing side of the House. This was highly significant since, as Farney outlines in detail, social conservatism played little or no role in the political culture of Canada until the end of the Mulroney era. This was primarily because, unlike the United States, its adherents made up such a very small proportion of citizens, and a small minority of conservatives. But it was also because their values and beliefs were outside the parameters of acceptable political action for both the Liberal and Progressive Conservative parties, which were the only political parties capable of forming a national government.

Under both the Liberal and PC parties, moral issues traditionally were seen as personal rather than political choices, and "the personal was not a suitable topic for partisan organizing ... political mobilization, or party discipline."[40] Hence such issues were treated as matters of conscience, with free votes on the rare occasions when they arose at all in parliamentary debate. In addition, of course, the very values of tolerance and compromise that figured so prominently in Canadian liberalism mitigated strongly against any party adopting moral positions that would inevitably be rigidly held. As a result, social conservatives had always found themselves marginalized from the political process.

It was only with the collapse of the Progressive Conservative Party in 2003, which led to the creation of two regionally based fringe parties – the Reform Party in western Canada and the Bloc Québécois (BQ) in Quebec – that an opportunity arose for social conservatives to "capture" a political party. While that fragment of the Progressive Conservatives that coalesced around the BQ was more concerned with nationalism and the federalist cause, those who remained in western Canada were more inclined to hold conservative social views and were easily able to capture the nascent Reform Party.

THE EVOLUTION OF THE REFORM / ALLIANCE / CONSERVATIVE PHILOSOPHY

It is important to note that Stephen Harper was not merely a member of the Reform Party but an original founder. He also was instrumental in developing its first platform when he served as Reform's director of policy before becoming a Reform MP in 1993. That original Reform platform, dubbed "the Blue Sheet," revealed the underlying concerns that prompted the creation of a new political party. Naturally there was an emphasis on reducing the size of government, relying on the invisible hand of the marketplace, and defending property rights. But an almost equal amount of time was devoted to social-conservative issues. Given that the final version already had been watered down by Harper and others to avoid the appearance of a wildly radical agenda, what remained is even more telling.

Among other things, the Blue Sheet proposed the elimination of formal official languages and multiculturalism policy and the gutting of the Indian Act, curtailment of the benefits of the welfare state in favour of assistance from families and charities, the promotion of "family values," and the imposition of a draconian law-and-order agenda. As party leader Preston Manning once remarked, "Our social conservatism is a combination of Rambo and Mother Teresa." Indeed, Reform's views could be seen as "far more reflective of the American right-wing conservatives led at the time by Newt Gingrich and the Moral Majority."[41] Not surprisingly, the platform was heavily criticized in the national media, and the nature of that criticism is instructive. *Toronto Star* journalist Charles Gordon described Reform's platform as "so far outside the Canadian consensus" that most Canadians "don't even think about the issues" that Reform had identified as important. Interestingly, western Canadian media also found the program too extreme, and for the same reasons. Described as "shrill and intolerant" by the *Edmonton Journal* and "repugnant" by the *Calgary Herald*, the last word can be left to the *Vancouver Sun* of 8 April 1994, which concluded "Reform is somewhat un-Canadian."

Even Preston Manning downplayed the importance of religion in the platform of the Reform Party, partly due to his overarching commitment to populism and partly because it continued to be seen by most Canadians as an unacceptable element in political discourse. At the same time, he recognized the importance of the large evangelical Christian component of Reform's supporters. In an apparent attempt to placate everyone, he once declared, "Sure, I believe in the separation of Chuch and State too, but I don't think that means the separation of religious values from political values."[42]

The subsequent transition from the Reform Party to the Canadian Alliance saw the social and moral conservative elements of the party's platform become ever more significant, culminating in the election of prominent "theocon" Stockwell Day as its first leader. A lay preacher in a fundamentalist congregation, Day's religious beliefs then became an important factor in the Liberals' successful strategy to convince voters of the party's "hidden agenda" in the 2000 election campaign.

By the time Stephen Harper became the leader in 2002, he had witnessed the failure of the Alliance Party to make any breakthrough in the 1997 and 2000 federal elections, despite Herculean efforts to moderate its positions. At this point, Harper was still seen both within the party and by Canadians in general as primarily an economic conservative, whose objectives involved dismantling government – and, above all else, reducing the role of the state in the marketplace.

This perception was only partly accurate. He certainly was committed to the laissez-faire economic conservative approach, with its emphasis on the unfettered marketplace, wealth-creation, and property rights. In a speech as leader of the Alliance Party, he again emphasized the role that Margaret Thatcher and Ronald Reagan had played in his thinking and, despite so much evidence to the contrary, he even argued that their economic agenda had been a success. "The Reagan–Thatcher revolution was so successful that it permanently undermined the traditional social-democratic/left-liberal consensus in a number of democratic countries," he declared in one of his speeches.[43]

But his hostility towards the welfare state clearly reflected his equally strong socially conservative views, although on this subject his most revealing comments were made when he was not in power. For example, in 1997 Harper was appointed vice-president of the National Citizens Coalition (NCC), a right-wing advocacy group whose motto is "more freedom through less government." Soon after he delivered a speech to the Council for National Policy, a right-wing American think tank, in which he referred to Canada disparagingly as "a Northern European welfare state in the worst sense of the term, and very proud of it." He urged his audience not to "feel bad" about Canada's unemployed, because "they don't feel bad about it themselves, as long as they're receiving generous social assistance and unemployment insurance."[44] (Although he subsequently tried to downplay some of these comments, he also told a *Globe and Mail* editorial board in 2006, "I don't think my fundamental beliefs have changed in a decade.")

Harper was also one of six signatories to an open letter to Alberta premier Ralph Klein known as the "Firewall" letter. It defended Klein's controversial medicare policies, which had been criticized by the federal Liberals during the 2000 election, and specifically supported Klein's creation of "truth squads" to promote the benefits of private health care, as well as his repeated demands that no conditions be attached to federal funding. The letter's recommendations included withdrawing from the Canada Pension Plan and "resuming provincial responsibility for health-care policy." The authors even argued "each province should raise its own revenue for health care," dismissing the problems of poorer provinces that relied on equalization. Finally, they urged the premier to fight any federal attempt to challenge the legality of these moves, especially concerning the

Canada Health Act. "If we lose, we can afford the financial penalties that Ottawa may try to impose," they wrote.[45]

Yet, back in politics, Harper continued to avoid any public emphasis on the social and moral conservatism of Preston Manning, Stockwell Day, and many of the Reform/Alliance MPs, assuming that any mention of these views would be politically disastrous. Eventually, though, the party's failure to make sufficient electoral headway using the strategic approach of targeting red Tories, alienated westerners, and Quebec nationalists – as revealed later by senior policy adviser Tom Flanagan[46] – finally motivated him to stress rather than downplay the social-conservative side of his thinking. A crucial component of a conservative victory in Canada, he now believed, was to follow the lead of New Right Republicans and form a coalition of right-wing interest groups.

In his seminal June 2003 speech to the Civitas Society, Harper therefore spoke directly to this point. He argued for a greater emphasis on the social-conservative side of the equation, because "serious conservative parties simply cannot shy away from values questions." This, he said, was because "on a wide range of public policy questions, including foreign affairs, defence, criminal justice and corrections, family and child care ... social values are increasingly the really big issues." Harper argued the party needed to emphasize the social-conservative aspect since "a growing body of evidence points to the damage the welfare state is having on our most important institutions, particularly the family." Even such disparate areas as defence and foreign affairs were affected by social conservatism, he stressed, stating that "emerging debates on foreign affairs should be fought on moral grounds" as well.[47]

The speech also highlighted Harper's vehement rejection of liberalism. He saw the "real challenge" posed by liberal cultures and governments to be their social, not their economic, agendas and, like Margaret Thatcher, he went on to decry the "social relativism, moral neutrality, and moral equivalency" of a liberal culture in which secularism, pluralism, and social justice are highly valued. He even equated liberalism with something "darker" than relativism. "It has become a moral nihilism," he argued, confirming Jonathan Haidt's definition of the righteous mind.

As Canadian philosopher Christian Nadeau demonstrates, underpinning Harper's world view is a Hobbesian approach to government and the role of the state. He believes his authority, and that of his government, are the source of legitimacy for all of his acts, and are sufficient justification for them. Like Margaret Thatcher, Harper sees many of the institutions of liberal democracy as obstacles for conservatives, impinging on their authority precisely because they were created by liberals to encourage diverse views and compromise, and therefore inevitably to promote liberal ideology. Similarly, he views many bureaucratic practices and parliamentary traditions with skepticism, because they allow for organized dissent. This is a dangerous concept, because it is at odds with the conservatives' view that they are right and those who oppose them do not simply disagree, but are wrong. As Nadeau puts it, they have "an extreme conception of the prerogatives of power." In this Hobbesian view, "pluralism, democracy, and freedom of expression only make sense if they do not impede the smooth functioning of government."[48]

This thinking was perhaps best demonstrated by a simple comment Harper made spontaneously when questioned by reporters during a stop on his 2010 Arctic tour. Having astonished even his security detail by mounting an all-terrain vehicle and driving off at high speed along an airport runway in Tuktoyaktuk, he was surrounded by reporters and photographers on his return. When one of them asked if he had a licence to drive such a vehicle, or to operate one in restricted airspace on a runway, he immediately replied, "I think I make the rules."[49]

But the Civitas speech also underlined Harper's pragmatism. He acknowledged the dominance of liberalism in Canadian political culture and admitted that this new value-driven conservative policy agenda might cause the party to lose some voters, such as Red Tories and members of the corporate elite in central Canada. Nevertheless, he concluded that "this is not all bad ... a new approach can draw in new people. Many traditional Liberal voters, especially from key ethnic and immigrant communities, will be attracted to a party with strong traditional views of values and family. This is similar to the phenomenon of the Reagan Democrats in the United States, who were so important in the development of the conservative coalition there." Harper agreed wholeheartedly with Tom Flanagan's cautionary approach to implementing this new conservative agenda. "The explicitly moral orientation of social conservatives," Harper declared, "makes it difficult to accept ... the incremental approach. Yet, in democratic politics, any other approach will certainly fail."

It is this pragmatism which sets Harper apart from his predecessors in the Reform/Alliance parties, as well as from the Republican Right. It is this pragmatism which has allowed him, in power, to maintain the support of his right-wing base while avoiding political problems – by moving slowly and gradually on some issues, by achieving some policy objectives quietly, and by flatly refusing to implement some conservative policies that would be patently unacceptable to the liberal majority.

But first, it was this pragmatism which allowed him to orchestrate the successful takeover of the PC Party, to win two elections against expectations, and, eventually, to win a majority government with only 39 per cent of the popular vote. Both the strategy and the tactics he employed to accomplish this owe much to his New Right role models and their technicians.

2

Strategic Thinking

I think about strategy twenty-four hours a day.

Stephen Harper, as cited in Lawrence Martin, *Harperland: The Politics of Control*

You can be a good Canadian and not vote Liberal!

Stephen Harper, 2000

Hit the Liberals when they're down!

Republican pollster Frank Luntz giving advice to the Conservative caucus in Ottawa, 2006

The key to the long-term success of the Liberals has been their cultivation of minority groups. Conservatives have to take away that advantage.

Harper adviser Tom Flanagan, 2007

When Stephen Harper's new Conservative Party formed a minority government in 2006, it was the culmination of efforts by right-wing conservatives over nearly twenty years. When he formed a majority in 2011, their wildest expectations had been met. To say that this victory was unexpected would be an understatement. Only a few years before, the possibility of the former Reform/Alliance Party winning an election had seemed not simply unlikely but impossible.

In fact the situation for Canada's right-wing conservatives in 1994 was strikingly similar to that of Republicans in the United States after Richard Nixon's fall from grace in 1974. The resounding defeat of the Mulroney Progressive Conservatives in 1993 had reduced them to only two seats in parliament and cost them their status as an official party. No one would have predicted that the right wing of the PC party could rise from the ashes on its own, let alone triumph in little more than a decade. Certainly the efforts of Preston Manning, the first leader of that breakaway right wing, had fallen far short. And when the appeal of his fledgling Reform Party stalled, leaving it on the margins and still considered a "fringe" party, the efforts of his successor, Stockwell Day, and the renamed Canadian Alliance were no more fruitful. Nor was there any reason to suppose that the subsequent merger of the Reform/Alliance Party with the defunct Progressive Conservatives, and the selection of the uncharismatic Stephen Harper as their new leader, would make much of a difference. As we saw earlier, political scientist Bruce Doern wrote shortly after the Chrétien Liberals had once again trounced their right-wing opposition and returned to office with their third consecutive majority government in 2000, "Jean Chrétien stands astride the Canadian political scene without much effective opposition of any kind at the federal level."[1]

Even when the Harper Conservatives formed a minority government in 2006, it was widely seen as an accidental victory, caused almost entirely by the missteps of the Paul Martin Liberals, and one that would not be repeated. But repeated it was. The Liberals lost the next two federal elections under two more leaders, Stéphane Dion and Michael Ignatieff, and fell to an unprecedented third-place finish in 2011, when Harper finally obtained his majority. By the time the dust had settled after that election, many observers were echoing the thoughts of a majority of Canadians when they asked themselves what had happened. How was it possible that a party whose fundamental values appeared to be at odds with those of most Canadians, and whose origins in western Canada appeared to make it an outsider on regional grounds as well, had managed to form a majority national government?

The simple answer is that the Harper Conservatives' victory was no accident. It was the result of a meticulously planned and carefully implemented strategy, one that eventually enabled them to form a majority government with only 39 per cent of the popular vote. And, although they adapted their approach to the realities of Canada's political system and culture, their strategy and tactics relied heavily on the experience of the Reagan Republicans and their New Right successors in the United States.

Indeed, just about everything Stephen Harper knows about winning elections he learned originally from the Republican Party strategists who delivered the White House to Ronald Reagan. Harper knows many of the backroom strategists, think-tank leaders, and communications experts who worked for Reagan and the New Right Republicans personally. As a university student, he attended a Young Republican summer training camp, and he has studied their campaigns and adopted their tactics with textbook-like precision.

Because Reagan's 1980 victory was viewed by most observers as little short of a miracle, the strategy and tactics that such veteran Republican organizers as Paul Weyrich, Richard Viguerie, Morton Blackwell, and Howard Phillips employed to orchestrate that victory were seen by many conservatives as nothing less than brilliant. Certainly they were an inspiration to Stephen Harper, who saw remarkable similarities between the underdog Republicans and the Canadian Conservatives, whose Liberal opponents were traditionally seen as the "natural governing party." Indeed, faced with the uphill philosophical battle outlined in the previous chapter, Harper realized early on that such carefully targeted strategies were essential in Canada if his Conservatives were ever to overcome their innate disadvantages and achieve electoral success.

Seen in this light, the influence of the New Right on Canada's new Conservatives, and the degree to which Harper's efforts have been modelled on their approach, is striking. Virtually all of the New Right's innovative strategies – such as their targeting of regional discontent, their mobilization of right-wing special-interest groups, their co-option of the religious right, and their use of wedge issues to attract traditional liberal supporters, have been copied with zeal and considerable success by their Canadian counterparts, as have tactics such as the introduction of attack ads and the use of direct-mail fundraising, which not only financed those ads but allowed for the implementation of the permanent campaign strategy.

The Conservatives began their strategic march to victory by building on regional discontent, playing on the perception of western alienation, just as the Republicans had taken advantage of southern discontent in light of President Lyndon Johnson's signing of the Civil Rights Act. For Stephen Harper, an original Reformer, this approach was not only self-evident but second nature. It is instructive to look at the various elements of the Conservatives' winning strategy: how they slowly and patiently put together an unprecedented coalition of voters sufficient to allow them to obtain a majority, while at the same time disregarding large segments of the Canadian electorate whom they knew would never be receptive to their message. It was in addition to these so-called "pillars" of Conservative strategy, as noted, that they made effective use of Republican tactics such as attack ads, direct-mail fundraising and the implementation of a permanent campaign to help them to achieve their electoral success.

IN THE BEGINNING: THE NEW CANADIAN CONSERVATIVES AND WESTERN ALIENATION

An important early element of the Reagan Republicans' strategy was to capitalize on regional discontent. In their case, this involved targeting alienated white voters in the Deep South, a region increasingly resentful of the federal government for its introduction of civil-rights legislation, desegregation, and affirmative-action programs. Reagan's emphasis on states' rights, and his promise to "restore to state and local governments the power that rightfully belongs to them"[2] (a commitment widely interpreted as code for his support for eliminating such programs), was crucial to the Republicans' success, and in fact cemented the party's support in the region for more than a generation.

From the beginning, Canadian conservatives found a useful parallel to this strategy in the growing phenomenon of western alienation. True, this regional alienation was based on perceived economic discrimination and central Canadian indifference, rather than the searing racial issues that estranged the American Deep South, but it was nevertheless significant, and it had increasingly caused problems for the governing Liberals. However, before Preston Manning's efforts to target this discontent with Reform slogans such as "the West wants in," the Liberals had managed to poll a fairly consistent 25 per cent of the vote in the region and elect some MPs in at least three of the four provinces (Alberta being the exception). Meanwhile, the protest vote against the Liberals, however significant, had often been split between the Progressive Conservatives and the NDP, so that there was no single beneficiary. And, with the bulk of the population located in central Canada, the inability of the Liberals to recover in the West had not seriously affected their ability to form majority governments.

By the time Stephen Harper took the helm of the new Conservative Party, however, Preston Manning had cemented conservative support in western Canada under the Reform Party. Manning's strategy was twofold. First, he proposed platform planks that he claimed would allow the West to acquire more influence in Ottawa, such as Senate reform and his Triple-E Senate plan. Secondly, he argued for a more decentralized federation, in which Ottawa would cede power to the provinces and recognize the areas of jurisdiction he believed had originally been intended for them in the constitution. Put simply, this was Manning's version of Ronald Reagan's states-rights argument that captured the American South.

Manning and Harper, as his research director, took another page from the New Right Republicans' manual when they added a social-conservative element to the Reform platform in order to expand the party's base and recruit active supporters from right-wing special-interest groups. They accentuated the social-conservative aspects of the platform through opposition to the welfare state and support for "family values," adding more Canadian context through planks opposing bilingualism, multiculturalism, and aboriginal self-government, all of which were unpopular with right-wing voters in the West. Their efforts here involved attracting support from such diverse right-wing social-action groups as the Canadian Taxpayers' Federation (the counterpart of Grover Norquist's American Taxpayers' Federation), the National Citizens Coalition (in which both Manning and Harper were directly involved), the National Firearms Association (modelled on the American National Rifle Association (NRA), to which Harper minister Vic Toews had extensive ties), REAL Women, the Canadian version of Phyllis Schlafly's anti-affirmative-action Eagle Movement, and numerous anti-abortion, anti-gay-rights movements in the US. In several cases, specific elements of Reform's platform corresponded directly with proposals made by these various right-wing American groups.[3]

Unlike Stephen Harper, Preston Manning was also a populist in the mould of Ronald Reagan. This was hardly surprising, given the record of his father, former Alberta premier Ernest Manning, and Manning senior's mentor, "Bible Bill" Aberhart, who had successfully introduced the right-wing Social Credit Party to the province by adopting populist policies. As a result, Manning added populist accountability measures to Reform's platform, such as citizen referenda and recall, along with commitments to allow more discretion for individual MPs and less party discipline. All of these were designed to appeal to western Canadians, whose mistrust of the federal government resembled that of the conservative Americans the Reagan Republicans were targeting.

To understand the success of this strategy in the West it is important to remember that the election of the Mulroney Progressive Conservatives in 1984, after almost twenty straight years of Liberal governments (the brief Clark interregnum having failed to make any impact), had led alienated westerners to assume their voices would finally be heard and their grievances addressed. Instead, it increasingly appeared to them that the Progressive Conservative Party, the only other major mainstream party that was capable of forming a national government, was equally insensitive to their concerns and equally focused on central Canada. In fact the PC leader, Brian Mulroney, had been elected in Quebec and was now spending much of his time and energy on Quebec's constitutional concerns. Moreover the Tory strand of the Progressive Conservatives' philosophy appeared to be in control, with little or no effort being made to rein in the welfare state or reduce taxation.

With the West's growing disdain for Mulroney's constitutional efforts on behalf of Quebec, and outrage at his plans to increase taxes through the introduction of the GST, Manning's new right-wing party began to receive some serious attention and support from well-known conservatives in Alberta, such as journalist Ted Byfield, author of the *Western Report,* and financier Francis Winspear, who bankrolled many party activities.

The Liberals were unable to benefit from this Progressive Conservative backlash in the West, and the Reform Party moved in to fill the gap. From winning one seat in a 1989 by-election, the new party quickly gained steam and helped to bring about the collapse of the Progressive Conservatives in 1993. As many analysts have outlined, this marked the beginning of a realignment of political parties in Canada, which Ken Carty, William Cross, and Lisa Young have referred to as the "fourth party system" in their book *Rebuilding Canadian Party Politics*.[4] Instead of the decades-long three-party scenario, the federal political scene now counted four parties, with the PC collapse having produced two regional fringe parties, Reform in the West and the Bloc Québécois in Quebec.

In 1993, when the PCs were decimated, the Liberals returned to power with the first of Jean Chrétien's three majority governments, taking 41 per cent of the popular vote and 177 seats. But they did not do well in the West. Reform took only 19 per cent of the overall popular vote, but due to its heavy concentration of support in the West, and an electoral system weighted in favour of rural ridings, this translated into a surprising 52 seats. All but one of these were in the four western provinces. The western base of the new right-wing conservative party was established.

But this western "pillar" alone was hardly sufficient if they wanted to become a national party and form a national government. True, with the 1997 federal election, having taken 60 seats, Reform's status did rise to that of the Official Opposition, and it did run candidates in all ridings across Canada. Moreover, its status in the West (where the Liberals' gun-control legislation proved an excellent wedge issue for Reform and allowed it – with considerable help from the NFA – to take many seats with more than 60 per cent of the popular vote), had been further solidified. Nevertheless, Reform's share of the overall popular vote remained stalled at 19 per cent, and it actually lost its only seat east of Manitoba.

For many observers this seemed to confirm Reform's status as a regional party, and – given several of the more extreme positions outlined in its platform and expressed by many of its MPs – a fringe party at that. Perhaps equally troubling for Reform's future prospects was the almost equal strength of the separatist Bloc Québécois and the resurgence of the Progressive Conservative Party under Jean Charest, which now held twenty seats and received only 1 per cent less of the popular vote than Reform.

This impasse led to a period of turbulence within the new party. Tensions rose between those like Manning, who were unwilling to compromise on policy to obtain votes, and those like Harper, who were far more pragmatic and intent on forming a government at all costs. Its organizers attempted to alter the party's image through a number of makeovers, but some early supporters, such as Harper, threw in the towel and left. Initially, this appeared to be a sensible decision. Despite having changed its name to the Canadian Alliance Party and recruiting a seemingly charismatic new leader in former Alberta finance minister Stockwell Day, the "new and improved" vehicle for right-wing conservatives still made no significant headway in the 2000 election. It also ran into considerable difficulty in that election by appearing to confirm the accusations of the Liberals and NDP that the party had a "hidden agenda," a tactic that memorably forced Day to "clarify" his position on medicare during the televised leaders' debates.

In addition, although Manning rarely spoke of his evangelical beliefs, Day had decided to place more emphasis on social conservatism, and especially moral conservatism. A lay minister in a Pentecostal church, Day inadvertently focused attention on his own beliefs and those of many in his party by his aggressively unapologetic "theocon" posture, for example with his announcement at the beginning of the election that he would not campaign on Sundays. His ultimate demise came at the hands of a Liberal pundit, Warren Kinsella, who successfully ridiculed Day's rejection of the theory of evolution with the help of a plush purple dinosaur that Kinsella claimed "is the only dinosaur to have walked the earth at the same time as man."

Although the 2000 election confirmed the Reform/Alliance lock on western Canada, Day was viewed as a failure. The party's very future seemed to be in doubt, especially when the continued presence of the PCs led to concerns that they were "dividing the right." Shortly after, Day was replaced as Alliance leader by Stephen Harper, who had been convinced to return to politics on the understanding that he was only interested in winning, and would do what was necessary to achieve his end.

STEP 2: THE REFORM / ALLIANCE "MERGER" WITH PROGRESSIVE CONSERVATIVES

In the US the New Right was able to simply take over the Republican Party, as Margaret Thatcher had done with Britain's Conservative Party. But those were two-party systems. Canada's new conservatives were obliged to undergo a much more time-consuming and complicated "merger" to achieve control of a political party that would be both potentially successful and truly national, and Stephen Harper was the man to do it.

It was here that the fundraising capacity of Reform/Alliance would play a major role. Their hugely successful use of direct mail to raise funds from members of sympathetic right-wing social-action groups had provided ample resources for the Reform/Alliance to operate. Meanwhile the cash-strapped PCs were considering shuttering their national office due to a lack of funds. In the end, it was their belief that they could not survive financially to fight another election that led some of the PC Party elites to respond favourably to the "Unite the Right" movement. In December 2003, this culminated in the creation of the new Conservative Party, after a formal agreement was reached between Alliance Party leader Stephen Harper and PC leader Peter MacKay.

As the first leader of the new party, Stephen Harper, despite cultivating the public image of a merger of equals, ensured that in reality it remained relentlessly right-wing. In a merger where the tail was wagging the dog, the new Conservative Party quickly abandoned the Tory aspects of the old PC Party philosophy, along with most of its political elites. The dominance of the new conservative agenda, both economic and social, was never in doubt. But the merger also led to Harper's pragmatic decision to downplay social-conservative issues in the party's first policy platform and to focus on his right-wing economic agenda, not only to have a better chance of achieving electoral victory, but also as a way of holding the new party together in the early days by avoiding philosophical clashes with the new PC members.

Once again Harper's pragmatism was based on a sound understanding of the Canadian political reality. As his former academic mentor and chief of staff, Tom Flanagan, once pointed out, "Canada is not yet a conservative or Conservative country. The party cannot win if it veers too far to the right of the average voter."[5] For Harper this reality heavily influenced his electoral strategy. It meant, for example, that there would be no discussion of eliminating medicare, despite his personal preferences, because it had been shown to be a fundamental element of Canadians' political psyche. Stockwell Day's desperate attempts to retrieve the situation after missteps on that front in the 2000 election had made this abundantly clear. Moreover, there would be a substantial watering down of Conservative platform proposals, on the clear understanding that any conservative victory could only be achieved through slow but steady incremental change – or policy by stealth.

This did not mean that Harper would fail to take advantage of the coalition that he and Manning had built, and which he would find invaluable in terms of fundraising and campaign organization. Harper fully expected to benefit from the numerous connections that already existed between his party and the various right-wing special-interest and citizen-action groups. In addition to providing valuable and seemingly "non-partisan" endorsements, the funds provided by individual members of these groups filled the coffers. Many of their members also chose to work as grass-roots party volunteers during election campaigns, providing instant organizational support in many ridings. The results spoke for themselves. In the subsequent 2006 and 2008 elections, these groups played significant roles in the growing Conservative margins of victory.

One reason for this electoral success was the large number of senior Conservative Party members who had themselves been involved in many of these groups, both in Canada and in the United States. Indeed, the linkages were striking. Having served as vice-president and president of the National Citizens Coaltion between 1997 and 2002, Harper's own contacts were excellent. To these were added the extensive network of Jason Kenney, who had become acquainted with former Reagan adviser Grover Norquist and his American Taxpayers' Federation (ATF) while studying in the United States. Kenney became the first director of the spinoff Saskatchewan Taxpayers' Federation in 1989, and president of the Canadian Taxpayers' Federation (CTF) in 1990.

Kenney's fellow caucus member John Williamson also served as president of the CTF before becoming an MP. In the same way that the ATF supported the Reagan Republicans, the CTF regularly supported the deficit-reduction and tax-cutting policies of the Reform/Alliance Party, and subsequently of the new Conservative Party. Meanwhile Calgary MP Rob Anders had worked for the Republican Party on the 1994 Senate campaign of Jim Inhofe in Oklahoma (according to his biographical notes, as a professional heckler), but he also served as the director of Canadians Against Forced Unionism, an organization related to the National Citizens Coalition.

Then there was the anti-gun-registry lobby, spearheaded by the Canadian Firearms Association with considerable assistance from the American parent National Rifle Association. MPs Vic Toews, Art Hanger, and Garry Breitkreuz had all been actively participating in the organization's activities and frequently appeared in the American organization's infomercials. In return, the NRA sent "advisers" to work with various Canadian groups on tactics during the lead-up to the 2006 election. Most observers agreed the gun registry played a key role in electing Conservative MPs in several provinces.

Nevertheless, Harper's 2002 return to politics, as Alliance and then Conservative Party leader, had been predicated on his determination to form a government. Unlike Manning he was not prepared to be the conscience of a government while languishing on the

Opposition benches. To succeed, he knew he would need to do more than simply play down the party's social conservatism after the merger. He would need to expand his strategic coalition if his new party was to make a breakthrough in vote-rich and seat-rich central Canada – and to do so he was prepared to sacrifice some principles if necessary.

STEP 3: EXPANDING THE NEW CONSERVATIVE COALITION

In a piece they co-authored in 1997, when Harper was out of politics and serving as president of the National Citizens Coalition, Stephen Harper and Tom Flanagan argued that no future conservative victory could be achieved without the support of western populists and Quebec nationalists, along with the "red Tory" Progressive Conservatives concentrated in Ontario and the Atlantic provinces. This was essentially the coalition that Brian Mulroney had forged, and which had collapsed.

They referred to this as their "three sisters" strategy. At the time, they saw no other alternative, because, as they specifically noted when referring to the Republicans' co-option of southern Democrats, Canadian politics were different from the United States, not only because of the greater commitment to liberalism, but because of the existence of Quebec.[6] However, like the New Right strategists, Harper and Flanagan were convinced that, by targeting the vote and ignoring all those who realistically could not be captured by the appeal of conservatism, they could eventually succeed.

Tellingly, they phrased their dilemma in terms of the two conservative role models who have so influenced Harper's thinking:

> Canadian conservatism is also a family of three sisters fated to perish in isolation unless they descend from their mountain tops and embrace more realistic expectations. In more prosaic language, the central question for Canadian conservatives is this: Can Canada ever have a version of the Thatcher-Reagan phenomenon – a broadly based, centre-right party committed to a definite and consistent conservative philosophy, and able to govern?[7]

Their answer was yes. With the western "sister" guaranteed and the PC "sister" supposedly accounted for by the merger, Quebec nationalists were the remaining pillar that required Harper's attentions. Quebec was an essential element of the Conservative strategy because of its importance in the electoral system. With 75 seats, it was second only to Ontario in size. No majority government had ever been formed without its backing. Yet this would be an inherently more difficult task for Harper, since his publicly stated positions on Quebec in the past ran directly counter to this objective. From his opposition to the Charlottetown Accord and rejection of any form of "special status" for Quebec, to his subsequent statement that "Quebec separatists are the problem and they need to be fixed,"[8] Harper was not known as someone who sympathized with Quebec nationalists, nor was he known to be concerned about the possibility of losing that province. Indeed, on more than one occasion he had implied that Canada could continue without Quebec, and for conservatives this would be the simpler option.[9]

As a result, whatever policy options Harper offered to attract Quebec nationalists would inevitably require that he put more than a little water in his wine. However the issue of how to handle Quebec was put on hold when the Martin government called the election only a few months after the merger and before the new leader and party had had time to consolidate. The platform, due to concerns about placating both sides in the merger, left much unspoken. In addition, a variety of impolitic comments by loose cannons in his caucus and among his candidates sank any hope the party might have had of appearing less radical and threatening. The Liberals under Paul Martin made good use of the "hidden agenda" argument once more. With Harper's refusal to address the abortion issue decisively – declaring on the one hand that he would not introduce legislation to recriminalize, but on the other insisting that private members' bills could do so – his efforts to appear more moderate and attract voters in Quebec, as well as red Tories in Ontario, were doomed. In the end, it was largely due to Martin's own troubles with the Gomery Commission that the Liberals were reduced to minority status.

True, Harper's new Conservative Party had increased its representation from a combined pre-merger total of 78 seats to 99, but this was due entirely to the 21 new seats captured in Ontario, and this number was hugely disappointing given the superior PC record in that province in past elections. As well, the new party actually lost five seats in British Columbia and took no seats in Quebec. Worse still, the combined percentage of the popular vote decreased from

37 per cent to 29 per cent. Clearly not enough Canadians were convinced the right had been united, or were happy with the result.[10]

Given the possibility of another imminent election, due to Martin's minority status, Harper almost immediately began to refine his tactics by taking control of the party and tidying up his operation. Many long-time Reform MPs were discouraged from running again or were not successful in nominations, and a somewhat more presentable group of candidates was assembled. A more professional war room and communications plan was put in place. But in terms of strategy, the situation did not change greatly. The leader would focus even more on Quebec and Ontario.

This time the Conservative platform attempted to increase the party's appeal to the two target groups by producing specific planks. For Quebec nationalists, the party offered Harper's concept of "open federalism." A federal government led by his new Conservative Party would strictly respect provincial jurisdiction and allow provinces to operate with much greater freedom. Meanwhile, to appeal to the Tory vote in Ontario, the platform emphasized economic conservatism, offering tax cuts to the GST and credits for specific items, such as sports equipment and workers' tools, along with the promise of a $1,200 cheque per child to families in lieu of government support for child care. As a minor concession to the social conservatives' concern about law-and-order issues, there were also promises to eliminate minimum sentences and statutory release of prisoners, as well as the perennial pledge to axe the gun registry. And, finally, in a nod to the populists in the party, and to take advantage of the Liberals' ongoing image difficulties with the Gomery Commission, the platform pledged to deliver transparency and accountability in government.

At the beginning of the 2006 campaign, few observers expected the election would produce significant change. Instead, this proved to be a turning point for the new Conservative Party, although it was not only their careful targeting of the two sisters, but events beyond their control, that helped them form a minority government. First, the RCMP unexpectedly announced that they were investigating Liberal Finance Minister Ralph Goodale's role in his government's recent decision on income trusts, a bizarre move that destroyed any chance the Liberals had to put the Gomery affair and allegations of corruption behind them. Secondly, a young woman was fatally wounded in a gang-related shooting spree in downtown Toronto. The Liberal fortunes plummeted, and the Conservatives – as a result of these two events – were the beneficiaries, thanks to their tough-on-crime and accountability planks.

As well, Harper's own performance during the campaign was greatly improved, while the Martin Liberals were in a state of almost total disarray. Polls began to suggest the Conservatives might be able to form a government. Then Harper unwisely commented on this situation, appearing overconfident by indicating that he was planning to appoint a transition team. When it seemed that a majority might not be out of the question, he added to the damage with his declaration that it was safe to vote for his party because the Liberals still controlled the Senate, bureaucracy, and Supreme Court. His support began to slip almost immediately as the "hidden agenda" fears resurfaced, but there was not enough time for the Liberals to spring back.

In the end, the new Conservative Party accomplished the unthinkable and formed a minority government. The party had taken seats in every province except Prince Edward Island. It even appeared that they might have formed a beachhead in Quebec, with ten seats. While Harper was given much credit for this by his colleagues, most analysts attributed the Conservative inroads to the Liberal collapse in that province because of Gomery, and felt it was too early to tell whether any permanent shift in support to Harper's party had occurred. Similarly the Conservatives had increased their support in Ontario, but it was impossible to know if this was only a temporary rejection of the Liberals as punishment, or the beginning of a voter realignment.[11]

The bad news was that the party had actually lost seats in the West, and did not win a single seat in Canada's three major urban centres, Montreal, Toronto, and Vancouver. In fact, the party remained solidly anchored in the West, whose MPs represented more than 50 per cent of the caucus. Worse still, with the total percentage of the popular vote and seat results still extremely close, in spite of the Liberals' disastrous campaign – at 36 per cent and 124 seats for the Conservatives, versus 30 per cent and 103 seats for the Liberals, it did not prove a convincing victory or one that many anticipated would last long.

SETBACK: THE FAILURE OF THE QUEBEC NATIONALIST STRATEGY

Now that Harper had formed a government, the tools of power were at his disposal to attempt to consolidate his party's coalition through further efforts to obtain the support of Quebec nationalists. In short order, he proceeded to demonstrate his willingness to set aside principles in pursuit of political expediency. To begin with, he appointed four of his ten Quebec MPs to cabinet. Then he added a fifth cabinet member from Quebec, to represent the Montreal region, which had not returned any Conservatives, by appointing his campaign co-chair, Michael Fortier, to the Senate. (Fortier would resign before the 2008 election to run in a by-election for a seat in the House of Commons, and be defeated.)

Meanwhile one of Harper's new Quebec MPs, Maxime Bernier, owed much of his overwhelming personal victory (an impressive 67 per cent of the popular vote) to his name and the reputation of his father, Gilles Bernier, who had served as a popular MP in the government of Brian Mulroney. Harper immediately appointed Maxime Bernier to cabinet as minister of industry. Barely eighteen months later, in August 2007, Bernier was promoted to a post with a much higher profile, minister of foreign affairs. This did not prove to be a success. He was almost immediately embroiled in a number of highly publicized controversies that culminated in his removal from cabinet a year later.

Harper also courted the province directly. He began by meeting with Quebec premier Jean Charest, the first premier with whom he held one-on-one meetings. At the press conference that followed the meeting, Harper repeatedly praised Charest's handling of medicare wait times, a subject that Harper had addressed during the election campaign.

Shortly afterwards, Harper reiterated a commitment made during the election campaign: to allow Quebec to participate directly in some international meetings, beginning with UNESCO. On 7 May 2006, Harper and Charest signed a formal agreement which stated, "This agreement is a clear illustration of our vision of open federalism. We are at the dawn of a new era, an era that will see us build a strong, united, free and independent Canada in which a confident, autonomous, proud and unified Quebec can develop its full potential." Coming from someone who had opposed any form of special status for Quebec, this move was seen by many as blatant opportunism, and by some in his own party as treason, but Harper persevered by assuring them that this strategy of pragmatic accommodation would provide them with a majority government.

Barely six months later, when the Liberals were in the midst of a leadership race to replace Paul Martin, Harper struck again. He seized on an opposition motion put forward by the Bloc Québécois, designed to recognize Quebecers as a "nation." Although Bloc leader Gilles Duceppe had not expected the motion to pass, he had hoped it would cause trouble among the Liberal leadership candidates, since one of them, Michael Ignatieff, had proposed a similar idea during the campaign, and other candidates had vigorously opposed it. Harper surprised everyone by tabling a government motion, with slightly altered language, the day before the Bloc item was scheduled for debate, thereby forcing the Liberals and the Bloc to respond to the motion on his terms. The motion passed, and Harper took credit for the initiative. Here again he firmly believed this measure, which was largely symbolic, would reap considerable benefit for the party in Quebec in the next election. Moreover it had cost him little. And former adviser Tom Flanagan, an even more ardent opponent of special status than Harper, had come to his defence, to everyone's surprise, praising his pragmatism and strategic sense.[12]

However, as a provincial election drew near, the strength of Harper's commitment to the Quebec nationalist strategy was challenged more substantially when Jean Charest played the fiscal-imbalance card, fearing that the opposition Parti Québécois was gaining in support. The argument that Quebec was not receiving its "fair share" of federal largesse, relative to its contribution to federal coffers, had been rejected by federal politicians of all stripes for many years. Even former Liberal finance minister and prime minister Paul Martin, who also had attempted to woo Quebec nationalists as part of his own failed re-election strategy in 2006, had categorically denied the existence of a fiscal imbalance. Yet Harper responded positively to Charest's argument and committed some $1.5 billion in the 2007 budget to "fix" the fiscal imbalance once and for all.

Unfortunately for Harper, Charest then proceeded to use nearly $700 million of that windfall to fund tax cuts for Quebecers as part of his provincial election campaign. This move not only infuriated western Canadians, but failed to give Charest any advantage. He was returned with a minority government, and the Harper Conservatives suffered a serious blow to their image as prudent fiscal managers.[13] The negative repercussions continued after the election, when Bloc leader Gilles Duceppe used the February 2008 federal budget to claim that Harper had not in fact "fixed" the fiscal imbalance, since he had not committed to withdraw all federal spending in areas of provincial jurisdiction. The dispute received considerable coverage in Quebec, and the Conservatives perversely came to be seen as anti-nationalist, despite their best efforts.

To Harper's chagrin, the party's situation did not improve during the fall 2008 election. Instead, Quebec became part of the problem for the Conservatives, not the solution. First the Bloc made much of the Conservatives' platform promise to reduce the age of young offenders and increase sentences. In Quebec, with its strong commitment to crime prevention and rehabilitation rather than the conservative preference for retribution, this proposal was viewed with horror. Harper did not help his cause when he rashly tried to repair the damage by claiming Quebec could enact a different age of majority than the rest of the country if it wanted, a clearly unconstitutional suggestion which raised eyebrows across the country.

The Conservatives' fortunes deteriorated further when Gilles Duceppe seized on their plan to cut some $45 million in federal funding for arts and culture grants, a move which most Quebecers saw as a direct attack on their culture. When Harper unwisely declared that this was a cut that most Canadians would support, since they "did not attend rich galas," as many artists who "depended on state support" did, his fate in the province was sealed.

As a result, despite the Liberals running what was arguably the worst campaign in their modern history with their weakest leader (Stéphane Dion, the victor in the party's December 2006 leadership race), the Conservatives still were not able to turn their government's record in Quebec and their coalition strategy into a majority victory. Although the Liberals were reduced from 103 to 76 seats, the Bloc held firm in Quebec and the NDP increased their support in Ontario, the Conservatives' overall share of the popular vote remained almost identical to 2006, and only the decrease in Liberal support allowed them to take a number of seats, because many traditional Liberal voters stayed home. Worse, although Harper's government increased their representation from 124 to 143 seats, they were still 12 seats shy of the minimum needed to form a majority.

In Quebec, the Conservatives held on to the 10 seats they had won in 2006, but made no gains in seats, and their share of the popular vote actually decreased. After so much effort, it appeared the Quebec pillar of their coalition was unattainable, and a new approach – and a new pillar – was necessary if they were ever to achieve a majority.

Ironically, the source of inspiration for this alternative pillar came from the pre-existing and most extreme element of the party's makeup, namely the moral conservative, or "theocon," segment that Harper had so assiduously downplayed for so long. While its role had long been crucial *within* the party, it would now become a springboard to a new outreach approach to minority groups, as the party used moral-wedge issues to pry loose from the Liberals the recent immigrants residing in the 905 region around Toronto and in exurban Vancouver.

Here too, Republican strategists had led the way, but in this case it was not a path that Stephen Harper originally expected to follow. The decision of New Right organizers to recruit Christian evangelicals was politically astute, given that America is overwhelmingly a Christian society. According to Gallup polling data, more than 80 per cent of Americans describe themselves as practising Christians. Some 43 per cent self-describe as born-again or evangelical Christians, a proportion not found in any other western democracy. With the Republicans' co-option of the religious right, or what Jerry Falwell termed the Moral Majority, they now form the rock-solid base of the party. (True, the guaranteed support of this element of their coalition came with a price, as the 2012 race for the Republican presidential candidate demonstrated, when several right-wing fringe candidates with strong evangelical support forced frontrunner Mitt Romney to move much further to the right in order to secure the nomination.) But Harper knew that Canadian political culture did not mirror the Americans in this regard, and was unwilling to take the risk until he was convinced there was no other alternative.

STEP 4: THE RELIGIOUS RIGHT AND THE NEW CONSERVATIVE PARTY

The role of the religious right in the Conservative Party was not well-known until recently, largely because of Stephen Harper's determination to avoid the subject at all costs. This is hardly surprising in terms of political strategy. As Canadian sociologist Reginald Bibby and pollster Michael Adams have demonstrated, Canada is a predominantly secular society, which is moving in many respects in the opposite direction from its neighbour to the south.[14] Only 12 per cent of Canadians identified themselves as evangelical Christians in the 2011 National Household Survey (the successor to Statistics Canada's long-form census), while twice as many, or nearly one-quarter of respondents, indicated they had no religion at all.

This might well have suggested to the casual observer that the New Right's successful co-option of the religious right in America was not a strategy that would bear fruit for the far right in Canada, and this was certainly Stephen Harper's original conclusion. But he eventually concluded that this was a mistake. Despite the religious right's minimal presence in Canada, as discussed, the willingness of the new political party to include their views in its platform had opened the door to their enthusiastic participation in Canadian politics. The result was strategically significant for the Conservatives and allowed the evangelical Christian community in Canada to punch far above its weight. Indeed, some analysts have concluded the participation of evangelical Christians and their various organizations were a key element of the Conservatives' 2006 electoral victory. The findings of the Canadian Election Study (a series of academic research papers published after each federal election for the past four decades) supported this claim, and confirmed the trend for evangelical Christians to support the Conservatives in the 2008 and 2011 federal elections as well.[15] In addition, as former NDP MP Dennis Gruending has noted in recent work on the role of the religious right in Canada, there has also been an organized effort by evangelicals to forge alliances with conservative Catholics on issues such as gay marriage and abortion, a phenomenon that has drained votes from the Liberals, who traditionally benefited from the Catholic vote.[16]

One reason for the efficacy of such a small group is their concentration in western Canada, and particularly in Alberta and the Fraser Valley region of British Columbia. This has allowed them to dominate ridings in rural and exurban areas, of which there are a disproportionate number, due to the weighting in favour of these ridings in the electoral system.[17]

A second reason is the influence and assistance provided by their American counterparts, who in many cases have been the template for the creation of Canadian equivalents. Some groups, such as Focus on the Family Canada and Promise Keepers Canada, are literally Canadian branches of their American parent organizations.

Others, such as the Evangelical Fellowship of Canada and the Christians United for Israel, have close ties with similar American organizations and many common board members. Almost all of the American organizations have actively participated in the Canadian debates on issues such as abortion and same-sex marriage, through media broadcasts, volunteer workers, and financial support. In 2006, their efforts to influence election outcomes in Canada using American tactics saw Canadian evangelical Charles McVety's Defend Marriage Coalition distribute "report cards" on political parties in churches, and target Liberal and NDP MPs whom it claimed supported "same-sex marriage, child pornography, and physician-assisted suicide."[18]

The connections between the Conservatives and the evangelical organizations of the religious right arguably began when Stephen Harper addressed the Council on National Policy (CNP) in 1997. The by-invitation-only event, whose speakers require the unanimous consent of its executive committee, was an opportunity to meet what the *New York Times* has called "a club of the most powerful conservatives in the country," and journalist Robert Dreyfuss has described as "a secretive group of wealthy donors that has funnelled billions of dollars to right-wing Christian activists."[19] The CNP is actually an umbrella organization founded by, among others, veteran Republican strategist Paul Weyrich and Tim LaHaye, an evangelical Christian and author of several bestselling apocalyptic novels. Its membership list includes individuals such as Jerry Falwell and groups such as James Dobson's Focus on the Family, Ralph Reed's Christian Coalition of America, Morton Blackwell's Leadership Institute, the League for Life, and the National Rifle Association. In 1997, the CNP executive director was none other than Morton Blackwell, who issued the invitation to Harper. As a result of the contacts Harper made there, and the people recruited to run for or work for the Reform/Alliance Party, the connections between Canadian organizations and their American counterparts quickly became even more numerous and significant.

A third reason for the disproportionate influence of Canada's evangelicals is the masterful way in which Stephen Harper has managed to attract and maintain their support while balancing the political scales. Here again, pragmatism has been the byword. Although Harper himself belongs to an evangelical denomination, the Christian and Missionary Alliance, he was well-known in the early years of the Reform/Alliance party for his insistence on publicly avoiding taking a position on the moral issues of interest to this group – such as abortion, gay marriage, reproductive technology, and other family-values concerns – because he was convinced it would be politically fatal to do so in the Canadian context. Given the self-destruction of Stockwell Day, there was initially good reason for him to believe that he had been correct. However, with the failure of the conservative right's efforts to make a breakthrough nationally after more than a decade, Harper delivered the famous Civitas speech in 2003 in which he concluded that only through expanding the social-conservative coalition and including moral issues as part of the Conservative platform could they hope to prevail.

An important distinction for Harper was that, unlike Day, he did not believe that he needed to speak about his personal beliefs. Indeed, there were some in the party who were convinced that he was merely an economic conservative and did not share their views. But Harper eventually decided he needed to focus on issues that would attract the moral conservatives and prompt them to become vigorous party supporters, both financially and in terms of recruitment and organization, all the while making sure to avoid a mainstream backlash.

As a result, Harper carefully targeted issues he believed could be managed. He was firmly opposed to any direct mention of abortion, just as he had been careful to avoid any discussion of weakening medicare, but he was prepared to go on the offensive about child pornography, affirmative action, and publicly funded child care. Moreover, in the 2006 election he promised to put the question of gay marriage to a vote in the House of Commons, despite the fact it had already been implemented as a result of several court decisions, and he knew the vote would not succeed. The result was an enthusiastic evangelical grassroots campaign in favour of the Conservatives, and an elated announcement on his program from David Mainse (Christian televangelist and founder of the *100 Huntley Street* television show) shortly after the Conservative victory, "We have a born again Christian prime minister!").

Harper's success in maintaining this fine line between cautious support for key issues promoted by the religious right and a firm refusal to consider others has paid considerable dividends. Once he obtained his majority in 2011, Harper increasingly allowed private members' bills to be introduced to address some of the most contentious issues, claiming that they were not government policy but that his caucus members were free to pursue them if they could receive sufficient support. Over time he also offered carrots such as the Office of Religious Freedom, and pursued a Middle East policy heavily weighted in favour of Israel, a policy diametrically opposed to Canada's traditional post-war position, but one that found great favour with many fundamentalist evangelicals, who viewed Israel's continued existence as an essential precursor to the Second Coming.

As award-winning journalist Marci McDonald has traced in painstaking detail in her book *Armageddon*, the interconnections between various evangelical organizations and interest groups and the membership and operation of the new Conservative Party are complex and legion.[20] Within Harper's actual caucus, one estimate by the *Vancouver Sun* placed the number of evangelical Christians at 50 per cent, or more than four times their representation in the general population.

Not surprisingly, then, the linkages between ministers in the Harper cabinet and these various religious groups are extensive as well. For example, in addition to Stockwell Day, both Jason Kenney and Vic Toews have less-well-known but close relationships with leading members of the American religious right. Kenney, a conservative Catholic, attended the Jesuit-run St. Ignatius College in San Francisco and participated in Ralph Reed's massive Christian Coalition rally of 1995 in Washington, DC. As a result, Kenney was instrumental in the creation of the first Canadian counterpart of that organization, located in British Columbia. He has also participated extensively in anti-abortion campaigns in both countries. As an opposition MP, Kenney posted a testimonial to well-known American anti-abortionist Scott Klusendorf, praising "his contribution to the pro-life movement in Canada," and stated that "having been involved in pro-life argumentation for most of my life, I nevertheless learned a great deal from Scott's techniques, which I plan to employ in the future."[21] In 2012, as minister of immigration in Harper's cabinet, Kenney ignored Harper's directive to oppose a Conservative MP's private member's bill which would have reopened the abortion debate. Kenney and seven other Conservative cabinet ministers, including Rona Ambrose, minister for the status of women, supported the bill, along with more than half of Harper's caucus.

Meanwhile Vic Toews, Harper's one-time minister of public safety, has been closely associated with both the Focus on the Family and Concerned Women for America, two groups that vehemently oppose abortion, stem-cell research, and gay marriage. He quoted their studies in the House of Commons and in a speech given to the League for Life, entitled "Abuses of the Charter by the Supreme Court," in which he attacked rulings on same-sex marriage.[22] Jim Flaherty, another conservative Catholic, also had long-standing ties to the religious right and the anti-abortion movement, and even received extensive support from Charles McVety and his Canada Christian College when he ran for the leadership of the Ontario Conservative Party in 2002. (Flaherty's unexpectedly extreme social-conservative positions came to the fore during that race with his proposal to make homelessness illegal.) Other leading members of the religious, right in Harper's caucus include MPs Rob Anders (a graduate of Morton Blackwell's Leadership Institute), Maurice Vellacott, Russ Hiebert (legal counsel to the Canada Family Action Coaltion), and Darrel Reid (a former president of Focus on the Family Canada).

As a result of these close connections, and the positive results the party had achieved to that point, the proposal to take advantage of the religious-right connection in order to craft a new third pillar to replace Quebec seemed less politically dangerous than it would have some years before. In fact, it seemed increasingly likely to be the solution to their problems.

STEP 5: TARGETING MINORITIES: WEDGE ISSUES AND THE "HARPER LIBERALS"

As Tom Flanagan wrote after the disappointing 2006 minority result: "The key to the long-term success of the Liberals has been their cultivation of minority groups. Conservatives have to take away that advantage."[23] Flanagan was on to something, but the question was how to do it.

Unhappily for the Liberals, former Reform MP and conservative Catholic Jason Kenney, then serving as Harper's parliamentary secretary, had the answer. The Republican New Right had already demonstrated that it was possible to win by targeting some groups of voters and ignoring others. They had also shown that it was possible to use wedge issues to lure voters away from the opposition. Building on the strategy they had perfected to recruit the so-called "Reagan Democrats," Kenney convinced Harper that the Conservatives could make similar inroads on the Liberals' traditional hold over recent arrivals to Canada by focusing on moral issues that the Liberals had either never addressed or on which they were now vulnerable.[24]

There was little doubt that the Liberals had long taken this immigrant group for granted, and had not paid sufficient attention to changing demographics. Generations of new immigrants had been welcomed to Canada by Liberal governments. Many had originally voted for the party out of gratitude for their acceptance here. Virtually all had become integrated into Canadian society within a generation, and absorbed the liberal values that the party promoted and which they saw as Canadian values. One indication of how successful this integration had been is the fact Canada has the highest percentage among OECD countries of immigrants who become citizens, and therefore can vote.

Yet the composition of newcomers to Canada had changed since the 1980s. New groups, primarily from Asia and the Middle East, brought new customs and new religions, which often included a new set of values as well, some of which came into direct conflict with Canadian laws and mores. While Liberals in the past would have promised these voters equality of opportunity and social justice, the new Conservatives saw an opportunity to focus on narrower concerns with respect to these values, which frequently, as with the same-sex marriage legislation, came into direct conflict with recent Liberal policies. This conflict therefore reinforced the Conservative message.

Kenney pointed out that these minority groups were politically important, because new immigrants to Canada routinely settle in urban areas, and it was in these urban areas where the Conservatives had failed to make headway in the last federal election. Indeed, they had been shut out of the three largest urban areas, all of which were home to substantial numbers of recent immigrants from Asia. Even more importantly, these groups tended to cluster in specific ridings in the suburban and exurban areas (the 905 region in Toronto and areas such as Richmond and Burnaby in Vancouver), so that the Conservatives could even more precisely target those ridings.[25] Last but hardly least, the most important concentration of these groups occurs in Ontario, the province that constituted their only other option in their attempts to find another pillar to achieve a majority government.

Kenney did not waste time, nor did he leave anything to chance. Having been handed this mandate by the prime minister personally,

Kenney soon created a detailed strategy for targeting and winning the so-called "ethnic vote," and maintained a gruelling personal schedule to implement it. Within the space of two years, the man his own colleagues dubbed "the minister for curry in a hurry" attended more than five hundred events at Sikh temples, Chinese New Year celebrations, and Muslim mosques. He also employed voter-profiling software to develop a sophisticated immigrant database, which was then used to target individuals with direct-mail campaigns and to offer groups regular meetings with the prime minister and other cabinet ministers.

In addition to the personal touch and access to government officials, Kenney – who two years later became minister of citizenship and immigration – was also able to deliver specific policies that reflected the Harper government's determination to win the support of these various communities. They included many symbolic acts, such as the prime-ministerial apologies for the *Komagata Maru* incident, compensation for the Chinese head tax, and motions in the House of Commons recognizing the Armenian and Ukrainian genocides. They were accompanied by concrete action on under-the-radar issues in mainstream Canada, such as marriage fraud. Similarly, while many Canadians may have been astonished to view photographs of the prime minister meeting with a Korean convenience-store owner in Toronto before the 2011 election, Jason Kenney was not. The shop owner had pursued and restrained a thief, and then been threatened with prosecution. The setting was chosen specifically to announce a criminal code amendment regarding citizens' arrests, an issue of great concern to many small shopkeepers in the Asian community.[26]

Despite this massive campaign, it is unlikely that the existence of Kenney's plan would have come to light had it not been for a leaked memo from his own office. Entitled "Breaking Through: Building the Conservative Brand," it contained sections on numbers, resources, and, most importantly, the costs of implementation, which were staggering in terms of the cost for ad purchases and media spots. (Some $200,000 was required for each ad sequence, according to the document, and this was in addition to the $750,000 in government funding that, it was later learned, was being spent on the monitoring of ethnic media by the minister's office.) The detail was impressive. Ridings were identified as "ethnic" or "very ethnic," and there were also sections on South Asian versus East Asian issues – "GTA Chinese

Voting Patterns" and "GTA South-Asian Voting Patterns" – as well as frank assessments of the uphill battle the party would be fighting in some instances.

The importance of this strategy of targeting the immigrant vote cannot be underestimated. In a first-past-the-post electoral system with more than two political parties, it is not only possible, but common, for a party to win a majority in parliament without having obtained a majority of the popular vote. But historically in Canada, this had not posed a serious problem, despite the long-standing existence of three political parties. Pierre Trudeau won three majority governments, with roughly 45 per cent of the popular vote each time. Brian Mulroney's first majority in 1984, the largest in Canadian history at 211 seats, was accomplished with 50 per cent of the popular vote. His second majority in 1988 returned to more typical numbers, at 43 per cent of the popular vote, and Jean Chrétien's three majority victories followed a similar pattern.

However, with the demise of the Progressive Conservatives and the advent of the fourth-party system, as described by Carty, Cross, and Young,[27] a new factor entered into play which had important consequences. With four parties, two of which were regional rather than national (the Bloc and Reform/Alliance), and then with five parties, as the Green Party grew in popularity if not in electoral success, the system became increasingly vulnerable to the formation of governments with much less of the popular vote. (In 1993, this is also what allowed the Reform Party, with 19 per cent of the popular vote, to receive 52 seats and come close to forming the Official Opposition, while the Progressive Conservatives, with 16 per cent of the popular vote, received only 2 seats.)

Hence Paul Martin's 2004 minority received 37 per cent of the popular vote, and Stephen Harper's two minorities, in 2006 and 2008, were achieved with only 36 per cent and 37 per cent of the popular vote. In addition, as political scientists Jon Pammett and Lawrence LeDuc note, the percentage of eligible voters who actually cast a ballot declined relentlessly during the new party era, a factor which again contributed to the Conservatives' success, as many Liberal voters stayed home, and young Canadians – the demographic most likely to oppose the Conservatives – did not participate.[28] In a pattern eerily similar to that which allowed the Republicans to win several elections (and Paul Weyrich to exclaim, "I don't *want* everyone to vote!") the Harper Conservatives benefited from voter-turnout levels that fell from the typical 75 per cent in 1988 to only 61 per cent in 2004, 59 per cent in 2008, and 61 per cent in 2011.

The 2011 election demonstrated that the minorities strategy was a success. Targeting the vote in ridings that "counted" produced a *majority* government with only 39 per cent of the popular vote. The Conservatives obtained their majority solely on the basis of the additional seats acquired in Ontario. As LeDuc and Pammett conclude, "The overall gain in the Conservative vote was only 2% but they benefited from where their gains and losses were realized, in part a function of the party's targeting of specific constituencies, particularly in the GTA." Put another way, the "loss of 5% in Quebec cost them five seats, but the gain of 5% in Ontario gave them twenty-one."[29] Although there were other factors involved in the 905 wins, including the collapse of the Liberals and the surge in the NDP, virtually everyone in the Conservative Party describes Jason Kenney as the architect of their majority.

Informed discussion has now turned to the issue of maintenance, as many observers question whether these "Harper Liberals" can be retained in the Conservative fold or whether, like the Reagan Democrats under Clinton and Obama, the Liberals will recapture these crucial voters. This is a particularly pressing issue for the Liberals. As pollster Darrell Bricker outlined, with the 2011 election, "for the first time since who-knows-when, the Conservative vote is more 'efficient' than the Liberal vote." Already at an advantage because of the disproportionate value of their western seats, the Conservatives now have an additional advantage in a five-party universe, especially where targeting the vote is possible. Bricker warned "Liberal dominance in areas with relatively few seats could create a situation in which the Liberals lose the next election even if they win the popular vote." As a result, both Bricker and Eric Grenier, the political scientist whose *threehundredeight.com* website assesses polling data, have concluded the next election "will probably be decided in Greater Toronto and Greater Vancouver," where the combination of the Conservatives' targeted seats and a potentially strong showing by the NDP could cost the Liberals the election.

The Conservatives have clearly recognized the importance of maintaining this voter base. In the July 2013 cabinet shuffle, Jason Kenney was moved to the post of minister of employment and social development (the former HRSDC), yet he specifically retained responsibility for "ethnic outreach," with the title of Minister Responsible for Multiculturalism. At the same time, Tim Uppal, the former minister of state for economic development, was named minister of state for multiculturalism, and newly minted cabinet minister Chris Alexander, who inherited the citizenship and immigration portfolio from Kenney, retained responsibility for the multiculturalism program and policies within government. On the surface, this seemed to be blatant overkill. But as one Conservative insider responded, with apparent sincerity, when asked why three ministers would be needed to tend to the ethnic-outreach file, "A certain portion of Jason Kenney's time will be spent doing HRSDC work – more than was spent doing citizenship work. That probably explains the need for a junior minister, because there's actually ministerial work to be done."[30]

Conversely, much less discussion has taken place concerning the Conservatives' diminished representation in Quebec, to say nothing of their failed Quebec nationalist strategy. Yet many observers have already noted the tendency for Quebec interests to be either ignored or directly challenged by the Harper government now that the party has achieved a majority without the support of that province for the first time in Canada's history. Clearly the implications for national unity could potentially be significant.

SWIFT BOAT REDUX: THE NEW CONSERVATIVE PARTY ATTACK ADS

Underlining the various elements of the coalition strategy that delivered a majority for the Conservatives are several tactics that the party employed to great effect to undermine their enemies while building their coalition, and they have continued to utilize these tactics with enthusiasm since taking power. Perhaps the most obvious of these tactics, and certainly the most divisive, has been the use of attack ads.

The Republicans' 2004 attack ads targeting Democratic presidential candidate John Kerry marked a turning point in American politics, and are universally cited as an example of legendary Republican fixer Karl Rove's best (or worst) handiwork. Although Kerry was a much-decorated Vietnam war hero, Rove is credited with the devastatingly effective "Swift Boat" attack ads, which convinced many Americans that Kerry was in fact an undeserving coward who had lied about his actions. Opinion polls demonstrated that the ads singlehandedly destroyed whatever chances Kerry might have had in the election campaign. Indeed, they were viewed as so successful that the term "swiftboating" has entered into the lexicon, referring to any situation in which someone is unjustly accused or railroaded out of a position on the basis of false information.

As his biographers concluded, "Under Rove, the politics of deception has become a conventional political tool."[31] Rove gave new meaning to the term "spin," and emphasized the importance of "going negative" against opponents. As many pollsters, including Canadian veteran Allan Gregg, have noted, negative campaigns work. With virtually unlimited access to funding, Rove's ability to use advertising as a nearly constant way to shape public opinion on issues – and about opponents – soon became the aspirational norm for all other candidates and parties, and has been well-documented in terms of its efficacy.[32]

A similarly aggressive approach to political campaigns has been taken by Frank Luntz, a highly regarded Republican pollster and media-relations expert whose self-described expertise is "manipulating language for political benefit." Among his better-known campaigns were those that opposed Democratic proposals by redefining them. For Republican "spin doctors," a proposed inheritance tax became a "death tax," global warming became the less worrisome "climate change," its primary cause became "ethical oil," and the Obama healthcare reforms were described as a "government takeover."[33]

For Luntz, a basic tactical truism is: "If you are not popular, make your opponents more unpopular." With an unpopular leader and a platform that still cast lingering doubts about a hidden agenda, the importance of attack ads in contributing to the 2006 and 2008 Conservative minorities can not be overestimated. Harper was aware of this. His 2011 success in achieving a majority, while a significant milestone, has not caused him to abandon this tactic, as he continues to work towards his ultimate goal of rebranding Canadian society and eliminating his Liberal opponents. In fact, the Conservatives' use of attack ads has actually increased.

Luntz is only one of several New Right politicians and tacticians to have met with Stephen Harper and other members of his cabinet and caucus in recent years, but most of these encounters were not publicized. However the presence of Luntz in Ottawa in 2006, and his meeting with the new prime minister, did become a matter of public knowledge. Luntz spoke at a Civitas meeting attended by Harper's then-chief of staff, Ian Brodie, and his former campaign manager Tom Flanagan, and also delivered a "campaign-style" lecture to the Conservative caucus on "how to win a majority in the next election." It included the advice to "hit the Liberals when they're down." When questioned, Harper admitted, "I have known Mr. Luntz for some years," but insisted he was not in the employ of the Conservative Party.[34] Yet much of what the Harper Conservatives have accomplished is due to their careful observation and faithful replication of his tactics, albeit tailored to Canadian circumstances. As Tom Flanagan has recently outlined in his book *Winning Power*, the Conservatives have embraced both negative advertising and the permanent campaign with enthusiasm and great success.[35]

Certainly the use of these new techniques marked a turning point in Canadian politics as well. Despite their increasing frequency and virulence in American politics, attack ads had not been common in Canada. In fact, the use of such an ad by the Progressive Conservatives during the 1993 federal election campaign (which seemed to mock the facial flaws of Liberal leader Jean Chrétien), provoked such a public outcry that for a time it appeared such ads would never again be used in this country.

In the lead-up to the 2000 election, which would be the first and last campaign as Alliance leader for Stockwell Day, the staunch evangelical Christian declared that he and his party would take the moral high ground and refrain from any type of negative campaign rhetoric, including in paid party advertising. His "agenda of respect" was not a success, however. The Martin Liberals took advantage of errant remarks by Alliance MPs and candidates to press their message about the party's hidden agenda. With only soft and reassuring messages in their own ad-campaign arsenal, the Alliance was unable to respond in time or effectively. Frustrated, by the final weeks of the campaign even Day had made a number of increasingly critical comments about Jean Chrétien.[36]

This was all to no avail, though, as was the subsequent campaign conducted by Stephen Harper in 2004, when he was forced to fight an election as the new party's leader before his newly merged Conservative Party was ready. Although he too began with a relatively positive approach, he soon adopted negative tactics that set a new tone, epitomized by an ad accusing Paul Martin of supporting child pornography. When the ad backfired and support for Martin grew, Harper was forced to recall it for changes and watch as his chances of forming a minority government melted away under more Liberal accusations of a hidden agenda.

In the 2006 election, a better-prepared Harper had both an aggressive war room and an aggressive campaign, which anticipated Liberal ads about the hidden agenda by warning Canadians to ignore them. Nevertheless, his party was ready with negative ads accusing the Martin Liberals of corruption and incompetence in the RCMP/Income Trust scandal and the bystander shooting in Toronto, the two major events of the campaign. Both appeared to have found their mark. Coupled with Harper's substantial platform and disciplined performance, to say nothing of Paul Martin's own disastrous campaign, the Conservatives obtained a minority.

The Conservatives were now in power, which theoretically gave them an innate advantage in terms of controlling the message. Moreover, they had more money than they knew what to do with. Already in 2005, when they were preparing for the 2006 election, they had revenue of $25.5 million, compared with only $18 million for the Liberals. But Canada is not the United States, and a substantial framework of financial regulations exists with respect to political fundraising and third-party advertising. With the party's election expenditures capped at $18.3 million by law, the Conservatives' real challenge in 2006 was to ensure they did not spend too much or, at the very least, to find creative ways of spending more. As will be discussed later, this led to their infamous "in and out" scheme to exceed legislated spending limits, which Elections Canada exposed and ruled illegal.

Given these legal limitations on campaign spending, and faced with what they saw as a hostile mainstream media biased in favour of liberalism, the Conservatives believed their obvious alternative was to invest heavily in paid advertising in the pre-writ period, when no regulations applied and when they would indeed be in control of the message. At the time, as the action of a minority government, this technique could perhaps be explained. Another election might take place at any time. But the Conservatives' campaign-style rhetoric and aggressive attack ads continued after the 2008 election, when Harper was returned to power with a larger minority. They actually escalated after Harper obtained his majority in 2011.

Indeed, ever since Stéphane Dion was selected as the Liberals' new leader on 2 December 2006, the Conservatives have wasted little time in attacking each new Liberal leader. Their efforts have been highly successful in discrediting these individuals, primarily by defining each new Liberal leader's image for the voters before he has had a chance to do so himself.

In the case of Dion, the Conservatives actually ran three different series of ads. The first set, unveiled on 27 January 2007, ridiculed Dion mercilessly, often by taking his comments and those of other Liberal leadership candidates out of context. The theme that Dion was "not a leader" was admittedly helped by his own low-key performance and difficulties with English, but many experts were nevertheless stunned by the heretofore unique approach the Conservatives had chosen: to personalize their attacks and focus on the individual rather than the party or its policies. Broadcast during the Superbowl game, an enormously expensive proposition that none of the other parties could have contemplated, this first series also received additional free coverage, as marketing experts debated their merits. One expert concluded, "They almost certainly contributed to the dismal leadership rankings that Dion quickly started to gather in the polls."[37] A Nanos poll in early April reinforced this view. Dion was selected as the best leader by only 17 per cent of respondents, while Harper received the support of 42 per cent. Since Dion had been a popular choice for the Liberals as leader only four months earlier, the quick turnaround in public opinion was all the more surprising.

Although the second set of ads, released in late May 2007, simply reinforced the initial message, a third set, released in June 2007, were another story entirely. Taking a page from Frank Luntz's book, the Conservatives managed to convince voters that Dion's Green Shift, the party's sustainable development platform, was a tax grab. Radio ads denouncing "Dion's tax on everything" and "Dion's tax trick" ran throughout the summer and early fall, even though the Green Shift actually included major tax cuts among its provisions. Although it is impossible to gauge the impact of these ads in isolation, it is noteworthy that the package was initially quite popular, but by September 2008 was opposed by the vast majority of respondents, while Dion's approval ratings had plummeted.[38]

When the writ was finally dropped in fall 2008, many observers felt the Liberals had already lost the election. During the campaign, the Conservatives reinforced the message that the Liberals were planning a tax grab, but went further and described them as "hapless incompetents" whose numbers did not add up. As one analysis of the election noted, not even a statement signed by one hundred prominent economists – declaring the Liberals' platform to be financially sound – was able to overcome the negative image already painted by the Conservatives.[39] The Liberals were reduced to 77 seats from 103, and Harper obtained a more substantial minority. Dion blamed the loss partly on the attack ads, and noted that the Liberals did not have the money to respond to them in the pre-writ era. Meanwhile Tom Flanagan concluded, "The Conservatives were no doubt satisfied with the results of spending millions of dollars on pre-writ advertising."[40]

Not surprisingly, the Conservatives redoubled their efforts when the Liberals quickly replaced Dion with someone who initially appeared more of a challenge for Harper, namely the former academic and internationally known public intellectual Michael Ignatieff. Confirmed as the Liberals' new leader in May 2009, Ignatieff was immediately the target of Conservative attack ads that accused him of being a carpetbagger. "Their 'just visiting' ads were viewed as particularly effective by advertising experts," one study noted, and succeeded in painting Ignatieff as "an elitist snob and opportunist who was out of touch by virtue of having been out of the country for most of the previous thirty years."[41] Given the drubbing Dion received at the hands of similar ads, observers were surprised that Ignatieff and his party initially opted to "take the high road" and dismiss the ads as "not serious."

The Liberals claimed to have sufficient funds to respond if they chose, but this was widely questioned. (Party president Alf Apps later confirmed they lacked the resources to respond.) Further doubt was cast on the party's claims when Liberal senator Dennis Dawson tabled a bill to include all advertising costs in the three-month period leading up to an election as part of campaign expenditures. This proposal was possible, since Harper's fixed-date election bill, introduced in 2009, meant that everyone would know what this time frame would be. Dawson's bill also proposed limiting the total amount of pre-writ advertising expenses, a suggestion that Jean-Pierre Kingsley, the former chief electoral officer, had already made. But Dawson's plan was dismissed out of hand by Harper's minister for democratic reform, Steven Fletcher, who declared "the advertisements are obviously hurting the Liberal Party and this is just an irrational, hypocritical reaction to the information commercials that the Conservatives are running." Fletcher went on to describe Dawson's proposal as "undemocratic, unCanadian, un-workable, and intellectually corrupt."[42]

When the Liberals finally did launch "response" ads in 2010, they were blandly ineffective, and widely criticized by even Liberal sympathizers. In any event the Conservatives launched another round of attack ads, some of which were personal ("Ignatieff. He didn't come back for you") and others deliberately misleading. For example, although Ignatieff had been the last caucus member to agree not to oppose Stéphane Dion's idea of forming a coalition government with the NDP, and had specifically said he would not do this himself if chosen leader, the ads suggested he was very much in favour of that plan ("Ignatieff and his ruthless coalition. He did it before and he'll do it again"). Subsequent Liberal ads were more hard-hitting, accusing the prime minister of undemocratic behaviour. One pollster declared, "This is what the Liberals should have done long ago. It may be too late now."[43]

With Harper still personally unpopular, his strategists had believed it was essential to create an even less attractive image of Ignatieff before voters were able to decide for themselves. According to pollster Nik Nanos, "The negative attack ads launched by the Conservatives did their job."[44] By February 2011, Ignatieff's approval rating was only 13.5 per cent. During the May 2011 election campaign, the Liberals were never able to overcome this disadvantage, despite a widespread consensus that the campaign had been more than competent and the leader had performed well. In the end, the Liberals turned in their worst showing ever. They fell to an unprecedented third place in parliament, behind the NDP, led by Quebec MP Thomas Mulcair. As a result, Mulcair himself soon came under attack from the Conservatives, who worried about his well-honed parliamentary debating skills as much as his Quebec roots. But the Conservatives did not let up in their partisan attacks on the Liberals either. As Carleton University journalism professor Christopher Dornan wrote in an assessment of the Harper government's behaviour shortly after achieving their majority, "The Conservatives think of the Liberal Party the way the Royal Navy thought of the *Bismarck*: Do not let it repair itself. Sink it when given the chance."[45] To make sure that this happened, the Conservatives made good use of another tactic employed so successfully by the American New Right, namely the permanent campaign.

THE CONSERVATIVES' PERMANENT CAMPAIGN

The Conservatives have had every opportunity to pursue their objective of eliminating the Liberal Party, due in large measure to their overwhelming financial advantage. With no limitations on spending outside of formal election periods, the Conservatives could spend money on advertising and other forms of communication at will. This they proceeded to do, the first time in Canadian history that such ongoing partisan activities were carried out. Simply put, the permanent-campaign mentality is now firmly entrenched in Harper's Conservative government. As political scientists Harold Jansen and Tom Flanagan concluded, "The Conservatives have invested so heavily in the pre-writ period that they have introduced a new model of campaigning in Canada – the permanent campaign – in which pre-writ spending and activities are just as important as what happens in the writ period."[46] In his subsequent work, *Winning Power*, written after he had been ostracized by the party over various inflammatory comments, Flanagan went further and concluded that it was precisely because of their ability to spend as much as they chose outside of the campaign period that allowed the Conservatives to claim victory in the first place, and to maintain their hold on power ever since.

In addition to their own considerable resources, the Conservatives have increasingly used government funds to promote their cause, for example through their Economic Action Plan advertisements and the controversial use of MPs' Householders (publicly funded pamphlets sent regularly by each MP to all his/her constituents) to attack the opposition. As one *Ottawa Citizen* editorial declared, the Harper Conservatives' "partisan handouts" have made a mockery of the Householders' original purpose of informing constituents about important new government programs and activities. The Conservatives, it argued, "appear intent on crossing the ethical divide with mail-outs that are nothing more than an extension of their attack ad campaign against the new Liberal leader" and, worse still, they do so "on the taxpayers' dime."[47]

Meanwhile the Liberals, reduced to 37 seats after the 2011 election, were again without a leader, Michael Ignatieff having been defeated in his own riding and immediately resigning. But this time they waited much longer to select their next leader. This did not stop the Conservatives. Liberal MP Bob Rae was serving as the Liberals' interim leader, and the Conservatives wasted neither time nor expense in crafting attack ads designed to create a negative image before he even contemplated running for the party's leadership. ("Bob Rae. If he couldn't run a province, why does he think he could run Canada?")

But their plan backfired. Rae became increasingly convinced that his political baggage as the former NDP premier of Ontario would be an insurmountable barrier to electoral success, and decided to remove his name from contention. Initially, this left a lengthy list of potential candidates who were no threat to Harper, but the situation changed when freshman MP Justin Trudeau entered the race. As discussed in the previous chapter, the liberal society that Stephen Harper is intent on dismantling owes most of its values and institutions to the Liberal Party, and in particular to the vision of Pierre Elliott Trudeau, the man whom Harper most resented and who prompted his entry into politics via the Reform Party. The presence of Trudeau's son in the Liberal leadership race could therefore be seen as waving a red flag in front of Harper, for whom "losing to a Trudeau would be the ultimate humiliation."[48]

When Trudeau was selected as the new Liberal leader in April 2013, Stephen Harper's communications team was ready. The speed with which they moved to discredit the latest Liberal messiah was striking, and quite possibly revealed the degree of their concern about his prospects. Within less than twenty-four hours, the Conservative spin machine was at work, branding Trudeau as "in over his head." A series of short television ads raised the stakes once again by using statements and photos out of context. Even a parliamentary Householder was devoted to attacking Trudeau, using the same language found in the party's television ads.

Trudeau responded by declaring that he would continue to take the high road, and that Canadians were sick and tired of such a negative approach. "This government knows how to do one thing, which is attack, which is low-blow, which is to try and incite fear and cynicism. The Conservatives are going to discover that the one thing they know how to do really well is no longer working for them."[49]

Some analysts agreed with Trudeau. Queen's University professor Jonathan Rose described the ads as "gratuitously malicious" and unlikely to impress viewers because they lacked a clear message, such as the ones used for Dion and Ignatieff. An EKOS poll released at the same time lent credence to Rose's argument, showing that

Harper's approval rating had fallen from 40 per cent in 2010 to 28 per cent in April 2013, with some 54 per cent of respondents stating that Canada was "moving in the wrong direction."

On the other hand, Ottawa image consultant Barry McLoughlin warned that some sort of response would be necessary on the part of the Liberals to counter the attacks, even if it was not an attack itself. "In these kinds of situations," McLoughlin noted, "silence is not golden. If they can frame the opponent before he frames himself, then they can be highly effective."[50] Luckily for Trudeau and the Liberals, money was not as much of a concern this time, given his own successful fundraising for the leadership race. The Liberals did respond, with ads that attempted to turn the tables on the attack ads by making fun of the perceived "weaknesses" the Conservatives wanted to highlight, such as mocking Trudeau's work experience as a teacher. With public-opinion polling showing the Liberals in the lead in July 2013, the consensus among observers was that Harper's attack ads at a minimum had failed to make a sufficient impression on voters. By February 2014, even Harper's former adviser Tom Flanagan was declaring that the negative ads "are not working" in Trudeau's case and argued the Conservatives should take another tack in their efforts to discredit the Liberal leader.[51]

Perhaps the most salient part of Trudeau's response was the reference to the Conservatives' efforts to intimidate and frighten their opponents. With their base support secure but still requiring frequent care and feeding, and so much time devoted to finishing off their principal opponents, the Harper government has resorted to the politics of fear to stifle all forms of dissent, both as a means of maintaining control and of implementing their agenda as quickly as possible. The philosophical roots of the party's thinking, which values certainty, and the conservatives' tendency to reject opposing views as wrong rather than different, have been given free rein since the party took power in 2006. This has led to a degree of control and intimidation which has only expanded since the majority victory in May 2011.

3

Stifling Dissent: Bullies in Power

We are intensely aware that we are and we must be the government of all Canadians, including those who did not vote for us.

Prime Minister Stephen Harper, Calgary, Election night, May 2011

Unfortunately there are environmental and other radical groups that ... threaten to hijack our regulatory system to achieve their radical ideological agenda ... they use funding from foreign special interest groups to undermine Canada's national interest.

Hon. Joe Oliver, Minister of Natural Resources, 9 January 2012

Information is the lifeblood of a democracy. Without adequate access to key information about government policies and programs, citizens and parliamentarians cannot make informed decisions and incompetent or corrupt governments can be hidden under a cloak of secrecy.

Opposition Leader Stephen Harper, 2003

The Harper Conservatives do not simply have an agenda, they are on a mission. As demonstrated earlier, they know they are right. They are convinced that they will face many challenges from "enemies" of their conservative agenda, and they believe they must be ever vigilant if they are to succeed. They must also act quickly, and often by stealth. Faced with this daunting challenge, and given Stephen Harper's take-charge personality, the only logical outcome is the one Canadians have witnessed since 2006 – a government determined to control and limit access to information, and to sideline all forms of dissenting opinion. The Conservatives are, in fact, operating under the very cloak of secrecy that Stephen Harper decried when he was leader of the Official Opposition.

The Conservatives' behaviour is all the more striking since they obtained their parliamentary majority in May 2011. In his victory speech, Prime Minister Harper promised voters he would govern in the best interests of all Canadians. He assured them that he recognized the need to listen carefully to opposing viewpoints. Many observers reacted optimistically to this unexpected election-night moderation. They even speculated that Canadians would soon see a kinder, gentler Conservative government.

They were wrong. At a time when the issue of bullying captured headlines across the country, the federal Conservatives provided Canadians with a display of bullying at its worst. While other levels of government were taking action to limit or eliminate the problem, the Harper government was busy rolling over any and all opposition. In fact, contrary to those wishful post-election expectations, the Harper Conservatives have spent the time since they obtained their majority exerting their influence wherever possible, pressuring or removing anyone they believe is standing in the way of their agenda. Fear is their primary weapon, and their success has been little short of astonishing.

Virtually every independent source of information or alternative viewpoints normally found in a democracy have been silenced. Internally, the Harper government has exercised strict control over its message with ministers, backbenchers, and bureaucrats through the prime minister's office (PMO). Externally, it has reduced the free flow of information by limiting media access to politicians and bureaucrats, closing government-run or -funded research organizations, "defunding" civil-society groups opposed to the government's agenda, and marginalizing political opponents through misleading advertising campaigns. It has also made a concerted effort to bankrupt opposition political parties. At the same time, the government has mounted an unprecedented advertising campaign to disseminate its own message in as positive a light as possible.

Like their electoral strategy, in power the Harper Conservatives' strategy to suppress information and silence their opponents is both deliberate and carefully planned. The process is a top-down one, driven by the prime minister himself and executed by his personal staff in the PMO. As former adviser Tom Flanagan revealed, Harper is prepared to leave several aspects of his role to others if he considers them to be competent, but communications is not one of them. As chief of staff when Harper was leader of the Alliance, Flanagan confided, "I just let Stephen be his own Chief of Staff with respect to messaging. That's where he has taken measures of centralization to new levels."[1] Indeed, while political scientist Donald Savoie's claim that previous Liberal prime ministers were becoming too powerful was problematic,[2] the same critique when applied to the case of the Harper PMO would be an understatement. Nowhere has this been more apparent than in the implementation of a centralized system of control for virtually all information emanating from government.

CONTROLLING THE MESSAGE

As an opposition MP and Leader of the Opposition, Stephen Harper regularly lamented the "oppressive" power of the prime minister and his office. In the 2006 election that saw him win a minority, Harper's first act was to introduce a Federal Accountability Act, which he described as an effort to increase transparency and accountability in government and limit the unchecked power of the executive. Since then, however, he has moved swiftly and unerringly to impose one of the strictest systems of prime-ministerial control ever seen, and certainly one that is unprecedented in Canada.

Although prime-ministerial power is exercised by this government in many ways, the most significant and concrete method is a new tool called the Message Event Proposal, or MEP. In theory, the process is simple. Virtually every announcement made by anyone in government – from a low-ranking bureaucrat to a deputy minister, and from a backbench MP at a riding event to a minister of the Crown giving a speech – must be vetted and approved by either the PMO or, more problematic in terms of the blurring of distinctions between partisan and bureaucratic functions, the Privy Council Office, which also reports to the prime minister. As one former Harper-era senior PCO official confided, "We discussed every single issue and managed every news release – everything."[3]

The MEP procedure involves a template that must be filled out by anyone contemplating a public statement of any kind, including spending announcements, public consultations, and even interviews. The template contains predictable sections, such as "headline," "key message," and "media lines," as well as more unusual and revealing ones such as "desired soundbites," "ideal speaking backdrop," "tone," "attire," and "rollout materials." Almost nothing is left to chance.

However straightforward this may sound in theory, in practice it presents a major challenge. Literally thousands of requests to hold public events are fielded by the central agency every year. While some can be submitted well in advance – for example, for conferences or other regularly held events – others necessarily arrive much closer to the event date. In the end, one frequent consequence of this tightly scripted process has been that many events simply do not take place, because approval is not received in time.

Not surprisingly, the number of communications officers in government departments has escalated dramatically since 2006, as have the number and seniority of communications directors and press officers in ministerial offices. A November 2011 report found that the number of communications officers had increased by 15 per cent since Harper took office in 2006, while the highest levels such as directors had increased by nearly 50 per cent.

Despite the micromanagement, there have been unintended consequences. One of the more interesting examples of public-service blowback occurred in the Department of National Defence, even though the public-affairs branch received a greater increase in funding and personnel than any other section of that department. A 2011 report prepared by Lt Gen. Andrew Leslie revealed that "there has been an exodus of experienced public affairs officers, with more than 30 per cent of the organization's senior officers leaving within the last two years," due to political interference and a reluctance on the part of political staff to provide accurate information.[4] As a result of the departure of veteran communications professionals, there has also been an increase in the number of inexperienced junior personnel in all departments who have been given the task of handling these functions. The result has often been a total blackout on information, either through the "no comment" option or simply a failure to respond to requests at all.[5]

Revelations about the existence of MEPS and the increase in communications personnel produced critical comments by retired public servants and media analysts. CTV journalist Craig Oliver, a fifty-year veteran of federal politics, concluded, "Stephen Harper has changed the ball game. He really has."[6] Former journalist and Liberal senator Jim Munson, warned that "It's much tougher these days for reporters to get to something ... I'm not so sure you're getting the information you want, you're getting the information they want to give you and nothing more." David Brown of the Public Policy Forum stated, "This stringent handling of issues and messaging is less reflective policy-making that's not as sensitive to different voices and what is actually going on in society"[7]

The government has also used its control over the message to prevent information from becoming public in a timely fashion. One classic example which came to light was the PMO's intervention with a supposedly arms'-length agency, the Transportation Safety Board, to delay the release of a report examining the government's regulations and oversight of the tall-ship industry. (The report was prepared in light of the death of the daughter of Montreal Canadians' former coach Bob Gainey in a sailing accident.) As a leaked series of emails revealed, not only was the release of the report delayed, but the PMO was to be informed of any "developments," and also whether any requests had been made under Access to Information legislation.[8]

In fact the whole issue of message control is one that has largely escaped public notice. Harper has been hugely successful in achieving this objective and has paid almost no political price for doing so. As one observer concluded, "The results have been spectacular ... The public, it is clear, doesn't give a hoot about this governmental attitude."[9]

CONTROLLING CABINET

But managing the message through MEPS was only the beginning. For Stephen Harper, trust is a difficult concept. Many of his closest advisers believe Harper's innate tendency to mistrust others was exacerbated by the 2004 election experience, when he believed maverick candidates going off-message cost him the election.[10] Even among his cabinet, very few ministers are allowed to speak publicly, and their formal speeches must be pre-cleared. (Apart from John Baird and Jim Flaherty, the most frequently mentioned ministers in whom Harper had a modicum of confidence included Stockwell Day and Jim Prentice, both of whom chose to leave government.) Many ministers never speak in public at all, while others simply read texts or talking points prepared by the PMO. Meanwhile, notices informing journalists of the time and place of cabinet meetings – a routine procedure under previous governments – were suspended soon after the Conservatives came to power in 2006, meaning journalists were unable to locate ministers to interview them. Nor was Harper interested in his ministers' views. According to one observer, cabinet meetings were "short and succinct," and no one intervened unless they had something very important to say. "The gavel wasn't necessary because Harper was an intimidating presence. People were uneasy around him."[11]

For those who doubted the degree of control Harper exercised over his ministers, a devastating interview with Maxime Bernier (returned to cabinet after the 2011 election) put the matter to rest. Waiting to appear on CTV's *Power Play* in November 2012, Bernier was seen by host Don Martin reviewing a hard copy of his PMO talking points and, more surprisingly, being prepped on his lines by a coaching assistant who accompanied him. Martin surreptitiously taped the briefing session, and after the interview he rolled the tape, showing how Bernier had stayed faithful to the lines – no matter what questions had been posed to him.

Perhaps the most clear-cut demonstration of Harper's lack of confidence in his own ministers, and his general distrust of bureaucrats and civil society, was seen in a PMO directive to ministerial staff, requesting that they prepare blacklists for new cabinet ministers after a July 2013 cabinet shuffle. The so-called "Enemies List" plan was leaked to the media by disgruntled ministerial aides who expressed outrage at the idea that stakeholders and bureaucrats should be classified as friends or foes from the outset. They refused to comply. As they said in their note to the media, "As Canadians, we are appalled by the paranoia that this request demonstrates." For their pains, they themselves were immediately classified as "politically unreliable" by the PMO and "cut out of the loop."

The government memo, prepared by PMO executive assistant of issues management, Erica Furtado, and issue manager Nick Koolsbergen, gave examples of potential "enemies." They included "environmental groups, non-profits, civic and industry associations" that had "different views than those being advanced by the government." Liberal MP and former Martin cabinet minister Ralph Goodale said the memo "betrays a very damaging mindset that characterizes the Harper government," which he found "not at all normal" for a national government, and one that made a mockery of Harper's election-night promise to listen to and respect diverse opinions.[12] Harper's own former environment minister Peter Kent went further in his criticism, declaring the whole episode reminded him of the Watergate scandal in the United States. "An enemies list ... was the nomenclature used by Nixon. His political horizon was divided very starkly into them and us."[13]

There is ample evidence that Harper's approach to decision-making is also driven by this need to control the message. For the few former Progressive Conservative ministers in Harper's early cabinets, this was something of a shock. According to one journalist, "veteran Progressive Conservatives could often be found on the Hill, cursing about having been told what to do by, as one of them put it, 'some debutante neocon in the PMO who knows nothing' but strategy."[14]

Undoubtedly the most interesting insight, however, comes from David Emerson, who was a minister in both the Paul Martin Liberal government and that of Harper. According to Emerson, Martin "seldom delved into the politics of an issue" and he "could not remember a single instance of Martin talking to him about how an issue should be handled politically," whereas under Harper "everything was put under the political microscope." In addition, "Harper and his team didn't hesitate, strategizing at cabinet meetings, for example, about how policies might be better 'contoured' to appeal to ethnic groups."[15] Equally important was the expectation that ministers would attack opponents at every opportunity, including during policy announcements.

As Canadians later learned, this approach was also in place in the Conservatives' caucus, the one place where government backbench MPs traditionally are allowed to have their say. A sounding board on policy proposals, and an early warning signal on political issues that may cause the party to lose support, national caucus for all political parties has been the inner sanctum in which everyone can speak his or her mind. Not so, however, for Harper. As Garth Turner, a former Conservative MP, revealed, Harper often did not wait until the end of the meeting for the traditional summing up by the leader, nor did he tolerate much dissent. On the issue of certain budget cuts, for example, Turner recalled "[Harper] said 'We've determined a series of cuts ... which will be announced ... They are our position. Anyone who has got a problem with that ... who says anything about it ... is going to have a short political career.' He said that in caucus! It was a threat."[16]

There is a dual purpose to such micromanaging of the message. On the one hand, it is designed to avoid trouble by ensuring that everyone is on the same page, whether on policy announcements or any other aspects of the government's agenda. On the other hand, as Jonathan Rose of Queen's University has noted, it is also designed as a pre-emptive measure, getting out ahead of an issue that has the potential to cause trouble for the government, regardless of its origins.[17]

Still another purpose of this message control is to promote a positive image of the government and thereby enhance its long-term prospects. For a government hoping to define the Conservative Party as the new "natural governing party," this objective has received an equal amount of their attention.

PROMOTING THEIR IMAGE

In keeping with their determination to realign the political culture in the long-term, the Harper Conservatives have employed a number of classic New Right tactics to reinforce their image as "the governing party." Most notable was their controversial directive to all government departments to refer to "Canada's new government," rather than "the federal government" or "the government of Canada," in press releases and other official communications. In 2006, Andrew Okulitch, a senior government scientist who objected to the use of the terminology, was actually fired because of this, although he was later reinstated.

After two years, the "new government" term was dropped, but by the fall of 2010 a new directive from "the centre" (PMO) required all departments to replace "the Government of Canada" with "the Harper Government" in all federal communications. This time, senior bureaucrats in several line departments refused to comply, but official communications from most departments – and especially key areas such as Finance, Treasury Board, and Revenue Canada – fell into line, despite the fact that the new term appeared to violate guidelines issued by the Treasury Board. When House Leader Peter Van Loan responded to criticism by saying "the Chrétien government" was a widely used term, critics were taken aback. Ralph Goodale pointed out in exasperation, "There is a huge difference between the media referring to 'the Chrétien government' in some article they have written, and the party in power trying to do this when operating as the government. We never did this. Period. This is entirely new."

Empirical support for Goodale's statement came from Sylvia Stead, an editor at the *Globe and Mail*, who examined the use of the term over time. According to Stead, her paper made two references to "the Chrétien government" and 3,156 references to "the federal government" in 2001. By contrast, in 2012 there were 1,947 references to "the Harper government" versus 4,131 references to "the federal government," which clearly "suggests that referring to the federal government as 'the Harper government' has exploded since Jean Chrétien."[18]

Critics argued Harper had stood his concerns about bureaucratic partisanship on their head. Having eliminated what he perceived to be a Liberal bias, he had now introduced a Conservative one. As Jonathan Rose noted, "It is one thing for journalists or even the public to use the more partisan 'Harper Government,' but it is another thing for the state to equate the Government of Canada with the leader of the governing party." Similarly former clerk of the Privy Council Mel Cappe declared, "It's not the Harper government. It's the government of Canada ... it's my government and your government," a sentiment echoed by political scientist Peter Aucoin, who declared, "It's the executive abusing the powers of government for purely partisan reasons."[19] Human-rights expert Errol Mendes was equally outraged. "The party is not the government," he exclaimed, noting that "countries that have conflated the governing party with the government of the country include the People's Republic of China, Zimbabwe, and Sudan."[20] Despite this overwhelming criticism, PMO spokesperson Dimitri Soudas defended the move, and the directive was not withdrawn.

Indeed, another very similar incident occurred in early 2011, when an aide to Immigration Minister Jason Kenney was found to have sent out a Conservative fundraising letter on ministerial letterhead. While this alone triggered accusations of violating public-service neutrality, the revelation that the letters were being sent to ethnic communities who would likely have dealings with the department raised the issue to greater heights.[21] The minister offered a formal apology, but lingering concerns about the willingness of the Harper Conservatives to use the tools and machinery of government for partisan purposes remained.

Other examples of the government's self-promotion have included the many changes to government websites and documents, including the prominent use of blue in headings, and even the removal of the red maple leaf on some occasions. Although only regular visitors to such websites would likely notice these differences, even a casual observer could not fail to notice the predominance of the Conservative blue background and the use of the phrase "the true north strong and free" – a prominent Conservative campaign theme and one that prime minister Harper has emphasized with yearly trips to the Arctic – on virtually all government websites.

The Conservatives have also expended considerable effort on attempts to position some of their more problematic policies in the most positive light possible. While this may well be a tactic that any political party would attempt to employ, the Harper Conservatives have gone much further than anything seen in Canada before. Rather than engage the public and convince them that their policy choice is the right one, they avoid discussion or debate whenever possible, and provide minimal, often misleading, information when forced.

Probably the best-known and controversial example of such subterfuge is their attempt to portray their support of the oil sands in a positive light, despite scientific evidence of environmental damage. When former Reform/Alliance staffer Ezra Levant published a book entitled *Ethical Oil* in 2010, the term was quickly picked up and used by none other than Environment Minister Peter Kent, as well as Stephen Harper himself. In an interview explaining his choice of term, Levant actually admitted that support for the oil sands was extremely difficult to defend politically, particularly since the actual reasons for that support are based on conservative values such as property rights, wealth creation, and the unfettered marketplace. Instead, Levant said, he decided to take advantage of Canadians' liberal culture. "Canadians see themselves as ethical ... People who try to do the right things, sort of the Boy Scouts of the world, the guys who help with foreign aid." As a result, he positioned the oil sands on the "liberal" side of the equation. Canadian oil is "ethical" because we are; by contrast, oil from countries such as Saudi Arabia, Iraq, and Nigeria is "unethical" because the countries are undemocratic, do not protect human rights, and so on.[22]

Until the "ethical oil" success, Levant's extreme views were controversial even among conservatives. He argued in favour of a Yes vote in the 1995 referendum on Quebec independence because he believed it would mean the end of multiculturalism and bilingualism, policies he and most original Reform/Alliance members of the new Conservative Party have long opposed. However, that opposition has been firmly blunted by Stephen Harper, because of his determination to avoid direct conflict with Canadians' liberal values whenever possible. As a result, Harper was obliged to demote one of his closest confidants, Scott Reid, when Reid suggested in a 2004 media interview that the Conservatives in power would make administrative changes to the Official Languages Act and withdraw the provision of bilingual services in some areas.[23] Since forming a government, however, the Conservatives have indeed taken numerous initiatives that weakened federal bilingual policy, while putting an alternative spin on the situation. The controversial appointments of a unilingual Auditor General and Supreme Court Justice, for example, were positioned as merit-based (choosing the most qualified candidate regardless of linguistic capacity) and as fulfilling concerns about regional representation.

But spin did not always work, and surprisingly it was ignored by several cabinet ministers. A case in point was International Cooperation Minister Julian Fantino, who became the subject of multiple news reports when his office issued a directive to officials that his letters were to be prepared in English only. Although Fantino was known to be accident-prone, this was hardly the case for his senior colleague, Foreign Affairs Minister John Baird, who persisted for some time in a highly public and determined confrontation with both Treasury Board guidelines and the Official Languages Act, which came to light when Official Languages Commissioner Graham Fraser issued a stern warning to the minister to replace his business cards. The minister, it transpired, had deliberately rejected the standard black-and-white format used by everyone in government, including cabinet ministers, in favour of a special, gold-embossed, unilingual card, on which the minister's name was highlighted and the departmental information (including the Lester B. Pearson Building address, Canada wordmark, and Canadian flag) were reduced or eliminated.[24] Adding insult to injury, the unilingual cards, funded by taxpayers, were nearly three times as expensive as the standard bilingual ones approved by the Treasury Board.

This should hardly have come as a surprise, since the Harper Conservatives have not shied away from the use of public funds for their own ends, and especially in order to promote their image. The cost implications of the MEP system alone were soon revealed to be substantial. For example a Public Accounts Committee report in 2012 noted that the budget for the PMO would increase to $10 million that year, an increase explained by Harper's own spokesperson as "primarily due to a larger communications staff in the PMO, so [the prime minister] can explain government policies such as the Economic Action Plan."[25]

The Economic Action Plan (EAP) is actually the federal budget, provided with an appropriately positive spin by another disciple of Frank Luntz. Although in 2009 it involved major cuts to many programs and services of the federal government, the budget was billed positively as a plan to create jobs and stimulate economic growth. Moreover, the term EAP has been used to describe every budget from 2009 to 2013, and each budget has benefited from a major expenditure of federal funds for promotional ads. In fiscal 2012–13, this amounted to some $16 million in the first quarter alone. Ironically, a Harris-Decima poll released in July 2013 found that only 6 per cent of those who recalled seeing the television ads had taken any further action, and it was hardly what the sponsors had hoped. Rather than contribute money to the Conservatives, most had actually "complained or expressed displeasure" at the ads, which critics have described as "thinly veiled propaganda."[26]

Another controversial spending practice was implemented by Jason Kenney in his role as "ethnic czar" of the Conservative election strategy and minister of immigration. In late November 2012, it was learned that some $750,000 had been spent by the Conservative government at Kenney's request to "monitor" the ethnic press between 2009 and 2012, a move which he defended as central to the government's adoption of various policies, such as the apology for the Chinese head tax, but which opposition critics charged was a blatant use of government funds for partisan purposes.[27]

Meanwhile the Conservatives' total advertising budget for 2010–11 was $83.3 million, or roughly twice the amount spent by the Liberals in their last year in office. Similarly, as the government-commissioned Paillé Report on polling irregularities inadvertently revealed, the Conservatives had already spent more on polling than their Liberal predecessors by 2007. Daniel Paillé also noted that the Conservatives had commissioned more than two polls per day in 2006–07, a figure he described as "quite astounding."[28] Since then, the government's advertising of its Economic Action Plan for partisan purposes has included some of the most expensive venues on television, including the Stanley Cup, the Superbowl, the Sochi Olympics, and the 2014 Oscars.[29]

The revelations of the Paillé Report were one of the few other public-relations setbacks for the Harper Conservatives, who not only have successfully maintained control of their message for most of their time in office, but have largely managed to control the media who report it.

MANIPULATING THE MEDIA

Like their Republican counterparts, Canadian conservatives have long viewed the mainstream media as an instrument of liberal propaganda. Although the CBC has been the lightning rod for this discontent, the Harper Conservatives came to power with a visceral dislike of the entire fourth estate at the national level, believing it represents a central-Canadian bias as well as a liberal one. As a result, the Harper government has worked hard to control and limit its interactions with the national media.

This has been accomplished through a variety of measures, each of which would have been not simply unprecedented but unthinkable in earlier times. To begin with, the prime minister refused to participate in traditional media scrums after parliamentary debates. Instead, scripted press conferences became almost the only venue in which journalists could pose questions. Then Harper insisted that a lineup of questioners be provided to his press secretary in advance. Those deemed "hostile" to him or his government often were not allowed to place a question on the list. (As CBC reporter Julie Van Dusen discovered, even being on the list did not guarantee a response from the prime minister, who on one notable occasion ignored her question and moved on to the next person on the list. When that individual refused to ask a question in deference to Van Dusen, the prime minister ended the press conference by walking out.)

Initially the parliamentary press gallery opposed these practices as unethical, and presented a united front in refusing to comply. This situation did not last long, however, and with surprising speed the national media fell into line. Only a handful of print-media columnists have dared to criticize or even report on this state of affairs.

Harper's office also began favouring local and regional media over the national media and the parliamentary press gallery. Given the Conservatives' strength in rural areas, they realized many Canadians there would not view national coverage on a regular basis and would be more likely to pay close attention to regional and local sources of information. Even among the national media, though, the PMO played favourites, granting exclusive interviews to private networks rather than the CBC.

As time went on, the PMO prevented any media access at all to some events. At a Conservative caucus retreat in Atlantic Canada in 2007, reporters claimed they were even prevented by the RCMP from entering the hotel where the event was taking place.[30] During the 2011 election, reporters were kept behind steel barricades during Harper's campaign stop in Halifax. In most venues, the press was limited to a total of four questions. In other venues they were not allowed to question the Conservative leader at all.

Then, in the fall of 2013, when parliament returned from yet another prorogation, cameras were invited inside the Conservative caucus room for a "photo-opportunity" during a speech by the prime minister, but reporters were barred. Camera technicians joined with the parliamentary press gallery and refused to participate. (An exception was Sun Media, which then claimed, as the only outlet to agree to the restrictions, to have "exclusive footage" of the speech.) Unfazed, the Conservative spin machine attempted to turn this media-relations debacle into an advantage by sending out a fund-raising letter to party faithful saying, "You won't believe what the press gallery just did in Ottawa." Sent by the party's director of political operations, Fred Lowery, it declared, "Some media decided to boycott an important speech by our Prime Minister – one where he laid out his vision for our country, before today's Speech from the Throne. Rather than send cameras to cover the Prime Minister's speech, they attended the NDP's meeting, and were welcomed with cheers and applause. We knew they wouldn't give us fair coverage – but this is a new low for the Ottawa media elite."[31]

Meanwhile the prime minister's communications team increasingly adopted the practice of providing prepared texts – and photos – to media outlets, who often have little choice about using them if they wish to "report" on the events. This practice is highly controversial, as recent academic studies have demonstrated, and is most problematic with respect to photojournalism, because of the technological advances of the digital age. An emerging conflict between smaller outlets, for whom the material is an invaluable time- and money-saving source, and larger organizations, who view the use of such material as unprofessional ("we decide what is news, not them") has become an ongoing debate.

Memorial University professor Alex Marland believes there is now an ongoing contest "between politicians, PR staff, and journalists, over news selection, pseudo events, framing, gatekeeping and priming."[32] Moreover, the use of these techniques by Mr Harper's communications team is extremely effective at portraying the prime minister in what they believe is a positive light. Classic examples include the free visuals they provided of Harper and his entourage during Arctic tours, with Harper variously posed in a military camouflage outfit on the rudder of an Armed Forces helicopter, shooting a rifle at a base practice range, and snowmobiling with Canadian Rangers. (As one cynical journalist commented privately, "next he'll be wrestling with a grizzly bear like Putin.")

Not surprisingly, Harper's communications adviser has frequently been described as the most important person in the PMO after the chief of staff. Given the position's revolving door, with eight occupants in under eight years, it is obviously a stressful one. Several of his former communications aides were criticized by Harper as being "too soft," and relations between the PMO and the press gallery are generally described as icy to non-existent.

One journalist in Atlantic Canada provided an insight into the typical interaction that characterizes this hostility when he revealed that he had received a call from Ottawa, demanding to know the source of his information for an article. When he declined to reveal his sources (the information was widely available in the public domain and never challenged), the caller angrily concluded with the statement, "The Government of Canada is unhappy with you!" The journalist, surprised by the aggressive tone, spoke to several Ottawa acquaintances about the incident and received the same reply from each. "That's them. That's them exactly!"[33]

In a 2012 column, journalist Jeffrey Simpson of the *Globe and Mail* highlighted how vulnerable an increasingly weakened fourth estate is to such tactics:

> The government understands what's happening in the media. Bureaus are stretched. Reporters have to deal with minute-to-minute deadlines. They seldom have time to probe, so that one or two lines of defence will suffice against them getting information beyond what the government wants to ladle out.

> They are on their BlackBerrys one minute, writing for online the next, filing some update next. Speed and urgency in the 24-hour news cycle is the enemy of reflection, analysis, and digging. Getting through or around the obstacles this government has erected takes time and persistence that few reporters are allowed, and the government knows it.[34]

Not content with this degree of control over the message, the Harper PMO has also intervened directly and indirectly in decisions of the Canadian Radio-television and Telecommunications Commission (CRTC), the supposedly arms'-length agency overseeing the media, for example concerning its decisions with respect to access to the Internet, and the allocation of a top-category licence (which would require carriers to include it in their basic package) to Sun News, the new Canadian version of Fox News. It actually overturned several decisions, including one on an application by a foreign wireless provider, Globalive. Industry Minister Tony Clement also stated that he would review and/or overturn the CRTC decision on the Internet if it was contrary to the government's position, resulting in the agency's announcement that it would review its own decision.[35]

In another unprecedented move, a communications adviser in the PMO was hired by the new Sun channel as its senior executive, a move that appeared to be in direct violation of Harper's own lobbying and conflict-of-interest legislation. In addition, the prime minister made it clear that the existing head of the CRTC, veteran public servant Konrad von Finkenstein, would not have his term extended. Harper then appointed a close friend of his communications director, Dimitri Soudas, to the number-two position at the agency, a controversial appointment, given that Tom Pentefountas, a lawyer and former president of the right-wing Action démocratique du Québec (ADQ) party, had no obvious credentials for the position.

As a result, many in the industry expressed concern about government interference. They pointed to the uncertainty this engendered concerning the regulatory structure under which they are expected to operate. However their complaints at least had the advantage of being aired in a public venue, due to the arm's-length nature of the CRTC and the well-established structure of public hearings. For those concerned about access to information located *inside* the federal government, or produced by government research agencies, the situation was even more worrisome.

SUPPRESSING INFORMATION

The Trudeau government introduced the Access to Information (ATI) Act in 1983. It gave citizens the right to obtain information controlled by federal government departments and other institutions, with limited exclusions related to privacy and national-security concerns. Such information was to be provided within a specific time frame. The act also established an ombudsman position called the Information Commissioner, who was charged with adjudicating complaints and attempting to mediate solutions. However the commissioner did not have the right to demand that a department release information.

While the act was a progressive measure when it was introduced, over time a number of technological and other developments made it less effective, and concerns emerged over its limited scope and the lack of sanctions available to the commissioner. A number of studies by parliamentary committees and former commissioners suggested ways to improve and modernize the act, but none of their recommendations was adopted.

In the 2006 federal election, the Harper Conservatives made reform of the Access to Information Act a key element of their promise to enhance transparency and accountability in government. Their actions once in office did not bear out this commitment. In 2006, the Harper government tabled a Federal Accountability Act, which introduced minor changes to the scope of the ATI act, but did not proceed with any further modifications. The incumbent information commissioner, John Reid, criticized the proposed changes to his office under the legislation, arguing that they would create unnecessary bureaucracy and actually delay response times. Once the Accountability Act was introduced in the House of Commons, Reid issued an emergency report, stating the legislation would actually "increase the government's ability to cover up wrongdoing, shield itself from embarrassment, and control the flow of information to Canadians." He also said no government had ever put forward "a more retrograde and dangerous" set of proposals for dealing with access-to-information laws.[36] Unmoved, the government promptly eliminated the registry for the Coordination of Access to Information Requests System (CAIRS), a move that observers argued would cause more delays and prevent accurate research.

Overall access to information, and the timeliness of that access, have indeed declined dramatically under the Harper administration.

One 2011 report indicated that the delay in response times was now so great that "major government departments have hired outside consultants to clear the backlog of delayed files, often by asking journalists and other requesters to simply abandon their requests."[37]

As a variety of parliamentary watchdogs, including Reid's successor as Information Commissioner have publicly stated, the government has also intervened directly within the bureaucracy to prevent access to information – in an unprecedented fashion. "Political interference in access requests has forced the resignation of a cabinet aide and the number of complaints received by the federal Information Commissioner is up 17 per cent since the Conservatives came to power." According to Information Commissioner Robert Marleau in his 2009 annual report, this situation was becoming chronic. "Too often, responses to access requests are late, incomplete, or overly censored. Too often, access is denied to hide wrongdoing, or to protect officials from embarrassment, rather than to serve a legitimate confidentiality requirement."

Marleau resigned shortly after tabling the scathing report, in which he accused the government of deliberately sabotaging the process. It was soon followed by international evaluations that placed Canada's ATI performance well below that of many OECD countries, and of previous evaluations. In fact, a study by British researchers Robert Hazell and Ben Worthy of the University of London, placed Canada "dead last" in transparency.[38] Marleau's successor, Suzanne Legault, responded to the study by stating, "I'm not surprise that they ranked Canada last ... We were seen as the leaders ... we have fallen behind." Legault's 2010 annual report, *Out of Time*, graded twenty-four federal institutions that fall within the purview of the act and ranked thirteen of them as "below average or worse."[39]

As Library of Parliament researchers have outlined, the Harper government is actually moving in the opposite direction from those who have suggested strengthening the ATI legislation. Instead, it is now pursuing "open government and open data" initiatives, which stress the proactive role of government in placing information on websites for public access. While there is widespread agreement that this is a positive move, it is seen as an unrelated measure and certainly not an alternative solution to ATI – as the Conservatives argue – since it is the government that controls what information will be made available on the sites.[40]

The Harper Conservatives' aversion to providing information should hardly come as a surprise, given their view that evidence is not merely irrelevant but often inconvenient for their agenda. Hence the government's refusal to provide information to either the Parliamentary Budget Officer or the opposition parties concerning the cost of twenty-one pieces of legislation proposed in the 2010 budget under the government's "tough on crime" agenda. One journalist reported "the government has stalled, stonewalled, and claimed the information is a matter of 'cabinet confidence.' Twice, under duress, it has released surprisingly low estimates for specific pieces of legislation ... which Liberal finance critic Scott Brison has called 'absolutely unbelievable.'"[41] Other examples include the Afghan detainee file, security for the G8 and G20 summits, and the cost of various corporate tax cuts.

The Harper government has also made use of tax cuts, and the resulting deficit-reduction exercise (Grover Norquist's "starve the beast" approach) in much the same way as the Reagan Republicans. It has selectively eliminated several research organizations created by, and wholly or partly funded by, previous federal governments, and which it viewed as likely to produce evidence contradicting elements of its agenda. Thus the funding for several defence research organizations was untouched, while it was cut or eliminated altogether for foreign-aid and foreign-policy think tanks and social-welfare agencies. This resulted in the shuttering of the National Welfare Council, the First Nations Statistical Council, the Canadian Foundation for the Americas (FOCAL), the Council of Science and Technology Advisers, and the Canadian Council on Learning. Others, such as the Forum of the Federations, now rely on domestic or international donations.

The cuts to environmental research were even more drastic. Among those eliminated were the highly regarded National Round Table on the Environment and the Economy, and the Experimental Lakes Area (ELA) research project. When the elimination of ELA proved politically embarrassing – prompting widespread provincial, commercial, and even international opposition – the government reluctantly agreed to "allow" provinces and stand-alone research agencies to take over its work, having already closed down the facility and laid off professional staff. Even the North was not spared, despite Mr Harper's personal interest in the area. Victims included federal funding for the cutting-edge research station in Kluane Park in the Yukon, and the Polar Environment Atmospheric Research Laboratory in Nunavut, an internationally recognized institute which was forced to close in April 2012 due to the withdrawal of federal funding.

Many similar government actions have gone under-reported, such as the decision to eliminate the position of National Science Adviser, or to appoint an economist as the National Librarian and Archivist. Daniel Caron's subsequent introduction of a new business plan for the organization, in which documents with "business value" would be maintained but others would be systematically eliminated, led Penni Stewart, president of the Canadian Association of University Teachers, to argue that the Harper government was organizing "a concerted assault on access to knowledge itself."[42]

This behaviour has introduced an entirely new element into the already tense relationship between Conservative politicians and their bureaucrats. In February 2013, Information Commissioner Suzanne Legault received a formal request from the Environmental Law Centre at the University of Victoria and the non-profit Democracy Watch to investigate what they termed the "systematic" efforts of the federal government to obstruct access to information and to limit its researchers. Calvin Sandborn, director of the centre, described the Harper government's actions as a "threat to democracy" and concluded "the name of George Orwell comes to mind."[43]

The government's decision to cancel the mandatory long-form census of Statistics Canada was even more controversial. It resulted in the resignation of Chief Statistician Munir Sheikh, who felt he had no choice, because the government was implying that he was in favour of the plan. An open letter from a large group of international experts criticized the decision to abandon the long-form census as "highly damaging" to the agency's world-class reputation. Neither this initiative nor widespread criticism from academics, NGOs, the premiers, and even the business community had any effect. The government continued to argue that the replacement – a voluntary National Household Survey – would do the job equally well.

Two years after the first voluntary form was introduced, the jury was in. The academic community and organizations dependent on the statistics for their decision-making and planning purposes quickly noted many problems with the results, including the very small, and hence unreliable, samples. The Federation of Canadian Municipalities concluded that most of small town and rural Canada had been effectively excluded. Social-welfare groups highlighted the under-representation of lower-income and less-educated Canadians. Carleton economics professor Frances Woolley concluded the damage already done was "irreparable," because no comparisons with previous results would be valid, due to the different samples. If the mandatory form was not reinstated immediately, she said, this damage would be "cumulative. As this policy continues we will be getting further and further away from the point where we have good information at all."[44] A team of researchers at the University of Toronto were less tactful. "We're concluding it pretty much is garbage," lead researcher David Hulchanski declared. Munir Sheikh, now an adjunct professor at Queen's University, was equally blunt. "The irony is, we've spent more money compared to a census to get data which is largely useless. Why anyone would want to do this is beyond me. Why would you spend $600 million for this?"

Adding insult to injury the new Chief Statistician, Wayne Smith, offered a lukewarm defence of the long form's replacement: "True, it's not a census, true, there's been some loss of small-area data, and true, there's more volatility in the estimates for small populations and small areas, particularly small populations in small areas. But the data turns out to be remarkably strong."[45]

Then, in 2014, the parliamentary budget officer revealed that Employment Minister Jason Kenney, having cut departmental spending on labour-market research by more than 20 per cent, was relying on commercial websites such as Kijiji for information on which to base his arguments about the need for a Temporary Foreign Workers Program (TFWP). In response, economist and former deputy minister of finance Don Drummond said, "Things are moving in the wrong direction." Decrying the lack of reliable data, Drummond declared, "Normally you create an information infrastructure and that informs the policy. Here we've had dramatic changes in policy with the TFWP and the Canada Jobs Grant, while we're undermining what little ... information infrastructure we already had."[46] His critique was echoed by a trio of noted Canadian scientists, including well-known environmentalist Thomas Homer-Dixon of the University of Waterloo, who stressed the need for government to have reliable data and, more importantly, for government to have the internal capacity to provide that data. "Modern nations that want to remain competitive and secure," they wrote, "need a solid foundation in government science, because universities and corporations can't undertake the kind of long-term, large-scale and interdisciplinary scientific studies the government needs."[47]

Not surprisingly, with the government's obvious lack of interest in expert opinion and evidence, not only government scientists, but public servants involved in policy-making across the federal government, began to experience serious morale problems. Long-term disability leave increased dramatically, leading the Global Business and Economic Roundtable on Mental Health to declare there was a "mental health crisis" in the federal public service. According to several observers, the primary culprit was the "climate of fear" that the government was creating, further damaging the bureaucracy's already strained relationship with the Harper government.[48]

MUZZLING THE BUREAUCRACY

The federal public service, like bureaucracies in all western democracies, is composed of professional experts. This is precisely because governments of the day, regardless of their political philosophy, are inevitably composed of politicians who are amateurs. Bureaucrats represent a wide range of disciplines because of the broad scope of government activity. The need for professional expertise, in turn, is the reason for the merit-based, non-partisan system of hiring and appointments in the public service. Politicians, by contrast, are elected based on their views and those of their party, and rarely if ever on the basis of their professional credentials. Moreover cabinet ministers must be chosen from the ranks of those elected within the governing party. They are typically selected by the prime minister to ensure regional, gender, and linguistic balance, in addition to their political skills and experience, but rarely because they have good managerial skills, nor are they likely to have a background in the portfolio for which they are responsible. In short, they are almost always likely to be amateurs when it comes to their department.

As a result, all political parties in Canada have historically placed a high value on the expertise of federal bureaucrats. They have understood and appreciated the role which the bureaucracy can play in assisting individual ministers, and governments, with policy formulation and implementation. Public servants, in return, have operated under a strict code of professionalism, neutrality, and anonymity, which ensures it is their political masters who are ultimately responsible for decision-making.

Although there have been some exceptions to this normally harmonious and mutually beneficial relationship, including a notable period during the first term of the Mulroney government when political interference and patronage played a significant role, this was the exception rather than the rule. Given their mistrust of scientific evidence, however, the Harper Conservatives have broken new ground in their troubled relationship with the bureaucracy. The expert knowledge and advice of bureaucrats is often seen as unhelpful. (Foreign Minister John Baird, for example, although widely seen as a diligent and hard-working minister who masters his files, is said to have told officials in the Middle East division of his department that he did not need briefing notes from them, since he already knew what he thought.)[49] More importantly, the body of accumulated knowledge within the bureaucracy could prove counterproductive to their plans if it were to become public. With this concern in mind, the Harper Conservatives have embarked on a massive campaign to muzzle public servants, one that has been widely reported and has caused considerable strain in the relationship.

In the end, the Conservatives' approach appears to have accomplished its short-term objective. The media, the academic community, and interest groups are all unable to obtain even the most basic information from government departments in a timely fashion, a situation exacerbated by the MEP process mentioned above, but not limited to it. At the same time, as Gary Corbett, president of the Professional Institute of the Public Service (PIPS) pointed out in an article titled "The Harper Government's Disdain for Science," the Conservatives' approach runs directly counter to the attitude of virtually all other western democracies, including the United States. "U.S. government policy," Corbett noted, "permits American scientists who work for the government to speak about their work to anyone at any time."[50]

Although this degree of hostility towards the public service is unprecedented, it did not come as a total surprise. During the 2006 election, it will be recalled, Harper argued he could be trusted with a majority because the Supreme Court, the Senate, and the public service would still be "Liberal" and would act as a counterbalance. As a result, when the Conservative Party came to power, many public servants were already wary of the new government. At the time, former senior mandarin Arthur Kroeger called Mr Harper's remarks "extraordinary" and predicted a "rocky" relationship between the new government and its bureaucrats.[51] The heads of major public-service unions, such as Nycole Turmel of the Public Service Alliance of Canada (PSAC) and Michele Demers of the Professional Institute of the Public Service (PIPS), expressed dismay that Harper would make such a comment before taking office. Similarly Michel Smith, director of the Association of Professional Executives of the Public Service of Canada (APEX), declared, "They may mistrust us, but what I bought into as a public servant is to serve the government of the day and we have a long track record to demonstrate we are a non-partisan public service." Smith continued, "I hope Mr. Harper will take time to build that relationship and get a sense of what it is like to govern, because his people have no experience in governing."[52]

Harper's comments were particularly significant, given that he had not campaigned against the public service as Brian Mulroney had done. In fact, Harper had not mentioned the public service at all until his fateful remarks. This was in sharp contrast to the enthusiastic campaign Mulroney conducted against bureaucrats in 1984, when he promised to deliver "pink slips and running shoes" to a large number of them, whom he described as overpaid and underworked. However, Mulroney soon came to appreciate the importance of expert advice. He increasingly relied on senior public servants such as Norman Spector, Simon Reisman, Mel Cappe, and Derek Burney to help him implement his agenda.

Stephen Harper did not follow suit. In a year-end interview with the CBC *Newsworld*'s Don Newman on 20 December 2006, several months after he had formed a government, Harper made that clear in his response when asked by Newman what had been the biggest challenge since assuming power. "Probably the most difficult job, you know difficult thing you have to learn as prime minister ... is dealing with the federal bureaucracy ... it's walking that fine line of being a positive leader but at the same time pushing them and not becoming captive to them ... I could write a book on that one."

The Harper Conservatives' management of the federal bureaucracy has confounded supporters and critics alike. Few anticipated the extent of the changes that would be implemented, especially in a minority situation, or the ruthlessness of some interventions to stifle dissent. Virtually no one foresaw how the prime minister and his government would simply ignore the bureaucracy most of the time, plunging it into irrelevance. As one observer concluded, work has "ground to a halt" in much of the public service.[53] Relations between the Conservative government and the federal bureaucracy are not simply rocky, as Kroeger predicted, but nearly non-existent. By 2011, numerous surveys confirmed that public-service morale was at an all-time low.

An initial sign of things to come was the Federal Accountability Act. Introduced in December 2006, shortly after the Conservatives were elected, it was almost universally panned. Public administration scholar Sharon Sutherland examined the legislation in her seminal work, "The Unaccountable Federal Accountability Act: Goodbye to Responsible Government," and concluded that the legislation was based on the premise that public servants could not be trusted; they must be severely constrained in their authority and threatened with a wide range of sanctions in order to ensure their loyalty and compliance. Apart from the fallacy of such thinking, which even anticipated "naming, blaming, and shaming" individual bureaucrats, Sutherland concluded that other aspects of the bill (which perversely assigned greater responsibility to senior bureaucrats for financial administration and implementation) had effectively shifted the blame for any government mistakes or failures away from ministers onto bureaucrats, thereby allowing politicians to avoid responsibility.[54]

Subsequent examples of information suppression are numerous and often bewildering. A world-famous expert on salmon stocks – whose report of dramatic new findings had already appeared in one of the world's top research journals – was forbidden to discuss her already public findings with Canadian media. A plant specialist in Environment Canada, who had written a fictional mystery thriller, was similarly ordered to refrain from attending his own book launch. Scientists in a number of government departments were told they could not attend conferences where they were scheduled speakers; others were prevented from speaking with the media to discuss factual data on everything from bear sightings in federal parks and weather patterns in the Atlantic to the discovery of fossils in a prehistoric ice pack in the Arctic – without seeking prior approval.

A leaked internal survey conducted within Environment Canada revealed that there had been a "dramatic reduction" in media coverage of climate change as a direct result of the 2007 rules introduced by the Harper Conservatives to prevent media interviews. "Scientists have noticed a major reduction in requests for any issue, particularly from high profile media who often have same-day deadlines," it said. More ominous still: "Media coverage of climate change science, our most high-profile issue, has been reduced by over 80%." The survey also noted that there had been forty-seven articles in Canadian newspapers since 2007 referring to the "muzzling" of federal scientists and other bureaucrats.[55]

Soon scientists, other academics, and the international scientific community began to react to this extraordinary situation. Their public comments highlighted the necessity of "knowledge-based" and "evidence-based" decision-making, and the need for the government to allow its experts to contribute to public debate. An international conference of biologists held in Ottawa in 2012 organized a one-time protest on Parliament Hill to highlight "The Death of Evidence." University of Ottawa biology professor Scott Findlay stated, "There is a systematic campaign to reduce the flow of scientific evidence to Canadians. As a result, the public hears and sees only information that supports federal government policy or ideology. That's not evidence, that's propaganda."[56] However the most scathing indictment of this policy came from the *New York Times*, whose editorial board published an article accusing the Harper government of seeking to "guarantee public ignorance."[57]

Where the Harper Conservatives' attempts to muzzle bureaucrats proved unsuccessful, they resorted to campaigns to discredit the source. For example, in response to media revelations that Afghan detainees who had been handed over to the Karzai government by Canadian forces were likely tortured, in violation of our UN commitments, the Conservatives attempted to shift the blame to particular bureaucrats in the Department of Foreign Affairs and International Trade (DFAIT). Denying all knowledge of the charges, both Harper and his ministers of foreign affairs and defence proceeded to publicly criticize the competence and veracity of a well-regarded senior DFAIT official, Richard Colvin. The government's attempts to paint Colvin as a rogue bureaucrat who was "spouting Taliban lies" were met with stunned disbelief, not only among his colleagues in the Canadian foreign service, but also within the international community. Open letters critical of the government's approach soon followed from Colvin's European counterparts and several aid-agency officials who had worked with him. More than a dozen former

Canadian ambassadors also wrote an open letter to the Harper government in which they denounced the personal nature of its attacks on a "dedicated" and "highly competent" employee, warning that "The Colvin affair risks creating a climate in which officers may be more inclined to report what they believe headquarters wants to hear, rather than facts and perceptions deemed unpalatable."[58]

This behaviour undoubtedly served to intimidate many in the bureaucracy, where fear of reprisals grew – and with good reason. The Harper government has not hesitated to dismiss public servants who run afoul of the government's agenda, often villifying them before and after their dismissal in a concerted attempt to paint the individuals as both incompetent and unstable. This was the case for several Agriculture Canada and Environment Canada officials concerned about the government's intention to bypass safety rules and regulations, including biologist Luc Pomerleau of the Food Inspection Agency, who had questioned the government's plan to let the meat industry regulate itself.

Over the next several years, the list of those dismissed by the Harper government grew dramatically. In some cases individuals were not reappointed, in others they were summarily fired. The Conservatives' first term of office from 2006 to 2008 was a harbinger of things to come. From the sudden "resignation" of Jean-Pierre Kingsley, the head of Elections Canada, to the peremptory dismissal of Alan Leadbeater (the Assistant Information Commissioner), Adrian Measner (president of the Canadian Wheat Board), and Dr. Arthur Carty (National Science Adviser), the pattern of direct intervention in areas where the government agenda was "threatened" by public-sector expertise became clear. The practice escalated in their second term, from 2008 to 2011. Information Commissioner Robert Marleau unexpectedly resigned. Parliamentary Budget Officer Kevin Page saw his budget slashed and was publicly warned that he would not be reappointed. Paul Kennedy (chair of the RCMP Complaints Commission), Peter Tinsley (chair of the Military Police Complaints Commission), Pat Stogran (ombudsman for Veterans Affairs), and Marty Cheliak (director of the RCMP Firearms Registry) were all dismissed.

Among the most blatant cases was Linda Keen, a former senior bureaucrat and the chair of the Canadian Nuclear Safety Commission, whose decision to shut down the Chalk River nuclear plant over safety concerns led to her dismissal in 2006. Although it was clear that her firing was the result of a dispute between her scientific expertise and the government's political priorities, Harper not only criticized her publicly but argued that partisan bias had influenced *her* decision-making. "Since when does the Liberal Party have a right, from the grave through one of its previous appointees, to block the production of necessary medical products in this country?" he mused.[59] As many experts noted, the government's decision to terminate her employment might have been defensible, but the subsequent attempts to paint the career public servant as a "Liberal appointee" who was deliberately challenging the government on partisan grounds were not. By 2011, perhaps leery of future problems with the regulator, the Conservatives' announced the privatization of Atomic Energy of Canada Limited (AECL), a move criticized by everyone from scientists and private corporations to the Ontario government. Michael Ivanco, vice-president of the Society of Professional Engineers and Associates, spoke for many when he indicated thousands of jobs and billions of dollars in private-sector revenue would be *lost* by the move. "The Tories are so eager to privatize AECL that they don't care if they destroy the whole industry," Ivanco declared.[60]

These conflicts with so many obviously qualified individuals in supposedly arm's-length agencies was frequently contrasted by the media with Harper's own tendency to make questionable appointments, a problem which reached unprecedented levels after the 2011 election. Among the more frequently cited problems were his decisions to parachute Chief of Defence Staff Walter Natynczyk into the position of president of the Canadian Space Agency and his appointment of the former head of his security detail, RCMP Superintendent Bruno Saccomani, as ambassador to Lebanon. But these paled in comparison with his nakedly partisan appointments of former Reform MPs Deborah Grey and Chuck Strahl to the civilian oversight body for the Canadian Security Intelligence Service (CSIS), despite their obvious lack of qualifications. They in turn were joined by another unlikely appointee, Montreal doctor Arthur Porter, whom Harper not only appointed as chair of the Security Intelligence Review Committee but invested as a member of the Privy Council, a position Porter held until he fled the country in early 2013 after being charged with numerous counts of fraud, abuse of trust, and money laundering.

In addition to their unprecedented interventions in the bureaucracy when they encountered specific instances of inconvenient opposition, the Harper Conservatives' attitude towards the federal public service as a whole has been largely one of indifference. Unwilling to accept advice from experts, their government has left thousands of policy analysts with literally nothing to do.[61] In many cases, a parallel political bureaucracy in the PMO and ministerial offices has taken up the slack, and the PMO has become the primary source of policy development. Policy implementation, meanwhile, is a one-way street, with top-down direction in minute detail controlling every aspect of their operations. In this respect, the Conservatives' ability to manage the bureaucracy and use it to pursue their own ends appears to have been quite successful.

SILENCING CIVIL SOCIETY

Perhaps even more remarkable is the impact the government's new conservative agenda has had on civil society and the various non-governmental agencies, interest groups, and academics who do not support that agenda. In the past the Mulroney Progressive Conservatives' aversion to funding social-action groups that were created by Liberal governments to "level the playing field" in areas such as consumer rights, women's, aboriginal, and human rights, and environmental protection, was well-known. However the Harper Conservatives have moved even further to hobble what they consider to be privileged or "special" interest groups.

To begin with, the Conservatives have exercised strict control over the funding of groups within federal departmental mandates. Established women's groups, for example, have been routinely denied grants for operating budgets or special activities. In her book *Women, Power, Politics*, University of Toronto professor Sylvia Bashevkin, draws a straight line between these refusals and the fact that the Harper government is "connected to organized anti-feminism" far more than any previous federal government, Liberal or Progressive Conservative, in the country's history.[62] In particular, Professor Bashevkin points to the disproportionate influence of REAL Women, which actually *did* receive federal funding, and to the actions of Status of Women Minister Rona Ambrose, who voted in favour of a private member's bill on abortion. Bashevkin also cites the number of contacts that groups such as REAL Women have with the PMO and with ministers, and the pattern of appointments of social conservatives to boards and agencies.[63]

One of the most controversial and high-profile examples of this unfolded with respect to the "defunding" of KAIROS, a well-regarded ecumenical aid organization that had received funding from CIDA for years. Although its directors had received assurances from officials that their annual application had been approved, they were suddenly informed in late 2009 that their group no longer met the required criteria for funding. Several other aid groups received similar explanations as their funding was reduced or eliminated. Concerns about government intervention in the grants process were expressed almost immediately, and in the case of KAIROS they were heightened by Immigration Minister Jason Kenney's comments in Israel, where he declared that his government was being vigilant about withdrawing support from any groups who criticized that country or supported Palestinian-rights groups.

In an escalating public-relations crisis, the Harper government insisted that the rules were being followed and the groups in question had been appropriately handled by bureaucrats, who had recommended against funding. When it eventually transpired that the minister, Bev Oda, had intervened after the fact on the KAIROS file to countermand the positive recommendation of her senior officials, the entire aid community vigorously criticized the process and stressed the need for openness and transparency. "This is not about a particular decision," one critic reiterated. "No one is questioning the government's right to set the criteria and decide as it sees fit. But without a rules-based system on which to evaluate applications, the system will deteriorate into chaos."[64]

Yet another of the Harper government's tactics to stifle dissent among such groups has been the threat that their charitable status will be withdrawn. The April 2012 federal budget actually allocated an additional $8 million to the Canada Revenue Agency over a two-year period to examine the files of various organizations, allegedly to ensure that they were not exceeding the 10-per-cent rule on annual expenditures for "political" purposes. According to Finance Minister Jim Flaherty, there had been "a lot" of complaints about charities, but he was not able to provide evidence of these complaints when asked. Critics drew different conclusions.

It soon became apparent that there was good reason to be suspicious. First, Natural Resources Minister Joe Oliver posted a broadside on his departmental website, declaring that "Unfortunately there are environmental and other radical groups that ... threaten to hijack our regulatory system to achieve their radical ideological agenda ... they use funding from foreign special interest groups to undermine Canada's national interest." This was followed by critical comments by Conservative senators in a Senate committee that was coincidentally examining the "issue" of political activities by charitable groups. Senator Percy Mockler referred to the Sierra Club and the Suzuki Foundation as "bad, not to mention ugly," while Senator Mike Duffy added "They're all anti-Canadian."[65] Environment Minister Peter Kent went even further a few days later, accusing an unnamed environmental group or groups of "money laundering." In an interview with Evan Solomon of the CBC the following day, Kent was asked to clarify whether he was speaking of criminal activity. Kent replied "There are allegations – and we have very strong suspicions – that some funds have come into the country improperly to obstruct, not to assist, in the environmental assessment process."[66]

Another minister in the Harper government entered the fray by issuing a new anti-terrorism strategy containing a list of perceived threats that included "eco-terrorists." To avoid uncertainty, Public Safety Minister Vic Toews stressed that domestic as well as foreign threats would be monitored under the new policy, and then provided examples of these threats, including "the promotion of such causes as animal rights, white supremacy, environmentalism, and anti-capitalism." The government's actions have had one obvious impact on civil society. As David Suzuki told reporters when he resigned from the board of his own organization, his group was "facing a chill" that was "leading it to pull back from important environmental debates" for fear of losing its charitable status.[67]

The chill facing civil society was also to be found in academic institutions, where scholars were targeted because of their research, public comments, or written work. Given the fundamental concept of academic freedom, the use of such tactics was described by one of the "victims" as "a McCarthy-like attempt to intimidate" and by another as "a concerted effort to put a chill on academic critics of the Harper government ... This government has a hostility towards people who think for a living or people who write for a living."[68] In one prominent case, the government leader in the Senate, Marjory LeBreton, wrote a letter to the chancellor of the University of Ottawa, demanding that history professor and fellow of the Royal Society Michael Behiels be disciplined for his criticism of the government's approach to federalism and national unity. When the university refused, she published a scathing letter in the *Ottawa Citizen*, attacking Behiels's competence. In another case, two prominent law professors who had been critical of the government's handling of the Afghan detainee file were the subject of an Access to Information request concerning their salaries, research expenses, and grants.

BANKRUPTING POLITICAL PARTIES

Given its zero tolerance for dissent and its single-minded pursuit of critics, it is hardly surprising that the Harper government includes opposition parties on its enemies list. What *is* surprising is the degree of success the Conservatives have had in convincing Canadians that their hard-line approach to their political adversaries is both reasonable and fair in a democratic society. Essentially, their approach has been to bankrupt the opposition and hopefully destroy the Liberal Party, which Harper continues to see as his principal opposition and the epitome of liberal thinking. As senior Harper adviser Keith Beardsley acknowledged, "He hates the Liberal Party, and I would say his aim from day one – and I don't think anyone would disagree – was to break the brand. The long-term strategy, that was it."[69]

Once again it has been the Conservatives' communications skill in portraying their targets in as negative a light as possible that has made this approach so successful. Yet even some conservatives – including former Harper adviser Tom Flanagan and former National Citizens' Coalition director Gerry Nicholls – have criticized the Harper government's approach as not simply ruthless and mean-spirited, but a potentially serious blow to democracy.[70] If even political parties cannot express dissenting opinions from the government of the day, what legitimate outlet for any opposition to their views will be left?

As was discussed earlier, the financing of political parties and elections in the United States is in such a chaotic state that even right-wing Republicans have recognized the need for state intervention. In Canada, such intervention has long existed, beginning with the Trudeau government's 1974 Election Expenses Act, which imposed overall spending limits on national parties, and on individual candidates, during election campaigns. In addition to ensuring that expenditures did not spiral out of control, the legislation had two other major objectives: to ensure a relatively level playing field for political parties and to provide a measure of transparency in political-party financing. For greater equity, it required television and radio outlets to provide fixed periods of time for paid political announcements by all political parties. For greater transparency, it required parties to reveal the source of any large donations.

Although the primary focus was on expenditures, another important aspect of the act was to provide tax credits to individuals for donations to political parties. Given the traditionally low level of financial support for political parties by Canadians, especially in comparison with other western democracies, it was hoped that this measure would encourage and enhance political participation.[71]

The act also provided publicly funded rebates for the national parties, and for their individual candidates, based on the number of votes received in elections. However, while this measure was helpful, it was insufficient to finance the ongoing operations of a national party, or indeed a national election campaign, and was not intended to do so. As a result, the major political parties continued to depend largely on corporate and union donations, as well as donations from small numbers of wealthy individuals, to finance their ongoing operations and the balance of their campaign expenses. It was not until 2003 that more attention was paid to placing limits on the other side of the ledger, namely, party *revenues*, when the Chrétien government introduced Bill C-24. First and foremost, the bill banned both corporate and union contributions at the national level, and limited them to $1,000 at the local riding level. Secondly, it capped donations by individuals at $5,000. Thirdly, the bill provided new measures to compensate for the revenue that parties would lose by these restrictions. It increased the amount of the tax credit for political contributions by individuals, and also the amount of the rebate to parties and candidates for election expenses. Most importantly, it introduced an entirely new mechanism of public funding for political parties, through a formula based on the strength of their electoral support in the previous election. Under this per-vote subsidy, parties would receive a fixed annual amount until the next election.

This last measure was considered essential, and was modelled on the practice in other western democracies where public funding of political parties has long been in place. Experts in electoral financing consider the per-vote subsidy mechanism to be the most equitable. By contrast, as Laval University political scientist Louis Massicotte has noted, parties with a high dependence on individual donations are often the most vulnerable to corruption or undue influence.[72]

Chrétien outlined several motives for introducing such legislation. In addition to bringing Canada's system in line with most of its counterparts, he was increasingly concerned about the trend in the United States, and said he did not want to see the Canadian system drift towards that model, where individual congressmen as well as presidential candidates spend nearly two-thirds of their time in office raising funds for their next campaign. As a result of this per-vote subsidy, all parties would have certainty. Moreover his unstated assumption was that this public funding would reduce the need for all parties to expend so much time and effort on fundraising from individuals, particularly since campaign expenditures were already capped by law. Given his imminent departure from public office, Chrétien also argued that the timing of such changes was ideal.

Interestingly, some of the greatest opposition to the bill came from within Chrétien's own Liberal Party. One reason was the degree to which the Conservative Party had already been able to raise funds through direct mail from the membership of right-wing special-interest groups. This was something the Liberals had not been able to replicate, since such groups generally form in opposition to government policies, not in support of them, and the Liberals had been in power for many years. As a result, they depended more heavily on large donations from a smaller number of wealthy donors, while the NDP received considerable financial support from unions. Consequently, many Liberals believed the legislation would negatively affect their party more than others, a fact that Chrétien acknowledged. At the same time, he argued that only the Liberal Party could introduce such legislation for that very reason.

Once it passed, the Liberals would have to improve their fundraising from individuals in a hurry. Nevertheless, the situation might have been manageable had it not been for the intervention of Stephen Harper once elected. Harper was well aware of the financial strain placed on the Liberal Party. In April 2006, he introduced the Financial Accountability Act, an omnibus bill which amended Chrétien's legislation, drastically lowering the cap on individual contributions from $5,000 to $1,000. This was a serious and completely unexpected blow, exacerbated by the additional ban imposed on corporate and union donations at the local level.

The importance of these changes was quickly apparent in the quarterly reports on revenue that Bill C-24 required political parties to provide. In the first half of 2007, the Conservative Party raised $8.9 million, *more than twice the combined total of all other opposition parties*. The Liberals raised only $1.8 million, despite their status as the Official Opposition, while the third party, the NDP, raised $1.9 million. Equally significant was the fact that the Conservatives' revenue came from 82,000 individual donors, while the Liberals had only 14,316, and the NDP 26,555. Even more revealing was the fact that, by 2008, both the Liberals and the Bloc derived the majority of their revenue from the annual per-vote subsidy, while the NDP was not far behind. Nevertheless, the opposition parties did little to protest these changes, apparently fearing the public would not understand their significance.

The federal election held in October 2008 strained all of the opposition parties' resources even further. Harper's surprise move to terminate the per-vote subsidy immediately after the 2008 election finally forced them to take decisive action. Having been returned with another minority government, Harper's decision to eliminate the subsidy in his November 27 Economic Update was all the more surprising. For once, it appeared his strategic skills had deserted him. As Flanagan and Jansen noted in an article on the implications of the proposed changes, all of the opposition parties would have been "profoundly affected" by the move, and he should have realized that he had gone too far. "In the short term," they wrote, "the move would have financially devastated the Liberals, NDP, and BQ, jeopardizing those parties' ability to pay off their campaign debts and their readiness to fight another election in the shortened timeframes of minority governments."[73] Columnist Murray Dobbin's analysis was typical of the negative media coverage. "It was a ruthless and transparent maneuver designed to crush the opposition before the next election was even called," Dobbin wrote. "And it was extremely cynical – he had never criticized the program publicly and nowhere in the party's policies was it even mentioned."[74]

Harper underestimated his opponents. Despite their immediate criticism and repeated demands that he remove the provision from the budget bill for a separate debate, he refused to bend, ignoring his own objections to omnibus bills when he was in opposition. Evidently he believed his opponents would have to support his budget, even though it contained that measure, because they would not dare to bring down his government so soon after a general election. But the opposition parties had a different plan: namely to defeat the government on a non-confidence motion and then form a coalition government, rather than force an election. It caught the Conservative leader by surprise and led to the now-infamous prorogation crisis. It also led Harper to remove the proposal from his budget when the House finally returned.

But he did not abandon his plan. With his 2011 majority secure, the elimination of the per-vote subsidy was a priority. Just three weeks after the election, he announced that the June 6 budget would terminate the scheme. As a minor concession, the removal of the subsidy was scheduled to take place gradually over three years, in time for the next federal election in 2015.

Experts have continued to criticize the move as fundamentally flawed. Former Chief Electoral Officer Jean-Pierre Kingsley noted that the Chrétien subsidy provided money for political parties based on votes, the most democratic scheme possible, and it also encouraged higher voter turnout. Duff Conacher of Democracy Watch concurred, adding that, with the subsidy's elimination, only the 1 per cent of Canadians who donate money to political parties will have any influence, and the incentive to vote may actually be diminished.[75] University of Ottawa law professor Errol Mendes was equally blunt. "You can see what's happening here. They're moving towards a process of eventually cutting the feet out from all the major opposition parties."[76] Mendes added that, while the Conservatives were eliminating the subsidy, they were leaving the tax credit in place, a move which would provide taxpayer-funded benefits to individual donors at the same time that Harper was arguing against the Chrétien subsidy because it was funded with taxpayers' money.

The reason for Harper's determination is clear. As one visiting head of state commented off-the-record to a reporter, "I don't like my opponents, but I don't hate them ... he *hates* his opposition, especially the Liberals!"[77] Certainly Harper's former National Citizens Coalition colleague Gerry Nicholls was in no doubt as to Harper's motive:

> Now ... Harper is free to deal a death blow to the Liberal Party. If you don't like the Liberals this might not concern you, but it

> should. For one thing, it's always disturbing when a governing party uses its legislative power solely for the purpose of undermining its political opposition. Secondly, if it's to work properly our democratic process requires opposition parties that are vibrant, effective, and well-funded.[78]

What has been the result? Although the Liberals managed to increase their revenue from individual contributors over the next two years, the gap with the Conservatives continued to widen. In 2013, under popular new leader Justin Trudeau, the Liberals raised a record $11.58 million, but the Conservatives received $18.16 million. With so much of an advantage, the Conservatives could continue to employ the tactics of the permanent campaign with impunity. Their attack ads became more frequent. Within *minutes* of his selection as leader, televisions ads were broadcast nationwide ridiculing Justin Trudeau. Moreover, and again taking a leaf from the Republicans, a number of Conservative-friendly interest groups have increasingly funded partisan advertising of their own outside the writ period. A classic example was an ad posted by the National Citizens Coalition in January 2012, attacking the Liberals' interim leader, Bob Rae.

Whether this huge imbalance in party finances will continue is perhaps a moot point, and one in which the role of Parliament might be expected to play a crucial role. However, even this avenue of democratic expression has been severely curtailed by the Harper Conservatives, who view the legislature as an inconvenience at the best of times.

4

Sidelining Parliament: Autocrats on the Hill

You win some you lose some. We have these debates all the time. But our focus can't be on parliamentary procedure. Our focus has to be on the big interests of Canadians and, in my judgment, that is the economy.

Prime Minister Stephen Harper,
10 March 2011, after his government became the first ever in Canada to be found in contempt of Parliament by the Speaker.

They will move with lightning speed to recreate and impose their reckless coalition on Canadians.

Prime Minister Stephen Harper,
27 March 2011

That guy would be happy with no opposition and maybe no Parliament.

Bloc Leader Gilles Duceppe, 1 April 2011

When he was a Reform MP in the Opposition, Stephen Harper often demonstrated a very good grasp of parliamentary rules and procedures. What was more, he was not in favour of the populist-inspired fiddling with parliamentary convention favoured by Reform leader Preston Manning. He was more than a little embarrassed by what he termed Manning's "silly" decisions to rotate his MPs' seating plan, to refuse to appoint shadow critics, and to delay responding to the government's budget until he had had time to consult with voters about their views. In the end, Harper resigned from Parliament and headed off to run the National Citizens Coalition rather than remain a Reform MP under Manning. For his part, Manning later wrote of his former protegé, "Stephen had difficulty accepting that there might be a few other people ... who were as smart as he was with respect to policy and strategy. And Stephen ... was not really prepared to be a team player or team builder."[1]

As prime minister, Stephen Harper has unquestionably become the most controlling party leader and the most autocratic head of a parliamentary government that Canada has ever seen. His approach has been neither conciliatory nor, on many occasions, has it been consistent with parliamentary conventions and procedures. As Bloc Québécois leader Gilles Duceppe complained (and as the earlier discussion of his philosophical underpinnings demonstrates), Harper seems to view opposition parties, and Parliament itself, as an inconvenience that must be tolerated rather than an essential element of our democratic system of government.

This perspective was evident from the beginning. Given his government's minority status between 2006 and 2011, he would normally have been expected to proceed with caution and a conciliatory attitude towards the opposition, who theoretically could bring his government down any time. True, Canada had not had significant experience with minorities since the Pearson/Diefenbaker era of the 1960s, being limited to Trudeau's short interlude in 1972–74 and Joe Clark's even briefer stint in 1979. Nevertheless, those minority governments paid considerable attention to the opposition, often adopting key opposition policies in order to placate them. But Harper managed to stand that minority tradition on its head, taking the offensive, keeping the opposition constantly on its guard, and making parliament itself subject to his will, rather than the reverse.

How was this possible? To begin with, it must be recognized that, in a Westminster-style parliament, the distinction between the power of the executive and that of the legislature can be effectively blurred if one is sufficiently determined.[2] Moreover, much of parliamentary procedure is dependent on traditional practice and conventions, rather than hard-and-fast rules. As former Canadian parliamentary official Philip Laundy wrote, "parliamentary procedure is a combination of two elements, the traditional and the democratic."[3] Some written rules do exist, collected in what are known as the Standing Orders. Rulings can be made by the Speaker on specific cases, and taken together form a set of precedents. But much of parliamentary procedure "is the result of centuries of practice – the unwritten rules of procedure which developed over time and have come to be accepted as the normal way of proceeding."[4] Yet compliance in effect is voluntary – there is no mechanism to enforce the following of traditions and conventional procedures, apart from the censure of opposition parties and the general public. As a result, those politicians who choose to ignore the conventions and traditions of parliamentary procedure – an exceedingly rare event in Canada until the Harper era – can often succeed without paying a political penalty.

By contrast, Stephen Harper's Conservative government has been prepared to ignore, bypass, and even ridicule many of the most basic and commonly accepted of these parliamentary procedures. Indeed, the Introduction to the 2009 Second Edition of *House of Commons Procedure and Practice* specifically (if somewhat euphemistically) noted that, in recent years, "the breadth of procedural evolution has been significant. There have been a number of rule changes and an even greater number of new precedents and practices."[5]

Taken together with a divided opposition in a multi-party system, the opportunities for someone aggressive enough to choose this route to control the agenda inside Parliament, and to work around it, are significant. Harper's tactics have been impressively ruthless, and his government's comportment both hyperpartisan and rigidly uncompromising. Moreover, as former adviser Tom Flanagan put it, Harper is "a predator. It's whoever is in his sights."[6] This extraordinarily disciplined and single-minded leader has, in turn, governed in a way that is anything but traditional or even normal. As journalist Andrew Coyne concluded, "This is not a normal government. It does not operate in the usual way, nor does it feel bound by the usual rules."[7]

Nothing could have highlighted the exceptional nature of the Harper Conservatives' parliamentary behaviour more clearly than the 2010 report of the British Institute for Government, entitled *Making Minority Governments Work*. The report, which examined several countries with Westminster-model parliaments, included a chapter on Canada entitled "Canada's Dysfunctional Minority Parliament." Its conclusions were blunt. The perceived failure of Harper's minority government was attributed partly to "The Prime Minister's personal style and tendency to behave as though he is leading a majority administration," and also to the tendency of the media and general public to see minority governments as weak aberrations, to say nothing of the fact that "many Canadians do not understand the basic rules of parliamentary democracy."

The report's solutions were equally blunt. In addition to the need for better civic education and a more informed media, it concluded, "For minority government to work in Canada there needs to be a dramatic shift in political culture which emphasizes cooperation and accommodation rather than conflict and partisanship. PMs leading minority governments should act with humility and recognize that they do not have a mandate to force their agendas through Parliament."[8] For Harper, this would have been unthinkable. His belief that his aggressive approach to parliament actually had been successful was confirmed at a Canadian Study of Parliament conference in October 2010, when senior Conservative adviser and Harper confidant Tim Powers told participants that the prime minister was increasingly convinced he could implement much if not most of his agenda without achieving a majority. In fact, he argued that a significant percentage of that agenda was already in place, implemented through non-legislative measures that circumvented parliament.

Despite this, there could be little doubt that Harper did indeed want to overcome whatever obstacles remained as a result of his minority situation. His 2011 election campaign was expressly targeted to achieve a "strong, stable, national majority" and end the "threat" of a "reckless opposition coalition." But the majority which he received in that election, while certainly stable, did not produce a more conciliatory or productive parliament in the traditional sense. If anything, it raised the temperature in the House of Commons and created a more dysfunctional legislature than before. It did, however, produce more emphasis on the legislative element of his agenda, as Harper was able to push through legislation without even attempting consultation or consideration for the opinions of the opposition parties.

Throughout his entire time in office Harper's stance in the House of Commons has been aggressive. From the partisan attacks on the opposition in Question Period, and the suppression of the oversight role of parliamentary committees, to the manipulation of procedure and use of omnibus bills, time allocation, and closure to limit debate in the House and pass their legislation in record time, the behaviour of the Harper government has been nothing short of remarkable. In several respects it has also been unprecedented. Most notable were the Speaker's historic findings, on two separate issues, that Harper's government was in contempt of Parliament, findings that Harper cavalierly dismissed as unimportant in the grand scheme of things. As one of his opposition critics declared, "You'd think he was talking about decorating advice. This is like calling a red light a suggestion. The Speaker has ruled, and these guys are in the wrong."

QUESTION PERIOD AS PARTISAN WARFARE

In many ways the elections of 2006, 2008, and 2011 continued to be played out in Parliament through the medium of Question Period.

As political scientist David E. Smith has so eloquently outlined, Canadians already had serious misgivings about the lack of civility that was developing in the House of Commons under the governments of Brian Mulroney and Jean Chrétien. Their concerns increased during the Martin era, when Harper was leader of the Official Opposition, and escalated rapidly once he had formed a government.[9] Many simply tuned out and turned off, as CPAC's declining viewership for parliamentary broadcasts demonstrated.

One of the first signs of things to come was Harper's choice of individuals to fill the crucial post of Government House Leader. This post was traditionally assigned to someone with expertise in parliamentary procedure, since the incumbent would need to argue points of order on the government's behalf before the Speaker of the House of Commons. Equally important, the individual would need to be a good strategist. The Government House Leader must negotiate with the House Leaders of the opposition parties to determine the legislative timetable, and perhaps make concessions to opposition parties in order to ensure quick passage of a bill or obtain opposition support for a bill. The position is especially crucial during periods of minority government, when the government must rely on the support of one or more opposition parties if it is to pass legislation and indeed to remain in power. It has increasingly been the custom to ensure the individual is bilingual, a facility that became even more important with the appearance of the Bloc Québécois in the House.

Harper's first choice for the post in 2006 was Rob Nicholson, a former Progressive Conservative MP who had served briefly in the government of Kim Campbell. As one of the few Conservative MPs in Harper's caucus who had any experience in government, this choice was perhaps not surprising, and could also be explained by the limited number of bilingual individuals in the Conservative caucus, as well as by Harper's need to include former Tories in his first cabinet. By most accounts, Nicholson was competent and reliable, but he served less than one year. It was widely believed that he had not proven tough enough for Harper, who was unhappy that several of his legislative plans had been delayed or rejected.

This view was reinforced when Nicholson was replaced by Peter Van Loan, a highly aggressive and partisan performer in the House, who set the tone for increasingly raucous sessions of Question Period. Van Loan's replies to opposition queries were almost unfailingly partisan and frequently involved personal jabs. He also could be counted upon to blindly repeat the talking points provided by the PMO, and to go on the offensive to divert attention from the subject at hand. Among his more infamous moments were his claim that Liberal MP Mark Holland was "an agent for the Taliban intelligence agency," that one of Holland's colleagues had "communist sympathies," and that Ontario premier Dalton McGuinty was "the small man of Confederation." Nor did his answers always make sense, as in his response that "it is not the fault of the rules that they were broken." What was always clear, however, was that Van Loan would not be providing an answer to any question posed by the opposition. As parliamentary expert Ned Franks commented, "I stopped watching QP some time ago for a variety of reasons, and he [Van Loan] was one of them."[10]

After barely six months in the post, Van Loan had so aggravated opposition MPs that even the normally unflappable and urbane Ralph Goodale, the Liberals' House Leader, could not resist heckling when Van Loan was engaged in yet another testy exchange during Question Period. "Do you know how stupid you look, Peter?" Goodale asked rhetorically. Interviewed by the press later, Goodale – who had served as Government House Leader himself for many years – stated, "In the relationship among House leaders there are bound to be tensions because House leaders see things through different ends of the telescope. But, frankly, Mr. Van Loan is not very helpful to the House."[11] As Goodale pointed out, and contrary to standard practice, Van Loan had particularly incensed him and the other Opposition House Leaders by failing to consult or even inform them of important developments until the last minute, and by reneging on agreements.

Van Loan was briefly replaced by the more moderate Jay Hill, but Hill's announcement that he would not be running in the next federal election quickly saw him replaced by John Baird, a Harper confidant as well-known as Peter Van Loan for his partisan and aggressive stance. Harper's choice was seen by most observers as a clear indication of his determination to play hardball with the opposition in parliament in the lead-up to the 2011 election. During the first prorogation crisis, Baird had taken an even more combative public stance than the prime minister. He declared the "reckless coalition" the opposition parties proposed was "undemocratic." Similarly, although the document they provided to the media clearly stated that the Bloc Québécois would not be part of the coalition government, Baird insisted that the other federalist parties had formed an "unholy alliance" and struck a "pact with the devil," namely the separatists. When asked by CBC reporter Don Newman what the government would do if the governor general refused to grant their request for a prorogation, Baird declared that, rather than "allow" the opposition to form a coalition, the Conservatives would take matters into their own hands by "going over the heads of the members of Parliament; go over the heads, frankly, of the Governor General; go right to the people."[12] This populist argument, although no doubt well-received by the party's core supporters, was in direct violation of the fundamental principles of a parliamentary democracy, as numerous legislative and constitutional experts were quick to point out.[13]

As one analysis concluded, "by putting such a divisive politician into the job, the Prime Minister may be signalling he wants to push full steam ahead on his agenda this sitting."[14] Harper told reporters, "I gave John a very clear message to implement our economic action plan and to ensure we stay the course. John has the confidence and respect of his colleagues to make things go forward."[15]

By now the front bench of the Harper government was occupied by a number of veterans who had mastered the art of the attack response under the tutelage of Baird and Van Loan. They even made frequent reference in their replies to any previous absence of the questioner, in contravention of a long-standing practice never to refer to the presence or absence of individual MPs in the House. This ministerial behaviour was accentuated by some of the more aggressive participants. For example, when Environment Minister Peter Kent, who had recently returned from a UN Conference on Climate Change in South Africa, was asked about Canada's formal position at that conference by the NDP environment critic, Kent criticized the member for not having attended the conference herself. This implied rebuke did not sit well with any opposition MPs, since it was because of the government's actions that no one else could attend. Newly elected Liberal MP Justin Trudeau even issued a statement in which he pointed out that "For the first time ever, this Government refused to accredit any member of the Opposition." The result was that opposition parties once again were prevented from participating in their legitimate legislative activities and denied access to information, the very concerns Stephen Harper had raised as Opposition Leader.

PARLIAMENT AS THREE-RING CIRCUS

In spite of the increasingly aggressive tactics in the House, few were prepared for what unfolded on 5 December 2012. When Conservative House Leader Peter Van Loan actually left his seat and crossed the floor, to engage in what was widely described as a vehement "verbal brawl" with NDP House Leader Nathan Cullen, more than dignity and civility flew out the window. Although the two men were "nose to nose," they did not come to blows, leading some to describe the incident as a tempest in a teapot. They could not have been more mistaken.

This development was important for much more than the amusing optics of Defence Minister Peter MacKay "escorting" a visibly furious Mr Van Loan back to his seat, while NDP MP Paul Dewar attempted to "calm" Mr Cullen and Speaker Andrew Scheer looked on helplessly. As the British Institute report had already concluded, it was indicative of a seriously dysfunctional parliamentary democracy, in danger of heading off the rails completely. It was this lack of civility that led opposition MPs to take more advantage of a legitimate tool for obtaining information from the government, namely Written Questions. This little-known mechanism had traditionally been used by MPs to obtain more detailed information from government departments than would otherwise be possible through the limited time allotted in Question Period. On many occasions in the past, such written questions would be submitted by a member in consultation with the minister responsible, who would be aware of the nature of the question and might even have suggested that the member take this route.

Under the Harper government, the use of written questions became one of the few means for the opposition to obtain any information at all, given the content-free ministers' responses in Question Period and the government's frequent attempts to undermine committee requests. But it was an obscure Conservative backbencher, Quebec MP Brian Jean, who filed a written question in November 2012 asking for an estimate of the cost involved in replying to written questions. His written request indicated that he believed there should be a fixed limit on the number of questions the opposition were allowed to file. The government happily complied with Jean's request. On December 18, 2012, it announced that responses for the first three months of that year alone had cost $1.2 million, and then produced a list naming individual MPs and detailing how much each of their questions had cost.

Opposition MPs were predictably furious. "Let me get this straight," Liberal MP David McGuinty said. "They've spent hours and hours figuring out how much these questions cost. They can put a price on the Order Paper [questions] but they can't seem to cost the F-35s." McGuinty went on to accuse the government of "classic Conservative politicking … They're attacking people who dare to ask them to do their job just like they attacked the Parliamentary Budget Officer when he asked them for the figures on the F-35s."[16] His colleague, MP Frank Valeriote, was equally blunt. "If they think it's too expensive to answer questions, maybe they should try being more forthcoming in Question Period. But they want to obscure this issue [of written questions] by putting a price tag on democracy. I mean, they might as well just cut off all of the funding to the opposition. That would save a lot of money, right?"[17]

But Question Period was not the only aspect of the legislature that the Harper Conservatives considered to be a hindrance to the implementation of their agenda. Parliamentary committees were targeted for special attention from their first day in office, and Conservative efforts to neutralize the oversight role of these committees was a matter of public record.

UNDERMINING PARLIAMENTARY COMMITTEES

Experts argue the real work of Parliament takes place in parliamentary committees, not in the hothouse atmosphere of Question Period. Traditionally, committees operate in a less partisan and more collegial fashion. The position of committee chair is automatically held by an MP from the government side of the House, and the prime minister's choices for chairs can be almost as important as his choice of House Leader. The procedures of committees are also governed by a set of rules, and each committee has its own non-partisan official, a committee clerk, to ensure those rules are followed. In a minority parliament, cooperation and good will are crucial, since the opposition members on the committee will outnumber those of the government and have the ability to defeat a motion. Yet few chairs appointed by Harper were conciliatory, and most were actively hostile to the opposition members on their committee. Many committees were hamstrung by their own chairs. Conflicts soon erupted over procedural issues, with clerks increasingly caught between the rules and the will of the chair.

In less than a year, the Conservatives had even shut down a committee. Trouble had been brewing for some time at the Official Languages Committee, where opposition MPs had wanted to hear witnesses to discuss the government's decision to eliminate the Court Challenges Program, which provided funding for individuals or groups to pursue challenges to government legislation that was potentially in violation of official language or other charter rights. Minutes before those witnesses were scheduled to testify, the chair, Quebec MP Guy Lauzon, cancelled the meeting, telling the NDP MP on the committee that the topic was "too political." Since the Official Languages Commissioner was scheduled to table his report to parliament that same day, arguing the Harper government had frequently "undermined" the Official Languages Act during its short term in office, the rationale for cancelling the committee meeting became evident. Former Liberal leader and committee member Stéphane Dion stated "The prime minister doesn't like the Charter, so he kills the program supporting it. He doesn't like official languages, he kills the program supporting it. He doesn't like to be questioned by members of this House, he kills the committee."[18]

Outraged, all the opposition MPs on the committee came together and voted to remove the chair from office. However, Harper refused to appoint a replacement, even though his chair had clearly lost the confidence of the members. The government Whip, Jay Hill, stated, "The opposition do not have the right to pick who the chair is," citing the very committee rules that some of his colleagues were ignoring. He also confirmed the government was effectively shutting down the committee, since it could not function without a chair. Days later, a leaked copy of a "secret" two-hundred-page guidebook prepared by the government for its committee chairs outlined "how to favour government agendas, select party-friendly witnesses, coach favourable testimony, set in motion debate-obstructing delays and, if necessary, storm out of meetings to grind business to a halt." It also provided advice for chairs on what to say when their authority was challenged, including "how to rule opposition MPs out of order during procedural wrangling and how government MPs should debate at a committee meeting when a 'hostile' motion was put to a vote."[19]

Shortly after, a major altercation developed between the PMO/PCO and the Public Accounts Committee over the interpretation of the new role of financial responsibility assigned to deputy ministers in the Harper government's Federal Accountability Act. Despite overwhelming expert advice that sided with the views of the committee and its chair that deputies could now be called as witnesses to explain and/or justify government spending, including an opinion from well-known parliamentary scholar Professor F.S. Franks, the Privy Council Office issued a contradictory interpretation that effectively limited the scope of the committee's authority to question top bureaucrats.

Other tactics came to light after the May 2011 election. One was a plan to conduct all future committee activities in camera, by redefining the term "committee business." Under the rules, committee business had always been conducted in camera, but there was no hard and fast definition of the term. In practice, the term had been interpreted quite narrowly to mean administrative matters such as the planning of future meetings or the discussion of a draft report. It had never been defined to include the hearing of witnesses or the clause-by-clause study of bills. But this was what was being proposed for the resurrected Official Languages Committee in a motion by one of the Conservative MPs, just as it was being proposed at several other committees where the government's agenda was perceived to be threatened.

The beauty of this tactic, from the government's perspective, was that any political points scored by the opposition during in-camera sessions would never be made public, since committee members are prevented from speaking publicly about an in-camera session. As the Green Party's Elizabeth May commented, "It's becoming increasingly evident that the Harper Conservatives dislike public accountability. They are already limiting debate in the House on a regular basis, and now they intend to make committee business secret." And they were doing so, May continued, "by running roughshod over past practice and doing away with any pretence of democracy."[20]

The nadir of this approach was the government's treatment of the Public Accounts Committee. The only committee chaired by an opposition MP, it had caused considerable difficulty for the Conservatives for their first five years in office. With their majority victory in 2011, though, they were able to make major changes in its operation, to attempt to limit the damage. Although the chair remained an opposition MP, the government now had a majority of members on the committee, and they used their new-found clout to make use of in-camera sessions as described above. At the same time they eliminated the steering committee, a tool previously used by all parliamentary committees to arrive at details of witnesses and subjects for examination in scheduled committee hearings.

As a result, NDP MP and committee chair Dave Christopherson said, "without a steering committee ... a large part of what we do in-camera is all the work we used to do in the steering committee," which used to be held outside the regular times the committee would meet. Liberal MP Gerry Byrne complained that, in those in-camera sessions, the Conservative majority used obstructionist tactics to prevent witnesses, delay hearings, and launch "esoteric fights and debates that [in the past] would have been settled collegially in a few minutes." In short, Byrne concluded, "the committee was designed to fail." This very point was raised by Harper-appointed Auditor General Michael Ferguson in his November 2013 report to Parliament. He noted "Engagement with parliamentary committees has again decreased: 30 per cent of our performance audits were reviewed, compared with 48 per cent in 2011–12 and 62 per cent in the 2010–11 fiscal year."[21]

Meanwhile, the prime minister's own parliamentary secretary, Dean Del Mastro, provided several examples of this type of interference when he sat as a member of the Ethics and Access to Information Committee, before he was ordered to cease and desist. The target of Del Mastro's efforts was the CBC. First he was repudiated for his attempt to have the committee call a judge as a witness, since the complete separation of judicial and legislative functions is fundamental to any democracy. Then he was criticized by the Bar Association for urging the committee to interfere in an Access to Information request involving the Crown corporation. Next he introduced a motion to have the committee demand unredacted documents from the CBC, a motion that was adopted, due to the

Conservative majority on the committee. Furious, NDP MP Charlie Angus, also a member of the committee, requested an opinion on that motion from the parliamentary law clerk, Rob Walsh. In his reply, Walsh indicated Del Mastro's demand was "well beyond the constitutional function of the House" and "could be found invalid and unenforceable by law." Angus provided a copy of the law clerk's letter to the media during a press conference in which he declared, "We have seen a full out attack by the Harper government on the ability of committees to carry out their work ... It's time the Prime Minister reins in Del Mastro – or risk turning parliamentary committees into kangaroo courts."[22]

Sadly, the Finance Committee provided another example of the Harper government's approach to procedure when James Rajotte, one of the few well-regarded Conservative chairs, was outvoted by his own members on a motion concerning the government's omnibus budget bill in November 2012. Rajotte, whose committee meetings were noteworthy for their civility and non-partisan nature, had ruled that opposition amendments not examined by the committee before a pre-determined deadline would have to be debated in the House of Commons. The Conservative members of the committee, however, were opposed to this development and voted to overturn the chair's procedurally correct ruling.[23]

This "might is right" approach to parliament and majority government was epitomized on a grander scale by the government's handling of budgets and financial matters generally, as demonstrated repeatedly through their use of massive omnibus bills.

FAST-TRACKING LEGISLATION

Once the Harper Conservatives obtained their majority, they immediately introduced a large number of controversial bills. Then they used every procedural tactic available to ensure the legislation was passed and implemented as quickly as possible. Most measures were long-standing platform commitments, which had been held back because Harper knew they would be opposed by the other parties. A few – such as the plan to eliminate the per-vote subsidy for political parties – actually had been introduced earlier and had to be withdrawn due to that opposition. Given their sense of urgency, the Conservatives made use of the omnibus bill. This tactic allowed them to do two things: first, it saved time, since they could introduce a plethora of measures at once, and, second, they could bury some of the most controversial measures within the larger bill.

Omnibus bills are typically used to group together various measures that are related or involve different aspects of a common subject. Historically, the use of such bills has been quite limited. One of the more well-known omnibus bills was the Trudeau-era Criminal Law Amendment Act, 1968–69, a 126-page, 120-clause amendment to the Criminal Code. Then, in 1994, the finance minister, Paul Martin, introduced a hundred-page omnibus budget bill which contained measures that would alter several different pieces of legislation, prompting the leader of the Official Opposition, Stephen Harper, to protest that the process was undemocratic. "I regret that we are proceeding with this omnibus approach to legislation," he said, "which, because it lumps in things we support and things we do not support, unfortunately deprives us of the ability to support the government in votes where that would be appropriate."[24]

Yet almost immediately after he formed a government in 2006, Harper introduced the Federal Accountability Act, the FAA, a piece of legislation so complex, and involving so many laws and agencies of government, that public-administration scholars specialize in one segment of the act. While there was considerable opposition to several measures, the fact that he had so recently been elected allowed him to proceed with impunity, as the opposition parties were in no position to bring down his government, particularly over a central election promise of his party.

This was not the case with the first budget bill tabled in February 2012 (C-38), nor again with the second budget-implementation bill of November 2012 (C-45). Both were omnibus bills of truly enormous proportions. Unlike the FAA, the opposition's response to C-38 and C-45 was vigorous and prolonged. They noted that the legislation Harper had objected to under Paul Martin was 100 pages, while his own omnibus budget was an astonishing 452 pages, contained 700 clauses, and affected 70 separate pieces of existing legislation. Worse still, the majority of the measures had little or nothing to do with financial matters. In fact, the bill made changes to everything from Employment Insurance and Old Age Security to immigration criteria, labour relations, national parks, animal welfare, railway and nuclear safety, fisheries, and environmental regulations.

Opposition leaders and representatives of First Nations, environmentalists, constitutional lawyers, and academics all described the bill as undemocratic. So did former Harper adviser Tom Flanagan.[25] The opposition parties introduced thousands of amendments to delay the bill, but the government persevered, forging ahead through the use of time allocation and closure.

The pattern was repeated in 2013, when the government introduced its budget-implementation bill in October and critics immediately highlighted unrelated measures "smuggled" into the legislation through this back door. The Conservatives' behaviour was described by one observer as Harper's "all-controlling methodology, in which he shows very little respect for the democratic system,"[26] a conclusion reinforced by the huge increase in hardball tactics, such as time allocation and closure.

CRACKING THE WHIP

There are a number of procedural tools available in Westminster parliaments to help a government manage time and implement its agenda. However they are intended to be used with caution, after opposition parties have had an opportunity to make their views known. The most serious tools – time allocation and closure – are generally considered a last resort, to be used only after lengthy debate in the House, and often to end a stalemate caused by opposition filibusters. While time allocation limits further debate to a fixed length of time, closure cuts off debate and forces a vote.

With a majority such as the Conservatives enjoyed after the 2011 election, any use of these measures would normally be very limited. But in their first sitting after the 2011 election, the Harper Conservatives used either time allocation or closure twelve times on seven bills. According to Peter Van Loan, they were justified, because their majority now meant they had a "clear mandate" to implement what he referred to as a "backwash" of legislation. Yet the June budget-implementation bill, containing many new measures, was cut off after only one day of debate. In addition, the Conservatives invoked closure to limit debate on an emergency motion to introduce back-to-work legislation for postal workers.

Opposition parties were livid, but powerless to prevent this "steamrolling" of the legislative agenda. NDP House Leader Joe Comartin noted that "no Canadian government has imposed closure on so many bills in such a short time."[27] Nor were federal opposition parties alone in their concerns. Quebec Justice Minister Jean-Marc

Fournier was "furious" that the Conservatives had limited debate on the omnibus crime bill before provincial objections could be heard, despite their efforts to meet with their federal counterpart to "soften" the bill. "Today we are not witnessing a move that is tough on crime," Fournier exclaimed, "but rather one that is tough on democracy."[28]

The situation deteriorated still further in 2012, putting paid to any thoughts observers might have had that a "kinder, gentler" Harper government would emerge once they had obtained their coveted majority. With the "backwash" cleared, the Conservatives continued to take advantage of closure and time allocation to implement the majority of the *new* legislation they tabled in the House of Commons. As early as February 2012, parliamentary expert Ned Franks predicted "they're going to set a record, that's for sure" in limiting debate in parliament. By June 2012, the government had indeed broken the previous record, using time allocation and closure to pass another ten bills. The trend continued, and in fact intensified. In June 2014, determined to pass a flood of new legislation with only days to go before a summer recess, the Conservatives first imposed emergency sittings until midnight each day, and then invoked time allocation seventeen times in nineteen days to push the legislation through. As parliamentary intern François Plante demonstrated in a paper published in the *Canadian Parliamentary Review,* the Harper government's use of these measures was even more exceptional when considered in the context of the low number of bills and high percentage of legislation affected.[29]

In addition, true to his word during the 2008 election campaign, Harper was encouraging private members' bills on a wide range of social-conservative issues, many of which his government would not want to be associated with directly. Nevertheless the PMO played a key role, leading one observer to argue the previously little-used and rarely successful mechanism had been "repurposed" by Harper for his own ends. Critics protested that the consequence of this strategy was that major changes to the criminal justice system were being implemented by the back door, with little or no parliamentary oversight. An unprecedented number of such bills were introduced, placed on the government priority list and then supported by the government in votes (which ensured their passage). By 2013, Public Safety Minister Vic Toews proudly reported that a record number of private members' bills had been introduced. Many of these bills were being pushed through the House of Commons in record time. By June 2014, fully twenty-five of thirty crime bills before the House or recently passed were in the form of private members' bills. Given Harper's cutbacks to the Justice Department, and the speed with which the bills were being processed, the almost inevitable complication of this unusual strategy was exposed when it was reported that, in the government's haste to process some of these bills before an adjournment, the Senate had been given incorrect versions of two private members' bills passed by the House, and both contained several provisions that experts warned would be found unconstitutional.[30]

Not content with limiting debate, Harper's government also began to make greater use of its ability to limit Opposition input through Opposition Days. By May 2012 there were accusations that the Harper government had begun to "punish" the opposition for their choice of topics, by scheduling their days at times which were highly unlikely to be noticed. One Opposition Day for the Liberals was set for a Friday, already a time of little interest, which was made worse by a shortened debate period, because the House would not sit in the afternoon. On another occasion it was also the day before a long weekend and a week-long parliamentary recess. Liberal House Leader Marc Garneau referred to the Conservatives' decision as "payback" for his party's criticism of an earlier government measure. "I think there's a message being sent," he said. Liberal leader Bob Rae agreed. "Canadians are now living in a democracy with dictatorial tendencies," he concluded.

STACKING THE SENATE

A different set of tactics was employed with respect to the Senate in order to further the conservative agenda. That body had long been described by the Reform/Alliance Party as illegitimate, because it was, as the phrase went, "unelected, unrepresentative and ineffective." Yet it quickly became one of Stephen Harper's most effective parliamentary tools. After his first attempt to change the Senate was rejected by the Supreme Court as unconstitutional, Harper embraced the appointments process. As Liberal-appointed senators reached mandatory retirement age, they were replaced with a host of partisan Conservative appointments, despite the party's original commitment to eliminate such practices. Once again, the argument used was that the government had no choice. In a Liberal-dominated Senate, Harper argued, he was obliged to appoint partisans to ensure passage of his legislation. Although he had no evidence to support that charge, by January 2010 the Conservatives had a plurality in the upper chamber, and by December they had an absolute majority.

This scenario allowed Harper to act with dispatch to eliminate troublesome legislation the opposition had put forward, which passed the House when the Conservatives were a minority government. Two examples stand out. First, in November 2010, a climate-change bill was effectively killed in the Senate – without a hearing or debate – for the first time in seventy years, on a procedural technicality eagerly seized upon by the Senate house leader. Senator Marjory LeBreton once again incorrectly described it as a "coalition" bill.

Similarly Bill C-393, a bill passed by an overwhelming majority of members in the House in order to provide cheap generic AIDS drugs for Africa, was deliberately stalled in the Senate and allowed to die on the order paper with the election. Conservative senators took direction from Industry Minister Tony Clement, who appeared before the Senate committee examining the bill to urge them to ignore it. According to Dr James Orbinski, an internationally recognized health expert, Clement's statement was based on "distortions, deceptions, lies and scare-mongering."[31]

The Conservatives' politicization of the Senate has been remarked upon by practitioners and observers alike. The previously civil and non-partisan nature of Senate debates steadily deteriorated under the firm hand of Senator LeBreton. Even more noteworthy was the overtly partisan behaviour of several recent appointees to the upper chamber, led by former members of the fourth estate Pamela Wallin and Mike Duffy. During the 2011 federal election, Wallin was a leading spokesperson for the Harper team, defending the party line in the media, while Duffy travelled the country speaking at candidates' events. Their subsequent undoing over housing and travel expenses, which resulted in a major scandal, raised questions about Harper's judgment in appointing and encouraging them in their activities, and in defending them for a considerable period before finally cutting them loose.

While Harper had appointed individuals to the Senate on condition that they would voluntarily resign if an elected Senate ever became a reality, several of his choices later declared publicly that they no longer felt bound by that commitment. Then some sixteen

Conservative senators ignored Harper's wishes and joined with Liberal counterparts to approve a number of amendments to an anti-union bill, C-377, which the government had passed in the House of Commons, thereby forcing the bill's return to the lower chamber. Harper, furious, replied through his spokesperson Andrew MacDougall, warning that, "as per Parliamentary convention, we expect that the Senate will respect the will of the House of Commons should the bill be returned to the Senate." Other signs of trouble in the Conservative Senate caucus included the determination of some Conservative senators, led by former Progressive Conservative Hugh Segal, to reject Harper's planned suspension of Duffy and Wallin, along with another Harper appointee, Patrick Brazeau. Segal's CBC interview of 18 October 2013, left no doubt what he thought of the PMO plan. "Some folks think the best way to deal with these problems is to throw everybody under the bus," Segal said. "Well guess what? You're going to run out of buses and you're going to run out of people."

FRIENDLY FIRE: THE BACKBENCH REVOLT

The government's authoritarian tendencies even extended to their own MPs, as Canadians learned firsthand in 2013 when an internal caucus revolt spilled over into the public domain. With the Whip's decision to remove Conservative MP Mark Warawa from the approved list for Members' Statements (also known as Standing Order 31s), in March 2013, Canadians learned just how great the control over Conservative MPs had become under the Harper government. Warawa had earlier tried to introduce a non-binding motion in the House of Commons condemning sex-selective abortions. Although a Library of Parliament researcher had provided expert opinion that the motion was well within the appropriate guidelines, a subcommittee on private members' business had ignored that advice and ruled it out of order, effectively killing it. Wawara had then sought to make a statement in the House, but the Whip informed him the subject matter was not acceptable and removed him from the daily list. Warawa's subsequent public protest was accompanied by a point of privilege, raised with the Speaker, and he was supported in this by a growing number of his backbench Conservative colleagues.

The Harper government's position, as outlined by the Whip and the House Leader, could only be described as a complete about-face from their campaign pledge to introduce greater transparency and openness in Parliament. For a party that had long criticized the Liberals for treating their backbench members as "trained seals," this was particularly striking. As one of Warawa's colleagues was overheard to say, "Trudeau said MPs were nobodies once they left the Hill. It seems we are nobodies even *on* the Hill."

Rather than promoting more independence for individual MPs, government whip Gordon O'Connor spoke of Parliament as a "team activity," and described his own role as a coach of that team, before informing the Speaker that "your role is a referee. It is not your job to tell the coach or manager which player to play at any given time."[32]

This meant MPs were being handed scripted questions and statements to read, produced by the PMO – when they were allowed to speak at all. By the end of March, the protest by Conservative backbenchers had gathered steam, and was being described by the media as an "open revolt." One report stressed "that members of Mr. Harper's caucus have been emboldened to stand in the Commons and publicly challenge the authority of the government whip, and by extension the prime minister, is extraordinary."[33] Mark Warawa's supporters had increased in numbers and prestige. Some twelve other Conservative MPs rose to speak on his behalf, including New Brunswick MP John Williamson, a former director of communications for Harper.

They were joined by Harper's former minister of intergovernmental affairs, Michael Chong, who rose in the House on 15 April 2013, to denounce the government's "command and control" approach and complain that members "can no longer ask questions of the government to hold it accountable, whether they sit on that side of the aisle [the opposition] or on this side. Chong went on to state, "The idea that the Executive is accountable to members of the legislature is a fundamental underpinning of modern political institutions in Canada. And the shift that has happened in Question Period, and is starting to happen in Members' Statements, is eroding this very fundamental principle."[34] When the Speaker finally did rule on Warawa's point of privilege, his decision was seen as a modest victory for the backbenchers. In particular, he specifically rejected the "team" concept. Shortly after this ruling, Brent Rathgeber, another outspoken Conservative backbencher, complained about the government's apparent decision to intervene in committee to "gut" his private member's bill C-461. Although it is not unheard of for a government to reject a private member's bill, it is unusual for members of an MP's own party to vote against his or her bill. In this case, Rathgeber's bill had been accepted and studied. As he pointed out, none of his caucus colleagues had objected to it or even mentioned the possibility of amendments at the time, yet in the end, all seven Conservative MPs on the committee voted in favour of last-minute amendments that altered the bill.

For Rathgeber, this was the last straw. He announced his resignation from the Conservative caucus on 6 June 2013, criticizing the government for its lack of transparency and accountability. "The more popular feeling, certainly at PMO and the whip's office, is that caucus members should essentially be cheerleaders for the government and spread the government's message, as opposed to being some sort of legislative check on executive power. I don't accept their premise," Rathgeber said. "I barely recognize ourselves, and worse, I fear that we have morphed into what we once mocked."[35]

Evidently determined to shut down the revolt as quickly as possible, Harper then circled the wagons during his July 2013 cabinet shuffle and turned to one of his early supporters, BC MP John Duncan, to take on the responsibilities of whip. Rather than allow for more flexibility to accommodate some of the backbenchers' concerns, Duncan made it clear in an interview that his job was literally to whip the dissidents into line.[36] If all else failed, however, there was still the option of shutting parliament down entirely, and Harper did not shy away from this.

SHUTTING DOWN PARLIAMENT

Prorogation is a more substantial type of adjournment than a recess. Parliament is shut down, and any legislation left on the order paper at the time that prorogation is announced will die, unless it is resurrected in the new session. Prorogation is a legitimate procedural tool available to a government in order to mark the completion of an agenda outlined in a Throne Speech, and to present another. Typically, in a four-year term of office, a prorogation would take place at roughly the halfway mark, meaning there would be only one in a four-year period. However, Stephen Harper used the mechanism of prorogation to shut down parliament twice within the space of a year, an unprecedented development in itself. Even more significant was the fact that his reason for invoking prorogation on both the first and second occasion was clearly partisan.

Only two months after the 2008 election resulted in another Conservative minority, Harper created a political crisis by introducing the measure in his omnibus budget bill to cut off all funding for political parties. This move was predictably and vigorously criticized by those opposition parties. Nevertheless, because defeat of the government on a money bill vote would have resulted in another election, Harper remained confident that he would prevail.

However the opposition parties, convinced that Harper would not budge, began to negotiate with each other to achieve an agreement on the formation of an alternative coalition government. This was a legitimate option, and one that could be expected in a parliamentary system.

But this is not how the Harper Conservatives understand parliamentary democracy. This was brought home to anyone who might still have doubted the new Conservatives' failure to appreciate the underlying principles of the system when John Baird made his declaration that, rather than "allow" the opposition to form a coalition, the Conservatives would take matters into their own hands by "going over the heads of the members of Parliament; go over the heads, frankly, of the Governor General; go right to the people."[37]

Indeed, as parliamentary scholar David Smith has pointed out, the perspective that the Harper Conservatives bring to Canadian parliamentary government is in fact an American one, in which they believe their source of authority is the people, not Parliament. A corollary of their approach is that the prime minister and the executive (cabinet) have an electoral mandate to act, and do not need to consider the views of the opposition parties in Parliament. (Smith also notes the inconsistency of their views, since, in many other respects, the new Conservatives actually place great emphasis on loyalty to the sovereign.)[38]

Unfortunately for the Liberals, their leader Stéphane Dion did not wait to defeat the government on a non-confidence motion before revealing that he and the NDP leader, Jack Layton, had come to an agreement in writing about forming such a coalition government, and that the Bloc Québécois had agreed to support that coalition for a specified period of time. Alerted in advance to their plan, and rather than hold the vote on the omnibus budget bill which he now knew would be defeated, Harper launched a pre-emptive strike by going to the governor general, Michaëlle Jean, and asking her to prorogue parliament. She agreed.

When they returned, Harper reintroduced the omnibus bill without the party-financing measure, in order to ensure its passage. But the matter did not end there. Harper made sure that it was the two opposition parties, and not the Conservatives, who paid a political price for the debacle. Here again he was remarkably successful. He was able to frame the debate in such a way that the legitimate constitutional option of the opposition parties forming a coalition government soon came to be seen by many Canadians as not simply "undemocratic," but a proposed coup d'état. Using their enormous financial reserves, the Conservatives launched a vigorous ad campaign attacking the very idea of a coalition. One radio spot argued, "Dion thinks he can take power without asking you, the voter. This is Canada. Power must be earned, not taken."[39]

Barely a year later, on 30 December 2009, Harper again advised the governor general to prorogue parliament. This time the ostensible reason was the XXI Olympic Winter Games to be held in Vancouver, British Columbia, in February 2010. Opposition members of parliament argued the move was a way for Harper to avoid ongoing investigations into the Afghan detainees affair, which was proving a significant public-relations problem for the government.

Once again Harper attempted to frame the debate, but on this occasion he was less successful. Canadians were well aware of the scandal unfolding in the parliamentary committee examining the Afghan detainees issue, and they also were now well aware of the consequences of prorogation: namely that the committee would cease to sit and no further news about the issue would be forthcoming for months, if at all. Reaction to his second prorogation move was in fact swift and intensely critical. Some citizens were sufficiently upset that an online petition protesting prorogation attracted thousands of names. Others organized demonstrations across the country. Even the *Calgary Herald* was highly critical of the move, which it described as a "cynical political ploy."

Meanwhile many academics signed an open letter to Harper, castigating him for what was termed a "flagrant breach of parliamentary practice" and "an assault on democracy." Nelson Wiseman, a political science professor at the University of Toronto, wrote a separate critique of Harper in which he declared that "no Prime Minister has so abused the power to prorogue."[40] Nor was the criticism limited to Canada. Even the venerable right-wing British magazine *The Economist* weighed in on the development. In a scathing editorial entitled "Harper Goes Prorogue," it described Harper as being a "competent tactician with a ruthless streak," whose decision set a dangerous precedent. "The danger in allowing the prime minister to end discussion any time he chooses," it said, "is that it makes Parliament accountable to him rather than the other way around."[41] Indeed, as University of Alberta political scientist Lori Thorlakson noted, "No other legislature among what Winston Churchill called the English-speaking peoples would tolerate such treatment. And since Westminster-style parliaments tend to have weaker legislatures than others, our House of Commons could (now) be described as the weakest of the weak."[42]

When parliament finally returned in March 2010, the Speaker delivered a clear rebuke to Harper's government over its handling of the committee investigating the Afghan detainees issue, and its refusal to hand over relevant documents that had been requested, by claiming they were vital to national security. The Speaker declared that the legislature did have the power to call witnesses and to demand documents, even if the government viewed them as confidential for security reasons. In his decision, Speaker Peter Milliken wrote, "It is the view of the Chair that accepting an unconditional authority of the executive to censor the information provided to parliament would in fact jeopardize the very separation of powers that is purported to lie at the heart of our parliamentary system and the independence of its constituent parts."[43] Yet despite this decisive finding, the government continued to stall.

In the meantime, further questions of parliamentary privilege were raised over the government's refusal to provide relevant financial information related to two major budgetary proposals, for the funding of the so-called "super prisons" and the purchase of F-35 fighter jets. As even traditional Conservative supporters noted, this behaviour had been unthinkable in the past. In an article in the *Globe and Mail* of 14 February 2011, columnist John Ibbitson went so far as to make the comparison between Harper and his Republican counterparts. "The Harper government is using 'cabinet confidence' the way the Nixon administration used 'executive privilege,'" he wrote, declaring that such an excuse was unjustifiable. His point was underlined by the parliamentary budget officer appointed by the Harper Conservatives, who declared parliament was "losing control of its fiduciary responsibilities" in testimony before the Finance Committee on 15 February 2011.

In both cases, in unprecedented rulings, the Speaker found both the government and the minister for CIDA to be in contempt of parliament, a scenario unprecedented in Canada and indeed in the fifty-four-member Commonwealth. (In the case of CIDA minister Bev Oda, this had been preceded by committee findings that she had not only misled them on the cutting of funding to the foreign-aid NGO KAIROS, as discussed earlier, but had retroactively altered the relevant cabinet document.) It was these findings, so disturbing to observers of parliamentary democracy in action, that Harper brushed off with the statement "You win some, you lose some."

The opposition then defeated the government on a non-confidence motion, resulting in another federal election and the return of a Harper majority, suggesting that the government had correctly calculated the public's lack of interest in such issues. Moreover, the government announced on its return that it would be proceeding with its proposed budgetary measures and had no plans to re-open the Afghan file. As Carleton University political scientist Jonathan Malloy pointed out, "In all of these cases the government took advantage of the degree of flexibility inherent in parliamentary conventions, tradition, and practice, even if no actual rules were broken." Moreover, the Conservatives were only too well aware that "public reaction on this rule-bending has been modest, and largely confined to huffy professors and committed partisans."[44]

In July 2013, when Harper announced that he was planning to prorogue parliament yet again, the move was immediately criticized by experts. This time it had been two years since the 2011 election, and his decision might have been less suspect had it not been for the fact that he and his party were suffering the slings and arrows of another aggressive opposition attack in the House of Commons, this time related to the growing Senate expenses scandal. Because of his track record, observers suspected that political reasons, and self-preservation were once again the real motivation for the move, rather than the "need to reset the agenda" as Harper claimed.

A number of expert observers argue that the progress made by the Harper Conservatives in stifling public debate in parliament was significant even before his majority. As professor emeritus W.T. Stanbury concluded:

> In his five years as Prime Minister, Stephen Harper has provided much evidence that he has serious authoritarian tendencies. He has established a governing culture based on a combination of secrecy, deceit, and contempt of Parliament. Harper has ruthlessly exploited the vast array of powers put into the hands of any PM by Canada's particular version of the Westminster model. But he has gone much further by governing "outside the box" of constitutional conventions that rely on custom, unwritten constitutional conventions, and self-restraint.[45]

His views were echoed by University of Toronto Professor Lorraine Weinrib, who concluded, "While Harper touts the democratic principle as his ideal, his actions align with another principle, an all-powerful executive authority that makes its own rules on a play-by-play basis."[46]

Why is such control necessary? Veteran journalist James Travers put his finger on the primary cause, namely Conservative determination to accomplish as much as possible in whatever time is available to them. "Determination and the patience to alter the country's course one incremental step at a time are core characteristics of a prime minister who is changing Canada more fundamentally than friends or foes often recognize."[47] And in so doing, Harper's government has called into question many of the democratic institutions of governance that Canadians have traditionally respected and trusted – of which parliament is the most obvious victim.

Political scientists Gary Levy and Paul Benoit have warned that the Conservatives' actions "threaten to undo the parliamentary fabric that has held the country together for nearly 150 years."[48] Their concerns are shared by political scientist Jonathan Malloy, who also noted that "passive disengagement" on the part of the general public – many of whom do not understand the issues, and even fewer of whom choose to vote in federal elections – allowed the Conservatives to take these actions with impunity, as evidenced by their 2011 electoral majority. "The bending of unwritten conventions and understandings may seem solely an academic matter with limited implications for an election," he wrote. "But Canadians need to take some time to reflect and inform themselves on this rule-bending, and only then can they express whether this is truly the way they want the system to operate."[49]

It remains to be seen whether this behaviour on the part of the Harper Conservatives will signal a permanent shift, or whether a future government will return to a more traditional approach to parliamentary procedure. Since the conventions that Harper has ignored are unwritten, there is no reason why his successor could not immediately restore them. Nevertheless, the ease with which such longstanding practices have been ignored and overturned may well lead to the conclusion that many of these traditional procedures should be formalized in Standing Orders or other written rules to prevent a recurrence. At the same time, as with the constitutional conventions related to minority government and coalitions, the Conservatives' unprecedented behaviour may also lead to greater efforts at public education by academics, the media, and political parties. As one conference dedicated to constitutional conventions, held after the 2008 prorogation crisis, concluded, "we need more public consultation and engagement with community, and public policy oriented organizations to begin to move forward … Broad dissemination of information through websites and public events will assist in informing politicians, academics, and voters about the role of such conventions in our parliamentary democracy."[50]

5

Making the Rules

I think I make the rules.

Stephen Harper, August 2012

We are agreeing to disagree ... We are amending our return under protest to reflect this.

Fred DeLorey, Conservative Party spokesman, after the party pleaded guilty to exceeding election spending limits and submitting fraudulent election records and agreed to repay $230,198 for violating Canadian election spending laws (March 2012)

[The court ruling] is a 'declaration.' We disagree with it.

Agriculture Minister Gerry Ritz after the Federal Court ruled he was violating the "rule of law" by introducing legislation on the Wheat Board before holding a plebiscite (December 2011)

Significant as it may be, the impact of the Harper government's agenda on parliament is unlikely to be as dramatic as its impact on the Supreme Court and the judicial system, both of which have long been stalking horses for the Conservatives' opposition to a number of constitutionally guaranteed rights and freedoms. Here, too, they have taken note of the approach of their Republican counterparts, who routinely criticize judges appointed to the Supreme Court by Democrats for their "liberal" interpretation of civil rights. Similarly, the Harper Conservatives rail against "activist" judges appointed by

Liberal and Tory governments, accusing them of "championing" the Charter of Rights.

The Harper Conservatives' ideological antipathy towards the Charter and the Courts is accompanied by their perception that their own authority is almost unlimited, because it comes from popular support. As a result, they believe that many if not most of the constraints imposed on governments by rules, officers of parliament, and even the Elections Act – all of which they see as the creations of liberalism – are no more binding on them than the decisions of the Speaker of the House of Commons. It is up to them to make decisions and, if necessary, to change or ignore the rules, conventions, or legislation that is in their way, in order to accommodate their agenda.

An examination of the Harper government's response to a number of adverse rulings by various officers of parliament and the Chief Electoral Officer, as well as decisions of the Supreme Court and the Federal Court, reinforce this conclusion. The irony of this situation is striking. Although their law-and-order agenda produced a multitude of hardline amendments to the Criminal Code to "get tough" on the crimes of others, the Conservatives themselves have played fast and loose with almost all of the other constraints on democratic governance in order to implement their agenda as quickly as possible. As one observer concluded, the Conservatives have "sail[ed] close to the wind when it comes to the ethics and legality of doing politics" since they were first elected in 2006.[1]

DEFYING OFFICERS OF PARLIAMENT

One of the first acts of the Harper government was to introduce the massive Federal Accountability Act, fulfilling their campaign pledge to increase accountability and transparency in government. One section created several new watchdogs. The Conservatives had been strongly in favour of all of these new positions when they were in opposition. Indeed they had clamoured for the Liberal governments of Jean Chrétien and Paul Martin to introduce such watchdogs in the aftermath of the sponsorship scandal. As a result, when the Conservatives were finally elected, they were committed to going ahead.

Their new oversight posts included:

- A Commissioner of Lobbying, a post which was to replace the existing Registrar of Lobbyists. It was to be a fully independent office with greater investigative powers, to enforce the new, allegedly more stringent, lobbying rules introduced by the Conservatives.

- A Public Sector Integrity Commissioner, whose role was to promote the reporting of wrongdoing in government and protect whistleblowers from negative repercussions in the workplace.
- A Conflict of Interest and Ethics Commissioner to administer the new Conflict of Interest Code for members of the House of Commons.
- And, most highly publicized, a Parliamentary Budget Officer, who was to provide parliament with objective analysis about government estimates, the state of the nation's finances, and trends in the national economy (a pre-expenditure role, to compliment the post-expenditure role of the Auditor General).

Yet, within short order, the Harper government had crossed swords with almost all of these new watchdogs, just as it had quickly come into conflict with the existing Access to Information Commissioner and the Official Languages Commissioner.

A case in point was the Conflict of Interest and Ethics Commissioner. Given Stephen Harper's vigorous criticism of the Chrétien government for perceived ethical lapses, few observers expected to see so many obvious violations of the conflict-of-interest rules by the Conservatives in such a short period of time. Yet that was exactly what happened, and in most cases it involved cabinet ministers rather than backbench MPs. Worse still, the incidents continued once the Conservatives had a majority in 2011, despite the greater experience of many ministers who had been rookies in 2006.

In 2011, for example, Immigration Minister Jason Kenney was found guilty of using his ministerial letterhead to solicit funds for the Conservative Party. Kenney admitted this had taken place, but blamed his staff, one of whom resigned as a consequence. In 2012, Quebec minister Christian Paradis was the subject of not one but two inquiries by commissioner Mary Dawson, but despite her findings, he refused to resign. Meanwhile, the international cooperation minister, Julian Fantino, was reprimanded by Dawson for the improper use of his departmental website for partisan purposes when two vitriolic statements attacking the opposition parties, signed by Fantino, were posted on the departmental website.

Unquestionably, the most surprising case of an ethical lapse was that of Finance Minister Jim Flaherty, a veteran of many years in the

Mike Harris Conservative government in Ontario before joining the Harper cabinet in 2006. Despite his previous experience, Flaherty found himself at the heart of a conflict-of-interest scandal in January 2013 when it came to light that he had written a letter to the CRTC supporting the licence application of a radio company in his riding. Dawson issued a stiff rebuke to the minister, indicating that he had breached both the conflict-of-interest legislation and the prime minister's own guidelines for office-holders. The opposition called for Flaherty to step down, as they had done in Paradis's case as well, but, like Paradis, the finance minister remained defiantly unrepentant. Dawson subsequently complained in testimony before a parliamentary committee that she had no authority under the act to issue sanctions, but could only find individuals guilty of breaching the legislation or not, leading some observers to conclude that Harper's legislation actually contained more loopholes than earlier Liberal versions of the guidelines.

Then there was the issue of lobbying, something the Conservatives had roundly condemned in a blanket fashion when in opposition. Soon after their election, however, the Conservatives discovered that not only former Liberal aides and parliamentarians took up this profession. One after another, important backroom operatives who had been instrumental in the Harper victory began to complain that they could not now enjoy the fruits of their labours by becoming lobbyists. Others, who had first gone to Ottawa to work with ministers or in the PMO, objected to the lengthy delay (known as a cooling-off period) imposed by Harper's new legislation before they could take up new jobs in the private sector. As a result, great emphasis was placed on a loophole in the bill which allowed those who supposedly did not actually function as lobbyists for more than 20 per cent of their time – despite working for consulting lobbying firms – to take up lucrative new posts immediately.

The so-called 20-per-cent rule soon came to be used by many with ties to the Harper government, including prominent former senior aides to Harper himself, such as Yaroslav Baran, a senior partner at Earnscliffe Strategy Group. Baran also led the way in demonstrating how to circumvent the new rules put in place by the Conservatives to ban lobbyists from their campaign. He simply "deregistered" as a lobbyist and took up a post with House Leader Jay Hill shortly before the 2008 election, in time to return to his post as director of communications in the party's war room during the campaign.

A different problem emerged with the newly created Public Sector Integrity Commissioner, whose primary role was to investigate complaints of wrongdoing within the public service and to protect the whistleblowers. Unlike Mary Dawson, Christiane Ouimet's legislative mandate provided her with ample scope. Nevertheless, Ouimet not only failed to exercise her authority, but actually sabotaged the work of her own office. Barely three years into her seven-year term, she abruptly resigned, shortly before a scathing report by the Auditor General revealed that, although some 228 cases had been filed with Ouimet's office during her tenure, only seven had actually been investigated. Five were closed with no finding of wrongdoing, while two others were still under investigation at the time of her departure. Evidence also emerged that Ouimet had often communicated directly with several cabinet ministers and officials in the Privy Council Office, despite her position as an independent officer of parliament whose relationship with the executive was supposed to be at arm's-length.

However it was the Parliamentary Budget Officer (PBO), the original jewel in the Conservatives' accountability crown, that caused Harper the most difficulty. Here the government's second thoughts over their initial enthusiasm were made clear from the beginning, and many efforts were made to limit the efficacy of the office. Their problem was Kevin Page, who soon became a household name. Over the course of his seven-year term, Page proved to be a consistent thorn in the side of the government, and one that they could not publicly undermine because of his popularity and the credibility of his work.

Nevertheless they also managed behind the scenes to restrict his access to information, in contravention of his legislative mandate, a point that Page raised publicly on several occasions before launching an appeal in Federal Court. The government made it clear that he would not be re-appointed, and when his term came to an end, they created a hands-on hiring process to choose his successor. But despite their plans to turn the watchdog into a lapdog, Page's successor Jean-Denis Fréchette appeared determined to fulfil his mandate with impartiality.

Still, these run-ins with various parliamentary watchdogs were hardly the principal cause of the government's declining credibility with Canadians. Instead, it was the Conservatives' deliberate manipulation of election legislation that caused them the most grief and led to a growing sense that the Harper Conservatives were prepared to ignore or bypass almost any constraints that prevented them from achieving their objectives. In fact, election legislation proved to be an area in which they were prepared to play especially fast and loose with the rules.

MANIPULATING THE ELECTIONS ACT

Stephen Harper introduced legislation establishing fixed dates for federal elections shortly after taking power. Bill C-16, An Act to Amend the Canada Elections Act, became law in May 2007. Its rationale, according to Rob Nicholson, the minister for democratic reform, was straightforward. "Fixed election dates," he declared, "will improve the fairness of Canada's electoral system by eliminating the ability of governing parties to manipulate the timing of elections for partisan advantage."[2]

The move was hardly unexpected, given that the Conservatives had campaigned on a platform of institutional reform to rectify the "democratic deficit" they believed was prevalent. Thus Senate reform and fixed electoral dates were both mentioned during the 2006 campaign. In addition, it was not difficult to understand the underlying motive for Nicholson's concerns, given the federal electoral record of the previous decade. In March 1997, Gilles Duceppe had been elected leader of the Bloc Québécois, and Prime Minister Jean Chrétien called a federal election for June 2 of that year. In July 2000, Stockwell Day was selected as the new Alliance Party leader and Chrétien promptly called the next federal election for November. Perhaps most importantly, Stephen Harper had been elected leader of the new Conservative Party in March 2004, and the next federal election was held on June 28, before he or the party had had a chance to find their footing.

As a result, the traditional prerogative of the prime minister to unilaterally determine the timing of elections was increasingly being seen as an abuse of power and an unfair advantage. Several provinces had already passed legislation setting fixed electoral dates before Harper's bill was introduced, and in theory many supported it. Nevertheless, a number of important constitutional and practical considerations were raised by experts about the Conservatives' legislation. Several amendments were proposed by them and by the opposition parties, but Harper rejected all of them. Without such changes, political scientist Gary Levy predicted Harper's legislation was "a constitutional crisis in waiting."[3]

That concern soon became academic when Harper astonished everyone by ignoring his own legislation. On August 27, 2008, he pulled the plug on his minority government, insisting the legislation still allowed him to do so if he chose. His subsequent victory suggested that Canadians were not too concerned with this issue, but Harper was not quite as lucky with another apparent effort to manipulate the Canada Elections Act, this time clandestinely. With far more funds available than they could legally spend in the 2006 election, senior Conservative campaign organizers Doug Finley and Irving Gerstein had devised a way to utilize more of their money, primarily for advertising purposes. The plan first provided a way for the party to spend an additional $1.2 million over and above the legal limit. Secondly, by claiming the expenses at the local level, candidates would be entitled to greater amounts of money as refunds from Elections Canada, which reimburses individual riding expenditures up to 60 per cent of the allowable limit. As a result, the party would actually *obtain* more than $300,000 in additional revenue.[4]

The scheme was discovered by Elections Canada, despite efforts to conceal it, and was ruled illegal. However, it was settled only in November 2011, after nearly five years of stalling, obstruction, and denial by the Conservative Party, and also after the May 2011 election gave the Conservatives a majority. A Federal Court ruling found the so-called "in and out" scandal violated the Elections Act in several ways. According to the Court findings, the national party already had come very close to spending its allowable $18-million limit when the scheme began.

In March 2011, having exhausted all avenues of appeal and delay, disaster loomed large. Four officials of the party, including the recently appointed senators Doug Finley and Irving Gerstein, were charged with violations of the Elections Act. If found guilty, they would receive major fines or prison sentences of up to five years. In addition, the commissioner of Canada Elections had referred the files of sixty-seven Conservative candidates to the Director of Public Prosecutions (DPP) for similar penalties. As a result, the party cut an eleventh-hour plea bargain with Elections Canada. All charges were dropped. In exchange, the party agreed to plead guilty to the charges, admitting they had submitted fraudulent expense claims, and repaying some $230,198. Nevertheless, defiant to the end, party spokesperson Fred DeLorey continued to maintain that the matter was really a disagreement between the party and the commissioner over the interpretation of the legislation, an argument that party officials repeated relentlessly.

Then, in early June 2011, Canadians learned that two Conservative MPs, Shelly Glover and James Bezan, were continuing to defy Elections Canada and refusing to submit revised expenditure claims. When they failed to comply with his final order to do so by 31 May 2013, commissioner Marc Mayrand wrote to the Speaker of the House of Commons, Conservative MP Andrew Scheer, requesting that the two MPs be suspended from the House as required under the Elections Act, which states that MPs "may not continue to sit or vote as a member until corrections are made." Surprisingly, Scheer did not inform the House of the letter. Its existence – and the ongoing dispute with the two MPs – became public knowledge only two weeks later through media accounts of leaked documents. A pitched battle ensued in the House, with opposition MPs claiming that Scheer should have informed them of the issue as soon as he received the letter. Their claim was bolstered by the opinions of a former procedural clerk of the House, Thomas Hall, and former law clerk Rob Walsh. Walsh also indicated that, in his view, MPs could vote to suspend the two, even though Scheer had not tabled the letter and refused to do so.[5]

Meanwhile, Peter Penashue, Harper's minister of intergovernmental affairs, who was first elected in 2011, had announced on 14 March 2013, that he would resign his seat after allegations of election spending irregularities surfaced. Penashue claimed the irregularities were the result of inexperience on the part of his campaign organization and vowed to run again in a by-election. (That by-election, held on 13 May 2013, saw Penashue defeated by the Liberal candidate, Yvonne Jones.) Equally troubling was the revelation that another Conservative MP, Ted Opitz, had spent $7,000 more than he was legally allowed in a 2008 election nomination campaign, a matter that surfaced years later and was not settled until October 2013, when Mr Opitz agreed to repay Elections Canada.

Still, all of these disputes paled in comparison with the saga of the prime minister's parliamentary secretary, Dean Del Mastro. Del Mastro's case was far more serious, because he was accused not merely of overspending, but of deliberately falsifying his expense claims and of participating in an illegal contribution scheme during the 2008 election. Del Mastro's troubles had only become public in June 2012. The situation rapidly deteriorated after that, and finally, on 26 September 2013, Del Mastro was formally charged with four counts of breaching the Canada Elections Act. He had resigned from the Conservative caucus the previous day to sit as an Independent MP, and less than a week earlier he was stripped of his post as parliamentary secretary to the prime minister, suggesting that Harper finally had lost confidence in Del Mastro's claims.

The resignation was yet another blow to the Harper government's credibility in terms of honesty, transparency, and accountability, a problem which had been developing for some time. Del Mastro's lead role in defending the government against the robocalls scandal, for example, was now called into question, and caused the Conservatives further public-relations problems. In fact, as one journalist commented, the robocalls scandal of the 2011 election was "the issue that won't go away." What began with concerns about efforts to manipulate the vote in one Guelph riding, soon spread to accusations of voter suppression tactics in more than fifty-six ridings. More than thirty-one thousand voters filed complaints with Elections Canada. The ongoing investigation into the deliberately misleading calls, made overwhelmingly to non-Conservative voters on election day in order to divert them to incorrect polling stations, led to strong suspicions that the national Conservative Party leadership was behind the scheme. The prime minister, Foreign Affairs Minister John Baird, and Finance Minister Jim Flaherty all strenuously denied the allegations on numerous occasions, claiming the party ran a "clean" campaign. Yet by November 2012, one Environics poll found that Stephen Harper's personal trust ratings were among the lowest of the leaders in twenty-six countries in the Americas.

Worse still, the revelations of widespread voter suppression tactics led to numerous court challenges, lawsuits, and lengthy media battles and threatened to cast a shadow over the credibility of the elections process itself. Chief Electoral Officer (CEO) Marc Mayrand summed up the situation in testimony before a parliamentary committee examining ways to tighten regulations in the Canada Elections Act. The calls, he charged, were "absolutely outrageous," and "strike at the integrity of our democracy," regardless of how many there were or how they were organized. Many critics believed the only saving grace for the Conservatives was the continuing inability of Elections Canada, after several years and thousands of dollars in investigative expenditures, to identify the key players in the scheme. Calls for Mayrand and his team to be given greater powers, to ensure no such scheme would be repeated, were the focal point of the committee hearings.

Yet it soon became clear that the Conservatives mistrusted Mayrand and were intent on minimizing future damage. One Conservative MP's campaign manager even accused Elections Canada of launching "a vendetta" against his party. As a result, when Minister of State (Democratic Reform) Pierre Poilievre tabled the long-awaited changes to the act, his "Fair Elections Act" was widely panned as being anything but fair. Seen as an outright attack on Elections Canada, it removed much of the agency's mandate and also limited access to voting for many Canadians. Then it was learned the provisions to outlaw robocalls in the future would not likely be in force for the next election.

Interestingly, many of the bill's provisions resembled those used by Republican politicians in many US states. President Barack Obama delivered a speech in April 2014 in which he warned "Across the country, Republicans have led efforts to pass laws making it harder, not easier, for people to vote," and accused them of "using voter fraud to … introduce strict identity checks to limit the Democratic core vote."[6]

Critics of Poilievre's bill included a consortium of 160 academics, who argued the reforms actually "undermine democracy." They declared some measures, such as the elimination of the voucher system (which allows individuals to vouch for someone they know who lives in their voting district but lacks formal proof of residence), were unconstitutional, a point also made emphatically by former Chief Electoral Officer (CEO) Jean-Pierre Kingsley. Even Preston Manning argued the government should "back off" on plans to "muzzle the CEO and weaken Elections Canada." Mayrand himself testified before a parliamentary committee, methodically attacking the proposed changes in a devastating line-by-line analysis. But the *coup de grâce* was delivered by Harry Neufeld, the author of a report that Poilievre had repeatedly cited to defend his measures. Neufeld categorically denied that he had claimed vouchers were a problem, and indeed predicted more than five hundred thousand voters could be disenfranchised by the move, which he said would only benefit

Conservatives. "To me, it appears like they are trying to tilt the playing field in one direction," Mr Neufeld said when asked about Poilievre's rationale. Asked to clarify in what way, Mr Neufeld said: "Their direction."[7] In response, Conservative Senate Leader Claude Carignan declared, "I don't think the comments from the experts are appropriate." Within weeks of its tabling, an Angus Reid poll found that some 62 per cent of Canadians believed "the Conservative government is motivated politically and dislikes Elections Canada."[8]

ATTACKING THE COURTS

The ultimate example of the Conservatives' willingness to challenge the rules of the game can be found in their attitude towards the courts. Before their election, Stephen Harper and other members of his future government, including his justice and public safety ministers, repeatedly demonstrated their disdain for decisions of the Supreme Court, the Federal Court, and indeed of many provincial Courts of Appeal. In fact, the Conservatives' resentment of the courts has been well-documented and is long-standing. Since the earliest days of Reform and its Blue Sheet platform, which Stephen Harper wrote, the Canadian conservative agenda has been intent on curtailing the influence of "activist" judges. Original Reform Party MPs, such as Art Hanger, Randy White, and Garry Breitkreuz, made numerous controversial comments about the need to rein in the courts and/or override their decisions through the use of the "notwithstanding" clause. The party's original platform called for the vetting of Supreme Court judges by a reformed, elected Senate with enhanced western representation, thereby ensuring a Reform-centric influence. Similarly Alliance MP and future Harper justice minister, Vic Toews, once told an ultra-conservative American interest group, Concerned Women for America, that in Canada "We have these radical liberal judges who have their own social agenda ... forgetting that their responsibility is to interpret the law and not to make the law."[9]

Harper himself was outspoken in his criticism of the courts when he was out of politics. As president of the National Citizens Coalition, he bitterly attacked the Supreme Court's rejection of his legal challenge to legislation limiting third-party election spending, claiming the court "displays a prejudicial bias." That decision, he insisted, "calls into question the court's neutrality and open-mindedness." A few years later, as leader of the Official Opposition, he decried the role of the courts when the government filed a reference to the Supreme Court on the proposed same-sex marriage legislation. Infuriated by the Court's finding that the Liberal approach was constitutional, he declared that the Liberals "didn't want to go to the Canadian people and be honest that this is what they wanted. They had the courts do it for them, put the judges in that they wanted, refused to launch an appeal."[10]

As prime minister, Harper came dangerously close to crossing the fine line between commentary and political direction to the independent judiciary when he stated publicly that he wished they would take a "harder line" on crime. This was followed by the extraordinary comments of Immigration Minister Jason Kenney, who did openly criticize judges for failing to follow the political direction of the government. The Canadian Bar Association fought back, defending the judges in an unprecedented open letter to Kenney: "Your public criticism of judges who follow the law but not the government's political agenda is an affront to our democracy and freedoms." Chief Justice Beverley McLachlin (a Mulroney appointee), then took an equally unprecedented step by publicly thanking the association for its "powerful" response to ministerial concerns over "judges who are insufficiently solicitous to government policy."[11]

The Conservatives' animosity towards the courts only increased after taking power, when one after another of their initiatives was struck down as illegal or unconstitutional. This string of judicial rebukes, in turn, gave rise to speculation about the advice Harper's justice ministers were receiving from their officials. Many observers began to publicly question whether this expert advice was deliberately being ignored. As it would turn out, and as discussed later, this speculation was well-founded. Moreover, on several occasions the actual decisions of the Court were simply ignored by the government.

IGNORING JUDICIAL RULINGS

A case in point was the Harper government's determination to eliminate the Wheat Board, the result of a long-standing campaign pledge. First it replaced the five government-appointed directors with individuals who favoured the disbanding of the board. Even so, the government's May 2011 announcement that it planned to unilaterally end the board's monopoly over grain sales was opposed by a majority of its board of directors, eight of whom were elected by farmers.

Board chair, Allen Oberg, launched a lawsuit against the government in Federal Court, claiming the Conservatives could not proceed with their legislation before holding a plebiscite among western farmers, as required by the existing Wheat Board Act.

Oberg claimed the government had acted "illegally and unethically" by failing to respect the legislation. Agriculture Minister Gerry Ritz argued that the Conservative's majority meant they could do so if they wished, since they could be sure of passing their own bill in parliament. "The government maintains the Parliament of Canada alone has the supremacy to enact, amend, or repeal any act," Ritz stated. Oberg retorted that "A majority government does not confer absolute power. Parliament cannot run roughshod over the wishes of directors duly elected by farmers."[12]

Ignoring the controversy, the government went ahead with its legislation, tabling a bill on 8 October, while the lawsuit was under review by the court and *after* a non-binding plebiscite held by the Wheat Board in lieu of government action found that 62 per cent of wheat farmers and slightly more than 50 per cent of barley farmers wanted to retain its monopoly.

Then, in early December, the Federal Court ruled that, despite its majority, the Harper government did *not* have the right to proceed as it had planned. In fact, Justice Douglas Campbell stressed that, while parliament could certainly introduce and pass legislation, "it must still follow rules established in laws by previous Parliaments in doing so." Failure to hold a referendum, Campbell stated, was "not only disrespectful. It is contrary to law." Adding insult to injury, Campbell declared the government's actions were "an affront to the rule of law, which is a fundamental constitutional imperative."[13]

A defiant Gerry Ritz said he would proceed with the legislation regardless. The ruling, he declared, "will have no effect on our continuing to move forward for freedom for western Canadian farmers."[14] Nor did it. In fact, when the Conservatives' bill came into effect in August 2012, Stephen Harper exercised what he referred to as the "ancient power" of Royal Perogative of Mercy by pardoning farmers who earlier had been convicted of illegally evading the Wheat Board by taking their grain across the border to sell in the United States. The highly unusual move, suggested by Saskatchewan backbench Conservative MP David Anderson rather than the ministers of justice or public safety, was immediately criticized by legal experts as an unintended use of the power. Critics also argued Harper had politicized the pardons process, and Harper himself said that he was righting a perceived wrong committed by the Liberals, who had charged farmers who broke the law in the past.

The Conservatives' defiance over the Wheat Board rulings was hardly unique. Two deportation orders overturned by the courts had already led to Jason Kenney's first outburst against the judiciary. Then, in June 2012, his sweeping new immigration law (Protecting Canada's Immigration System Act) was passed, which University of Toronto law professor Audrey Macklin described as "flagrantly unconstitutional" and the Canadian Civil Liberties Association called "unCanadian." Among other things it gave the minister, rather than a group of experts, the power to determine which countries were "safe," and then denied the right to appeal, delayed the granting of permanent resident status, and imposed arbitrary distinctions on refugees coming from such "safe" countries, as well as introducing biometric identification for anyone applying for a visa to Canada. A number of court challenges followed, and Kenney's public response – that no doubt there would be a number of "stupid Charter challenges" – was by now predictable.

Harper himself weighed in on court rulings rejecting his government's Minimum Mandatory Sentencing legislation, which removed judicial discretion in sentencing. In 2012 two Ontario Superior Court judges struck down the legislation as unconstitutional. Justice Anne Molloy also described the legislation as "fundamentally unfair, outrageous, abhorrent, and intolerable," but Harper defended it as "reasonable" and "essential" and vowed to appeal.[15] In April 2014 he lost that appeal, as the Supreme Court ruled unanimously against his government on three cases related to the legislation.

A similar defiance followed the Supreme Court's unanimous decision condemning the Conservatives' efforts to shut down the internationally acclaimed Insite supervised injection site in Vancouver. In this case, the court ordered the government to exempt medical staff and clients from prosecution, an extraordinary rebuke in itself. Moreover, the court's ruling left the door open for the creation of other supervised injection sites across the country. Harper declared, "We're disappointed. We have a different policy. We'll take a look at the decision."[16] In October 2013, the Conservatives returned to the charge. New health minister Rona Ambrose defied the Supreme Court by essentially reintroducing the same bill. "Bill C-2 is an (obvious) attempt to circumvent the Supreme Court ruling of 2011," senior policy adviser Constance Carter of the Canadian Drug Policy Coalition wrote, noting that Ambrose wilfully ignored the input of experts as well as the court. Only two weeks earlier, Carter and representatives of some fifty other health agencies across the country had written an open letter to Ambrose in which they stated, "It is unethical, unconstitutional, and damaging to both public health and the public purse to block access to supervised consumption services which save lives and prevent the spread of infection."[17]

However these cases quickly faded from view, unlike the government's lengthy and highly public legal wrangling over the fate of Omar Khadr, the fifteen-year-old child soldier and Canadian-born citizen who was imprisoned and tortured in the American military facility at Guantanamo. To begin with, all other countries had repatriated their nationals who were imprisoned there, but Canada did not request Khadr's return. In fact, Khadr was the last foreign national to leave, and even then it was only due to newly elected President Barack Obama's forceful appeal to the Canadian government to do so. In Guantanamo, under the Bush administration, Khadr had not been allowed to speak with a lawyer for the first two years of his detention, violating the fundamental legal principle of habeas corpus. Nor did the administration treat Khadr as a minor, in violation of international conventions to which Canada is a signatory. In addition, Canadian officials from the Canadian Security Intelligence Service (CSIS) and Foreign Affairs Department not only participated in interrogations of Khadr, knowing he had been tortured, but they met with him separately and shared what they learned from these encounters with their American counterparts.

Before Obama's election, Khadr's lawyers had filed an application with the Federal Court, requesting that the Harper government be ordered to bring Khadr back to Canada. The Federal Court agreed, noting that Khadr's Charter rights had been repeatedly violated. Harper appealed, but the Federal Court of Appeal upheld the ruling, as did the Supreme Court. In fact, the Supreme Court ruling took the government to task, stating "This conduct offends the most basic Canadian standards about the treatment of detained youth suspects." Still, the government continued to stall. Nor did it pay a political price. Ordinary Canadians were unfamiliar with most of the details, and the Conservatives were successful at framing the discourse. Every government spokesperson described Khadr as a terrorist, not a child soldier, and an interloper rather than a native-born

Canadian. No mention was made of Charter violations, or international conventions that Canada was ignoring. As a result, reflecting their philosophical preference for retribution-based justice, the Conservatives remained adamantly obstructionist.

Convinced that no progress would be made in time, Khadr's lawyers then urged him to agree to a plea bargain with the Americans. This was done on the understanding that all but one year of the remaining eight years of his sentence would be served in Canada, an understanding based on a written commitment to the Americans from Foreign Affairs Minister Lawrence Cannon. Yet after the deal was finalized, the Harper government reneged. Only after media exposés, letter-writing campaigns, and a massive petition finally caused some public concern did Public Safety Minister Vic Toews make the request for Khadr's return. On his arrival in Canada, Khadr was arbitrarily placed in a maximum-security prison, despite corrections officials ruling that he posed no security risk and the Office of the Correctional Investigator insisting that he be reclassified at a lower security level. Once again his lawyers approached the Federal Court, this time to request that Khadr be transferred to a minimum-security facility as someone whose crimes were committed as a young offender. Khadr's lawyer declared, "He has now been imprisoned for twelve years. He's been behind bars since he was fifteen. I have represented guys who did terrible things and they were back on the streets in five, six, or seven years."

Even many conservatives were taken aback by the government's behaviour. Well-known right-wing columnist Dan Gardner was outraged by their "cavalier" disregard for the law. "The government has disregarded the Constitution and the Supreme Court," Gardner exclaimed "Arguably it has even been contemptuous of both. Omar Khadr is a citizen of this country. What you think of him doesn't matter ... If the government can do this to him, they can do this to any citizen."[18]

STACKING THE BENCH

Faced with such a spate of unfavourable decisions from the courts, it is hardly surprising that the Harper government demonstrated a keen interest in the appointments process for the various federal courts. But in fact, it had done so from its earliest days in office, having observed the success of the Reagan Republicans in stacking their

Supreme Court. This is particularly important, since the consequences of a partisan approach to judicial appointments can easily be seen in the United States, where the Supreme Court now routinely splits decisions 5–4, based on their Republican majority, and some critics have argued that George W. Bush owed his second term in office to this conservative strategy.[19] Until recently, Canada's judicial appointments have been pre-screened by impartial appointments committees and successive federal governments, whether Liberal or Progressive Conservative, appointed individuals generally considered to be unbiased. The proof of this assertion is found in the inability of experts to predict the outcome of contentious cases before the Canadian Supreme Court.[20]

Yet the Harper Conservatives clearly were convinced that they must remake the courts in their image, and they wasted little time beginning the process. Just as Ronald Reagan had found himself in office at a time when Supreme Court vacancies were appearing, so Stephen Harper had the good fortune to take office at precisely the right time to influence the shape of the Canadian Supreme Court, potentially for decades to come. And, with Canadian judges forced to retire at seventy-five, rather than the American practice of lifetime tenure, Harper had considerable advance notice of upcoming vacancies and was able to plan his replacement choices with great care, as well as an eye to upcoming cases.

Among the first acts of the minister of justice was to change the selection and appointments process for the 1,100 federal judgeships across the country. In November 2006, Vic Toews added a police representative to each of the judicial advisory committees, the role of which was to vet candidates for the posts, thus increasing the total membership from seven to eight. He also removed the vote of the judicial representative. Since only two of the original seven members represented bar associations and law societies, and there was only one provincial representative, the three "at large" appointments of the federal minister in the previous seven-member committee could therefore conceivably constitute a majority voting block with the addition of the new police representative to the eight-member committee.

Critics argued the move was a blatant attempt to impose attitudinal bias in the courts by the back door. The changes were vigorously opposed by the Canadian Bar Association, the Canadian Judicial Council, and the Federation of Law Societies of Canada. Extraordinarily, even the Chief Justice of the Supreme Court weighed into the debate, issuing a press release in which she urged the minister to consult with the Judicial Council before finalizing his plans. "We believe this is necessary to protect the interests of all Canadians in an independent advisory process for judicial appointments," she wrote.[21]

As of late 2012, Harper had already appointed some 439 judges to various federal courts across the country. However, little attention was paid to these appointments by the media or the general public until early 2014, when Harper appointed his former justice and public safety minister, Vic Toews, to the Manitoba Court of Queens Bench. As various experts noted, this was an unusual appointment, not only because Toews was a long-serving federal politician with strong partisan ties, but also because, as federal minister, he had introduced much of the legislation on which he would be ruling. They also noted that his appointment could put Toews in line for a Supreme Court seat in little more than a year, when Justice Marshall Rothstein of Manitoba would be obliged to retire, even though, by convention, the next appointment would be from Saskatchewan.

Certainly it is at the Supreme Court that Harper is most likely to make a lasting impression. In less than eight years in office, he already had replaced six of the nine justices, with two more scheduled to retire in 2014 and 2015. This dramatic turnover is one of the fastest and most substantial in the history of the court. Moreover, given the relative youth of his appointees, the implications of a "Harper Court" could be in effect for twenty years.

Harper's first three appointments (Thomas Cromwell, Marshall Rothstein, and Richard Wagner) were widely considered to be reasonable, if somewhat conservative, choices, but his subsequent two appointments (Andromache Karakatsanis and Michael Moldaver) were more controversial. Both were described as either "tough on crime" or "anti-Charter," as well as being more deferential to executive power. Karakatsanis was viewed as a mediocre jurist, lacking experience, while Moldaver was also cited for his lack of bilingualism.

But it was Harper's sixth choice, an obligatory selection from Quebec, that proved disastrous. Ignoring a long list of highly qualified candidates, he selected an obscure semi-retired judge from the Federal Court of Appeal, Marc Nadon. This choice caused great concern, given that Nadon was not a member of the Quebec bar and had not practised in the province for two decades. Indeed, less than a day after he took his seat on the court he was obliged to step aside after a legal challenge to his appointment was filed. Toronto lawyer Rocco Galati argued that Nadon was not eligible to sit as a Quebec judge, because the Federal Court of Appeal is not mentioned as a source of candidates in the Supreme Court Act. Soon the government of Quebec joined in, as Intergovernmental Affairs Minister Alexandre Cloutier announced the province would contest the nomination as well. As a result, the government's December 2013 omnibus budget bill actually contained a measure to change the legislation governing Supreme Court appointments to include the Federal Court, a move one opposition politician described as "closing the barn door after the horse is out."

Some observers questioned why Harper would risk making such an unusual choice. The answer emerged from a review of Nadon's rulings during his time on the Federal Court of Appeal. He had written a dissenting opinion on the Omar Khadr case, vigorously defending the government's actions and denying that Khadr's Charter rights had been violated. With the terrorism case of Mohamed Harkat scheduled to reach the Supreme Court in the near future, Nadon's presence on the court could have proved crucial to the court's decision, as it was already known that Charter rights would play a key role in the plaintiff's arguments. But the Supreme Court's ruling, released 21 March 2014, dealt a devastating blow to Harper's plans. By a vote of 6–1, the court ruled Nadon was not eligible to sit on the bench, and moreover that Harper's effort to change the appointment legislation was unconstitutional. Harper indicated he was surprised and disappointed by the court's decision, but in the end he conceded he would abide by its ruling.

Yet no action was taken on Nadon's replacement for more than three months, leaving the Supreme Court short-handed and leading observers to question Harper's real intentions. Their concerns were heightened when Harper and Justice Minister Peter MacKay then engaged in an unprecedented attack on Chief Justice Beverley McLachlin, whom they accused of interfering in the appointments process. Their move backfired when it was learned that she had merely alerted the justice minister to the problem of Federal Court ineligibility after being shown their shortlist. As virtually all sectors of the legal community rushed to her defence, it emerged that the real reason for Harper's delay was his lack of options, which also explained McLachlin's concern. The shortlist containing Nadon's name had also included three other justices from the Federal Court, all of whom would evidently be found ineligible by the Supreme Court on the same grounds. In the end, attempting to make the best of a bad situation, Harper decided to take the advice of the government of Quebec and, on 17 June, he appointed Clément Gascon, a well-regarded judge of the Quebec Court of Appeal. However, whatever goodwill was salvaged by the positive response to that appointment quickly disappeared when it was learned that another judge on the Federal Court of Appeal, Robert Mainville, had been moved by Justice Minister MacKay to the Quebec Court of Appeal. Immediately speculation turned to the possibility that Mainville had been selected as the replacement for Quebec Supreme Court Justice Louis LeBel, whose retirement was scheduled for December 2014. Determined to prevent what he considered to be another "end run" of the system, lawyer Rocco Galati quickly launched another challenge, this time to ascertain in advance whether MacKay's attempt to ensure Mainville's eligibility would be successful. However, most experts considered Galati's appeal unlikely to succeed. Moreover, Mainville, an expert in aboriginal law, was widely praised for his competence by Quebec and Canadian bar members. At the same time, the Conservatives' determination to proceed with Mainville suggested that their concerns over upcoming constitutional and Charter battles on aboriginal rights was a prime motivating factor.

DISMISSING THE CHARTER

The Reform Party's early platforms, drafted by a young Stephen Harper, opposed many of the rights entrenched in the 1982 Charter of Rights and Freedoms introduced by the Trudeau government. Specifically, Reformers opposed women's rights, gay rights, multicultural rights, aboriginal rights, and linguistic rights. The 1993 Blue Sheet declared the party "supports the repeal of the *Official Languages Act*," despite the fact the entire act was by then entrenched in the Charter. Similarly, the party pledged to "end funding of the multiculturalism program and abolish the Department of Multiculturalism," despite the commitments outlined in Section 27 of the Charter. And, finally, the Blue Sheet stated the party would:

- Discontinue federal affirmative-action and employment-equity programs.

- Support the repeal of Section 15 Subsection (2) of the Charter that permits the government to engage in affirmative-action legislation and other forms of "reverse discrimination."

During the 1997 and 2000 federal election campaigns, a number of Reform/Alliance candidates made derogatory comments about the Charter. However the quintessential conservative perspective on it was articulated by a former Reform justice critic and senior caucus member under Stephen Harper, BC MP Randy White, just prior to the 2004 election. White advocated invoking the "notwithstanding" clause whenever a Charter provision caused a problem for the Conservative agenda, and concluded with a dismissive "to heck with the courts" remark. His interview with filmmaker Alexis Mackintosh was widely circulated during that election, contributing to the Conservatives' defeat and Harper's long-standing distrust of renegade caucus members. In the interview White declared:

> Well, my position and the Conservative Party's position are identical … If the Charter of Rights is going to be used as a crutch to carry forward all of the issues that social libertarians want, then there's got to be for us conservatives out there a way to put checks and balances in there. So the notwithstanding clause … should be used, I would think, not just [for] the definition of marriage, but I think you'll see more uses for the not-withstanding clause in the future.[22]

White was hardly alone in his views. Other influential Conservatives, including several members of the Calgary School from whom Harper took his inspiration, have made their antipathy to the Charter known. Chief amongst them are professors Ted Morton and Rainer Knopff, authors of several articles criticizing the role of the Courts and the Charter, as well as their seminal work, *The Charter Revolution and the Court Party*. Similarly Ian Brodie, a former chief of staff to Harper, is the author of *Friends of the Court*, a highly critical assessment of the impact of the Charter on judicial activism.

Interviewed by *Maclean's* magazine in 2012, former Reform leader Preston Manning made it clear that he shared those views. "Does the Charter encourage and empower the courts to be activist?" Manning was asked. His answer was categorical. "I think the answer is, yes it does." But Manning did not stop there. "The bigger question is whether judicial activism using the Charter is out of sync with society." Ignoring the concepts of minority rights and judicial independence, Manning continued, "The election of a Conservative majority government means Canadians generally share its values. When the court goes against those, the court is not only going against the government, but also going against the values that are alive and well in society."[23]

As we have seen, the Conservatives believe one way to minimize this activism is to change the players on the bench. Another is to make it more difficult for anyone to avail themselves of the costly judicial process. In 1982, the Court Challenges program was established by Prime Minister Trudeau. Its purpose was to "level the playing field" by providing financial assistance to individuals or groups with significant judicial arguments to raise concerning Charter issues. The program was always viewed with deep distrust by conservatives, including Ian Brodie, who referred to it as "the state at war with itself." Prime Minister Mulroney eliminated the program as one of his first acts in office in 1984, and Prime Minister Chrétien reinstated it in 1993. Not surprisingly, then, the program was immediately eliminated by the Harper government in 2006.

Another way to minimize the impact of the Charter is to encourage special-interest groups to bring forward alternative cases. In the first decade after the Charter took effect, various social-action groups, such as the Women's Legal Education and Action Fund (LEAF), were instrumental in shepherding landmark cases through the legal system. As McGill law professor Chris Manfredi noted, those groups often accomplished their objectives, but many disappeared due to a lack of funding after the elimination of the Court Challenges program. A number of extremely wealthy, privately funded, conservative groups took their place.[24] The Canadian Constitution Foundation, for example, typically raises more than $1 million annually. Along with the Justice Centre for Constitutional Freedoms, they have pursued an agenda diametrically opposed to that of the earlier groups, launching court challenges opposing affirmative action, Charter definitions of human rights, and other measures promoting equality.

Perhaps equally important is the government's determination to ignore the Charter. Since the 2006 election, Harper and his ministers have made virtually no references to it. The thirtieth anniversary of the Charter's adoption, in April 2012, was no exception. Although it was celebrated in many venues across the country, the federal government was conspicuous by its absence. Prime Minister Harper was out of the country at the time, but in answer to a reporter's question, he first dismissed it as some sort of extension of the Bill of Rights introduced by Progressive Conservative prime minister John Diefenbaker, and then added that the event was not worth celebrating, since the Charter was part of a constitutional package that was not formally approved by the government of Quebec.[25]

However, in early 2013 it became apparent that, behind the scenes, the Charter was *not* being ignored by the government. On the contrary it was the subject of considerable concern. A senior Department of Justice counsel, Edgar Schmidt, filed a suit against the department in Federal Court in which he noted it is the legal responsibility of the department's deputy minister to advise the minister if a proposed piece of legislation is unconstitutional or in conflict with other legislation. The minister of justice is then obligated to inform the House if any bill tabled by the government is likely in violation of the Charter or the constitution. According to Library of Parliament researchers, no such declaration has ever been filed. Because the Trudeau and Chrétien governments had pledged never to invoke the notwithstanding clause, they would not have tabled any legislation that required such a notice. But after the Schmidt revelations, some academics speculated that Harper too might have shied away from using the notwithstanding clause, albeit for political reasons.

They were partly right. It soon became clear that Harper had decided to take his chances in the courts. In his lawsuit, Schmidt alleged that lawyers in the department had been told to refrain from flagging any bill which had even a 5-per-cent chance of being successfully defended against a Charter challenge. According to Schmidt, this was one of the reasons why so many of the Conservatives' bills had been struck down by the courts.[26] Schmidt stressed that he raised this issue with senior management repeatedly, and only resorted to whistleblowing when all internal avenues had been exhausted. Yet the day after he filed suit, he was suspended without pay, contrary to whistleblower protection in Harper's Federal Accountability Act. In Schmidt's first appearance before the Federal Court in January 2013, Judge Simon Noël was highly critical of the department, and in April he ordered the department to pay Schmidt's legal costs.

The Conservatives' behaviour in flouting rules, legislation, and court decisions can only be explained by their autocratic approach to government and the perceived urgency of their agenda. The Harper Conservatives have already made considerable progress on that agenda, in large measure without the knowledge or understanding of many Canadians, but it has come at considerable political cost to them and the country. Interestingly, the Conservatives' lack of respect for the rulings of officers of parliament, and their overt hostility towards the Chief Elections Officer and the Chief Justice of the Supreme Court, have had the perverse effect of bringing the existence of these democratic safeguards to the attention of the Canadian public. Here again, therefore, it is unclear that the long-term consequences of the Harper government's behaviour are significant in terms of undermining democratic institutions. Nevertheless, one option for a future government may be to strengthen existing legislation and/or enhance the mandates of various watchdogs to prevent any future recurrence. Meanwhile Harper's unsuccessful efforts to shape the decisions of the courts through his appointments, as the recent spate of unfavourable rulings by the Supreme Court on his various legislative measures demonstrate, suggest that the Canadian legal profession is much less vulnerable to partisan influence than their American counterparts.

PART TWO

Taking a Stand

6

Shrinking Government: The Economic Agenda

I believe that all taxes are bad.

Stephen Harper, 2005

I think there are probably some great buying opportunities out there in the stock market.

Stephen Harper 2008, speaking about the global economic crisis

Now more than ever our future prosperity depends on our natural resources.

Harper government Throne Speech, October 2013

Kyoto is essentially a socialist scheme to suck money out of wealth-producing nations.

Stephen Harper, 2002

In public-administration theory there is something called a "focusing event." It is an unexpected and dramatic development, such as a natural disaster or an externally driven shock, which forces a government to take action it would not otherwise have contemplated. Focusing events are considered inevitable; they will affect any government that remains in power for more than a short while. In recent decades, such events have included the 9/11 terrorist attacks and the resulting wars in Iraq and Afghanistan, the H1N1 and SARS crises, and the 2008 global economic recession.[1]

Scholars argue that these events can either provide a "window of opportunity" for policy change, or derail the policy agenda of a government,[2] and some governments are able to handle these major unexpected developments better than others. Perhaps not surprisingly, the Chrétien government – with its experienced prime minister and cabinet and close working relationship with the professional bureaucracy – was exceptionally well-positioned to weather such storms without losing sight of its own agenda. The five events mentioned above, all of which occurred on Chrétien's watch, led to a wide range of increased national-security measures involving Canada's border agency, transportation, and immigration departments, along with updated Emergency Measures and Quarantine acts, the appointment of a federal medical officer of health, and improved federal-provincial cooperation and communication mechanisms, to name just a few. Yet, despite the large number of measures and their complexity, they were put in place efficiently and expeditiously, without delaying implementation of the Liberals' own platform commitments. Nor did they wreak havoc on the federal budget, despite the fact that all of the initiatives posed unexpected costs to the federal Treasury, some of them quite significant.[3]

By contrast, the Harper government, new to power and unwilling to take advice from its bureaucrats, was thrown badly off course by several focusing events during its time in office, and none more so than the 2008 global economic crisis, which blindsided the Conservatives, and Stephen Harper in particular. They hastily implemented several measures that were antithetical to their conservative philosophy, as many of their critics on the far right were quick to note.[4]

They spent vast amounts of money on so-called economic action plans to provide economic "stimulus," bailed out various industries, and created ad hoc programs such as the Temporary Foreign Worker Program, despite Harper's visceral dislike of all such measures, and ended up intervening in the economy in more ways than many previous Liberal or Progressive Conservative governments. Moreover, overall government spending, and the size of the federal bureaucracy, actually *increased* under Harper, despite his firm intention to cut both drastically.

At the same time, the Conservatives continued to implement a number of their campaign pledges, regardless of their credibility or cost. They persisted with deep cuts to consumption, income, and corporate taxes, deregulated and/or eliminated numerous environmental, health, and safety programs, and forged ahead with plans to support the natural-resources industries of western Canada at the expense of the manufacturing heartland. This in turn lead to a number of other unanticipated and highly problematic consequences, including the return to a deficit position in federal finances, the crippling of the Ontario economy, and mounting opposition from aboriginal groups, environmentalists, and provincial governments.

In the end, the Harper government's record on economic policy can only be described as a failure, by their own measure and that of experts, even though their communications machine managed to convince Canadians that economic policy was actually their greatest strength. This perverse gap between perception and reality, meanwhile, played a key role in allowing Harper to achieve an electoral majority in 2011, and may yet permit him to recover from his party's serious drop in popular support since then – in time to win another term in 2015.

STARVING THE BEAST: THE HARPER TAX CUTS

The Harper government's approach to taxation followed the standard economic conservative line: taxes were too high and should be lowered, and certainly never raised, in order to relieve the "burden" on individual citizens. But an underlying purpose was to force government to retrench. This first rule of the new conservative economic mantra was exemplified by Harper's acquaintance Grover Norquist, the former Reagan adviser who coined the term "starve the beast." Norquist's plan was to deprive the federal government of revenue by cutting taxes, or "starving the beast" until it was "down to the size where we can drown it in the bathtub." Superficially, the logic was impeccable. If government lacked sufficient revenue, it would be obliged to cut programs and scale back its activities until its role was reduced to that of a "nightwatchman state," rather than a constant intervenor in the private sector. The second rule of the new conservative economic mantra is that deficits are unacceptable and must be avoided at all costs, again justifying the need to eliminate programs if there is a revenue shortfall. Taken together, the two rules virtually ensure major reductions in the size of government.

The problem with this plan, of course, is that citizens are almost always unwilling to give up programs and services to which they have become accustomed. This is particularly true in liberal societies such as Canada, where the welfare state is sacrosanct. As a result, the new conservatives have been forced to develop a deliberately misleading discourse to persuade voters that their plan is a good one. On the whole, this discourse involves playing fast and loose with the facts, promising that it is possible to cut taxes and balance budgets without affecting the delivery of any important government services or programs, claiming they can "do more with less." They insist cuts will be made by "trimming the fat" in programs, eliminating "inefficiencies" and cutting out "administrative" elements, or by firing "backroom personnel," rather than "front-line employees" who actually deliver services. With skill and determination, such language may allow these conservatives to go quite some distance towards achieving their purpose – to shrink government and eliminate as much as possible of the welfare state – before it becomes clear how things are being affected.

In the case of the Harper Conservatives, the tax-cut side of the equation was well-publicized and undoubtedly played a role in their three electoral victories. They began with a reduction in the Mulroney GST, followed by cuts to personal and corporate income tax. In the 2006 election, for example, their "Stand Up for Canada" platform pledged to provide "real tax relief" for Canadians by cutting the GST by 1 per cent immediately and then by another 1 per cent within less than five years.[5] They implemented the first cut in their maiden budget just months after their election, and the second shortly thereafter, despite the fact that economists were unanimous in their criticism of the move as fiscally irresponsible and a "terrible piece of public policy." In fact, Harper's former chief of staff Ian Brodie admitted the cut was simply intended for political gain when he spoke at a conference at McGill University in 2009. "Despite economic evidence to the contrary, in my view the GST cut worked," Brodie said. "It worked in the sense that by the end of the '05–'06 campaign, voters identified the Conservative party as the party of lower taxes. It worked in the sense that it helped us to win."[6]

By 2011, the *annual* lost GST revenue was reported by Finance Canada to be $13 billion. By 2013, the Parliamentary Budget Officer (PBO) reported that the lost revenue for the two percentage points amounted to slightly more than $14 billion, or nearly enough to wipe out the federal deficit of the day singlehandedly. As analyst

Barrie McKenna noted, "not having $14 billion delays what the Conservatives now insist is Job # 1 – erasing the deficit by 2015."[7]

Having lowered Brian Mulroney's hated consumption tax as a top priority, the Conservatives then turned their attention to personal income tax. First they raised the personal exemption limit, and then they implemented two rounds of tax cuts in 2008 and 2009. By 2010, these measures alone had resulted in a loss of $3.2 billion in federal revenue.

However, this was not the only set of changes to the personal income-tax system. Far more significant, and far more detrimental to the fairness and equity of the tax system, were the countless special tax credits and exemptions introduced by Finance Minister Jim Flaherty. Ideally, an income-tax system should have as few exceptions as possible. This is to simplify the process for taxpayers and accountants, but also to ensure that all income is treated the same way (horizontal equity) and to keep rates as low as possible. By contrast, the Conservatives, in their efforts to target and attract the support of specific categories of citizens who constitute their electoral base, introduced so many special niche measures that the system became hopelessly complicated. First they created an alternative to the long-established RRSP, the Tax-Free Savings Account (TSFA). Then they introduced a plethora of tax credits – the medical-expense credit, public-transit credit, children's fitness and arts credits, textbook credit, child-disability credit, and family-caregiver credit, the first-time homebuyers' credit and the volunteer firefighters' credit. In addition they introduced several new "benefits," such as the universal child care benefit. Finally, they created a host of new deductions for things such as apprenticeship job creation, tradespersons' tools, and long-haul truckers' meals. As one critic noted, no item was too small or insignificant to be considered.

Not surprisingly, the effect of all of these boutique tax provisions was to make the system more complicated, more subject to fraud, and far less efficient. Nor did they benefit large segments of the population. In the end, these tax cuts also resulted in considerable loss of revenue. According to a study by the Canadian Centre for Policy Alternatives, in fiscal 2011–12 alone, the changes to personal income tax cost the federal government $13.6 billion.[8]

Last but hardly least, the Harper Conservatives tackled the issue of corporate taxation, partly through major reductions in rates, and partly through another creative set of credits and deductions. They quickly lowered the small-business rate to 11 per cent, while the general corporate tax rate – 22 per cent in 2006 – was reduced every year and stood at 15 per cent by January 2012, or by almost half of the 28-per-cent prevailing rate in 2000. According to OECD reports, Canada's corporate tax rate (federal and provincial combined, at 25 per cent) is now the lowest of the G7 countries, and far lower than the American federal-state combined rate of 39.2 per cent. Perhaps understandably, *Forbes* magazine declared Canada the best country in the world to do business, "credit a reformed tax structure."[9] Meanwhile the total revenue foregone by the federal government, as calculated by the PBO, amounted to roughly $60 billion. Yet the government also continued to argue that it could afford to maintain the programs and services that tax dollars pay for, and which Canadians consider essential. Only the fat or administrative costs would be cut, they insisted. But the increasingly lengthy delays citizens encountered in obtaining passports, employment insurance, and welfare benefits or in processing immigration applications, to say nothing of closed weather stations, coast-guard offices, and lighthouses suggested otherwise.

Meanwhile economists maintained a running battle over the six years of corporate tax cuts, debating whether they had stimulated the economy and created jobs, as the Conservatives claimed, or whether the money would have been better spent in shoring up social programs, investing in post-secondary education, or completing the national broadband network. Perhaps the most telling criticism came, indirectly, from Mark Carney, governor of the Bank of Canada, who criticized large corporations for sitting on unprecedented amounts of "dead cash" rather than investing in research, equipment upgrades, or employee training, as was traditionally the case when such a tax stimulus was offered in the past. Even Stephen Harper commented on this anomaly at the end of a G20 meeting in France. Frustrated by their inaction, he declared that now was the time for business to step up to the plate. His critics replied that it was necessary for governments to spend, rather than cut taxes, to provide business with the stable climate in which it would be willing to invest.[10]

By 2013, Canada had the singular distinction of the lowest corporate and consumption taxes in the G7. Looking forward to another election in 2015, Finance Minister Flaherty predicted still further corporate tax cuts, and reductions in the income-tax system through the implementation of income-averaging and the collapse of the existing five income brackets into three and then two, moves roundly criticized by most economists as highly regressive.

Interestingly, the Harper government's October 2013 Throne Speech, which received much attention for its glorification of natural resources as the primary driver of the economy, actually made more mention of its tax record. "Overall," the speech declared, "the federal tax burden is at its lowest level in half a century." Since the federal government (like all western democracies) is involved in far more activities than it was fifty years earlier, this decrease in revenue is even more significant. According to the government, their income-tax cuts resulted in savings of $3,200 per year for the average family, but public-opinion polls suggested it went largely unnoticed by individual taxpayers. Yet the cost to the federal treasury did not go unnoticed by those who had benefited from the countless programs and services that suffered reductions or elimination as a result of the revenue shortfall. To fully appreciate the magnitude of the revenue loss, one need only consider the situation in comparable countries. At 14 per cent, the federal revenue-to-GDP ratio in Canada is now 4 per cent lower than in 2006. This is considerably less than that of Australia (21 per cent), a country with similar population and resources, and even of the United States (19 per cent), despite their many years of Republican tax cuts.[11]

THE CONSERVATIVES' 2008 ABOUT-FACE: THE ECONOMIC ACTION PLANS

By the time the writ was dropped for the October 2008 federal election, the Harper Conservatives had been in power for nearly three years and had tabled three budgets focusing on tax cuts. At that point PBO Kevin Page already was predicting that the combination of the government's major spending commitments for the military and its "tough on crime" agenda, along with the greatly reduced revenue from the tax cuts, would likely tip federal finances back into a deficit situation.

Meanwhile the 2007 subprime mortgage debacle in the United States had developed into a full-blown international economic crisis, worse than any seen since the Great Depression. Yet even though the ripple effects of the collapse of two huge financial houses, Lehman

Brothers and Bear Sterns, and the bailout of federal mortgage companies Freddie Mac and Fannie Mae, were increasingly being felt around the world in the summer of 2008, Prime Minister Harper was still unconcerned. Declaring that Canada was much better prepared to weather the economic firestorm than any other G7 country, Harper told one interviewer that he saw the downturn as a good opportunity for Canadians to invest in stocks that were undervalued.

On the one hand, Harper was correct in his evaluation of the Canadian situation. The various rules and regulations concerning the financial sector that had been put in place by previous Liberal governments – almost all of which the Harper Conservatives had criticized in the past and promised to remove – were still in place, and they alone prevented a meltdown of the magnitude that occurred elsewhere, rather than any action on the part of his government. On the other hand, the new reality of globalization's interconnected economies meant that, although there were no bank failures in Canada, there were certainly private-sector defaults, layoffs, and a credit crunch. Moreover Finance Minister Jim Flaherty's decision to introduce forty-year mortgages with zero down payments began to produce a potential housing crisis in Canada, before cooler heads prevailed and the moves were rescinded. Still, the government ordered the Canada Mortgage and Housing Corporation (CMHC) to approve high-risk borrowers in order to keep credit levels up. According to CMHC records, the approval rate for risky loans rose from 33 per cent in 2007 to 42 per cent in 2008 alone, resulting in a 9.3-per-cent increase in Canadian household debt between June 2008 and 2009. As Harper critic and economist Murray Dobbin opined, "Every single US lender specializing in sub-prime has gone bankrupt. The largest subprime lender in the world is now the Canadian government."[12]

Most importantly, as their mortgage initiative suggests, neither Harper nor Flaherty appeared to grasp the seriousness of the situation. During the fall 2008 election campaign, Harper initially dismissed the idea of any form of government intervention to minimize the impact of the downturn. Rejecting calls by economists, provincial premiers, and opposition party leaders for stimulus measures, he once again suggested that now was the time to take advantage of undervalued stocks. By the mid-campaign televised national leaders' debate, he was still taking this position. "We have a plan," he told an audience at a Conservative campaign event in Victoria, BC. "We do not get caught up in market panic."[13] However the party's dramatic slide in public-opinion polls after that debate, in which his laissez-faire approach was attacked vigorously by Liberal leader Stéphane Dion and NDP leader Jack Layton, convinced Harper that he would have to change his strategy. He decided to abandon ideology in favour of political expediency, and began to emphasize stimulus measures in his speeches. His party's platform, released several days later, also committed an additional $400 million to support the manufacturing industry, which had been hit the hardest by the downturn.

Harper managed to win a second minority for his Conservatives, despite his early mistakes.[14] Nevertheless the public's concern with the economy had been clearly expressed, and Harper listened. Flying in the face of his philosophical preferences, he demonstrated the pragmatism for which he would become so well-known. The Conservatives' budget of 2009 was given another name – the Economic Action Plan (EAP) – and promoted not as a cost-cutting exercise but as a plan to create jobs and stimulate the economy. For the next three years, each of the Harper government's budgets was referred to as an EAP, and the communications plan associated with each of them was relentlessly focused on those themes, regardless of other content. Every minister, and every backbench MP, referred to the EAP and to the government's priority of creating jobs and stimulating the economy. In fact, the three budgets between 2009 and 2012 were specifically referred to as "the stimulus phase" of the Conservatives' "economic plan."

In the end, the Harper government allocated some $45 billion to specific stimulus projects, including support for infrastructure renewal, manufacturing, and the so-called "knowledge-based economy." A bailout of the automobile industry, something Harper initially rejected as well, eventually cost the federal and Ontario provincial governments a combined $13.7 billion. The measure of Harper's discomfort with the bailout could be seen in the lack of information provided about the deal, and the complex and ambiguous nature of the federal contribution. As the *National Post* editorial of 20 December 2008, declared, the proposed deal "goes against every ideological bone in his body," but the prime minister evidently felt he had no alternative, and it was finally announced in June 2009. Although some money was recouped with paybacks from Chrysler and General Motors, a critical article in the *Financial Post* some four years later argued that the Canadian taxpayer was still on the hook for more than $1 billion in lost federal revenue.[15]

Interestingly, one way in which conservatives normally could have expected to *raise* revenue was never available to the Harper Conservatives. When they took office they could not privatize Crown corporations, because the Mulroney government had already done so. Of the roughly seventy Crown corporations and agencies in existence when Mulroney took office in 1984, fully one-third had been eliminated by the time of his departure. Almost all of those that remained were neither significant nor likely to be of interest to the private sector, with the possible exception of the CBC. Here again, pragmatism prevailed. That Crown corporation, a perennial target of Conservative invective, was nevertheless viewed as too politically problematic to eliminate, but both Mulroney and subsequently Harper inflicted significant budget cuts (more than 10 per cent in 2012 alone), which they correctly expected would accomplish much of their objective by rendering it impotent or irrelevant.[16]

The Harper Conservatives did, however, manage to sell the nuclear-reactor division of Atomic Energy Canada Limited (AECL) shortly after they obtained their majority. But this was actually an expenditure rather than a revenue-making venture, and was sharply criticized by the PBO. The parliamentary spending watchdog found that the unit was sold to private-sector giant SNC-Lavalin for $15 million, only months after the Harper government had invested $114 million of taxpayers' money in it. NDP critic Nathan Cullen declared, "It may be the dumbest sale of anything in the history of Canada. We're spending money in the process of losing even more money."[17] The move was even more perplexing until the Conservatives' ideological imperative was factored into the equation, particularly since the government's deficit was becoming a serious problem.

THE DEFICIT DILEMMA

Given the massive stimulus effort, which had been preceded by the massive tax cuts, it was hardly surprising that the federal fiscal situation deteriorated rapidly. Yet the very idea of running a deficit was anathema to Harper. The situation was particularly galling, since he had been handed a $13-billion surplus by the departing Liberals, who had restored the federal government to fiscal health after the huge deficits racked up by the Mulroney government.

Indeed, when Jean Chrétien took office in 1993, he inherited a serious fiscal problem. Despite Brian Mulroney's stated priority of eliminating the deficit, the situation deteriorated badly on his watch. Over nine Mulroney budgets, the federal deficit increased from $37.2 to $39 billion and the national debt nearly doubled. More importantly, the debt-to-GDP ratio reached a dangerously high level at more than 70 per cent. When the Liberals returned to power, Chrétien and his finance minister, Paul Martin, convinced Liberal colleagues and Canadians that the situation was serious enough to warrant tough measures. As a result of their concerted efforts, the federal government was back in the black by 1997. But it was not an easy task. Many observers, including a number of left-wing Liberals, felt the measures taken were too severe.[18] Regardless of the merits of their approach, however, the Liberals did restore the federal government's fiscal credibility. They delivered ten successive budget surpluses, and paid down more than $81.4 billion on the national debt, which stood at only 32 per cent of GDP when the Harper Conservatives took over.

Under Stephen Harper, the $13.2 billion surplus inherited from Paul Martin quickly turned into a string of eight budget deficits. In 2009, the deficit actually ballooned to $58.2 billion. Three years of stimulus, therefore, were followed by significant efforts to cut spending. By 2012, the deficit had been cut in half, to $25.2 billion, but only by taking extreme austerity measures, cutting both government programs and services and public-service jobs in large numbers. Still, in 2013, Finance Minister Jim Flaherty predicted the government would not be able to post a surplus until 2015. Even more significant were the PBO projections indicating that, by 2014–15, the Harper government would have *added* $176.4 billion to the national debt.

Yet the Conservatives managed to win a majority government in May 2011, in large measure on the basis of their claim to be good fiscal managers. Public-opinion polls repeatedly showed that Canadians believed this claim. They also showed that the Conservatives successfully took credit for the Liberal rules and regulations that had saved the economy from freefall after the 2008 crisis, and for the recovery that followed. Conversely, most economists argued the recovery had been neither as strong as expected – nor as the Conservatives claimed. Moreover, the new jobs created after the recession, while significant, masked an equally significant and growing problem, namely that they were in different sectors from those that had been lost. This resulted in ongoing high levels of unemployment and calls for an end to the government's austerity.

These calls were bolstered by a Statistics Canada report indicating that the country's trade deficit was much worse than expected, due to the high value of the Canadian dollar and the ongoing American recession. But during a four-country trade mission tour to Latin America, Harper reacted to the bad news by insisting that further cuts to government spending and a renewed emphasis on enhanced international trade, not a new round of stimulus measures, was the best way to ensure Canada's economic recovery. "It continues to be our view that the Canadian economy will grow," he said. "It will grow slowly and gradually, along with the world recovery. As long as those remain the circumstances, [I believe] the policy mix of the government of Canada is the appropriate one."[19]

By the end of 2013, the balance-of-trade situation had deteriorated still further, and the jobless rate remained stubbornly high at 7.2 per cent, a full percentage point higher than it had been before the recession.[20] Still, renewed calls for the government to relax its tight austerity measures and invest in areas such as infrastructure to ease the unemployment situation fell on deaf ears. In fact, the government was continuing to look for ways to cut more programs and benefits.

SHRINKING GOVERNMENT: PROGRAM CUTS WITH A PURPOSE

Initially the Conservatives expected to take advantage of their tax cuts to eliminate the programs and services they disliked, using the lack of revenue as an excuse. Although the 2008 recession interfered with their plans by creating a stimulus-inspired deficit, it also allowed them to move forward with more cuts, citing austerity as the reason. As a result, the first round of the Harper government's cuts and closures can be seen as revealing their top priorities and targets. By contrast, the second – more comprehensive and draconian – round of spending cuts, which began in 2012, was motivated more by their desperate desire to balance the books by the 2015 election. As a result, even departments such as National Defence felt the pain in that second round.

In the initial stages of the Harper government's cuts, however, the outright elimination of specific programs or significant reductions in their funding clearly reflected the Conservatives' concerns and dislikes. Predictably, as we have seen, the Charter Challenges Program was among the first to be eliminated. This was quickly followed by other federal programs involving human rights, democratic development, or almost any form of policy research. The doomed programs included such Liberal landmarks as the Law Reform Commission, the Forum of the Federations, the Canada Policy Research Networks, the Canadian Institutes of Health Research, the National Welfare Council, the Canadian Council on Social Development, and the Canadian Council on Learning. There were also significant cuts to Statistics Canada, quite apart from the elimination of the long-form census. In addition, the National Roundtable on the Environment, created by Brian Mulroney in 1988, was unceremoniously eliminated. Other programs suffered substantial funding cuts, including Status of Women Canada, the Canadian Conference of the Arts, the Native Womens' Association, and the Social Sciences and Humanities Research Council. Even research-oriented programs related to defence, such as the RADARSAT Constellation Mission (RCM) and the Canada Centre for Remote Sensing, were wrapped up.

Meanwhile, federal departments, such as the Canadian Food Inspection Agency, Human Resource Development, Health, Justice, Heritage, Foreign Affairs, and the Canadian International Development Agency (CIDA) suffered significant reductions in overall funding, at the same time that the Department of National Defence received massive injections of cash for capital expenditures and the ongoing costs of the various armed conflicts in which Canada was involved. Similarly, Public Safety received increased funding for prisons, and funding was ramped up for the so-called "war on terror" through Emergency Preparedness Canada, the RCMP, and Immigration Canada.

Unquestionably, the hardest hit departments were the Environment, Natural Resources, and Fisheries and Oceans. By 2011, Environment Canada had virtually ceased to provide any money for grants and contributions, and its operating budget was drastically reduced. Moreover, within these departments some programs were specifically targeted. For example, by 2011, Environment Canada's budget had been cut by 20 per cent, but climate-change and air-pollution programs in that department saw their funding reduced by 60 per cent. Programs to protect endangered wildlife, and to clean up toxic waste sites, also suffered substantial funding cuts. Many cuts had ripple effects that were devastating for research and for Canada's participation in international cooperation. The closing of the Canadian Foundation for Climate and Atmospheric Sciences, for example, meant that the world-famous Polar Environment Atmospheric Research Laboratory was also forced to close its doors due to lack of funding, along with the equally renowned Experimental Lakes Area (ELA) research station.[21] At Natural Resources Canada, programs to promote research on alternative energy, sustainable forestry practices, and housing construction were eliminated. Meanwhile, at Fisheries and Oceans, programs such as the Institute of Ocean Sciences, various water-pollution labs and marine-science libraries, the Ice Information Partnership and the Freshwater Institute ceased to exist.

Once they had eliminated the programs they most disliked, and the departments whose mandates they did not support had been neutralized through reduced funding, the Harper government turned its attention to social programs that were not part of the federal-provincial shared-cost transfers, because they fell under exclusive federal jurisdiction. Here the problem for the Conservatives was more complex. For example, Brian Mulroney's ill-fated attempt to de-index pensions for seniors (giving rise to the infamous "Goodbye, Charlie Brown" incident, in which senior Solange Denis confronted Mulroney on the steps of the Centre Block) had made Stephen Harper extremely cautious. As with his other efforts to dismantle the welfare state, he believed that stealth and a healthy dose of pragmatism were essential in order to avoid political fallout. In a classic demonstration of these methods, he used the occasion of a speech at the World Economic Forum in Davos in January 2012 to raise the issue of a "crisis" in federal retirement funding and to propose an increase in the age of eligibility for Old Age Security payments from sixty-five to sixty-seven, a move that incidentally would save the federal government billions.

Yet both a 2009 Department of Finance report, and a 2011 PBO report had argued that there was no crisis. According to them, the cost of retirement programs for the aging Boomer population was not only sustainable but temporary, reflecting the blip in the demographic profile of the country. In addition, as many earlier academic studies had noted,[22] the situation in Canada in terms of the ratio of working-age citizens to seniors was much better than in most other western countries, including in Europe. Canada's financial situation was also much stronger. And, as PBO Kevin Page noted, the rise in the percentage of seniors in the population was hardly unexpected and could easily be accommodated with advance planning. In an unusually aggressive statement, Page asked, "The Prime Minister, when he was cutting taxes in the 2006 and 2007 budgets, do you think he did not know that we were going to be dealing with a rising old age dependency ratio? ... He knew that. But he reduced the GST by two points. He cut corporate income taxes. He cut personal income taxes. We had spending going at a fairly rapid rate."[23] Nevertheless, the government proceeded with the change, gradually raising the age of eligibility to sixty-seven over six years, and indicated that further changes might also be in the works.

Soon after, the full impact of the stimulus spending and lost revenue became glaringly evident. The looming 2015 election caused the Harper government to launch the second, more broadly based, deficit-reduction effort. Both the 2012 and 2013 budgets contained massive cuts in federal expenditures and public-service jobs, although the details were sadly lacking. In the 2012 budget, some $5.2 billion in cuts and nineteen thousand job reductions were announced, but one year later the PBO – and Canadians – still had no idea where those cuts would fall. In an unprecedented move, the Conservatives maintained a cone of silence over the entire process. Requests to individual departments by the media and others for information on the specific areas of cuts were met with consistent refusal, often on the pretext that decisions had not yet been made.

Eventually the PBO, frustrated by the lack of cooperation he was receiving from departments, decided to take the entire issue to court. On 24 April 2013, the Federal Court upheld his right to demand information from those departments as an integral part of his mandate, and ruled that only a legislative change to the mandate of the PBO could absolve the government and its departments of that responsibility. That ruling came after Page's term had come to an end, but his replacement, Jean-Denis Fréchette, continued to pursue departments and agencies for information. In some cases, minimal information about the cuts finally began to appear in scattered announcements, timed for release before weekends and holidays. Still, by late 2013, sufficient information had been released for experts to conclude that more than twenty-nine-thousand public-service positions were at risk, and more than one hundred additional programs were slated for elimination, although many observers felt the ultimate tally might well be greater.[24] In January 2014, a frustrated Fréchette revealed that thirty-three access-to-information (ATI) requests had been filed by his office since his appointment in August 2013, in an attempt to obtain further information from delinquent departments. While twenty-four had responded, only one had provided information that was even "somewhat useful," and nine had failed to respond at all. Worse still, his office was being charged an exorbitant fee for the ATI requests, even though the provision of such information was obligatory under his mandate. "It's an absurd, almost Orwellian, notion that the Parliamentary Budget Officer should have to file ATI requests to get information," an outraged NDP MP Pat Martin, chair of the House of Commons ATI, Privacy, and Ethics Committee, declared.[25]

Among the more problematic revelations for the Conservatives were those concerning the Coast Guard and the Department of National Defence. Army training programs were being cut back, military housing closed, and the purchase of new equipment, such as tanks, TOW launchers, and missiles to upgrade the air-defence system – a move touted by the Harper government only three years earlier when it dedicated $100 million for that purpose – was being scrapped.[26] Equally problematic were the huge cuts to the Canada Revenue Agency, the very organization the Conservatives had earlier enhanced in order to capture what they claimed were substantial amounts of lost revenue from fraud, overseas accounts, and other tax scams.

Other cuts demonstrated the vulnerability of any government to public protest over seemingly insignificant reductions in funding. Parks Canada, for example, implemented a reduction in the boating season for the popular Rideau Canal waterway and for national parks, as part of its effort to cut costs. These moves prompted considerable negative publicity from municipalities and businesses reliant on the tourism industry. This was particularly frustrating for the Harper Conservatives, who above all were operating on the assumption that their government was in power to help business.

PUTTING BUSINESS FIRST

The Harper government's determination to reduce the size of government was not simply an end in itself. Eliminating certain government programs was one element of a larger plan to restore as much autonomy as possible to the private sector. As discussed, the new economic conservative philosophy is grounded in the belief in the supremacy of market forces. A free market, unfettered by government regulation or other forms of intervention, will produce the best results for society, guided by Adam Smith's "invisible hand." That the followers of Friedrich Hayek and Milton Friedman continue to believe in this model, despite developments in the twentieth century, including the Great Depression, is surprising to say the least. That Stephen Harper, despite the 2008 global recession, continues to share their views is indicative of the strength of his convictions. As one of Harper's critics put it, "Harper still believes in homo economicus," a "neat, clean, simple theory," in which economic man always makes rational decisions based on self-interest, and the economy always rewards merit and distributes wealth equitably. But almost no one still believes in economic man, least of all modern economists.[27]

Yet, as late as January 2012, Stephen Harper went to Davos, Switzerland, and extolled the merits of capitalism and the free market economy. Delivering a not-too-subtle lecture to his European counterparts on the many economic accomplishments of his government, and their own failure to deal with the euro crisis, he pointedly criticized their prioritization of the welfare state and urged them to adopt austerity measures and get their euro-zone house in order. He also repeatedly emphasized the role of governments in creating wealth and prosperity, rather than "focusing primarily on services and entitlements." His comments were particularly striking, since the Occupy movement was in full swing at the time, and the founder of the World Economic Forum, Dr Klaus Schwab, had declared only days before that "capitalism in its current form has no place in the world around us" and "we must begin by restoring a form of social responsibility."[28]

Harper's government constantly demonstrated the importance it placed on the private sector, beginning with the major cuts to corporate taxes. In addition, it introduced or extended tax subsidies and tax credits for the oil sands and other natural-resource industries (while eliminating tax breaks for renewable resources and "green" industries), and in 2013 introduced a new "action plan reboot," by providing a tax break for the manufacturing sector.

Then there were the policy reversals. These most often resulted from a conflict between the populist rhetoric of the original Reform/Alliance party roots, and the practical demands and concerns of business. An early policy casualty was the Passengers' Bill of Rights. In response to growing consumer concerns about the lack of information and appropriate compensation provided by airlines for delayed flights, lengthy tarmac delays, or lost luggage, the then-transport minister, Lawrence Cannon, announced the launch of Flight Rights Canada, just days before the start of the 2008 federal election. At the time, he also promised passenger-rights posters would soon be prominently displayed in all airports. However, the Flight Rights Canada initiative turned out to be only an obscure Transport Canada website with little detail, and the poster promise still had not materialized more than five years later. Nor, as several consumer groups and passenger-rights activists noted, was there an actual Passenger Bill of Rights. This was in stark contrast to strict EU-wide regulations adopted in 2005, similar regulations in Asia and even the situation in the United States, where airlines can be fined and significant passenger-compensation rules are strictly regulated.

One immediate reason for the Conservatives' failure to act was financial. In yet another apparent example of reactive ad hoc policy-making, the senior Transport Canada executive in charge reported to Cannon that "there is no new money for this initiative."[29] But Cannon proceeded anyway. However the broader issue was the significant lobbying by the three major Canadian carriers – Air Canada, WestJet, and AirTransat – all of whom voluntarily filed "compliance" forms with the Canadian Transportation Agency as an alternative.

But the clearest and certainly the most revealing explanation of the government's rationale for inaction, which flew in the face of its alleged "consumers first" policy, could be found in the comments of Conservative MP Pierre Poilievre. As parliamentary secretary to the transport minister at the time, Poilievre spoke in the House of Commons about an NDP proposal for a passenger bill of rights, which was first tabled in 2009. Despite the regulatory provisions already in force in Europe, Asia, and the United States, Poilievre insisted that such a measure would leave Canadian airlines at a competitive disadvantage and inevitably increase airfares. Then he invoked the sanctity of the marketplace: "The ideal of free enterprise, free exchange, has delivered humanity the most unprecendented buildup in prosperity in all known history. That can only happen when we limit government to doing the things that people cannot do for themselves, which brings me to the question before the House today, and the overall airline industry and its service to customers."[30]

Many of the Conservatives' cuts to government programs and services also reflected their emphasis on government serving the interests of the private sector. Nowhere was this more evident than with respect to the once world-renowned National Research Council of Canada, an institution whose basic research in the past had led to countless discoveries, such as the vaccine for meningitis, rust-proof wheat, canola oil, and the development of the Canada space arm.[31] Yet under the Conservatives, the institution's budget was slashed dramatically, reflecting their lack of interest in scientific data and evidence-based decision-making. Equally important, though, was their decision to shift what funding remained from a relatively equal balance between pure and applied research to an almost exclusive focus on applied research (which would serve industry), and away from the basic research that scientists know to be essential to discovery. Indeed, Harper's long-serving Minister of State for Science and Technology, Gary Goodyear, actually referred to the council as an organization that now would provide a "1-800 concierge service" to industry.[32] As one anonymous critic scoffed, "the NRC has been reduced to testing light bulbs for GE."

Another series of cuts – to Agriculture Canada and the Canadian Food Inspection Agency – appeared at a minimum to be careless if not wilfully reckless, although few critics were prepared to argue that they had been made with the deliberate intent of aiding business. Nevertheless, they soon created that impression. The Harper Conservatives had already presided over the largest food recall in Canadian history in 2008, when a listeriosis outbreak at Toronto-based Maple Leaf Foods was responsible for twenty-two deaths and thirty-five cases of serious illness. Not since the Harris Conservatives' Walkerton tainted-water disaster in Ontario had there been such a major health-and-safety crisis, and it would normally have driven any government to exercise more caution rather than less in future. Yet the 2012 budget, which launched the Harper government's major deficit-reduction exercise, hit hardest at the department and the agency responsible for maintaining safety standards in the food industry. Although it was unclear how many positions would ultimately be affected, due to the government's own reluctance to release details, it was learned that nearly five hundred food inspectors, veterinarians, and scientists who operated testing facilities had received notices that their positions were at risk. When these revelations came to light, the agency immediately issued an official press release, declaring that "No cost-saving measures will affect food safety." However Bob Kingston, the president of the relevant PSAC union, responded, "It's impossible to cut that many people and not affect safety."[33]

Unfortunately, Kingston's words soon proved prophetic. In September 2012, an E. coli outbreak at an Alberta beef plant, XL Foods (the third-largest in Canada), caused at least eighteen serious illnesses and resulted in massive product recalls. Canadian beef was also blocked from export to the United States and much of Asia. Amazingly, Agriculture Minister Gerry Ritz declared that "the timeline actually backstops the fact that our system does work. There is no endemic situation out there from E. coli."[34] Staff at the inspection agency, speaking on condition of anonymity, disagreed with that interpretation and maintained that, if the system had worked, the poor procedures which caused the outbreak at the plant would have been detected and corrected long before the problem arose. Lack of staff, they argued, was forcing them to allow some companies to essentially police themselves.[35]

Award-winning medical journalist André Picard was one of the few who openly criticized the government's attitude in the aftermath of the debacle. In a scathing article in which he described the federal minister's response as "buffoonery" and the government's line as "beef good, regulation bad," Picard decried the government's strategy of shifting responsibility to consumers. "Gerry Ritz has played the industry booster well," Picard wrote, "repeatedly expressing his concern for XL Foods, the cattle industry, and the economy of Brooks, Alberta. But he has been all but silent on those who have been sickened, and the safety of consumers generally." In particular, he lambasted a subsequent Health Canada press release entitled "Information for Canadians on cooking mechanically tenderized beef," pointing out that, quite apart from the obvious abdication of responsibility on the part of government, the absence of mandatory labelling regulations meant there was no way for consumers to know which products fell into that category. "The government's clear message on tainted beef," Picard declared, "is that the interests of business matter more than the health of consumers."[36]

ABANDONING THE ENVIRONMENT

An equally important move by the Conservatives to assist industry was their deregulation of most of the major environmental protection measures that had been put in place by successive federal governments over several decades. Since the Harper government had already demonstrated its lack of concern for environmental issues by withdrawing from the Kyoto Accord on climate change, this was perhaps not surprising. Certainly Stephen Harper's earlier statement that "Kyoto is essentially a socialist scheme to suck money out of wealth-producing nations" was no doubt indicative of his feelings. Given the government's priority of aiding the private sector to create that wealth, the deregulation of environmental-protection measures was an obvious next step. However, Harper's minority status until May 2011 prevented him from taking this action sooner, since he knew he would face strong opposition from the Liberals and New Democrats. As a result, the first years of Conservative government instead saw him adopt a pragmatic approach based on cuts to programs and departments, and the elimination of a number of key environmental research facilities described above, all measures that could be accomplished outside the glare of parliament.

The majority changed everything. It was barely six months after the Conservatives' May 2011 victory that Stephen Harper pulled Canada out of the Kyoto Accord. Then, in the April 2012 omnibus budget, the remainder of Harper's agenda for the environment was spelled out in graphic detail. Buried in the four-hundred-page document – which the government refused to split, despite repeated opposition requests to do so – were measures to repeal the Canadian Environmental Assessment Act, 1992 introduced by Brian Mulroney, and replace it with a new, less rigorous, act, as well as hundreds of amendments to the Canadian Environmental Protection Act, the Species at Risk Act, the Fisheries Act, the National Energy Board Act, and the Canadian Nuclear Safety Commission Act.

The new Canadian Environmental Assessment Act, 2012 was described by environmentalists as a serious backward step and an obvious attempt to curry favour with natural-resource industries. It narrowed the scope of projects captured by the act, limited the number of potential intervenors in the assessment process, and transferred responsibility for many projects to the provinces. In addition, it allocated considerable discretion to the minister responsible to determine the scope of a particular assessment. It also proposed that only three agencies – the Environmental Assessment Agency, the Nuclear Safety Commission, and the National Energy Board (NEB) – would conduct such reviews. With all energy and pipeline project approvals transferred to the NEB, opponents argued, the government was literally opening the door to oil and gas projects such as the oil sands.

Even more revealing was the overt hostility directed towards environmental groups in the bill. It limited interventions to those directly affected, or with specific expertise related to the project in question. As such, it effectively limited public interventions to local stakeholders (if any, given that most projects would be slated for relatively uninhabited areas), while *closing* the door on national, regional, or provincial environmental groups with expertise, almost all of whom would be based in large urban centres, far from the actual projects. Then, adding insult to injury, the new legislation also required groups with charitable status to provide more detail on their sources of funding, including foreign funding, and any activities that could be described as political activism, thereby threatening their charitable status.

Meanwhile, the hundreds of amendments to other important environmental legislation, such as the Species at Risk Act and the Fisheries Act, had the effect of limiting coverage by selecting only certain major species, or certain major habitat areas, for coverage. Indeed, the Fisheries Act changes actually specified that coverage would only be extended to "important" species, meaning those that were "valuable for commercial, recreation, or first nations purposes."[37]

In a pointed repudiation of the government's plans, four former federal fisheries ministers issued an open letter, questioning the government's motives for including environmental-protection changes to the Fisheries Act in the Budget Implementation Act. The four – Mulroney-era Progressive Conservatives Tom Siddon and John Fraser, and Chrétien Liberals Herb Dhaliwal and David Anderson – argued that the government had not provided a reasonable explanation for the changes, rejecting its defence of eliminating red tape. They also urged Harper to allow the Fisheries Act provisions to be reviewed by the parliamentary fisheries committee and not a subcommittee of finance. They concluded, "Quite frankly, Canadians are entitled to know whether these changes were written, or insisted upon, by the minister of fisheries or by interest groups outside the government. If the latter is true, exactly who are they? We find it troubling that the government is proposing to amend the Fisheries Act via omnibus budget legislation in a manner that we believe will inevitably reduce and weaken the habitat protection provisions."[38]

Ignoring this criticism entirely, the government surprised almost everyone a few months later by scrapping the Navigable Waters Protection Act in Bill C-45, its second piece of omnibus legislation, which was tabled in the fall of 2012. The hundred-year-old piece of legislation had come to function as an important piece of environmental protection, but it was replaced with a new Navigation Protection Act, which failed to mention water and did not cover more than 99 per cent of either rivers or lakes. Although Transport Minister Denis LeBel attempted to attribute the changes to numerous requests from municipalities, it later transpired that the actual source of the suggested changes was the Canadian Energy Pipeline Association (CEPA) in a meeting with the then-deputy minister.[39] Moreover, in January 2013, Greenpeace Canada revealed that it had obtained a letter under Access to Information which outlined virtually all of the changes made by the Harper government. It was signed by CEPA, the Canadian Association of Petroleum Producers, the Canadian Gas Institute, and the Canadian Petroleum Products Institute, leading most observers to conclude the Harper government was indeed more concerned with helping industry than protecting the environment, just as the former fisheries ministers had feared. In fact, the budget's relevant subheading was not environmental protection but "Responsible Resource Development." Chapter 3.2 of the Budget stated "The Government is committed to improving the review process for major economic projects to accelerate investment and job creation."

CRUSHING UNIONS

A logical corollary of the Conservatives' affinity for the private sector was hostility towards unions. Following once again in the footsteps of Margaret Thatcher and Ronald Reagan, the Harper government took on several of the major private-sector unions in the country, as well as its own public-service unions, with significant success. Shortly after obtaining their 2011 majority, for example, they tabled back-to-work legislation twice in less than six months, to avert two potentially major strikes at Air Canada and Canada Post.

In the case of Air Canada, the labour strife resulted from the company's plans to enact a major overhaul to its services and create a new, low-cost division, which would entail decreased salaries and benefits for many of its unions, such as those for flight attendants, mechanics, and pilots. The attendants' threatened strike in the fall of 2011 was followed by looming strikes by pilots and mechanics in March 2012, and a threatened lockout in retaliation by Air Canada management. Labour Minister Lisa Raitt acted swiftly. First she referred both cases to the Canada Industrial Relations Board for a review of health-and-safety issues, a temporary ploy which immediately put all labour action on hold and prevented a strike over the March break. Then she promptly tabled legislation which would impose a permanent settlement by a government-appointed arbitrator, effectively precluding any strike. Speaking to her legislation in the House of Commons, Raitt made the government's reasoning crystal clear. "The government is very concerned that a disruption at Air Canada will damage Canada's fragile economic recovery," she said. "We will take the swift action that is needed to ensure that Canada's economic recovery is not negatively affected."[40]

Union leaders and opposition parties criticized the moves as unnecessary and ultimately harmful to labour relations in Canada. Professor Ian Lee of Carleton's Sprott School of Business went further, arguing that the Harper Conservatives had "*de facto* amended the Canada Labour Code to prevent strikes in the transportation and communications sector, while leaving the legislation untouched *de jure*." This "new normal" in Canadian labour relations, he maintained, had also involved the unprecedented use of a government's majority situation to "use executive authority to ... amend a statute of Parliament."[41] Similarly, several labour experts and academics pointed out that previous back-to-work interventions overwhelmingly involved the public sector. Professor Anil Verma of the University of Toronto's Rotman School of Management noted not only that Air Canada is a private company, but also that it does not have a monopoly or provide an essential service. "Unlike the ports or the railways, there is ample competition in the airline industry both domestically, with WestJet Airlines Ltd. and Porter Airlines, and abroad with any number of international carriers. Air Canada does not fit the typical category at all."[42]

When a strike loomed at Canadian Pacific Railway shortly after, Raitt again threatened back-to-work legislation, a tactic which Verma and others argued was not even beneficial to management in the long run, since necessary restructuring would not take place and labour unrest would be merely postponed. A study by right-wing think tank the C.D. Howe Institute concurred, finding that a back-to-work bill "triples the likelihood that in the next round of bargaining, legislation or arbitration will again be needed."[43]

Already, in October 2011, the Conservatives had upped the ante in their more general attack on unions, possibly as a political move to counter what they perceived to be the growing threat from the NDP as the Official Opposition. Given the unions' traditional support of the NDP, Conservative backbencher Russ Hiebert tabled a private member's bill which sought to change provisions of the Income Tax Act in order to force unions "to apply financial disclosure rules," a move which many independent observers considered reasonable, until the details of the bill were disclosed. Instead of merely requiring disclosure of revenue, as was already the case for registered charities, the legislation called for detailed lists of all transactions and disbursements, names and addresses of those involved, and even the purpose of such transactions. As one public-service-union president exclaimed, "this is an astounding request coming from one of the most secretive and controlling governments in Canadian history," and because it was strongly supported by Ottawa MP Pierre Poilievre, "whose constituents overwhelmingly work for the federal government and benefit from its unions."[44] The proposal was also rejected by several provincial governments. As Ontario Labour Minister Linda Jeffrey indicated in a letter to the Senate committee examining the bill, "the Government of Ontario wishes to convey to you and to the Government of Canada our serious concerns regarding the inexplicably intrusive nature of Bill C-377's financial disclosure obligations."[45]

Nevertheless, the government supported the bill and used the whip to ensure its passage in the House of Commons, a move described by Canadian Labour Congress president Ken Georgetti as a "bully state" tactic. However, in an astonishing development, the

Conservative-dominated Senate broke ranks and voted against the bill, sending it back to the House. Interestingly, the opposition to the bill was led by Tory senators.

That bill was followed in 2012 by MP Pierre Poilievre's call for legislation aimed at allowing both public servants and employees of companies falling under federal legislation to opt out of joining unions or paying union dues. As a parliamentary secretary, Poilievre was ineligible to present a private member's bill himself, and so he publicly called on one of his colleagues to present such a piece of legislation, which he described as similar to American "right to work" legislation. NDP critic Nathan Cullen vigorously opposed the idea, and agreed that it would turn Canada into a so-called "right-to-work" state such as Georgia or Alabama, with the inevitable lowering of wages, working conditions, and job security.

Meanwhile, the Harper government had launched what Professional Institute of the Public Service president Gary Corbett described as an all-out war on public servants. It included successive, and progressively more serious, initiatives to end legal strike actions, impose contract settlements, and arbitrarily remove or alter sick leave, severance pay, and pension benefits. These efforts did not always succeed, however, and certainly not without significant repercussions. For example, in September 2013, the Federal Court ruled that then-heritage minister James Moore violated the union's procedural rights and "ran roughshod" over existing collective agreements when he ordered the Public Service Labour Relations Board to conduct a vote of Canada Border Services employees on the government's "final" contract offer. The offence was particularly egregious, since it was later learned that Moore's order had come one day after the government-appointed conciliator's report recommended significant improvements to that "final" offer to employees.

The toxic work environment in the public service led to an unprecedented number of grievances and use of sick leave for stress-related illness. It culminated in 2013 in the first of a series of potential strikes by major unions, as the existing contracts of more than two-thirds of employees were set to expire. An initial strike by the Professional Association of Foreign Service Officers (PAFSO) was symptomatic of the hostility, since that union had long been seen as non-militant. The strike, which began in May, involved a number of highly public escalations in action and rhetoric by both sides. Then, on 13 September the Public Service Labour Relations Board ruled that the federal government had been bargaining with the striking diplomats in bad faith. In its twenty-five-page decision, the board found the government "violated its duty to bargain collectively in good faith and make every reasonable effort to enter into a collective agreement." Shortly after the ruling, Treasury Board president Tony Clement and PAFSO president Tim Edwards signed an agreement that the union considered an unqualified victory. Nevertheless, barely two months later, at the Conservative Party convention in Calgary, both Clement and Harper made it clear that one of their next big battles was with "big labour." "We're not here to buy labour peace through caving in to every single public-sector union boss's demands. We're not here to do that. We're here to represent the taxpayer," Clement declared.

The Harper Conservatives' hostility towards unions was not shared by a majority of Canadians. In fact, a Harris-Decima survey, conducted in late December 2013, after several years of Conservative attacks on labour unions, found that some 56 per cent of Canadians still considered unions to be a positive influence in society, while 13 per cent remained neutral. Fully 70 per cent of Canadians agreed that unions were "still needed today," while two-thirds agreed that everyone in a workplace should pay union dues if they benefit from union activities. Most revealing of all, the survey found that 53 per cent of Canadians said they were "suspicious of governments and politicians who try to limit collective bargaining and the power of unions."[46]

This type of information once again was not a concern for Harper, who famously indicated in his own convention speech in Calgary that "I couldn't care less what they say," when referring to his critics. As usual, and especially since his May 2011 majority victory, Harper and his advisers were intent on maintaining the core support necessary for them to be able to forge another electoral victory, and adding a small number of outliers motivated by wedge issues. For the Harper Conservatives, whose November 2013 convention was not held in Calgary by accident, that core support remains in western Canada and in the private sector. Indeed, more than one analyst has concluded that much of the government's economic agenda – and certainly that portion not predetermined by the new conservatives' philosophical focus on reducing taxes – is driven by western concerns surrounding the natural-resource base of that regional economy.

PROMOTING AN ALBERTA AGENDA

In addition to his conservative philosophy, it is important to note that Stephen Harper considers himself to be an Albertan and a western Canadian, despite his Ontario roots. His early involvement with a Reform Party whose slogan was "the West wants in," his deep-seated dislike of Pierre Trudeau, his conviction that the National Energy Program was one of the worst policy decisions ever made, his authorship of the Firewall Letter to then-premier Ralph Klein, urging him to adopt an Alberta-first policy, and his decision to represent a Calgary riding, are only a few indicators of the importance he attaches to his regional identity. This identity, in turn, was reinforced over time by the evolution of the Reform/Alliance/Conservative Party, whose own roots are entrenched in the region and many of whose original proponents continue to dominate his government in Ottawa.

As much of this discussion has demonstrated, decisions by the Harper Conservatives to deregulate the environment, reduce corporate taxation, and provide incentives to the natural-resource sector for mining, energy, and forestry, have benefited western industries far more than the central Canadian manufacturing sector. In fact, some of the government's policies, as both the Ontario and Quebec governments have repeatedly protested, have actually been detrimental to the country's industrial heartland.

This apparent bias towards western Canada, even if it were admitted by the Conservatives, would undoubtedly be viewed as a realistic response to the real-world economy in which the country must operate. Harper himself once declared that the Canadian economy was based on hewing wood and drawing water, and his economic agenda has reflected that belief, in spite of other increasingly important realities. His continued defence of his policies as having provided economic recovery, for example, is based on the success of the oil and gas industry, the exports of which increased dramatically in 2012–13, for a surplus of $62.9 billion. At the same time, however, the remainder of the economy suffered an export deficit of more than $72 billion.

One obvious problem with this scenario is that the vast majority of Canadians live in central Canada. Another serious concern is the temporary nature of the natural-resources boom, which inevitably will be followed by another bust. Yet the Conservatives appear content to benefit from short-term financial gains, and show virtually no interest in recommendations by some of their own advisers, such as then-chair of the Industry, Science and Technology Committee and Alberta MP James Rajotte, whose committee's report on the manufacturing sector urged the government to invest in value-added technology and diversify the western economy as much as possible.

Undoubtedly the most important pillar of the Harper government's Alberta-centric economic agenda has been their support for the oil and gas industry and, in particular, their determination to provide new markets for the industry through the development of a north-south pipeline to the United States (the Keystone XL project) and to Asia via the West Coast (the Northern Gateway project). As early as 2008, Harper referred to Canada as an energy superpower, and many of the measures implemented in the early years were dedicated to making this statement a reality. It came as no surprise, therefore, to learn that Harper's choice for a new president of the National Research Council (NRC) in 2010 was a petroleum engineer, John R. McDougall, or that the council's reorganization in 2011 created the research portfolio of mining, energy, and the environment, designed to assist clients in the oil-and-gas and mining sectors.

The Conservatives' efforts accelerated after their majority victory in 2011, with a high-profile public-relations campaign to defend the exploration and development of the Alberta oil sands as "ethical oil," because of Canada's democratic regime and reliability. The oil sands are widely viewed as highly polluting, and a government report predicted their development would singlehandedly neutralize all progress made in reducing greenhouse gas emissions from coal-based electricity in Canada. Nevertheless, in response to an open letter from eight Nobel laureates urging Harper to stop the oil-sands expansion and the proposed pipeline to the US, Energy Minister Joe Oliver defiantly declared, "Our government will continue to promote Canada, and the oil sands, as a stable and secure source of energy to the world."[47] It was shortly after, that Canada withdrew from the Kyoto Accord, whose targets the government admitted it had no possibility of meeting.

Meanwhile, on the domestic front, the government was ramping up its deregulation of environmental-protection measures, which resulted in the removal of more than two hundred projects involving the oil sands, fossil fuels, and pipelines from any environmental-assessment process. In some cases, as a leaked memo demonstrated, these projects were allowed to proceed, despite warnings from government scientists that water sources could be at risk and fish habitats harmed.

In August 2012, having recognized the importance of showing some evidence of concern for the environment if they were to succeed in convincing the Obama administration to proceed with the Keystone project, the Harper Conservatives finally began drafting a set of national regulations related to greenhouse-gas emissions. However, when Alberta premier Alison Redford protested that their approach would have a devastating impact on oil-sands development, they agreed to let the province continue setting its own guidelines for emission standards. Those standards were particularly problematic, since they were based on emission limits per barrel of oil produced, rather than on the industry as a whole. The result, as environmentalists were quick to note, was that the oil sands would be free to double their production. According to several reports, the federal government also agreed to focus on the construction of new plants, rather than imposing tough regulations on existing plants.[48]

However, the pipeline projects were proving far more difficult to control than the oil sands. Despite repeated trips to Washington by Harper, John Baird, Joe Oliver, and Alison Redford, the Obama administration repeatedly delayed its decision. Even the all-Canadian route was proving to be a major political challenge for Harper. On the one hand, the move to assign responsibility for approval of the Northern Gateway project to the National Energy Board had worked out well, and approval in principle had been delivered in late 2013. Similarly the "environmental terrorists" Joe Oliver had attempted to demonize, as discussed in an earlier chapter, had been restrained by changes to the assessment process to do with intervenors, and by various measures in the Income Tax Act that had produced what environmentalist David Suzuki referred to as a "chill" on environmental activism. On the other hand, Oliver had thrown unwanted fuel on the fire during one April 2013 interview by questioning the actual climate-change science and suggesting that Canadians were not that concerned about a two-degree increase in global warming. In addition, many other jurisdictions were involved in the pipeline, including two provinces and countless aboriginal communities. Moreover, the vaunted Temporary Foreign Worker Program, although it had been well-received by the natural-resource industries initially, was proving to be a poisoned chalice, in which the increasing number of problems that were identified and publicly exposed required numerous modifications to legislation, each one more embarrassing than the last.

In the end, however, it was the aboriginal problem that appeared to be most intractable. As former Harper environment minister Jim Prentice indicated in a speech delivered at the University of Calgary on 27 September 2013, and in an open letter to the government published in the *Vancouver Sun*, the federal government had a constitutional responsibility to consult with aboriginal peoples before making any decisions on the issue, and it had not done so. Prentice's blunt letter struck at the heart of the problem:

> The constitutional obligation to consult with first nations is not a corporate obligation. It is the federal government's responsibility. Second, the obligation to define an ocean management regime … is not a corporate responsibility. It is the federal government's responsibility. Finally, these issues cannot be resolved by regulatory fiat – they require negotiation. The real risk is not regulatory rejection but regulatory approval, undermined by subsequent legal challenges and the absence of "social licence" to operate.[49]

A year later, Harper's own special envoy on aboriginal and energy issues tabled his final report and delivered a speech in which he stated Ottawa "must shoulder most of the blame" for the substantial and growing opposition to the Northern Gateway project. Rather than negotiate in good faith, Doug Eyford said, "I've been surprised at the extent to which the federal government has been content to allow project proponents like Enbridge to engage aboriginal authorities with little or no Crown oversight, direction, or assistance."[50]

The need for the government to negotiate was brought home forcefully yet again by an unfavourable Supreme Court decision a few weeks later. In a unanimous decision written by Chief Justice Beverley McLachlin, the court confirmed the existence of aboriginal title – that is, it found that native Canadians still own their ancestral lands, unless they signed away their ownership through treaties with government. This historic ruling was particularly important for the Harper government, since treaties were never signed in most of British Columbia, through which the Gateway pipeline must pass. As a result, the court ruled that governments and companies must obtain consent from aboriginal title-holders, *and from aboriginal communities who have asserted ownership of land which has not yet been established* (the case for most of the land claims in BC), before proceeding with resource-development projects or other economic development.

But negotiation has not been part of the Harper government's strategy, and the pipeline is likely to remain a major problem as the Conservatives near the end of their mandate. Moreover, Harper's most recent attempt at pragmatism – in which his government used the May 2014 National Energy Board recommendation to approve the project, and then once again abandoned responsibility by telling the private sector to work out the details in negotiations with stakeholders – is even less likely to succeed, nor is it likely to distance his government from the inevitable fallout.

Still, as we will see, this is hardly the only unexpected development the Conservatives faced in implementing their agenda. Other key elements of their domestic agenda have also been overturned by the courts. Nevertheless, it may be in the area of economic policy that the Harper Conservatives have the most significant long-term impact. Regardless of whether their pipeline project is ultimately successful, their changes to the tax system and cuts to government programs have created a substantial economic imbalance among regions and individuals in Canada, closely mirroring the consequences of the Reagan and Thatcher economic agendas in their respective countries. An OECD study released in April 2014, for example, showed that the gap between rich and poor, while widening in many industrialized countries, had increased more in Canada than any of the thirty-eight other members states, except the United States. In fact, it found the top percentile of income earners in Canada accounted for 37 per cent of pre-tax growth, compared with only 23 per cent in Britain and Autralia, and 47 per cent in the US. Worse still, the higher the income, the faster the gains. Although the report identified several possible causes of the growing income gap, it paid particular attention to tax policy, noting that rates for upper-income earners had been reduced dramatically by the Harper government, and recommended that "top income earners contribute their fair share of taxes."

Similarly, a number of economic analyses in 2014 demonstrated the growing polarization between the booming resource economies of western and northern Canada, and the downward spiral of the Ontario manufacturing economy, which led to its qualification for federal equalization payments as a "have not" province in 2009–10 for the first time in its history. Ontario has continued to receive equalization payments ever since, and in 2014 the Parliamentary Budget Officer concluded that the province, which is home to 40 per cent of Canadians, was entitled to greater payments than it currently receives. For this downward trend and growing disparity to be reversed, an increase in federal revenue would be an essential first step, yet this solution is one that opposition parties have been unwilling to promote because of the perceived political costs, making any attempts by future governments to rectify this situation exceedingly difficult.

7

Restoring Order: The Domestic Agenda

Canadians have found, through a costly forty-year experiment with liberalism, that big government is not an instant answer to everything … it cannot substitute for personal responsibility, self-reliant families, and strong communities.

We have always said that we would put the protection of Canadians ahead of the rights of criminals … At the same time as we focus on the fight against criminals, we shall work to put government on the side of victims and law-abiding citizens.

We owe these men and women who put on the uniform and risk their lives for our country a huge debt of gratitude. So, our Conservative government, regardless of criticism, will go on giving the Canadian Armed Forces the equipment they need, and the respect that they deserve.

Rt Hon. Stephen Harper, Calgary, July 2011

When Stephen Harper addressed his Calgary riding association at a barbeque in July 2011, just months after his May election win, he could hardly contain his delight at finally obtaining the "strong, stable majority government" he coveted. Nor could he conceal his glee at having presided over the apparent demise of the Liberal Party. "I believe the long Liberal era has truly ended," he told supporters. "As with disco-balls and bell-bottoms, Canadians have moved on." Then he proceeded to outline the objectives of his government, objectives which he said had not changed since long before his party was first elected in 2006. Only the lack of majority, he insisted, had prevented him from doing more. Nevertheless, he concluded "Canada is stronger, safer and better" because the Conservatives had been and were still in power.

The choice of those three words was instructive. For many observers, the absence of terms such as "fairer" or "more tolerant" was noteworthy, as was his failure to mention the social-policy challenges still facing his government, such as poverty, homelessness, the plight of aboriginal Canadians, or the many hurdles confronting new immigrants. Unlike Jean Chrétien's speech after winning a third majority government, when he acknowledged "we have work to do," the Harper Conservatives appeared to take the view that not much more was left to accomplish. This was hardly surprising, given their belief that their most important contribution would be to minimize the role of the state in the social union, not expand it.

Under previous federal governments, a chapter on domestic policy would undoubtedly have focused on social-policy initiatives, a reflection of the strong commitment of Liberals and Progressive Conservatives to the collective well-being of Canadians, and to the values of fairness, compassion, and equality of opportunity. Both mainstream parties also shared the view that the federal government had an important role to play in nation-building and the development of a unique Canadian identity. As a result, they launched many cultural programs and other initiatives that were designed to foster that identity. In short, successive federal governments traditionally played a positive and proactive role in the areas of social and cultural policy, and any chapter on domestic policy would have covered their initiatives.

By contrast, the new Conservative Party philosophy of minimalist government was nowhere more evident than in social and cultural policy. By any traditional definition, the Harper government did not have a social-policy agenda. Nor was it interested in cultural policy. As a result, the arrival of the Harper Conservatives in Ottawa marked the beginning of a lengthy and unusual hiatus, in which the federal government was simply missing in action on a number of important files. This absence can be seen in their very thin legislative legacy in those areas, and the lack of meaningful political debate on pressing issues of the day. As journalist James Travers noted, it is possible to identify the priorities of a government as much by what is *not* being discussed, as what is.[1]

This is not to suggest that there was no domestic agenda whatsoever. On the contrary, the Harper Conservatives brought with them a classic set of social-conservative priorities, and seemed determined to ignore what the majority of Canadians considered important. Instead, Harper's agenda envisaged a return to the Canada of the 1950s. His priorities were restoring family values, getting tough on crime, cracking down on immigrants, and celebrating the military. Predictably, it was an agenda that met with considerable resistance from opposition parties, academics, non-governmental organizations, and ordinary Canadians.

Just as their economic agenda had been preoccupied with scaling back government intervention in the private sector, so the Conservatives' domestic agenda was a negative one as well. It focused primarily on eliminating government programs and agencies, cutting funding for civil-society groups, and deregulating or withdrawing entirely from certain activities. And in the same way that their economic policy was symbolically framed around "hard-working Canadians," so their domestic agenda was centred on "traditional Canadian families" and "law-abiding Canadians." Perhaps most importantly, it was in the area of social and cultural policy that the Conservatives' preference for values and beliefs over factual evidence was most visible, as was their emphasis on tradition, loyalty, and justice over fairness, compassion, and equality of opportunity. Indeed, it was in this area that the evangelical and fundamentalist values of the new Conservatives were most clearly reflected, producing a polarization of views within the general public not seen for more than fifty years.[2]

RESTORING FAMILY VALUES

One of the first and most controversial of these social-conservative values was the importance of the family, and more specifically the traditional "nuclear" family, with two parents, two or more children, and a mother who stayed at home. Many of the policies put in place by previous governments, and especially their initiatives on government-sponsored not-for-profit child care, were considered dangerous to the well-being of the traditional family and an unfair slap in the face to single-income families. As Harper himself said, the Conservatives knew who the real experts were, and they were not bureaucrats, academics, or interest groups. No, "their names are mom and pop."

Consequently, in their first budget, the Conservatives cancelled a $5-billion, multi-year child-care plan announced by the Martin government. In its place they created the stand-alone federal Universal Child Care Benefit, which provided a child-care allowance of $1,200 per year for every child under the age of six. Although the measure was billed as an alternative to the Liberals' formalized child-care plan, there was no requirement that the funding be spent on child-care services of any kind. Moreover, experts argued that not a single new child-care space would be created. Eventually the government set aside $250 million for a problematic program that expected the private sector to create new spaces. Estimates placed the annual cost of the child-care allowance at $3.7 billion; the remaining $1 billion in funds was returned to general revenue.

The Conservatives also provided a range of boutique tax breaks for "hard-working families" in their 2006 budget and several that followed. Chief among them was the Children's Fitness Tax Credit, which allowed parents to claim up to $500 (each) for their children's participation in organized and often-costly sports such as hockey. Later, under pressure because of accusations of gender bias, they extended the credit to activities such as dance or kung fu lessons. Although experts generally oppose all such narrowly based tax measures on principle, it might have been possible to defend if the credit was aimed at lower-income families who otherwise could not afford the fees. But several studies demonstrated that nearly two-thirds of all claimants earned more than $50,000. More importantly, a study by an Alberta professor found that the measure was almost totally ineffective in assisting the very low-income families it might have been designed to help. Unrepentant, the government reconfirmed its support for the measure, at an estimated cost of nearly $70 million annually.

Meanwhile there were a number of values issues looming over Harper when he was first elected, a legacy of the Chrétien and Martin governments. One in particular, same-sex marriage, had caused enormous difficulties for him, his party, and many of his candidates during the 2004 election. It had been legalized by Martin in 2005, after lengthy debate and a reference to the Supreme Court, which found that anything short of the term "marriage" – such as civil union, a term favoured by Harper personally but opposed by many in his party – would be unconstitutional. Having learned from the mistakes of 2004, Harper sought to avoid political fallout during the 2006 election by promising at the start of the campaign that he would allow a free vote on the rejection of the Liberal legislation if elected. This was disingenuous but effective. It followed the long-standing practice of the Liberal and Conservative parties to consider moral issues as non-partisan, and hence subject to free votes. In another classic example of the conflict between ideology and pragmatism that confronted him regularly, Harper chose pragmatism. He devised a solution that allowed him to placate his social-conservative base, which vehemently opposed the Liberal measure, by allowing them to try to organize a majority of votes, at the same time that he managed to reassure the majority of Canadians who supported it, since – despite the best efforts of the social conservatives – he knew that a free vote was virtually guaranteed to fail. The vote took place on 7 December 2006, and the motion to reject the Liberal legislation was indeed defeated, 175–123. To the chagrin of some of the most committed members of his party and caucus, Harper then stated that he considered the issue to be closed and that he would not pursue the matter further.[3]

Perhaps in a bid to offer solace to those disappointed with the result, his government promptly cut funding to a number of social programs and cultural festivals that had come under fire from the religious right. For example Heritage Canada was suddenly denied funding for the annual Montreal Black and Blue Festival. Described by organizers as the world's largest charity gay dance festival, in the past it had received $50,000 annually from the department. A frustrated Robert Vézina, president of the non-profit group in charge of the festival, told journalists that bureaucrats responsible for the grants had told him confidentially that the event was not considered "family-oriented enough," although this had never been mentioned before as a criterion. Liberal MP Mauril Bélanger, a member of the Canadian Heritage committee, indicated that the cuts were not a surprise. "I think we've seen that time and again from this government – ideology trumps objectivity, trumps respect, trumps treating all of us equally. [This is] a government that makes decisions by ideology that is basically targeting some segments of our population unfairly, and that is not the country I know."[4]

A similar fate befell Toronto Gay Pride Week, but not before a slightly more moderate member of Harper's cabinet caused an uproar among her socially conservative colleagues. Diane Ablonczy, minister of state for tourism, awarded $400,000 to the event under the new Marquee Tourism Events Program announced by Industry Minister Tony Clement in the 2009 budget, and then attended it herself. The program's mandate was spelled out in Clement's statement: "By the summer of 2009, Industry Canada will provide initial funding to marquee events that significantly promote tourism, in time to respond to the many events that bring tourists to Canada during the summer vacation period." Organizers pointed out that Toronto's Pride Week clearly qualified, since it attracted tens of thousands of visitors each year, and more than a hundred thousand spectators for the parade that was the highlight of the event. Nevertheless, a furor erupted when Ablonczy made the announcement, and shortly thereafter responsibility for the new program was placed directly with Clement.

Conservative MP Brad Trost left no doubt as to the cause and effect. Outraged by Ablonczy's behaviour, he told an alternative Christian media network, LifeSiteNews, that she had been punished. "Almost the entire Conservative caucus," including "most of the Prime Minister's Office were taken by surprise ... The pro-life and the pro-family community should know and understand that the tourism funding money that went to the gay pride parade in Toronto was not government policy, was not supported by – I think it's safe to say, by a large majority – of the MPs," Trost said, adding that the funding was "a very isolated decision" and that "most of the caucus is still strongly pro-traditional marriage."[5] His comments were echoed by Dave Quist, executive director of the Institute of Marriage and Family Canada, a well-known Conservative supporter, who told journalists he objected to grants for Pride events on principle, because they were not "family friendly."

Another perceived threat to family values was also addressed by the Harper government soon after its election, when it cut funding to various women's-rights groups. One of the Conservatives' most prominent supporters, REAL Women, had taken the lead for years in attacking federal grants for women's organizations. REAL argued they were special-interest groups, which represented only one perspective on the issue of women's rights. President Gwen Landolt and many of the officials in her organization were original members of the Reform Party. Vice-president Judy Anderson described the close relationship as one based on mutual self-interest. "We're both against equal pay for work of equal value. We're against so much government intervention into family and private life, which is what the radical feminists want ... the Reform Party seems to support many of the same philosophical ideas that we have."[6]

Anderson's perception certainly appeared to be accurate. Many Reform/Alliance members of Harper's future caucus outlined their views repeatedly during election campaigns, often causing considerable frustration for their leader. From unsuccessful candidate Hugh Ramolla's reference to his NDP opponent as "Ms Giroux and her femi-Nazi supporters" to MP Garry Breitkreuz's claim that "We should keep our mothers in the home, and that's where the whole Reform platform hangs together," and fellow MP Paul Forseth's astonishing statement that "in domestic conflict more women than men are likely to resort to using a weapon against a spouse," it was evident that the Conservative base did indeed share many of the views of REAL Women. Another Conservative MP, economist Herb Grubel, contributed his view that "programs in support of single mothers cause mothers to be single and to need support." Nor were these comments limited to men. None other than Harper minister Diane Ablonczy once objected strenuously to a Liberal proposal to provide child tax benefits to pregnant women, arguing that it would encourage women to become pregnant.[7]

Once in power, the Conservatives' 2006 budget immediately cut funding for Status of Women Canada (SWC) by nearly 40 per cent, and closed twelve of sixteen regional offices. In addition, the criteria for SWC's program to fund groups was changed, to prevent any form of advocacy or lobbying. The definition of those activities was so stringent that most groups, including women's rape crisis centres, were effectively prevented from applying. REAL Women promptly issued a press release, stating that "This is a good start, but we hope that Status of Women will eventually be eliminated entirely, since it does not represent women, but only represents the ideology of feminism."

In 2010, in advance of Harper hosting the G8 summit, where his maternal and child health initiative was to be discussed, some eleven foreign-aid and women's groups who received support from SWC suddenly found themselves cut off, apparently because they had been critical of the government's position to fund family planning but not abortion. Once again it was a Conservative who confirmed the causal link. Senator Nancy Ruth used characteristically blunt language to warn others to let the issue slide and "shut the f...k up" if they hoped to continue to receive any federal funding at all.[8]

On the issue of affirmative action, the link was equally clear. Reform MP Deborah Grey, whom Preston Manning once called "the Margaret Thatcher of the Prairies," had often made it clear that she believed affirmative action – and especially pay equity – simply gave women an unfair advantage over men. Stephen Harper concurred. As head of the National Citizens Coalition in 1998 he had called for the federal government to scrap "its ridiculous pay equity law," which he claimed "has everything to do with pay and nothing to do with equity. It's based on the vague notion of 'equal pay for work of equal value,' which is not the same as equal pay for the same job."[9] In 2006, despite a campaign pledge to consider the recommendations of a federal task force, Harper instead ignored the issue and the recommendations entirely. Then in 2009 his government introduced the Public Sector Equitable Compensation Act, a misnamed piece of legislation, which experts warned would effectively "empty the right to pay equity of any meaning" and "reintroduce gender discrimination in pay practices, rather than eliminate it."[10]

This was followed in 2010 by a review of employment equity in the public service. While pay equity involves concerns about equal pay for work of equal value, employment equity is designed to ensure equal opportunity and diversity in the workplace. With the decision to cancel the long-form census, announced by the Harper government in June 2010, the review of employment equity quickly followed. Public-service union leaders immediately made a connection between the two developments, noting that it would be impossible in future to determine whether progress was being made on employment equity, since the relevant data would no longer be collected. They also stressed that both the Employment Equity Act and the Public Service Employment Act required all hiring to be done on the basis of merit and qualifications. "The government claims to support diversity," a National Union of Public and General Employees (NUPGE) press release said, "but its [actions] imply the opposite. It reinforces the misconception that equal opportunity is threatened by employment equity measures, and that such hiring policies are not based on merit." The release also noted that fewer than 2 per cent of job competitions in the public service were designated for employment-equity hiring processes. Meanwhile a Senate committee issued a report which found the federal public service was actually falling behind the private sector in terms of representation.[11]

Nevertheless, the Conservatives were determined to neutralize the impact of the existing employment-equity legislation. First they cut funding for the compliance program and closed all regional offices. Then they proceeded to ignore the criteria in many cases, despite a letter from Public Service Commission chair Maria Barrados reminding line-department managers that they were legally required to do so. In the 2012 and 2013 omnibus federal budget bills, changes were made to the requirements concerning private-sector contractors bidding on federal jobs. Fewer companies would now fall under the legislation. Some estimates suggested more than 40 per cent of existing contractors would be exempted.

The Conservatives also wasted no time eliminating the Court Challenges program, which had been established to allow individuals and groups to pursue legal challenges of Charter violations. The program was seen as allowing left-wing radicals such as feminists to make their case before a liberal-minded court, to the detriment once again of traditional family values. Successful court challenges concerning women's rights, gay rights, pornography, and prostitution had all served to anger the social-conservative elements of the party. Indeed, the program was a flashpoint, revealing the philosophical differences over the Charter of Rights and Freedoms between the new Conservatives and the mainstream political parties, and its history perfectly reflected those differences. It was created by the Trudeau government, immediately eliminated by the Mulroney government, re-established by the Chrétien government, and then once again disbanded by the Harper Conservatives after their election in 2006.

The program was particularly galling to them because it was seen as responsible for Supreme Court rulings on same-sex marriage, the Omar Khadr case, and numerous Criminal Code measures they introduced. As a result, the Court Challenges program also served to demonstrate that, while the family-friendly policies were important to the Conservatives, they were not the bedrock upon which their domestic agenda rested. Probably no policy area was of greater importance to them than their "tough on crime" platform, which the Court repeatedly thwarted. Indeed, more than one-third of all the legislation introduced by the Harper government was concerned with the criminal-justice system in one way or another, and the only non-budget omnibus bill they introduced contained a raft of anti-crime initiatives. Not surprisingly nine former or serving police officers were present in Harper's caucus (as well as two former officers appointed to the Senate), a number which represents nearly half of all police officers elected since Confederation. Here too, the influence of the religious right among Conservative Party supporters was obvious. The new measures ignored all available evidence and were seemingly motivated by a desire to exact retribution rather than ensure rehabilitation.

GETTING TOUGH ON CRIME

One of the most prominent examples of policy failure in many decades must surely be the Chrétien Liberals' gun registry. Conceived as a response to the 1989 Montreal massacre, the legislation was promised in the Liberals' 1993 Red Book, and introduced in 1995. The concept of a gun registry originally had the support of the majority of Canadians, especially in central and Atlantic Canada, as well as the Canadian Association of Police Chiefs, various police unions, legal societies, and a panoply of other experts. But the devil was in the details. The apparent failure of drafters and politicians to consider the different situations of western, northern, and rural Canadians led to widespread opposition to the rules and regulations in those very regions from the beginning. However, it was the horrendous cost overruns – caused by administrative difficulties and technological nightmares – that allowed the Harper Conservatives to turn the policy failure into a full-fledged political disaster. In 1997, the issue singlehandedly cost the Liberals their few seats in Saskatchewan, and by 2000 its importance as an issue in western Canada had riven both the Liberal and NDP caucuses along rural-versus-urban dividing lines.[12] More to the point, the Conservatives had recruited the entire anti-gun lobby to their side, as well as opponents such as the Canadian Taxpayers Federation and other right-wing lobby groups outraged by the costs, providing Harper's party with more money and memberships than it knew what to do with.

In order to retain that crucial support, the Harper government was intent on dealing with its commitment to eliminate the long-gun section of the gun registry as quickly as possible after its 2006 electoral victory. However this was not to be, as they soon discovered the limitations of a parliamentary minority. In June 2006, they introduced a bill designed to put the onus on retailers, rather than owners, to register non-restricted long guns, but the bill died on the order paper when parliament was prorogued. A similar bill was tabled in late 2007, but failed to pass before the December 2009 prorogation. Finally, using a technique for which they had become well-known, the Conservatives next supported a private member's bill, introduced by rural MP Candice Hoeppner, to eliminate the requirement for owners to register non-restricted long guns. That bill came to a vote in September 2010, at which point the Conservatives had increased their representation in the House, but were still shy of a majority. With all opposition parties joining forces, the bill was narrowly defeated by a vote of 153–151. As he was leaving the House after the vote, a bitter Harper told reporters "we will continue our efforts until this registry is abolished."

True to his word, when his party achieved a majority in the 2011 election, Stephen Harper moved quickly to eliminate the long-gun requirements for non-restricted weapons. This was expected, especially since he had reiterated his commitment during the election campaign. However, Harper and his public security minister, Vic Toews, went much further than anyone had anticipated. On 25 October 2011, the government introduced legislation to scrap the Canadian Firearms Registry (Bill C-19), and observers were shocked to learn that the bill provided for the destruction of all records. Supporters of the registry described the move as a vengeful, over-the-top move to ensure that no future government could ever reintroduce such a measure. Conservative insiders concurred. Toews was convinced that both the NDP and the Liberals would use the data to recreate the registry the moment they were in power, despite a commitment by the NDP not to do so. Harper himself declared that he would not facilitate a "backdoor registry." Yet some 66 per cent of Canadians surveyed in an Ipsos Reid poll a few months earlier still supported the registry, ranging from a predictable 81 per cent in Quebec to a surprising 53 per cent in Alberta.[13]

But the gun registry was only the tip of the iceberg in the Conservatives' "tough on crime" agenda, which can be seen as the outward and visible symbol of their Old Testament–style determination to impose order on a world they view as lawless and dangerous, despite all evidence to the contrary. Indeed, their perception was so strong that it caused Stephen Harper to ignore such evidence and decry the "epidemic" of rising gun, drug, and gang crimes.[14] Similarly, his former chief of staff and mentor, Tom Flanagan, referred to an "explosion of crime."[15]

Throughout their time in office, the Harper Conservatives continued to use such inflammatory rhetoric as they focused on their law-and-order agenda, and they did so despite the existence of at least four factors that would have led a normal government, of any political stripe, to lose interest in the subject. The first was public opinion. Although there had been a gradual increase in public concern over crime rates and individual safety (a disconnect that many experts attributed to the Conservatives' increasingly alarmist rhetoric), a December 2011 Statistics Canada report demonstrated conclusively that this was no longer the case. Fully 93 per cent of Canadians were "satisfied with their personal safety," virtually identical to the situation in 1994. An Environics poll in January 2012 confirmed this finding as well. Violent crimes, Canadians now understood, were trending downward, and had been doing so for more than twenty-five years. Equally important, fully 63 per cent of Canadians favoured *crime prevention* over law enforcement as the primary means of crime reduction.[16] Yet when Harper faced intense public pressure to establish a commission of inquiry into the disappearance of countless aboriginal women – an issue which had been brewing for several years – he forcefully rejected the idea by returning to his familiar Old Testament approach that "we should not view this as a sociological phenomenon." Instead, he said, "we should view it as a crime."[17]

A second factor was the evidence itself, provided by the government's own sources. According to a 2009 Public Safety Canada report,[18] homicides were at their lowest level in four decades. The overall crime rate was at its lowest level since 1991, the Crime Severity Index (CSI) had decreased by 22 per cent since 1999, property crime had declined by 50 per cent since 1991 and auto thefts by 40 per cent, while the use of weapons in robberies had declined as well and the use of firearms accounted for only 15 per cent of cases in 2008. Equally interesting were the data relating to specific situations. In Toronto, where one gun-related death in 2008 had spurred the Conservatives to introduce a steady stream of amendments to the criminal code, Statistics Canada data showed that the use of firearms had actually *decreased* by 10 per cent since 1999. Moreover,

Toronto's CSI ranking was the *third lowest in the country*, among the thirty-three largest metropolitan areas.

A third factor, and one which would normally have been considered very important by fiscal Conservatives, was cost. When the Harper government passed its first comprehensive package of crime legislation in 2010, it set aside $89 million to cover the changes. But Parliamentary Budget Officer (PBO) Kevin Page produced a report indicating that the real costs would be up to $8 billion. Subsequent measures added to the potential costs. Liberal critic Mark Holland cited the government's own figures for the cost of incarcerating one individual, which ranged anywhere from $86,000 to $160,000. With the estimated addition of some 3,400 prisoners a year due to new Conservative measures, such as mandatory minimum sentences, the *additional* annual cost of maintenance alone therefore would be between $292 and $544 million. Yet the Harper government continued to stress that they were prepared to do the "right" thing, protecting law-abiding citizens and helping victims, whatever the cost. In the battle against crime, it seemed, ideology would always trump pragmatism.

The fourth factor which might have been expected to give any government pause was, of course, expert opinion and experience. But the Harper Conservatives were prepared to ignore the input of countless experts who had demonstrated that crime prevention and deterrence were far more successful at producing safe streets and safe communities, if that was the true goal. Moreover, longer sentences and tougher prison conditions had been conclusively proven to *increase* the likelihood of individuals reoffending, rather than decrease it. In short, by virtually any scientific measure, the Conservatives were moving in the wrong direction entirely if their real purpose was public safety.

Instead, their actions would seem to confirm that their primary motivation is indeed retribution, driven by the values and beliefs outlined earlier. Yet, as political scientist W.T. Stanbury has pointed out, the "theory" behind retributive justice is never clearly spelled out. Evidently punishment is an end in itself in this "just desserts" approach to crime ("do the crime, do the time") which allows "law abiding" individuals to express "righteous indignation," but it is also "a form of vengeance: wrongdoers should be forced to suffer because they have forced others to suffer." Still, it is not clear how, or on what basis, supporters of retributive justice such as the Harper government can make decisions about changes to the Criminal Code on sentencing.[19] By contrast, the field of criminology, which Mr. Harper has vocally disdained, provides three standard objectives and guidelines for sentencing. Punishment is certainly one, but deterrence and rehabilitation are the others. Normally, students are taught that the loss of freedom is the "punishment" component. Once incarcerated, the role of correctional services, as the name implies, is to work with offenders to ensure deterrence and ultimately to achieve rehabilitation in order to permit reintegration into society.

However, the Conservatives wasted no time after taking office in 2006 in demonstrating that they had little use for rehabilitation or reintegration, as they proceeded to implement an agenda that focused exclusively on punishment. First they tackled the situation of existing offenders by establishing a Correctional Services Review Panel in 2007. It was comprised of known conservatives and chaired by Rob Sampson, a former minister of corrections under the Mike Harris Conservative government in Ontario. The panel promptly issued a report entitled "Roadmap to Strengthening Public Safety," which recommended a number of stern and regressive changes, none of which were supported by evidence. Their recommendations were immediately adopted by the government, without any debate or enabling legislation.

Reacting to these developments, UBC law professor Michael Jackson and Graham Stewart, former executive director of the John Howard Society of Canada, prepared a scathing critique of the Roadmap, entitled "A Flawed Compass: A Human Rights Analysis of the Roadmap to Strengthening Public Safety." "It is a flawed moral and legal compass," Jackson said at a press conference in Ottawa. Stewart said the changes "dismantle a generation of reform painstakingly put in place by both previous Conservative and Liberal governments, and will make a mockery of Canada's claim to leadership in the vindication of human rights."[20] The last word was left to Conrad Black, the disgraced former newspaper publisher and ex-convict who had recently returned to Canada. A known conservative, his remarks were perhaps the unkindest cut of all. "The Roadmap is the self-serving work of reactionary, authoritarian palookas," he wrote. "It is counterintuitive and contra-historical. The crime rate has been declining for years and there is no evidence cited to support any of the repression that is requested. It appears to defy a number of Supreme Court decisions and is an affront, at least to the spirit of the Charter of Rights."[21]

Nevertheless, the government continued to pursue the idea of *increased* punitive measures. They appointed more like-minded conservatives to the Parole Board, most with no relevant experience. Soon dramatically fewer requests for full parole or even day passes were being granted.[22] Over the next several years, the Conservatives chipped away at anything that could be seen as a modest perk or benefit within the prison system. They began by closing six prison-farm programs across the country, programs that had been widely hailed as groundbreaking and hugely successful at promoting rehabilitation. Outraged experts and correctional personnel protested to no avail, and no reason was ever given for the closure by Vic Toews or the government. Another "counterproductive" and "mean-spirited" measure, according to the Canadian Bar Association, was a little-known provision in one of the omnibus crime bills that would prevent or reduce the number of visits to inmates by family and friends. International evidence had demonstrated that family visits played a demonstrable role in preventing recidivism, but that advice, too, was ignored. Instead this change was followed by a decision to cancel the contracts of all part-time prison chaplains, eliminating forty-nine positions that served a variety of non-Christian inmates and leaving only full-time, almost exclusively Christian, chaplains to serve the entire inmate population.

A rapid succession of even more picayune changes was introduced, including eliminating the ability of inmates to occasionally order pizza or other fast food. Since these rare events were usually tied to the visits of family and friends, they had no doubt become redundant for many. Well-known ethicist Margaret Somerville declared Toews's measures were ethically and humanely difficult to justify. "Rehabilitating inmates is not 'going soft' on crime; rather it's 'going hard' on protecting society ... Creating settings in which prisoners can experience love and joy with their families and friends, or companionship with their fellow inmates, is more likely than not to assist in their rehabilitation."[23]

Far more serious and potentially dangerous moves included the elimination of rehabilitation programs, medical programs, and access to education. So was the decision to charge inmates more for their room and board and make them pay for phone calls, a decision taken at the same time their pay rates were slashed. Vic Toews declared the measures were an attempt to "restore balance" to the criminal justice system and "increase accountability." Critics charged they were a violation of the Canada Labour Code and the Charter of Rights and Freedoms, and would, once again, have the perverse effect of encouraging recidivism. Catherine Latimer, head of the John Howard Society, stressed that "the accountability for wrongdoing is the sentence that's imposed by the courts and it concerns me that the minister thinks he should be adding to the measure."[24] Criminologist Leah DeVellis added that the changes violated the United Nations Standard Minimum Rules for the Treatment of Prisoners.[25] However a statement from the minister's office was unapologetic, saying the cuts and other changes would save some $4 million annually and reduce the amount that "law-abiding Canadians incur for these types of expenses."

The recently retired director general of Corrections and Criminal Justice at Corrections Canada, Mary Campbell, was an even more severe critic of the government's "failed policies and slogans." She delivered a scathing indictment of the Harper government in a speech to a criminal-justice conference in Vancouver in October 2013. Noting that twenty years earlier Canada had been considered a world leader in the corrections field, Campbell warned it had now reached its "lowest point." Decrying the lack of evidence for the policies, Campbell cited political considerations and "deeply embedded nastiness" as the primary drivers of the Conservatives' "regressive" decisions, which "do nothing to address crime or victimization." In addition to "ever more punitive carceral conditions, erecting barriers to re-integration and never letting the offender be more than the worst thing they have ever done," Campbell cited a "chilling" comment by Stephen Harper earlier that year, when the government unveiled new and tougher penalties for pedophiles. "The fact is we don't understand them and we don't particularly care to," he said. "We understand only that they must be dealt with."[26]

The consequences of the Conservatives' approach did not take long to materialize. According to the independent Correctional Investigator for Canada, Howard Sapers, by August 2011 there was ample evidence that prison violence was on the rise. Apart from the various cutbacks to programs, Sapers identified the cuts to prison budgets as an important factor. "Overcrowding is definitely an issue," Sapers declared. With more people being incarcerated, and fewer outlets for prisoners for rehabilitation, the decision by prison officials to resort to "double-bunking" (the placement of two prisoners in a cell originally meant for one), not surprisingly led to "strain on the aging prison infrastructure, on prison inmates, and on prison personnel." Sapers reported that federal prisons were "more crowded, more tense, and more polarized between old and new inmates," and these problems were contributing to "an increase in violence and deaths behind bars." Toews denied this was the case. "I haven't seen that statistic," he declared.[27]

After the 2011 election, the Conservatives also returned to the charge on the issue of sentencing. They had introduced a number of bills in earlier parliaments, almost all of which had died on the order paper, and as a result they bundled them together in an omnibus crime bill in the fall of 2011. With their majority assured, they were able to force the bill through, despite fierce opposition from the other parties, as well as lawyers, judges, correctional services, and provincial premiers. Indeed, it was impossible to locate any experts who supported the measures.

One category of changes made almost all criminal offences more serious by increasing the length of time to be served. Changes also were introduced to tighten parole provisions, reduce the credit for time served before sentencing, tighten the definition of "not criminally responsible," and make pardons far more difficult to obtain. Conditional sentences were eliminated, and a minimum amount of time was set that judges must assign for a particular crime. These so-called "mandatory minimums" were a principal reason why the number of incarcerated prisoners was rapidly growing, as was the number of mentally ill inmates with no access to treatment. Judges increasingly viewed the changes as foolhardy, self-defeating, and a violation of their constitutionally guaranteed independence. The situation deteriorated to the point where Ontario Justice Melvyn Green took the extraordinary step of publishing a scathing criticism of the federal government's actions in a Criminal Lawyers Association newsletter, arguing the Conservatives "are driven by an ideology of unabashed Puritanism, marketed through fear-mongering."[28]

Next came the abolition of the "faint hope" clause – a provision which, while rarely granted, allowed those serving life sentences to apply for parole after fifteen years. It was a provision that prison guards had enthusiastically supported when it was introduced, because it was shown to reduce prison violence. Its elimination was imposed without consultation. Then, in a tense question-and-answer period with members of the Canadian Bar Association at their annual meeting in Halifax, Justice Minister Rob Nicholson stubbornly rejected the lawyers' pleas to "tone down" the legislation in the omnibus bill to prevent "clogged courts and handcuffed judges." Instead, he insisted that their majority meant the Conservatives had a mandate to do what they pleased. Their determination to ensure retribution continued unabated, as evidenced by Prime Minister Harper's unexpected pledge during a campaign-style speech to supporters in September 2014 that his government would move to eliminate the only remaining possibility of parole for life sentences after twenty-five years.

Tougher penalties for child predators, including a provision for consecutive sentences, were followed by a plan to designate offenders found "not criminally responsible" as "high risk." The Conservatives also introduced new limitations on the rights of convicted sex offenders *after* their release. Then they launched several court challenges to uphold legislation preventing prostitution. (It must be noted that prostitution itself was not illegal.) The Supreme Court ultimately ruled against the government on this latter issue. In essence, the court struck down three provisions in the legislation, because they had the effect of denying sex workers safe working conditions, but it also allowed the government a one-year window to rewrite the legislation.

As a result, in June 2014, Justice Minister Peter MacKay introduced the government's response, Bill C-36, The Protection of Communities and Exploited Persons Act. The legislation, which surprised most experts with both its moralistic tone and regressive content, was quickly and almost universally condemned for two reasons. First, it did not address the issue of worker safety raised by the court. Indeed, as several critics pointed out, it would have the opposite effect, making the sex trade more dangerous.[29] Second, by introducing a large number of new prohibitions, it effectively criminalized sex work. Most experts predicted the new law would be viewed no differently than the old one by the court, and would be soon overturned. Given this widespread consenus, the rationale for the Conservatives' approach therefore could best be explained as a *combination* of pragmatism and ideology. On the one hand, it was intended to promote their practical political strategy of creating wedge issues among voters, and on the other hand, it did so by promoting an extreme conservative ideology. As one observer noted, with the 2015 election approaching, the Conservatives viewed the legislation as a perfect opportunity to reinforce their support from "their social conservative and Reform Party roots ... it is evidence [they] realize they need more than just their old mantra of tax cuts to motivate their base and hold off a liberal resurgence."[30]

Another unexpected initiative was Prime Minister Harper's personal intervention to make citizens' arrests easier. Seeming to base their policy on a single case and anecdotal evidence, the Conservatives followed through on Harper's verbal commitment during an earlier visit to Toronto. The measure was unveiled at a photo opportunity of the prime minister standing with a convenience store owner who had faced charges after physically kidnapping and abusing a shoplifter in Toronto.[31] A similar surprising change was proposed soon after a widely publicized homicide by stabbing in Toronto. In this case it was intended to make the use of a knife an additional offence for sentencing purposes. As one observer asked, "Isn't it already illegal to kill someone? Does it matter what weapon they use? If knives are going to make for a longer sentence, maybe everyone will start using hammers or bows and arrows!" In both cases, critics expressed concern that criminal law was being made on the fly for partisan gain.

One of the most problematic of the government's policies was related to victim fine surcharges. Although victim fines were introduced in 1989 by the Mulroney government, during an earlier period when conservatives took up the cause of victims' rights, their application to convicted offenders was at the discretion of judges. Funds acquired through these fines were to be collected and used by provinces to pay for services provided to victims of crime. In 2007, the Harper Conservatives added the surcharge, to be either 30 per cent of the fine imposed, or a flat rate of $100 for offences punishable by summary conviction and $200 for offences punishable by indictment if no fine was imposed. However judges still had discretion. They could exempt individuals from paying a fine or the surcharge if they believed it would cause undue hardship. In reality this was very often the case, and they were rarely imposed. But the Harper government received numerous complaints from REAL Women and victims'-rights groups about this judicial resistance. As a result, and despite evidence that restorative justice programs were far more effective and helpful to victims as well as perpetrators, the government introduced Bill C-37, the Increasing Offenders' Accountability for Victims Act, in June 2013.

Critics said the bill neither increased accountability nor did anything for victims. What it did do was close the loophole allowing judges to dispense with the surcharge. Moreover, it doubled the amounts involved in the fines. Many predicted a huge increase in unpaid fines. Lawyer Neha Chugh's response was typical. "If the purpose of the changes to the victim fine surcharge provisions of the Criminal Code is to devalue the role of the courts in the sentencing process, and to highlight and exacerbate social problems, this new bill may be the solution." York University law professor Alan Young concurred. "Let's be realistic," he said. "The majority of criminals are from a lower socio-economic class where waivers was a responsible way of addressing an impoverished situation ... You can't squeeze water from a stone."[32] Across the country, judges began ignoring the mandatory ruling, or finding creative ways to circumvent it. They levied fines of $1, with a surcharge of 30 cents. If that was not possible, then they gave the convicted felon fifty or sixty years to pay.

The government was forced to confront the prospect of a full-scale mutiny by the judiciary. Peter MacKay had replaced Rob Nicholson as justice minister, but MacKay was equally adamant that he would impose the surcharge. He accused judges of showing "contempt" for the law, and raised the possibility of filing complaints against individual judges with provincial judicial councils.[33] In an interview MacKay went further and suggested offenders could sell property to pay their fines if necessary. This comment infuriated many stakeholders, but none more so than an Ontario court judge, Colin Westman, who accused the minister of a "bully mentality. It's kicking people when they are down," Westman said. "I think someone has to remind the minister there are broken people here who don't have anything to give. The people we are dealing with, believe me, a high portion of them are just broken souls."[34]

Last but hardly least, there was the Harper government's relentless battle against drug use. As one columnist quipped, "If a drug policy works, Harper wants nothing to do with it."[35] The subject of the debate was the world-renowned Vancouver-based Insite safe drug injection facility, the only one of its kind in North America. Numerous studies, including one by the prestigious British medical journal *Lancet*, had demonstrated that the site saved lives, reduced crime, and encouraged the use of detox and addiction-counselling services. The site had been operating under a special exemption authorized by an earlier federal government, but was in danger of closing, because the Conservatives were planning to withdraw the exemption. A series of court challenges and appeals ensued, ending finally with the Supreme Court of Canada emphatically and unanimously coming down on the side of the site. The court ordered Health Minister Leona Aglukkaq to issue an exemption "forthwith." The decision was blunt. "The Minister's refusal to grant Insite [another] exemption was arbitrary and grossly disproportionate in its effects, and hence not in accordance with the principles of fundamental justice."

Nevertheless, the decision was a narrow one. A future attempt by the federal government to prevent the creation of other similar facilities might succeed. Although the court laid out a concise list of factors that would be taken into consideration, at least one analyst argued it would not be difficult for the federal government to argue that it had done so.[36] In the end this is exactly how the Harper Conservatives responded, tabling a new bill in the House of Commons outlining the requirements for new sites, requirements which would also apply to the Insite facility when it was next up for review of its exemption. Both opposition parties immediately charged that this was a backdoor effort to eliminate Insite and circumvent the courts.

Meanwhile, the government had also been making changes to the Criminal Code regarding drug use. One reason for the overcrowding in prisons was the number of individuals being caught by the "mandatory minimum" provision when convicted of simple possession. In many cases, police were refusing to lay charges, issuing warnings instead. In other cases, those charged were electing to go to trial rather than plead guilty, since the penalty for a conviction now resulted in prison time. This in turn explained the huge backlog in the courts. More than one criminal defence lawyer pointed out this might well allow those charged with more serious crimes to be discharged, by virtue of a Charter challenge under Section 7, because their case had taken too long to reach trial.

These points were also raised by an American expert who had been involved in the introduction of mandatory minimum sentences and their application to drug use in that country. Eric Sterling urged senators to reject the government's proposal. The former assistant counsel to the American Senate committee that had passed the legislation warned "mandatory minimums severely damaged the credibility and reputation of the justice system and put innocent people behind bars." The fallout for victims and witnesses was also substantial, he said, because the consequences for offenders were far more serious. Sterling informed Canadian senators that "Perjury increased dramatically … threats and killings of civilian witnesses became epidemic … and non-drug legal matters were squeezed out of strained court systems."[37] In short, Sterling said, Canada was about to repeat the mistakes that the United States had made, and the implications would likely be as bad or worse.

CRACKING DOWN ON IMMIGRANTS

In her critique of the "tough on crime" agenda, criminologist Paula Mallea described the Harper Conservatives as "fearmongers."[38] This view was shared by none other than former Progressive Conservative MP David Daubney, a lawyer and former chair of the House of Commons Justice Committee, who spoke out against the government's "tough on crime" policies. Criticizing them for "taking Canada backward," Daubney added, "their policies are based on fear – fear of criminals and fear of people who are different."[39]

This attitude was mirorred in the Harper Conservatives' approach to a number of other policy issues, including immigration and refugee determination. In a country which had once accepted hundreds of thousands of refugees, such as the Vietnamese "boat people," with open arms and compassion, under both Liberal and Progressive Conservative governments, the Harper Conservatives were charting an entirely new course. It appeared to be based at least partly on fear, and even more on indignation about "phony" refugees, "queue jumpers," "part-time Canadians," and other perceived malfeasance that required additional punitive measures.

Although the Conservatives actually maintained or even exceeded the numbers of immigrants accepted under previous Liberal governments, they did so on their own terms. This meant, first and foremost, that a new emphasis was placed on economics. "This government is focused on the priorities of Canadians," Jason Kenney declared, and those priorities "are economic growth and prosperity … We need more newcomers working and paying taxes and contributing to our health care system."[40] Speaking with reporters later, he expanded on that theme. "We want the next Bill Gates or the next Steve Jobs," he said. "We want high-value innovators." While few could disagree with that proposal, experts noted that such a priority was likely to exclude immigrants from many areas of the developing world. At the same time, the government reduced access under the family-class category, making it even more difficult for individuals from poorer regions to reunite with their families. Queen's University Dean of Law Sharry Aiken echoed the views of many experts when she noted that this was potentially a serious problem, since "being able to bring over family members is the underpinning of successful integration."[41]

Despite his stated commitment to an economic emphasis, by 2012 Kenney had frozen the highly regarded Skilled Workers Program, and introduced a moratorium on the Immigrant Investor Program, which he eventually eliminated in 2014. Kenney's subsequent Temporary Foreign Worker Program (TFWP), announced with great fanfare and initially well-received by the business community, made matters worse, accepting more people but with fewer qualifications than the skilled-immigrant category he had frozen. Clearly introduced to accommodate specific sectors of the economy (and western industry), it resulted in large numbers of immigrants arriving to work in the energy, restaurant, and domestic-service sectors, and evidence mounted that Canadian workers were being replaced with cheap foreign labour. The TFWP soon became a policy disaster as the implications of the hastily thrown together plan became clear, forcing his retreat on several occasions and numerous amendments to the plan over time. And, as with his closure of the investor program, his additional decision to impose stricter linguistic requirements for economic-class immigrants had the predictable result of once again limiting access from many parts of the developing world.[42]

While economic advantage drove the pragmatism that caused the Conservatives to support immigration, their political need to respond to the ideological concerns of their social-conservative base led them to impose a number of extreme sanctions on various categories of "offences," and on refugees. A case in point was the arrival of asylum seekers on the MV *Sun Sea* in 2010. In stark contrast with the Mulroney government's acceptance of 150 Tamil asylum-seekers found drifting off the coast of Newfoundland in 1986 (who were released and issued work permits within days), the Harper Conservatives took a hard line against the 492 Tamils who arrived on the cargo ship off the coast of British Columbia. All those on board filed refugee claims, but instead of being released within days, they were transferred to "accommodation and detention" centres. Then the Conservatives created anxiety rather than sympathy among ordinary Canadians by stating publicly that they believed many of the claimants were members of the Tamil Tiger group, which they had classified as a terrorist organization in 2006. They demanded exhaustive evidence of identity, opposed individuals' release as mandated by the Immigration and Refugee Board, and even contested release orders in Federal Court.

By February 2011, Harper's government had spent $25 million on the case. Despite this effort, they had almost nothing to show for it. By May 2012, nearly two years later, only nineteen individuals had been deported, over considerable public opposition and looming legal concerns related to Canada's obligations under international conventions. Two more were in police custody. The remainder had been released, pending the hearing of their refugee claims, and were not expected to encounter difficulties. Nevertheless, the government did not back down or indicate that it would process future cases differently. On the contrary, according to Peter Showler, director of the Ottawa-based group Refugee Forum, "the government clearly has admitted that they have this aggressive detention policy because they want to deter additional boats from coming."[43]

Immigration Minister Jason Kenney had already introduced a bill to address what he referred to as human smuggling. The Preventing Human Smugglers from Abusing Canada's Immigration System Act was introduced in October 2010, but died on the order paper with the federal election. Still, it had been soundly criticized by legal and immigration experts, many of whom argued it violated Charter rights as well as Canada's international obligations. Kenney maintained that it was fair but firm. In his view, asylum-seekers who had paid others to help them arrive on our shores were in fact queue-jumpers, who should all be detained for up to a year and then most likely deported, while the smugglers themselves should be prosecuted and given minimum mandatory sentences. According to one expert, this language was deliberate. "The Conservatives are creating a kind of slander about people on boats, using words like smuggler and criminal," he said, "to cause Canadians not to see refugees as human beings. They aren't refugees fearing persecution, they become something associated with crime and terrorists."[44] One of the most substantive critiques of the bill was prepared by the Mennonite Coalition for Refugee Support, who stressed that, under Bill C-4, "most of the provisions punish refugees, not smugglers." Their brief pointed out that the bill's sweeping provisions contradicted international law and conventions, which Canada had signed

– notably by providing for arbitrary detention and imposing repressive conditions on release, by denying permanent resident status, even if refugee status is granted, and by denying the right of appeal of negative decisions. It also noted that strikingly similar tough measures had been tried in Australia unsuccessfully, and had been sharply criticized by the Australian Human Rights Commission. As their brief concluded, "Under Bill C-4, refugees will be victimized three times: first by their persecutors, secondly by the smugglers, and finally by Canada."[45]

After their majority victory, the Conservatives wasted little time reintroducing the bill, which was then guaranteed passage. But it failed the legal test, as did so many of the Conservatives' legislative efforts. In January 2013, a BC Supreme Court judge struck down the section of the bill dealing with human smuggling, forcing the Conservatives back to the drawing board and delaying their case against several of the accused from the *Sun Sea*.

Another example of the government's grudging acceptance of refugees was made clear in the 2012 omnibus budget bill, which included a provision to eliminate health-care coverage entirely for certain refugee claimants and to eliminate supplemental benefits for others. The unexpected move resulted in protests by health-care workers in nineteen cities across the country. Doctors argued the cuts were putting even basic health care out of the reach of many vulnerable individuals, who might in turn pose a health risk to the general public. Nor did the cuts make sense economically, since, according to several sources, the roughly $20 million saved by the federal government would end up costing hospitals and provincial governments up to ten times more. As Ontario health minister Deb Matthews put it, there is only one taxpayer. She described the cuts as "a serious abdication of the federal government's responsibility towards some of the most vulnerable people in our society. And because Ontario has the majority of refugee claimants in Canada, we have been disproportionately affected by these changes."[46] By January 2014, Ontario and five other provinces had moved to fill the gap, vowing to "do the right thing," by funding the services for free, even if the federal government would not.

Meanwhile, Kenney announced a string of other punitive measures designed to crack down on immigration and refugee "cheats." For example, he announced in December 2011 that the government would launch a massive "crackdown" on "bogus citizens." First this appeared to be aimed at "dual citizens who commit terrorist acts in other countries," but it soon became clear that this included other, much larger, categories, such as those who did not fully comply with residency requirements. While it has always been possible for the federal government to revoke the citizenship of an individual on specific grounds, this rarely happened. Between 1967 and 2011 there were only sixty revocations, virtually all of them related to war criminals, and specifically to individuals making false identity claims to conceal those crimes. But Kenney's plan, as he himself said, would capture ordinary individuals who had somehow failed to comply with all requirements. Kenney, however, referred to them as "fraudsters," implying that everyone captured by the broad sweep would have done so deliberately. "We're taking action," he told reporters, "to strip citizenship and permanent residence status from people who do not play by the rules and who lie or cheat to become Canadian citizens. Canadian citizenship is not for sale."

In September 2012, Kenney announced that nineteen individuals had already had their citizenship revoked as a result of his plan, while some 3,139 individuals were being investigated. In addition, some 5,000 permanent residents had been "flagged" and another 2,500 recent arrivals were being "watched closely." While no one disputed the existence of fraudulent practices, most critics argued that the problems were minor and that Kenney should be spending far more time and effort on the immigration consultants who perpetrated the bulk of the fraud, rather than on the individuals who were their clients and in many cases were unknowing victims. Undeterred, Kenney announced the creation of a "snitch line" to help authorities locate "fraudsters."

By early 2013, it became clear that Kenney's optimism was misplaced. Departmental officials confirmed only twelve of the nineteen deportations had involved fraudulent claims. Worse still, of the 3,000 individuals being investigated, only 286 had actually been located, and ninety per cent of them had filed appeals with the Federal Court. According to several reports, the government's focus on this issue was creating a backlog, while proceeding at a snail's pace. Meanwhile the snitch line had received 22,000 calls, resulting in a paltry 132 referrals to investigators. "No matter how long it takes," Kenney said defiantly, "we will ensure that the full strength of the law is applied to anyone who lied or cheated to obtain Canadian citizenship."[47]

Meanwhile, in late 2012, Kenney testified before a parliamentary committee to explain why he required additional power to ban individuals from coming into Canada for "public policy" reasons. The proposed new power was contained in the government's Faster Removal of Foreign Criminals Act, which also imposed even stiffer terms for non-Canadians who committed crimes in this country. Since Kenney had already barred British MP George Galloway from entering Canada in March 2009 under the existing legislation – an event that made negative headlines around the world – it was difficult for many opposition MPs to justify the extension of the minister's powers, especially when the new powers were to be based on non-binding "guidelines." Galloway had been scheduled to deliver two talks in Toronto, but was deemed "inadmissible" on national-security grounds. This was allegedly because of his opposition to the war in Afghanistan, in which Canada was an active participant. However, when explaining his decision, Kenney inadvertently revealed the real reason, which had more to do with Galloway's position on Israel than on Afghanistan. "We're going to uphold the law, and not give special treatment to this infamous street-corner Cromwell who actually brags about giving financial support to Hamas … a terrorist organization banned in Canada," Kenney said. Galloway replied simply that "this idiotic ban shames Canada."[48] Critics noted Kenney did allow Geert Wilders, a far-right Dutch politician who compared Islam to Nazism, to enter Canada and speak at two events.

Less than a year later, there was at least one glaring example of what might develop if the minister were granted additional powers. First it was learned the government was attempting to deport a Canadian-born petty criminal – who possessed both an Ontario birth certificate and a Canadian passport – after he completed his two-year sentence. His social insurance number was destroyed by officials and his passport revoked. The government attempted to make the case that he was actually an Indian citizen, although he had never lived anywhere but Canada, and his parents were naturalized citizens. Deepan Budlakoti eventually hired a lawyer, who successfully filed a claim in Federal Court for his client to be given a work permit after the government refused to issue one. Then his lawyer learned that the government was suppressing information from the Indian government, which categorically rejected the claim that Budlakoti was an Indian citizen. "It's insane that the Harper government is taking this position against a Canadian man who has lived his entire life here," Yavar Hameed told reporters as he launched another claim in Federal Court, this time to have Mr. Budlakoti declared a Canadian citizen.[49]

Unrepentant, Kenney turned his attention to the backlog in immigration files, a perennial problem, which other governments had also tackled. For previous governments, though, the solution had been to introduce various fast-tracking scenarios. Kenney adopted a different approach. In the 2012 omnibus budget bill, the government announced that 280,000 existing immigrant applications – some of which had been in the system for years – would simply be eliminated. Not surprisingly, that move was immediately condemned by virtually everyone concerned, and a group of claimants in British Columbia launched a court challenge. Still, Kenney claimed victory in March 2013, declaring that the backlog had already been reduced by 40 per cent, from nearly one million outstanding applications to roughly six hundred thousand.

The Harper Conservatives' approach to immigration, like their approach to family values and the criminal-justice system, was not affected by facts or expert opinion. As one retired senior bureaucrat revealed, "the minister's [and the government's] general skepticism about social policy research," their reliance on anecdotal evidence and "disdain for the 'downtown activists' who had forged deep ties with bureaucrats" meant there were "two starkly different evidence bases" being drawn on "by the political and bureaucratic levels."[50] And, like the crime agenda, the discourse of the Conservatives on immigrants and refugees was overwhelmingly negative.

CELEBRATING PATRIOTIC MILITARISM

By contrast, the one priority of the Conservatives' domestic agenda where their rhetoric was consistently positive was the military. The government's commitment to restoring a patriotic militarism in Canadian political discourse was well-known long before the 2006 election. Harper's own enthusiasm for military adventures was also self-evident. In the opinion piece he co-wrote with Stockwell Day in 2003, criticizing the Chrétien government's decision not to participate in the Iraq war, Harper's position was crystal clear. "Modern Canada was forged in large part by war," he maintained, "not because it was easy but because it was right. In the great wars of the last century … Canada did not merely stand with the Americans, more often than not we led the way. We did so for freedom, for democracy, for civilization itself."[51]

After one brief year of disastrous stewardship of the defence department by Gordon O'Connor, Peter MacKay settled in for a lengthy stint there from 2006 until 2013. With MacKay as defence minister, Harper found the perfect complement to his views, just as Vic Toews had shared his views on crime. The post, which might have been seen as a minor one in other administrations, proved to be a prominent one under the Conservatives. MacKay was personable and immensely popular with the troops. It was often said that he truly enjoyed the post, and was loath to leave it for the justice department in the summer of 2013.

MacKay was also an enthusiastic proponent of patriotic militarism. In 2011, when he made a simple announcement about the word "royal" being reintroduced for the titles of the navy and air force, the press release for his brief remarks was titled "Restore the Honour!" MacKay declared, "We Canadians are blessed with a proud military history – a legacy of service and sacrifice that established on these shores a land of freedom, democracy, and justice … a country that has grown to stand tall on the world stage, a defender of freedom … a country that is, a century later, the envy of the rest of the world!"[52]

Soon the government introduced initiatives to heighten the visibility of the military on the home front. These included a uniformed presence at citizenship ceremonies, professional hockey matches, and basketball games, and even flypasts at the annual Grey Cup. Similarly, Harper was quick to expand the "Wear Red Friday" campaign, started by family members of soldiers from CFB Petawawa in 2006 to show support for Canadian troops abroad. It became an annual event sponsored by his government, with rallies held across the country. His personal interest in the military was reinforced by his political objective of identifying the Conservatives with the military in order to distinguish his party from the long-governing Liberals, who in Harper's view had presided over a "decade of darkness" for the armed forces.

"I'd like to thank you for the incredible amount of strength and support you have displayed over the last twelve months while hundreds of members from CFB Petawawa were deployed in Afghanistan," Harper said at the 2007 Wear Red rally in Petawawa.

According to the official press release, he "spoke of their heroic acts in Afghanistan, noting that nine soldiers from the base were recently honoured for their service. The Prime Minister went on to speak of the importance of ensuring Canadians from coast-to-coast are made aware of their stories of professionalism, bravery, and selflessness." And then, turning his problems with Afghan detainees into an advantage, he added, "Unfortunately, these soldiers didn't get the attention they deserved, because their stories were eclipsed by arguments in the House of Commons over the allegations of Taliban prisoners. I sincerely hope their stories get told when the Governor General formally awards their decorations."

Other ministers took up the cause as well. For example Immigration Minister Jason Kenney told an audience in 2012 that "no government in the modern history of Canada has done more to invest in giving the equipment necessary to our men and women in uniform." Similarly Peter MacKay was joined by associate defence minister Julian Fantino and Veterans Affairs Minister Steven Blaney in writing an opinion piece which claimed the Conservatives "have increased our investment in our bravest Canadians ... to unprecedented levels."[53]

Certainly financing of the military was considered a top priority in the 2006 election, and for a time the Conservatives backed their promises with hard cash. In their first budget they maintained the Liberals' promise to increase defence spending by $12.8 billion over five years (which brought the Chrétien/Martin government's commitment to roughly $20 billion by 2010), and then added another $5.3 billion for military projects. In 2008 the Conservatives produced a blueprint for defence policy, entitled the "Canada First Defence Strategy," which committed the government to spending a massive $490 billion on equipment over twenty years. However, these funds included the purchases already projected by the previous Liberal government for Hercules transport planes, Cyclone helicopters, and navy frigates. Still, the Conservatives did add major commitments of their own, namely the purchase of a fleet of F-35 fighter jets, Arctic patrol vessels for the navy, and an icebreaker for the Coast Guard.

By 2011 the Conservatives' defence budget stood at $21 billion, or $1 billion higher than the dollar commitment of the previous Liberal government. But several military analysts, such as Craig Stone of the Canadian Forces College and Ugurhan Berkok of the

Queen's University Defence Management Studies Program, questioned whether the situation could realistically be referred to as "unprecedented." Both experts underlined the fact that major defence acquisitions require long-term planning and multi-year expenditures, so that much of the Conservative record reflected the Liberal agenda of the previous decade. They also noted that equipment purchases are cyclical in nature. Previous highs had existed in the 1960s under Lester Pearson and in the 1980s under Brian Mulroney. In fact, in 1968 Pierre Trudeau had inherited a defence budget that represented 14.4 per cent of total government expenditures, in comparison with a low of 5.6 per cent during the Chrétien deficit-reduction era, and the Harper Conservatives' 7.9 per cent in 2010–11.

The reality of the 2008 global recession, with the federal budget falling back into a deficit situation, soon put considerable strain on the government's commitments. One by one the purchase of various items was scaled back (naval vessels) or delayed by spreading the cost over a longer period of time (F-35s). More importantly, the F-35 purchase became a political hot potato after a series of revelations about cost overruns and growing concerns about the viability and safety of the product. A February 2013 report commissioned by the Pentagon contained almost universally negative comments by test pilots over safety and performance issues. Other NATO countries planning to purchase some of the fighters began to pull out. Then, in a press conference in Washington, DC, to discuss the report, Lt Gen. Christopher Bogdan, the head of the F-35 Joint Program Office, told an audience that his biggest concerns with the plane "were not technological, but rather sustainment issues." He referred to affordability as "the big gorilla" in the room, suggesting "if Operational and Sustainment costs were not reduced," the plane could "potentially be unaffordable in the future."[54]

Meanwhile the Conservatives were facing serious problems in the House of Commons, where their refusal to provide detailed costing for their military purchases led to numerous confrontations. The government finally agreed to kill the sole-sourcing of the F-35 program and launch what it termed a "reset" in December 2012. One columnist declared "The F-35 're-set'" is an unmitigated disaster for the Tories," and constituted "a wholesale repudiation of the government's core military procurement policy of the 2011 [election] campaign."[55] Perhaps not surprisingly, by April 2014 the

Harper government indicated no final decision on the purchase would be made until after the next federal election in 2015.

The Conservatives' deficit dilemma eventually forced them to make cuts to the departmental budget as well, including roughly $500 million in 2012–13 and $1 billion in 2013–14. According to the minister, the cuts would affect civilian support staff, government contractors, and reservists, and be accomplished as much as possible by attrition. However, union spokespersons noted that, without civilian support staff, many frontline activities could not be sustained. Moreover, a plan by Peter MacKay to merge headquarters and operational commands immediately faced resistance from senior command accustomed to the structure that had been introduced by General Rick Hillier during a period of campaigns abroad.

Over time more problems emerged. One leaked memo from the head of the armed forces in Ontario, Brig. Gen. Omer Lavoie, explained that his position was "somewhat unstable," because he was being forced to lay off civilian staff in accordance with announced cuts, only to be obliged to rehire them due to critical skills shortages. "We are losing valuable skill sets or complete core services which are necessary to support our mandate," he warned.[56] By October 2013, some 1,100 civilian jobs had been eliminated by DND. Another ninety frontline jobs at a maintenance depot in Montreal were slated for cuts, despite the government's earlier assurances that only "backroom, administrative jobs" would be affected. The situation did not escape the notice of NATO allies. A report in the British *Economist* magazine noted that the Canada First blueprint had described the Canadian military as "Strong, proud, and ready," but concluded "the third is now in doubt."[57]

Other efforts to find "efficiencies" in departmental spending led to unintended consequences. For example, government spending on military equipment traditionally had been seen as a way of ensuring jobs and pumping money into the domestic economy. As a number of military analysts noted, this approach "cut across party lines over the years regardless of which party was in power." But the government's abrupt and seemingly ad hoc decision to pull out of two NATO aerial-surveillance programs, in order to save $90 million annually, was in direct conflict with that policy. Reports indicated Canadian high-tech industries had received nearly $150 million annually in service and maintenance contracts related to the two programs, but would be unable to bid on further work, or renew existing contracts, once the government withdrew from the programs. Liberal defence critic John McKay noted that Canada had participated in the programs for nearly twenty years, and had taken a leadership role in their utilization in the Libyan campaign. A Canadian was also in charge of the operation in Germany. "The way this government seems to be going about this is slapdash," McKay said. "Particularly when you consider that in other areas it has billions of dollars in unspent budget funds."[58]

More serious still was the government's dismissive attitude towards individual members of the armed forces. This became increasingly clear over time, as fiscal restraint imposed more conditions on the department. Early signs of trouble included a decision to eliminate "danger pay" for some categories of personnel serving in Afghanistan, although this move was quickly reversed by the minister after a public outcry, and after he had blamed the whole incident on the military.[59] But the minister did not change his mind about another controversial decision related to the 2012 cutbacks. Attempting to avoid "frontline" layoffs, the defence department was planning to cut the number of medical personnel involved in treating post-traumatic stress disorder (PTSD) and in suicide prevention. The minister stood firm in supporting that decision, despite a leaked memo from senior officers at CFB Petawawa – the very base at which Harper had made his appearance to commend the troops for their service only a few years earlier – stating that "emotionally damaged Afghanistan war veterans at the base [were] being neglected by a mental health treatment system already in crisis."[60] In 2012 the number of reported suicides by war veterans had increased to twelve, with another eleven known attempts, although experts stated that the actual number of attempts was likely much higher. By 2013, the situation had become sufficiently serious to warrant personal statements by the Chief of the Defence Staff, General Thomas Lawson, and the Governor General.

Meanwhile veterans had been criticizing the government for some time for a variety of other policy decisions that they argued left them isolated, impoverished, and forgotten. Chief among these was the New Veterans Charter (NVC), introduced by the Harper government in 2006 to replace the existing system of a pension for life for disabled veterans. Veterans Ombudsman Guy Parent had repeatedly said the new system, which provided a one-time-only lump sum, would leave most of the recipients in poverty in their old age. A class-action suit was filed by a group of disabled veterans. The Canadian Legion described the government's attitude as "reprehensible" and accused them of "trying to shed a decades-old commitment to troops who defend the country ... they have a moral obligation."[61] In addition, the department had begun discharging some disabled veterans from the service involuntarily, before they reached the ten-year mark, which meant they would not receive any pension or lump-sum payment at all. Adding insult to injury, only veterans whose income was lower than $12,000 annually would receive assistance from a veterans' burial fund.

Meanwhile, Veterans Affairs offices in nine communities across the country were being closed as a cost-cutting measure. Internal documents obtained by media sources indicated that senior management in the department was seriously concerned about the impact of the closures, the result of cuts that meant a loss of eight hundred employees. "Units will need to look at what they can do differently, and what they can stop doing," one memo declared, while another argued the department and its clients would need to rely heavily on automated, self-serve facilities.[62] Isolated protests over the cuts were followed by a spectacular public-relations disaster for the Conservatives when Veterans Affairs Minister Julian Fantino dismissed a veterans' delegation that had travelled to Ottawa to meet with him, and he continued to defend the cuts as well as his own performance, suggesting that many veterans were taking advantage of the "generous" system in place. Calling the minister "disrespectful," outraged veterans groups called for his resignation, but to no avail.

The "nickel and diming" of veterans was roundly criticized by the Canadian Legion as well, and in November 2013 silent protests were held at Remembrance Day ceremonies across the country. Given the important role that the Harper government expected the armed forces to play in developing the Conservative image, this disconnect between rhetoric and reality was particularly surprising. For once Stephen Harper's ability to impose pragmatic solutions over ideology appeared to have backfired, and was even costing the government critical support with their base.

More importantly, like their family-values and tough-on-crime agendas and their punitive approach to immigration, the Conservatives' policies towards veterans were drawing enough negative attention among the general public that it was increasingly likely a future government would reverse their decisions. Since those decisions that did not result from spending cuts were the result of changes to regulations or ordinary legislation, a future government could in fact change course relatively quickly, particularly if it chose to follow the precedent set by the Harper government and make use of omnibus legislation.

8

Taking a Stand: The Foreign-Policy Agenda

I don't know all the facts on Iraq, but I think we should work closely with the Americans.

Stephen Harper, 2002

There are, after all, a lot more votes in being anti-Israel than in taking a stand. But as long as I am prime minister ... Canada will take that stand, whatever the cost.

Stephen Harper, 8 November 2010

Canada's principled foreign policy is not for sale for a UN Security Council seat.

Minister of Foreign Affairs John Baird, May 2013

Foreign policy has rarely been an important issue in Canadian election campaigns, unlike the United States. One reason for this difference has been the engagement of American troops in a series of armed conflicts after the Second World War, while Canada pursued a peacekeeping role through the United Nations. Another is the significant difference between the two countries in terms of their sheer size and clout on the world stage. America was the Western world's champion during the Cold War years, and assumed the mantle of only remaining superpower after the fall of the Iron Curtain, while Canada followed a more modest path as middle power.

Not surprisingly, American presidents were often preoccupied with events far from home. Kennedy's travails with Cuba, Nixon's trip to China, Reagan's "Evil Empire" theme and mining of harbours in Nicaragua, Carter's success brokering the Camp David accords and failed Desert Storm rescue are all hallmarks of their time in office. More recently, newly elected President Barack Obama received a Nobel Prize for his efforts to achieve a settlement in the Middle East. The United States, quite simply, has been expected to take a leadership role in the world, and American voters have evaluated their presidential candidates accordingly.

Canada's leaders, meanwhile, always recognized their limited capacity to influence international events. Canadian prime ministers tended to focus on peacekeeping, democratic development, and human rights. Nevertheless, the country traditionally punched above its weight through their proactive pursuit of compromise and negotiation. From Lester Pearson's Nobel Prize for his role in settling the Suez Crisis to Brian Mulroney's role through the Commonwealth in ending apartheid in South Africa and Jean Chrétien's role in establishing the UN Convention on Land Mines and the International Criminal Court, Canada's "soft power" approach was widely recognized and appreciated. For many, this country was the "honest broker," whom both sides would trust in negotiations to end disputes. Canada was also widely respected for its contributions to the United Nations, as a founding member and seventh-largest contributor, its increasing role as a foreign-aid donor, particularly in Africa, and its even-handed approach to the Middle East.

However, while Canadians may have appreciated these efforts, they did not normally consider foreign affairs when selecting their party leaders or prime ministers. As a result, mainstream political parties usually made only a passing reference to those issues in their platforms. The Reform/Alliance party also made little mention of foreign policy under Preston Manning and Stockwell Day, not least because they, unlike their counterparts in the major parties, had little or no experience with the world outside North America.

This situation changed abruptly with the election of Stephen Harper as leader of the Alliance Party and then of the new Conservative Party of Canada. Although Harper too had travelled very little, he had firm views on foreign-policy issues. He served notice in his 2003 Civitas speech that a new era in Canadian foreign and defence policy would begin the moment his party formed a government. The era of compromise and accommodation would be over, and a new era of "hard power" would take its place, based on conservative values. As he told his audience, "Conservatives must take the moral stand, with our allies, in favour of the fundamental values of our society, including democracy, free enterprise, and individual freedom. This moral stand should not just give us the right to stand with our allies, but the duty to do so and the responsibility to put 'hard power' behind our international commitments."[1]

Stephen Harper's determination to see Canada play a more aggressive role on the world stage was evident long before he became prime minister. In 2003, for example, a furious Harper wrote an article in the *Wall Street Journal* denouncing the Chrétien government's refusal to participate in the American-led Iraq invasion. Later he told a reporter "We should have been there shoulder to shoulder with our allies" and was forced to apologize in the House of Commons for calling the Liberal defence minister, John McCallum, an "idiot" for not supporting the war effort.

Harper's hawkish stance was accompanied by a deep-seated mistrust of a variety of multilateral organizations in which Canada had long been a member, including the United Nations. As he remarked quite candidly in his 1997 speech to the right-wing American Council for National Policy, "many Canadians fancy [Canada] as some kind of a third force ... that's where you get the strong support for the United Nations. Canada contributes a great deal to the UN relatively, and takes a great deal of pride over always being praised by UN bodies. This distresses conservatives like myself quite profoundly."

The actions of Harper's government have been remarkably consistent in demonstrating disdain for bodies such as the United Nations, which is viewed as irrelevant and inefficient, and which his foreign affairs minister, John Baird, once described as a "gabfest for dictators." They have also demonstrated a relentlessly aggressive approach to foreign policy, characterized by blunt talk, snap decisions, and very little interest in traditional diplomacy. In fact, diplomacy is clearly seen as yet another morally bankrupt liberal construct, which they have replaced with "principled" policy decisions.

This dramatic about-face in Canada's foreign policy has been widely remarked upon by Canada's allies and enemies alike, with negative consequences. The changes are so significant that former Progressive Conservative prime minister Joe Clark, who later served as Brian Mulroney's minister of foreign affairs, was moved to write a scathing critique. Clark's book *How We Lead* was widely viewed as a direct rebuke of Harper and his government's rejection of traditional Canadian foreign-policy objectives.

Yet the vast majority of ordinary Canadians remain largely ignorant of the major shift that has taken place in the country's policy stance and international reputation. According to numerous public-opinion polls, Canadians continue to support peacekeeping, development assistance, and efforts to reduce global warming, and are surprisingly uninformed about many of the federal government's diametrically opposed policy positions. As mentioned earlier, more than two years after Canada pulled out of the Kyoto Accord, nearly 60 per cent of Canadians were still unaware of this move. This lack of awareness has played into the Conservatives' hands, allowing them far more room to express their ideological preferences than has been possible in domestic policy, and eliminating much of the need for pragmatic compromise. The result has been unrestricted conservative rhetoric and deeds, and nowhere more so than in their approach to the Middle East, a key concern of the religious right.

TAKING "PRINCIPLED" POLICY STANDS

One of the first and most obvious ways the Harper Conservatives demonstrated their commitment to "doing the right thing," regardless of the cost, was in their stand on the Middle East. Historically, both Liberal and Progressive Conservative governments had supported Israel, while at the same time promoting peaceful efforts by Palestinians to obtain their own state. Both parties had also been willing to criticize both sides when necessary. As a result, Harper's unequivocal support for the state of Israel, and insensitivity to Palestinian concerns, marked an abrupt end to more than fifty years of Canadian strategy in the region. Instead of the balanced approach, which stood Canada in good stead with both sides in the conflict, the country quickly became a pariah in the Arab world and a marginalized non-player at the United Nations.

While Harper's long-standing support for Israel could be traced at least in part to his evangelical Christian roots and his evangelical core supporters,[2] Baird had often admitted that he was not a religious man. His views, he declared, were based on conservative values. "In this region there is only one liberal democracy, only one place that values and respects democracy, human rights, and the rule of law," he told the *Jerusalem Post*, "and that is our ally Israel." As one veteran journalist explained, "Mr. Baird disdains the moral relativism that, he believes, often equates Israel with some of its enemies."[3] Baird confirmed this explanation by repeatedly recounting a story from his time in Ottawa in the 1990s as a young aide to an earlier Conservative foreign affairs minister, Perrin Beatty. According to Baird, he tired of the daily briefings on Israel by a senior bureaucrat. "He told me it's not easy to tell the black hats from the white hats, so we keep quiet," Baird told his audience. "I took a pad of paper and drew a white hat on one side and a black hat on the other, and under the white hat I wrote 'Israel' and under the black hat I wrote 'Hezbollah' ... Beside Israel I wrote democracy and 'our friend' and beside Hezbollah I wrote 'global terrorism' and 'our enemy.'"[4]

The Conservatives soon had a chance to put this theory into practice. Only months after they were elected in 2006 the Israel–Lebanon conflict broke out. Harper referred to Israel's "right to defend itself" and described its subsequent invasion of Lebanon as a "measured response" to Hezbollah incursions. Others were less sanguine, particularly as civilian casualties mounted in Lebanon. Interestingly, the Middle East appeared to be one region which caught the attention of Canadians. Public-opinion polling by the Strategic Council found that Harper's unqualified support for Israel was unpopular with many. Nationally some 45 per cent thought the government's support was too uncritical, while that number rose to 61 per cent in Quebec. Nevertheless, Harper told reporters that he believed his position was "in tune" with Canadians, and that he would be maintaining it. "I think the position we have, properly understood, is exactly the position of Canadians," he said.[5]

The same year the Harper government cut funding to the Palestinian Authority (PA) due to the electoral victory of Hamas, which had been defined as a terrorist organization by Canada. Indeed, Harper's view of Hamas and its Lebanese counterpart, Hezbollah, was made crystal clear in an interview in which he stressed that both groups refused to recognize Israel's right to exist. "Hezbollah's objective is violence," he noted, declaring that Canada would be there to defend Israel if necessary. "Hezbollah believes that through violence it can create, it can bring about the destruction of Israel. Violence will not bring about the destruction of Israel."[6]

The following year the government's position appeared to moderate slightly when Foreign Affairs Minister Peter MacKay actually met with Palestinian leaders on a visit to the region. In addition, MacKay questioned Israeli prime minister Ehud Olmert about the wall Israel had constructed between that country and the PA, and underlined his hope that it would not become a permanent fixture. But MacKay was replaced after barely a year by a series of three ineffective and equally briefly serving ministers (Maxime Bernier, David Emerson, and Lawrence Cannon), during which time Stephen Harper effectively acted as his own Minister of Foreign Affairs. Only with the appointment of John Baird in 2011 did the department acquire a strong voice at the helm, and he not only shared Harper's views but expanded on them. As mentioned, according to several sources, Baird even instructed his bureaucrats to refrain from providing him with briefing notes on the Middle East file, since he and his government had already made up their minds on that issue.[7]

Perhaps one of Baird's most surprising moves was to travel to Israel for an entire week of meetings, accompanied by Rabbi Chaim Mendelsohn, the director of public affairs for an ultra-orthodox Hasidic movement known as Chabad. Based in Ottawa, the group was known for its firm position that there should be no "land for peace" agreement or negotiations based on Israel's 1967 boundaries, two points which formed the very basis of virtually all recent plans put forward to settle the Middle East question. Queried about his choice of travelling companion, Baird declared Canada's position was "all about values." Baird's effusive praise and support for Israel in a subsequent dinner speech led Israeli finance minister, Yuval Steinitz, to jest that Canada "is an even better friend to Israel than Israel."[8]

During the visit, Baird deliberately went to the West Bank with his colleague, Finance Minister Jim Flaherty, to discourage the PA from its campaign to obtain recognition as a state at the United Nations. In a good cop–bad cop routine, Flaherty offered a carrot to his counterpart, Jihad al-Wazir, noting that the free-trade agreement Canada had signed with Israel could offer financial benefits to the PA. Meanwhile Baird's public comments after meeting with President Mahmoud Abbas and Foreign Minister Riad al-Malik took "a harder line than any of Canada's allies," including the United States. Baird repeatedly described the Palestinians' efforts as "profoundly wrong" and emphasized that negotiations with Israel were a primary step toward eventual statehood.[9] One veteran Canadian observer described Baird's comments as "not simply conservative," but "reckless" and "dangerous."[10]

Baird responded to criticism by suggesting Canadians supported his position, despite a major *Globe and Mail*/Environics poll that found 36 per cent of Canadians supported the Palestinians' request for statehood and 53 per cent said they had no opinion. His comment was likely based on a separate question that found fully 48 per cent of Canadians believed the government's policy on the Israel–Palestine question "strikes the right balance." For many observers, this apparent contradiction reflected a lack of knowledge of the changes made under Harper. Another argued "most Canadians turn off. It's complicated and intractable in their eyes and ... they don't see a white hat."[11]

Baird was so determined to take a stand against PA state recognition that he travelled to New York in November 2011 to personally vote against the motion. But the United Nations General Assembly overwhelmingly passed it, approving the PA as a "non-member observer state." Canada was one of only eight countries other than Israel to vote against the motion, including Palau, Nauru, the Marshall Islands, and Micronesia, while allies such as Britain and Australia abstained.

The next year the Conservatives took a similar hard line on the question of Iran. In March 2012, Israeli prime minister Benjamin Netanyahu visited Canada to convey his growing concerns over Iran's nuclear capacity. Soon Canada's rhetoric was more extreme than any of Israel's other allies, including the United States. In September, when Stephen Harper was in New York to receive a World Statesman of the Year Award from the Appeal of Conscience Foundation (established by a prominent American rabbi), he delivered a decidedly unstatesmanlike speech. He described Iran as a country "where evil dominates" and its Islamic regime as a "truly malevolent ideology." He also referred to its human-rights record as "appalling" and urged those present not to "shrink from recognizing evil in the world for what it is."[12]

By November 2012, Canada had closed its embassy in Iran, cutting off diplomatic relations and expelling all remaining Iranian diplomats from Canada. "Canada views the government of Iran as the most significant threat to global peace and security in the world today," Baird said.[13] Observers noted that his American counterpart, Hillary Clinton, had been far more measured in her statements about Iran, and did not take the same actions as Canada diplomatically. Harper even appeared to support Israel's threats of a first strike against Iran, while Clinton and President Obama were consistently pressuring Israel to exercise restraint and working through third parties to deter Iran's efforts. (A year later, those efforts had borne fruit when Obama announced Iran's agreement to disband its most advanced nuclear facilities, but Baird remained publicly skeptical and adamantly critical of the regime, despite elections there which saw a moderate win the presidency.)

Meanwhile Baird had once again come out swinging in defence of Israel. In September 2012, when a rocket-and-missile campaign was launched by Hamas in an effort to stop further Israeli settlements on the West Bank, Israel retaliated with incursions into Gaza. Baird delivered a resounding defence of Israel in a speech at the Jewish National Fund's Negev Dinner, where he was the guest of honour. Blaming the entire conflict on Hamas and the Palestinians, Baird declared, "Canada ... stands by Israel. True friends are measured by whether they are there for you when you need them most."[14] The speech echoed one Baird had recently given at the United Nations, which he allegedly wrote himself, full of fiery rhetoric and touching only briefly on the subject at hand, namely the settlements Israel was developing in disputed territory.

Many academics and retired diplomats disagreed with the Harper government's approach, and they were becoming increasingly vocal in their dissent. One such critic was former ambassador Michael Bell, who had spent seven years heading the Canadian embassy in Israel. Bell argued that "trust is the most essential thing needed to bring Palestinians and Israelis together to resolve the conflict. In my experience one has to have a certain amount of credibility and be viewed as legitimate by both players," something he said Canada now lacked.[15] The criticism was put more bluntly by another former diplomat, Gar Pardy. "War does not need cheerleaders, especially wars in the Middle East. Yet this has been the essence of Canadian policy in the region for the last six years." His views were reinforced by one expert observer who summarized Baird's "simplistic, naïve" speech as "Israel Right, Others Wrong."[16]

Not surprisingly, the Canadian stance was not appreciated by the Palestinians. Senior PA officials warned publicly of "consequences" for Canada. At a meeting of the Arab League in December 2012, the PA asked member states to consider reprisals as well. The PA's chief negotiator, Saeb Erekat, argued that voting against the UN member-state motion was one thing, but Canada's vehement public opposition was another, and simply too extreme. As he told delegates, "I believe this government is more Israeli than the Israelis, more settler than the settlers. I think they have disqualified themselves from playing any role in the Middle East peace process."[17]

After a hurried meeting with Canadian diplomats posted in the region, Baird initially appeared to soften his stance, backing away from an initial pledge to consider "all available next steps," including the complete withdrawal of financial aid. But in March 2013, on yet another visit to Israel, Baird met with Justice Minister Tzipi Livni in her office in East Jerusalem. This marked a significant deviation from established policy, since Canadian officials had refused to cross into that area because it was viewed as "occupied" territory by both the PA and the UN. Predictably, the PA described the move as setting a "dangerous precedent." Baird's response was equally predictable. "Where I have coffee with someone is irrelevant," he declared. "I'm just not interested in getting into the semantic argument about whether you have a meeting with one person on one side of the street or the other."[18]

One repercussion of Canada's hardline approach emerged in May 2013, when the state of Qatar launched a surprise bid to move the headquarters of the International Civil Aviation Organization (ICAO) to Doha. The organization, which had been situated in Montreal since its inception in 1947, employed more than five hundred people and contributed more than $100 million to the local economy. The move was seen by most observers as a concerted effort by Arab and Muslim countries to embarrass Canada and the Harper government. A resolution passed unanimously in the House of Commons calling for the ICAO to remain in Montreal, but NDP critic Ève Péclet left no doubt as to her assessment of the situation. "Canada is now paying the price for repeated errors in the government's foreign policy," she said. "Qatar is benefiting from the Conservatives' lack of credibility on the international scene." The government launched a vigorous campaign and eventually succeeded in retaining the site in Montreal, but the damage to Canada's reputation was done. Nor was it helped when Baird made several heated accusations about Qatar and issued a statement in which he said "this government will not apologize for promoting a principled foreign policy."[19]

Meanwhile Harper announced in late 2013 that in 2014 he would be visiting Israel for the first time. The announcement was made at the annual Negev Dinner, where this time it was Harper who was the guest of honour, described as someone who took the high ground in debates, "an extraordinary leader who has raised awareness in the international fight against anti-Semitism."[20]

TAKING THE MORAL HIGH GROUND

The Middle East may have been the most obvious example of Stephen Harper's morality-based approach to foreign policy, but it was hardly the only one. One of the earliest examples involved China, where Harper was being urged to develop closer relations to benefit from its growing economy. On his trip to Hanoi for the APEC Summit in 2006, Harper was initially refused a face-to-face meeting with Chinese president Hu Jintao, allegedly because the Chinese had insisted the discussion be limited to trade, with no mention of human rights, and Harper had demurred. Ignoring harried Canadian officials who were trying to paper over the discord, Harper famously told reporters, "I don't think Canadians want us to sell out important Canadian values, our belief in democracy, freedom, and human rights. They don't want us to sell that out to the almighty dollar."[21]

Liberal leadership contender Michael Ignatieff immediately criticized Harper for what he termed "megaphone diplomacy" and told reporters "Mr Harper, I think, believes you can go to one of the greatest civilizations on earth, a superpower of the twentieth century, and give them a little lecture on human rights." Instead, Ignatieff argued, "the best way for Canada to raise those concerns is to get in a room with the Chinese president and say 'Here are the files, here are the issues where we have specific disagreements with you; how can we work to get these things resolved?' [It] doesn't mean you don't stand for your values but you don't engage in megaphone diplomacy. It just doesn't work with the Chinese."[22] In the end, it would be five years before Harper returned to China, having been on the receiving end of several embarrassing tit-for-tat slights from the Chinese government in the interim, while Canadian businesses yearned for the return of Jean Chrétien's trade missions.

The Harper government took similar "righteous" stands on a number of lesser issues as well, further isolating Canada from many of its allies and rapidly decreasing its standing at the United Nations and other multilateral organizations. In October 2012, for example,

Harper attended the annual Leaders' Summit of La Francophonie in the Democratic Republic of Congo, even though he said he had "grave concerns" about human-rights violations in the country and "would express those concerns very clearly" in the meeting. Interviewed by reporters before leaving at the end of the summit, Harper said he hoped "that in the future, La Francophonie and other major organizations will decide to hold a summit only in countries with democratic standards."[23] Observers were quick to note that such standards would eliminate many if not most of the countries who were member states.

Another striking example of moral indignation was Harper's decision to boycott the biannual Commonwealth Heads of Government meeting in Sri Lanka in November 2013. Harper decried "serious violations of human rights and international humanitarian standards during and after the civil war," and concluded there had been "no improvement" in the four years since the war ended. He also hinted that the government might cut off its funding to the organization. Then he referred to "overwhelming opposition" domestically to his attendance at the meeting. This surprising claim led some to conclude that the importance of the Tamil community in Toronto-area electoral ridings may have played a role in the decision. In any event, the move once again placed Canada offside with most of its allies. New Zealand prime minister John Key told reporters "[Harper] knows our position. It is rock solid. We will be going," while Australian prime minister Tony Abbott criticized Harper's decision as a failure of diplomacy. "You don't make new friends by rubbishing old friends," he said.[24]

This moralistic approach to foreign policy continued in 2014, when Harper delivered an election-campaign-style speech to Conservative supporters in Ottawa on 15 September, to mark the return of parliament from its summer break. In that speech Harper described the world as a "dangerous place," and defended his decision to send troops to Iraq to combat the Islamic State (ISIL) fundamentalists who had recently beheaded several western hostages. "We know their ideology is not the result of social exclusion or other so-called root causes," Harper said, reminding listeners of his earlier accusation about Justin Trudeau's response to the Boston Marathon bombings. Then, sounding much like Ronald Regan railing against the "evil empire" of Russian communism, Harper declared that the ISIL is "evil, vile, and must be unambiguously opposed."

DELIVERING LECTURES

The Harper government's rejection of traditional diplomacy soon became a well-known fact of life in international circles, but the prime minister's tendency to lecture friends and enemies alike was something for which few were prepared. As the new man on the stage, many of the world's leaders expected Harper to take a back seat to more experienced individuals until he had a chance to learn the ropes. This was not to be. From the outset, Harper did not hesitate to criticize his hosts or colleagues publicly whenever he disagreed with them. And, after his appointment as minister of foreign affairs, John Baird reinforced Harper's behaviour at every possible opportunity.

Nor were the lectures limited to moral issues. Harper was also keen to articulate his conservative views on economic policy. For example, using the setting of the annual meeting of the World Economic Forum in Davos, Switzerland, in early 2012, Harper publicly "admonished" his European counterparts for their overly generous social programs, and their "complacency about economic growth and affordable spending." His minister of state for finance, Ted Menzies, elaborated on this theme. "When you look at Europe right now," he told reporters, "the reason that many of those countries are in the situation they're in ... is unsustainable retirement promises to their citizens."[25] Harper and Menzies then proceeded to announce likely increases to the age of eligibility for Canada's Old Age Security program, despite the reports demonstrating that there was no serious problem in Canada. Meanwhile, in Ottawa, Harper's former parliamentary secretary, Pierre Poilievre, told the House of Commons that "this prime minister will not force hard-working Canadian taxpayers to bail out sumptuous euro welfare-state countries and the wealthy bankers that lend to them."[26] One senior spokesperson for the French government was quoted anonymously as declaring irritably "we have no lessons to learn from Canada."

Less than six months later, Harper placed Canada offside with almost all of the G20 countries. He continued to reject calls for Canadian participation in a special IMF fund related to the European financial crisis, despite the commitments of all other member states except the United States, where President Obama was facing a massive domestic financial crisis and intense Republican opposition to his recovery policies. At the G20 leaders'meeting in Mexico,

Australia announced it would allocate $7 billion, Japan $60 billion, and even Saudi Arabia pledged $15 billion. Harper remained adamant that Canada would not participate, but he did not stop there, telling reporters "Europe is one of the wealthiest parts of the planet. We would hope it doesn't get to the stage where the rest of the world has to rescue Europe."[27]

Then he added fuel to the fire by declaring that the EU should get its act together and pursue deeper financial integration as quickly as possible. That message was reiterated by Finance Minister Jim Flaherty at a G7 meeting with his counterparts, when he declared that the "weakened debt-fighting resolve" of European nations was "mistaken."[28] During an interview with CBC anchor Peter Mansbridge, Harper went further. "I don't want to sound alarmist here," he said, "but we are running out of runway." Asked to elaborate, he added, "In terms of the structure of the euro-zone and in terms of addressing some of their problems, we need to see the broader game plan … We can't just say 'Let's wait until after the Greek election, … In a time of crisis, to sustain the euro they have to do a much bigger job of integration than they have done until this point."[29]

European leaders were quick to express their unhappiness with Harper's uninvited interventions. Germany's ambassador to Canada told reporters, "We find it indeed somewhat irritating and somewhat disappointing that Canada is so adamantly refusing to help. A major problem in the euro-zone world would have major negative economic repercussions for Canada, so solidarity is needed … We still hope Canada would be ready to contribute, like so many of our other partners."[30]

But the Harper Conservatives did not change their minds, nor did they soften their aggressive language. In London, just days before meeting with newly elected French president François Hollande, a well-known opponent of the strict austerity measures Harper proposed to deal with the euro crisis, he declared, "I know that in many countries there is a considerable debate between austerity and growth. Let me tell you, this is a false dichotomy. You need good measures of both."[31] The fact that Harper was attempting to secure a Canada–EU trade agreement at the time, and that Hollande was already on record as opposing key elements of that deal, evidently did not deter Harper from expressing his views.

However those comments paled in comparison with Harper's blunt public statements a few days later, as he prepared to attend a

G8 summit in Northern Ireland. There, Harper launched a broadside against Russian president Vladimir Putin over his support for the regime of Syrian president Bashar al-Assad. Arguing that the other G8 member states would not be able to influence Mr Putin, who alone among them was supporting the Syrian regime, Harper first said they should ignore the issue at their meeting and let NATO take the lead, something which few would have found surprising. However, Harper continued by insulting Putin and Russia directly. "I don't think we should fool ourselves," he declared. "This is the G7 plus one. That's what this is. G7 plus one. Mr Putin and his government are supporting the thugs of the Assad regime for their own reasons that I do not think are justifiable, and Mr Putin knows my views on that."[32]

With the emergence of the Crimean crisis in the Ukraine in 2014, Harper and Baird upped the ante by not only criticizing Putin repeatedly but by sending six CF-18 fighter jets and accompanying military personnel to a NATO base in Eastern Europe. Announcing the decision on April 14, Harper declared, "I believe this to be a long-term serious threat to global peace and security and we're always prepared to work with our allies in NATO and elsewhere to try and bring whatever stability we can to the situation."[33]

The Harper government's approach was made manifest with the creation of the Office of Religious Freedom in 2012. Fulfilling a commitment made in the Conservatives' 2011 platform, its stated purpose was to "publicly criticize regimes that mistreat religious minorities."[34] The controversial move saw the government allocate some $5 million in funding for the agency, and create a place for it in the Department of Foreign Affairs, with its own ambassador and staff of five.

Some opponents argued that it blurred the lines on the separation of church and state, and also that it was inappropriate to focus on protecting individuals from religious persecution as opposed to the broader issue of protecting everyone from all human-rights violations. Others argued it was a crass political move to placate the Conservatives' evangelical support base in Canada, and would be used to prevent the persecution of evangelical Christians on missions abroad. Former Liberal leader Michael Ignatieff declared that the office would only be acceptable if it defended all religions, and "not just those that are bothering domestic constituencies." Meanwhile, Carleton University political scientist Jonathan Malloy provided a lengthy analysis linking the office with the Christian right's influence on the Conservatives in a piece entitled "Hidden in Plain Sight: The Tory Evangelical Factor."[35]

The government encountered considerable difficulty filling the post of ambassador, a source of some embarrassment to them. Public servants in the department were considered "not strong enough" on the issue of religious freedom, while those involved in the evangelical community were ruled out as either too well-known for particular stands or too biased in favour of their brand of Christianity. In the end, it took the Conservatives nearly two years before they finally chose Andrew Bennett as the first Ambassador of Religious Freedom. Bennett was a former public servant who was teaching the history of Christianity and serving as volunteer dean at an obscure liberal-arts college in Ottawa. With a PhD from Edinburgh University and community service as a sub-deacon and cantor with the Holy Cross Eastern Catholic Chaplaincy in Ottawa, Bennett was a pragmatic choice who possessed sufficient academic credibility along with his religious conviction.

Still, the office maintained a relatively low profile in its first years in operation. Although the ambassador did indeed criticize various regimes, he was scrupulous in condemning acts of persecution and violence against any and all religious groups. But his even-handed approach to the post, which some observers attributed to the steadying hand of veteran diplomats in the department, was not reflected in the views of the Harper government towards other international organizations, and especially the United Nations.

MARGINALIZING CANADA AT THE UNITED NATIONS

Stephen Harper's blunt talk and John Baird's over-the-top rhetoric found their ultimate expression in their attitudes towards the United Nations. As a result, an unusual behavioural pattern emerged, best characterized as strident criticism combined with studied disinterest.

In the fall of 2006, for example, Harper attended the opening of the General Assembly in New York, an annual occasion for national leaders from all member states to address the gathering. His speech, however, was not typical. The bulk of his allotted time was spent congratulating Canada for its role in the armed conflict in Afghanistan. Then, after a brief mention of the humanitarian crisis in Haiti, he turned his attention to the internal administration of the United Nations. Expressing serious concerns about the legitimacy of the new Human Rights Council, he pointedly asked, "And what will be done about management reform?" Then he told the assembled members "Earlier this year, Canada's New Government was given a mandate to make our national government more accountable and more effective, to ensure taxpayers get full value for their money, and to pursue a clear, focused agenda that produces tangible results." Warming to his topic, he declared "the United Nations should accept nothing less. This organization must become more accountable and more effective. Management reform must continue, and at an accelerated pace."[36]

Perhaps because the room was half-empty when he delivered this address, but more likely because of his preconceived notion that the UN was both ineffective and weak-kneed, he decided to shun the international body in future, in favour of organizations he considered worthwhile. Harper did not speak to the General Assembly again until 2010, when Canada was seeking a seat on the UN Security Council. Nevertheless his officials attempted to compare his attendance record favourably to that of previous prime ministers, noting that Brian Mulroney had spoken to the Assembly only three times in eight years. (Harper spoke twice in eight years.) But Jean Chrétien addressed the body five times in slightly less than ten years, and Paul Martin did so both years his government was in power. Harper's critics also pointed out that the dates of the annual UN meetings sometimes conflicted with other important commitments of those earlier prime ministers. But Harper was actually in New York at the time of the meetings on several occasions, making his absence far more obvious and more egregious. In 2009, for example, he had been travelling in the US for several days, but chose to leave New York on the morning of Barack Obama's address to the Assembly. Instead, he visited a newly opened Tim Horton's franchise in Oakville, a decision that led to considerable controversy.

This pattern was repeated in 2012. Harper was in New York to receive the Statesman of the Year Award at an event the evening before. There he rejected the "typical" diplomacy of the UN, which requires countries to "court every dictator with a vote or ... just going along with every emerging international consensus, no matter how self-evidently wrong-headed." The following day he remained in the city, but chose to meet with businessmen, including Bill Gates, instead of speaking to the Assembly. Harper left that task to John

Baird, who delivered one of the most scathing rebukes ever heard there. Baird criticized what he saw as the "endless, fruitless, inward-looking exercises" and "preoccupation with procedure and process over substance and results." He denounced the Security Council's failure to impose binding sanctions on the Syrian regime, and the failure of many of the member states to protect human rights for their citizens. He also warned that, in future, Canada would forge ahead on a number of issues with its allies, through NATO or in bilateral treaties.[37]

Harper's snub of the UN, and Baird's attack, were roundly criticized in an opinion piece by Fen Hampson, director of the Global Security Program at the International Centre on Governance Innovation, and Derek Burney, former trade negotiator and Canadian ambassador to the United States. The two wrote that Harper was "turning his back" on the UN, and reversing sixty years of Canadian commitment to the body Canada helped to create. Their views were shared by Roland Paris of the University of Ottawa, who argued that the Harper Conservatives' preference for bilateral discussions, and for dealing only with allies "rather than potential protagonists," was the result of ignorance and fear. "This reliance on high-minded principle is a way of dealing with complexity by simplifying it down to something that's comfortable and less confusing," he said.[38]

Harper repeated the pattern in 2013. He again skipped the General Assembly meeting, even though he was in New York, participating instead on a panel arranged by the Canada–American Business Council, and attending a committee meeting on maternal and child health of a UN subsidiary. This time a group of seventeen former ministers of foreign affairs, diplomats, and academics organized events around the country, calling on Harper to "re-engage" with the United Nations. They also released a booklet entitled "The UN and Canada: What Canada Has Done and Should Be Doing at the UN." One of the articles in the booklet was written by Ian Smillie, a former director of Canadian University Service Overseas (CUSO) and president of an international development consulting firm, who told reporters Canada's reputation was in tatters and "Canada couldn't get elected dogcatcher at the UN today."

This was hardly surprising. Apart from the controversial speeches of Baird, and Harper's deliberate absences, the Conservatives had taken many other actions which devalued the country's image with other UN members. They were increasingly late in paying their dues.

Amazingly, Canada's contribution to peacekeeping had fallen by 2012 to only 56 individuals in a UN force of 83,000. Moreover, Canada had withdrawn from two international conventions, an unprecedented development. In December 2011, as discussed earlier, Canada pulled out of the Kyoto Accord, apparently to avoid financial penalties due to missed targets. Then in March 2013 Canada pulled out of the international Convention on Desertification, making it the only country in the world outside the agreement. This time the decision was taken by cabinet but not formally communicated to the UN authority, and officials were "stunned" when they learned of the move from reporters.[39] Nor did the government elaborate on its reasons.

Later the same year, Harper made it clear that he would not be signing a landmark UN treaty regulating the small-arms trade, a move that astonished many observers who viewed the document as uncontroversial. However in Harper's case the problem was his base support in Canada. Having courted the gun lobby as part of his social-conservative coalition, he was now constrained by their (incorrect) conviction that the treaty would have a negative impact on their ability to import and own guns. The situation was considered so important politically that the president of the Canadian Shooting Sports Association (CSSA), Steve Torino, was accredited by John Baird as an official member of the Canadian delegation to the UN talks about the treaty, while all other NGOs – such as anti-gun lobby Project Ploughshares – were left to pay their own way and attend as observers. Ploughshares senior officer, Ken Epps, told reporters "When Canada goes to the negotiating table, it's doing it exclusively from the perspective of Canadian firearms owners" whose far-fetched concerns were destabilizing the talks.[40] The government's efforts to portray Torino as an expert consultant, unrelated to his role with the CSSA, were seriously undermined when the CSSA sent out a newsletter to its members declaring "Foreign Affairs Minister John Baird, CSSA President John Torino (who serves on Canada's UN delegation) and the rest of the Conservative caucus have our backs as they alone hold back the crushing tide of UN intervention."[41]

Behind the scenes, Canada's position on various UN committees and boards was often unhelpful and sometimes counterproductive. A case in point was the effort by the World Health Organization to produce updated guidelines related to fat, salt, and sugar content in foods, and to the use of alcohol and tobacco. According to one participant, "Canada's position is, at best, persistently ambivalent and, often, energetically opposed to using government regulation in Canada or elsewhere to help limit the economic and health burdens of diseases caused by tobacco, food diet, and alcohol." Likewise British scientist Deborah Cohen, editor of the *British Medical Journal,* told reporters that "Canada has been particularly bullish, even more bullish than the US, in protecting industry. They surprised us because you typically think of Canada as being quite into public health."[42]

Little wonder, then, that Canada failed, and failed dramatically, in its 2010 attempt to secure a rotating seat on the UN Security Council. In the past it had succeeded without difficulty each time it put forward its candidacy, six times – or roughly once per decade. In 2010, however, when Canada was competing with Germany and Portugal for one of the two seats available, it lost the first round to Germany and then, after two rounds of ballots for the remaining seat, it trailed badly behind Portugal. The Harper government announced it was withdrawing its bid.

Undoubtedly one reason for Canada's humiliating defeat was poor preparation. The Harper government failed to take an interest in the issue or participate in a "campaign" for one of the two seats available until far too late in the day, despite repeated urging by bureaucrats. But when Harper did journey to New York in September 2010, to address the General Assembly for only the second time, he made a serious pitch for the post, accompanied by ministers and bureaucrats, as well as Mounties in red serge outfits and bottles of maple syrup for delegates. However his speech did not help matters. He spoke primarily about the "heavy price" Canada was paying as part of the NATO mission to Afghanistan, a choice of topic that surprised many delegates, as did his not-too-subtle digs at the United States for its protectionist trade policies.[43]

Far more important as a factor in the defeat, however, was the damaged state of Canada's international reputation. With European states likely to support at least one of the two other candidates, Canada could count on little support from them for the second seat, after having insulted or lectured most of its leaders. It was therefore even more important for Canada to be able to rely on Third World support from Africa and Asia, areas which would traditionally have come through for the "honest broker" and leader in foreign-aid assistance. However Canada had cut much of its aid to Africa in recent years, and its position on the Middle East had alienated many of the Muslim countries of Africa and Asia.

After the embarrassing debacle, opposition parties and experts criticized Harper for having lost the vote. He in turn criticized Liberal leader Michael Ignatieff, who a week before the vote had commented negatively on Conservative foreign policy. "Mr Ignatieff chose to oppose his own country," Harper's spokesperson, Dimitri Soudas, declared, while Foreign Affairs Minister Lawrence Cannon told reporters "I can say that Michael Ignatieff's statement hurt us."[44] Ignatieff retorted that "the blame game is the sign of a government that is unwilling to accept the lessons of defeat."[45]

After that defeat, all pretence of cooperation with the UN was put aside. When Professor James Anaya, an internationally recognized human-rights expert serving as the UN Special Rapporteur on Aboriginal Peoples, lamented the state of housing on the Attawapiskat reserve in late 2011, the government dismissed his concerns as a "publicity stunt." His subsequent request to visit Canada to observe the situation in various parts of the country met with stony silence for nearly two years. Meanwhile, in another embarrassing first for Canada, the UN Special Rapporteur on the Right to Food targeted Canada for his first investigation of a wealthy nation. Belgian law professor Olivier de Schutter announced that he had selected Canada because of similar concerns over the lack of potable water on aboriginal reserves, the exorbitant cost of food in northern and isolated regions of the country, and the lack of access to nutritional food among those living below the poverty line in major urban centres. All were seen as problems which had been exacerbated by the Harper government's cuts to a variety of social programs and other policies that impeded the fight against poverty.

After tabling his critical report with the United Nations Human Rights Commission in Geneva, de Schutter commented that "Canada, like any other country, is only credible when it preaches human rights to others if it is irreproachable itself." Health Minister Leona Aglukkaq retorted that the rapporteur's report was "one-sided and biased," "ill-informed," and "patronizing," while Immigration Minister Jason Kenney termed it "completely ridiculous." Aglukkaq delivered what she obviously saw as the *coup de grâce* by stating that "implementing this report would have a devastating impact on

Canadians, including a $48-billion tax hike," but she did not elaborate on the source of her numbers.[46]

Appearing before a parliamentary committee in 2013, Foreign Affairs Minister John Baird was asked if Canada would be making another attempt to obtain a Security Council seat when one became available in 2015. A defiant Baird declared that "Canada's principled foreign policy is not for sale for a Security Council seat," and said Canadian efforts to "take a stand" against Syria and Sri Lanka were far more important than "wasting time" on such a campaign.[47] The statement confirmed that Canada was basically washing its hands of the United Nations, and also that it was uninterested in the opinions of those who did not share its views.

Interestingly, his government, so intent on taking stands and exerting moral influence on world affairs, was also inclined to withdraw from Canada's traditional role as a keen supporter of development aid. The apparent contradiction can perhaps best be explained by one aide's comment that Harper was more concerned about "slush funds and Swiss bank accounts," and also wanted to make sure that Canada's prestige and international reputation were enhanced by any such assistance.

SLASHING AND REALIGNING FOREIGN AID

Canada's reputation as a committed member of the foreign-aid community was hard-earned over many administrations, including that of Progressive Conservative prime minister Brian Mulroney. Each placed a different emphasis on the nature of development assistance, but the ideal of Canada as a player in the field remained strong, even when the reality of financial assistance did not always match the rhetoric. The inspiration for a 0.7-per-cent-of-GDP commitment by states in the developed world came from the 1969 report of a United Nations expert commission. That commission was headed by none other than retired Canadian prime minister Lester Pearson. Although no Canadian government has ever reached that level (nor have any other states except the Netherlands), until Harper it had generally maintained a respectable 0.04-per-cent rate, and each successive government had supported the 0.7-per-cent goal as its theoretical objective.

It was under Pearson that the federal government created the Canadian International Development Agency (CIDA), whose first president was Maurice Strong, a future senior UN bureaucrat. Under Pierre Trudeau, the emphasis of Canadian aid was placed on "the poorest of the poor," and focused on Africa and certain countries in Southeast Asia. Under Brian Mulroney, Canada's funding reached its highest level as a percentage of GDP (0.5 per cent), but under his successor Jean Chrétien that level of funding actually declined in the early years, the victim of a serious deficit-reduction exercise. However, with the elimination of the deficit in 1997, Chrétien placed renewed emphasis on Canada's foreign-aid role and dramatically increased the country's level of contributions. He also paid particular attention to Africa, and launched the New Partnership for Africa's Development (NEPAD) program as part of his leadership role as chair of the G8.

By contrast, apart from their ongoing concerns about "wasting money" on ineffective programs that might also be tainted with local corruption, the Conservatives devoted little time or effort to the foreign-aid file in their early years in power. They were the first to abandon the 0.7-per-cent target, and the appointment of such cabinet lightweights as Josée Verner, Bev Oda, and Julian Fantino to the post of minister responsible for the file reinforced the impression that foreign aid was an afterthought in the Conservative agenda.

Nevertheless, in 2007 Harper's government did outline a new priority in selecting recipients of Canadian aid, namely that preference would be given to those countries where Canada could be among the top five donor countries. Verner stated publicly that only a slight increase in existing levels of funding would be necessary in some cases. The declared purpose of this change was to increase Canada's prestige in the recipient countries and enhance its international reputation.[48] This line of thinking set a precedent, and one that was increasingly evident, as large amounts of Canadian aid were funnelled to Afghanistan.[49] In fact, by 2011 Afghanistan was the single largest recipient of Canadian aid, at $200 million.

Also in 2007, while attending a G8 Summit meeting in Germany, Harper told his astonished counterparts that Canada's emphasis would shift from Africa to Latin America. This decision was reinforced in 2009, when another change resulted in CIDA's identification of twenty "core" countries. This move dropped many African countries entirely and added many (wealthier) English-speaking Caribbean countries and countries in Latin America. Significantly, many of the new target countries (such as Peru and Colombia), were also those in which Canada had a vested interest in terms of trade deals and other commercial negotiations.

Behind the scenes, other informal changes in government policy were also taking place. Among the most noteworthy were several controversial decisions to withdraw funding from a number of well-regarded and long-standing non-governmental organizations (NGOs) dealing with foreign aid, including the multi-faith aid group KAIROS, which Immigration Minister Jason Kenney had described as anti-Semitic, because of its aid activities in the Palestinian Authority. At the same time, a study by the Canadian Research Institute on Humanitarian Crises and Aid found that, between 2006 and 2010, religious NGOs had increased their CIDA funding by 42 per cent, while funding for traditional NGO recipients had increased by only 5 per cent. Among the religious groups was an evangelical Christian organization – Crossroads Christian Communications – whose website described homosexuality as a "sin" and a "perversion." It received $550,000 from CIDA to fund projects in Uganda, a country known for virulent anti-gay activities.

Then, in the 2010 federal budget, the Harper government froze all foreign-aid funding for three years. Two years later, even this promise was broken, as they actually cut funding. The Conservatives were desperately searching for ways to reduce spending to balance their books, and foreign aid was considered a "safe" target for cuts, since there were few votes to be gained by being generous donors. CIDA suffered a 7.5-per-cent reduction in funding, and saw three hundred positions cut, while Foreign Affairs lost an additional $170 million earmarked for aid programs. An anonymous source within CIDA indicated that the cuts meant twelve of the world's poorest countries would see their Canadian assistance eliminated entirely. As Liberal senator Colin Kenny, former chair of the Senate Committee on National Security and Defence noted, Canada's contribution level had fallen to 0.31 per cent of GDP. Kenny also noted that David Cameron, British prime minister, was increasing his own country's foreign-aid budget to 0.56-per-cent of GDP at a time when the British economy was in far worse shape than Canada's.[50]

A few months later, International Cooperation Minister Julian Fantino delivered an address to the Economic Club of Canada, in which he announced yet another dramatic shift in Canada's aid policy, making it clear development assistance was now a tool to further the government's economic agenda. Fantino told a receptive business audience that future decisions by CIDA would see it "align itself more closely with the private sector and work more explicitly to promote Canada's interests abroad." The minister specifically referred to Canada's mining sector, and speculated that it might be in the vanguard of the new approach, since the government expected the private sector to drive economic growth in the developing world.[51] Within months it was also learned that $300 million in foreign aid had gone unspent by CIDA the previous year, something experts decried as "additional budget cuts by stealth."

Perhaps inevitably, the March 2013 federal budget announced that CIDA was being disbanded and folded into the department of Foreign Affairs and Trade. Although the government insisted that CIDA's work would continue, most observers believed that foreign aid would now become an incidental appendage to Canada's increased emphasis on international trade. Former CIDA president Maurice Strong argued the drastic changes would not achieve the Conservatives' objective of enhancing Canada's reputation abroad. "It has always been true," he wrote, "that development assistance contributes in various indirect ways to Canada's own economic interest. But making commercial interests the main purpose of our program will undermine its effectiveness, quite apart from its damage to our credibility and influence."[52] After more than eight years in power, the Harper government still believed aggressive measures were superior to diplomacy in getting things done. As former Canadian ambassador Jeremy Kinsman concluded, "This government has no feeling for 'soft power' because it still has little feeling for the world landscape except from the standpoint of Canadian business interests." "Internationally, it believes only in trade promotion and military expeditions like Afghanistan."[53]

DEFENDING FREEDOM AND DEMOCRACY

In fact, one of the first things the Harper government did after taking office was to extend the Canadian mission in Afghanistan to 2009. Then it was extended a second time, to December 2011. The importance Stephen Harper placed on the mission was emphasized when he chose to go to Afghanistan in March 2006 for his first trip abroad as prime minister. Despite his aversion to foreign travel (later confirmed in a Wikileaks memo), he subsequently visited Canadian troops stationed there twice more, in 2007 and 2011.[54] His ministers of defence, Gordon O'Connor and Peter MacKay, did so as well, as did governors general Michaëlle Jean and David Johnston.

Afghanistan was a top priority for Harper in the early years, driven by his desire to change Canadians' image of their country. He would make Canada a world leader in defending freedom and democracy, by force if necessary, rather than simply standing by like the Liberals, wringing their collective hands. In his 2006 speech to the troops, he described Canada's role in Afghanistan as "crucial," and one where "our security concerns, our values and our capabilities come squarely together." He assured them they were contributing to the creation of a new democratic state in place of the old failed state and leading the way in bringing hope and freedom to Afghan citizens and the world. He also told them Canada would not "cut and run" as long as he was prime minister. "You can't lead from the bleachers. I want Canada to be a leader," he said. "Your work is about more than just defending Canada's national interests. Your work is about demonstrating an international leadership role for our country."[55]

But national-security concerns, rather than leadership, were highlighted on his second trip, when he told the troops "terrorism will come home if we don't confront it here." He also placed less emphasis on the groundbreaking role of the mission in terms of democratic development. As time passed, the references to Afghanistan in Harper's speeches at home declined dramatically. By the end of the second extension, he had evidently recognized the harsh reality of mixed results and ongoing conflict, a stark contrast from his earlier expectations. With little evidence of a positive resolution in sight, he declared that, after nearly a decade, there was a finite limit to how much more Canada could be expected to contribute. In the end, fighting troops returned home by late 2011, and a third and final extension to early 2014 was confined to the provision of 950 specialists for a training mission.

Despite the disappointing result in Afghanistan, Harper was keen to participate in a 2011 military expedition to Libya, as part of another allied effort under a UN Security Council Resolution. This time the objective was to protect civilians and Libyan rebels from military attacks by the Gaddafi regime as it fought a bitter civil war against the insurgents. Newly minted foreign affairs minister, John Baird, declared with certainty, "the one thing we can say categorically is that they couldn't be any worse than Col Gaddafi," while

Harper confidently declared Gaddafi "simply won't be able to sustain his grip on the country. He won't last very long."[56] By early March, NATO had taken charge and Canada contributed extensively to that effort. In the end a total of 440 Canadian Forces personnel participated in Operation Mobile, the code name for the Canadian expedition. The RCAF deployed seven CF-18 fighter jets, two Polaris refuelling airplanes, four transport planes, and two maritime patrol aircraft. By the end of May, the CF-18s had flown hundreds of sorties and dropped more than 240 bombs on Libya. There were also unconfirmed reports that special operations were being conducted by the Canadian Joint Task Force 2 (JTF2) in association with Britain's Special Air Service (SAS).

Despite all of these efforts, it became clear that Gaddafi was perversely "lasting" much longer than Harper had expected. At a pre-G8 Summit meeting in Paris on 28 May, the allied leaders unanimously demanded Gaddafi's resignation, and Harper announced that he would ask Parliament for an extension of the mission if this did not come to pass. The extension was approved the following month, first until late September and then until early November, when, with the death of Gaddafi, the NATO mission came to an end. In total, Canadians flew one thousand sorties and dropped seven hundred bombs, contributing more than 10 per cent of the allied total, a record that led Defence Minister Peter MacKay to claim "Canada once again punched above its weight as part of an international coalition. The men and women of the Canadian Forces confirmed their leadership position at NATO and the role they can play in successful international operations."[57]

Harper's enthusiasm for the mission remained strong. He described Canada's involvement as "a great military success" and organized a special ceremony on Parliament Hill in November 2011. Harper and Governor General David Johnston presided over the special tribute to the military in the Canadian Senate, where commanding officer Lieutenant-General Charles Bouchard was awarded the Meritorious Service Cross. "Let no one question whether Canada is prepared to stay the course in the defence of what is right," Harper said. "We believe that in a world where people look for hope and cry out for freedom, those who talk the talk of human rights must from time to time be prepared to likewise walk the walk."[58]

Interestingly, two major public-opinion polls released the following November indicated that Canadians, and young people in particular, were more inclined to view Remembrance Day ceremonies as an occasion to emphasize the need for peace, rather than to highlight famous Canadian battles and victories – a perception at odds with the Harper government's determination to stress such military achievements. Conversely, despite their strong support for military engagements, the Conservatives showed little interest in declaring November 11 a statutory holiday, something polls indicated veterans and ordinary citizens had long viewed as an appropriate symbolic gesture.[59] The principal reason given for Harper's reluctance was the opposition of the business community. This internal party conflict between economic and social-conservative values emerged again on trade policy, where economic interests eventually came to predominate over human rights.

PROTECTING VESTED INTERESTS

When the Conservatives took office in 2006, they identified free trade as a top priority of their economic agenda. However a conflict quickly arose between this objective and their philosophical concern with democratic freedoms. Indeed, as mentioned earlier, when pressured into courting China as part of a trade initiative, Harper had killed any chance of improved relations through his criticism of China's human-rights record. The result was a multi-year standoff, during which the relationship between the two countries was variously described as "chilly" or "non-existent."

This was particularly noteworthy, since Canada under Pierre Trudeau had been among the very first western states to bridge the divide and establish diplomatic relations, an advantage that both Brian Mulroney and Jean Chrétien continued to pursue. With China's economy having vaulted over Japan's to become the second largest in the world, and Canada's dependence on the American economy reaching dangerously high proportions, the severity of the problem for the Conservatives was obvious. Despite this, the situation did not improve for several years. In October 2007 Harper met with the Dalai Lama in Ottawa, resulting in China's angry cancellation of a planned meeting between high-level bureaucrats from the two countries. The following year, Canada threatened to take China to the World Trade Organization (WTO), because China refused to negotiate a tourism deal with Canadian businesses, even though it had similar arrangements with 138 other countries. Then, in April

2008, Harper announced that he would not attend the opening ceremonies of the Beijing Olympics, a move that was considered a direct snub.

Meanwhile his government was feverishly concluding bilateral trade deals with a number of Latin American countries, such as Peru (2008), Colombia (2008), Honduras (2013), and Panama (2013). In addition, deals were negotiated with the European Free Trade Association states (Iceland, Liechtenstein, Norway, and Switzerland), and with Jordan (2012). Yet all of these countries taken together did not represent a significant increase in access for Canadian businesses, or a major boost for the Canadian economy. Critics were also quick to note that many Latin American states could have been censored for human-rights violations as much as China; the major difference appeared to be the fact that they were right-leaning regimes rather than communists. However the government defended its strategy, in part because it was helping to secure Canada's place at the table for the more significant set of free-trade negotiations, the Trans-Pacific Partnership (TPP), a highly controversial and secretive process dominated by the United States, which one noted economist described as "neither free nor fair."[60]

Then in early 2011 the government announced it was increasing its emphasis on Asia, and would be pursuing a new round of meetings and discussions with India, Thailand, and South Korea. But Harper's two-day visit to Thailand in February left many puzzled. Canadian businessmen in Thailand were unable to obtain any meetings with the prime minister, but he met with the head of the Thai national energy company (which had invested heavily in the Alberta oil sands the previous year), and visited a police station and a boxing gym. As economist Eric Reguly of *Report on Business* pointed out, Thailand was Canada's largest trading partner among the ten-member ASEAN group, yet Harper's low-key visit did little to promote trade or speed up negotiations.[61]

The objectives of his trip to India in November 2012 were equally perplexing, but his week-long stay was anything but low-key. From the decision to ship over armoured vehicles for "security reasons," at a cost of more than $1 million, to his stern lecture to Indian prime minister Manmohan Singh about the slow pace of the free-trade negotiations that had been under way for nearly eight years, Harper's visit was widely but negatively reported in India and Canada, particularly as the hoped-for Foreign Investment and Protection

Agreement (FIPA) did not materialize, although side deals on social security and nuclear materials did.

In retrospect, this visit could perhaps have been considered a public-relations success, at least in comparison with Harper's trip to Malaysia in October 2013. A victim of poor planning, Harper's official three-day visit to promote trade was totally overshadowed by the simultaneous visit of Chinese president Xi Jinping. Nevertheless, several Malaysian trade experts argued that "Canada also needs to step up its game." Tang Siew Mun, of the Malaysian Institute of Strategic and International Studies, emphasized that Canada had made claims in recent years that it wanted to focus on Asia. But "it only talks ... when it comes to programs and concrete actions, it is missing ... CIDA was here for many years, but now it is gone and it seems as if Malaysia does not matter anymore."[62]

Meanwhile, the Conservatives had been persuaded that they would have to offer conciliatory gestures towards China in order to make progress there. This was becoming an even more pressing issue as the Chinese economy expanded, to the considerable benefit of western Canada, where exports of lumber and natural resources were producing an economic windfall. In the fall of 2008, Harper was aided by a court decision that allowed the deportation of a wealthy Chinese refugee claimant whom China had accused of massive fraud. Then, in May 2009, Lawrence Cannon, foreign affairs minister, startled observers by stating that Canadians should recognize China had "made progress" on human rights, a move that was noted with approval in Beijing.

Finally, in December 2009, Harper made his first visit to that country. This point was underlined by his host, Premier Wen Jiabao, in his welcome speech. In front of Canadian, Chinese, and international media, Jiabao told Harper "this is your first visit to China and this is the first meeting between the Chinese premier and a Canadian prime minister in more than five years. Five years is too long a time for China–Canada relations, and that's why [you will see] there are comments in the media that your visit should have taken place earlier." A "stone-faced" Harper listened to this thinly veiled criticism without comment. A senior Canadian reporter covering the event noted that "for the premier to embarrass his guest by reminding him of his decision to allow a strong relationship that started in the Trudeau era to deteriorate badly is a highly unusual and pointed breach of domestic protocol."[63]

Nevertheless, the relationship did improve, and by September 2012 Canada had signed a FIPA with China, something that Canadian businesses had long requested. While the Conservatives described the deal as important for protecting the rights of private-sector businesses in both countries, they also made it clear that they did not consider it to be something that required parliamentary approval before it was ratified. They considered it to be a simple commercial agreement, of which thousands already existed internationally. However, critics argued that such a deal was worrisome, not only because it involved China, but because it contained measures to allow secret investor-state tribunals to hear complaints and assess fines, and was to be in force for thirty-one years. Given the Chinese government's control of many Chinese corporations, they added, this deal might also involve a request from the Chinese government for special protection, while Canada would not similarly benefit.

Lobby groups such as the Council of Canadians and LeadNow brought the issue to the public's attention. They noted that Australia had indicated it would reject investor-state tribunals in future economic agreements with developing countries. Within months, hundreds of thousands of Canadians had signed petitions and written letters to their MPs protesting against the FIPA. Opposition to the deal appeared to be strongest in western Canada, leading Harper to delay ratification, although he still did not agree to parliamentary scrutiny of the deal.

As a result, with trade as their stated economic priority and little to show for their efforts after more than five years, the Conservatives put increased emphasis on the Canada-EU deal which had been in negotiations for some time. Throughout 2013, the urgency of signing a deal before the Europeans moved on to negotiations with the United States, heightened the pressure on Harper's government to make concessions on a range of issues, including marketing boards. At the same time, the delays and lack of progress increasingly frustrated Harper. In June he went to Brussels, expecting to sign a deal, but one did not materialize. This was a huge blow to his credibility with the opposition parties, as well as his own caucus, especially when the two sides began trading barbs over who was responsible for the delay.

Finally an agreement in principle was reached in October 2013. Harper described it as even more significant than the Canada-US Free Trade Agreement (FTA), and worth more than $12 billion a year to the Canadian economy. Critics argued it would cost up to 150,000 jobs, and remove Canadian control over vital areas such as pharmaceutical patents and telecommunications. However the devil was in the details, which were not yet finalized. The government originally indicated it would be several months before the actual text was available, but by June of 2014 no deal had been completed. As the EU turned its attention to the United States and the deal it was negotiating with that country, critics increasingly expressed concern that, despite progress, Canada would not follow through on this agreement. And, with the next federal election scheduled for fall 2015, the Conservatives admitted that Canadians might not be able to express their views at the polls, as was the case with the FTA, although they once again noted their government had received a majority in the last election.

Then in March 2014 the Harper government signed their first free-trade deal with an Asian state, South Korea. That deal was widely seen as another positive move, which greatly enhanced export opportunities for agricultural producers – notably beef farmers, salmon fishers, and whisky makers – as well as for liquified natural gas. However, here too it soon transpired that the deal had been announced before detailed negotiations were completed. Several months later, a concrete agreement was still unavailable for scrutiny. Nevertheless, significant concerns were raised by the Ontario-based auto industry, based on what was known through statements by ministers – concerns that Harper cavalierly dismissed out of hand, leading to accusations the deal favoured western Canada. Indeed, the Conservatives' seeming lack of willingness to engage those who did not share their views about the deal was striking, given the importance of economic issues to their agenda, and this apparent indifference even extended to their take on Canada-US relations.

CONFRONTING THE UNITED STATES

If there was one area of foreign policy where the new Conservatives *should* have been expected to deviate from the traditional Canadian approach, it would surely have been in their dealings with the United States. Although Canadians had always enjoyed a cordial relationship with their nearest neighbour, the fact that it was a superpower had not escaped them. Nor had the fact that its political culture was significantly different, especially in its views on social policy. As

Pierre Trudeau once commented, living next to the US had its advantages, but it was also "somewhat like sleeping with an elephant. No matter how friendly or temperate the beast, one is affected by every twitch and grunt."

As a result, a series of Liberal prime ministers in the twentieth century, from Pearson and Trudeau to Chrétien, had carefully avoided the appearance of too close a relationship with American presidents. On some occasions, as with Trudeau's visits to China and Cuba, or Chrétien's refusal to participate in the American-led Iraq War, they had insisted on demonstrating Canada's independence. By contrast, Progressive Conservative prime minister Brian Mulroney declared that an "excellent" relationship with the United States was a primary objective of his foreign policy. At first Canadians were merely skeptical, but when Mulroney sang "When Irish Eyes Are Smiling" with US President Ronald Reagan, they became apprehensive, with good reason. One result of this close relationship (which Reagan often demonstrated was more important to Mulroney than to him), was the free-trade agreement that Mulroney once declared Canada "would have none of," and which nearly 60 per cent of Canadians rejected in the hugely divisive 1988 federal election. Nevertheless, even Mulroney continued to pursue an independent foreign policy on a range of issues, including his criticism of Reagan's mining of the harbours in Nicaragua and his own support for sanctions against South Africa, despite the hesitation of both Reagan and Thatcher.

Yet Ronald Reagan, as earlier chapters demonstrated, remained a larger-than-life role model for the Reform Party and for the Reform/Alliance politicians who came to form the nucleus of the new Conservative Party and its leadership, including Stephen Harper. It therefore came as no surprise to see that Harper's foreign-policy objectives included maintaining close ties with the Americans, and especially following their lead on military matters. Apart from Canada's willing participation in Afghanistan and Libya, this sentiment manifested itself in Harper's personal attendance at the tenth-anniversary 9/11 ceremonies in New York in 2011, and his willingness to negotiate a deal on border security related to terrorist threats.

What *did* come as a surprise, therefore, was the extent to which Harper was prepared to cross his American friends. Indeed, Harper's apparent lack of concern for maintaining good relations with his American counterpart, Barack Obama, led to the inevitable conclusion that it was the Republican Right, and not the United States, with which Harper and his followers were enamoured. Harper's misfortune, it seemed, was to finally achieve power in Canada at the very moment when the Republicans' star was on the wane and Obama, the left-wing Democrat, was in charge. The potential for a clash between his conservative values and the liberal rationalism and evidence-based decision-making of Obama was obvious.

One area where the two clashed was in their approach to Israel. Early in 2011, Obama proposed that the pre-1967 borders of Israel be used as the basis for new peace negotiations, although he also indicated that a land swap could be part of the plan to compensate for this. A few months later, when Harper was attending a G8 summit, he insisted that any reference to the pre-1967 border issue be removed from the leaders' communiqué endorsing Obama's plan before he would sign it. That fall, as mentioned earlier, Harper once again avoided the opening of the UN Security Council session in New York, choosing to leave the city on the very morning when Obama was scheduled to deliver his address.

A similar clash based along philosophical lines had occurred during Harper's own chairmanship of the G8 the previous year. Although he had made "maternal and child health" the signature issue of his tenure, the early support he enjoyed for that move quickly turned to controversy when it was learned that his government was determined not to fund any groups that offered contraception methods or abortions.

When US Secretary of State Hillary Clinton visited Canada for a meeting of G8 foreign ministers in March 2010, she wasted little time making her critical views known. "You cannot have maternal health without reproductive health and reproductive health includes contraception and family planning and access to legal, safe abortions," Clinton said. "I do not think governments should be involved in making these decisions. It is perfectly legitimate for people to hold their own personal views based on conscience, religion, or any other basis. But I've always believed that the government should not intervene in decisions of such intimacy," she added.[64]

By April, the Harper Conservatives were scrambling to find a solution so that the Americans would sign their communiqué. In the end, they sidestepped the issue by saying that Canadian efforts would focus on safe drinking water and vaccination programs. Opposition parties accused the government of reversing Canada's position on maternal health in poor countries, policies that had been in place for almost three decades. International NGOs and women's groups argued any omission of abortion also would be at odds with the G8's established goals at previous summits. Meanwhile interim Liberal leader Bob Rae argued the move "reopened" the whole abortion debate, while NDP critic Paul Dewar called the government "ignorant."[65]

But philosophical differences based on moral values were not the only bone of contention between the Harper Conservatives and the Obama administration. As the Harper government intensified its efforts to develop the Canadian economy through the exploitation of natural resources, the issue of pipelines for the transport of oil became a crucial one. And here it was their differing views on environmental protection and sustainable development that caused the difficulties. Although the proposals were controversial in Canada as well, the primary difficulties involved plans for a north-south pipeline through the American heartland, constructed by Canadian-based corporation TransCanada. Although Obama was clearly concerned about the potential environmental impact of the Keystone XL project, the Harper government initially did little to assuage his fears except to insist that they were making progress on their efforts to limit greenhouse-gas emissions, a claim that could not be substantiated. Given Canada's withdrawal from the Kyoto Accord, and the attacks of Joe Oliver and Peter Kent on "foreign environmental terrorists," it was little wonder that American environmentalists and the governing Democrats were leery.

Harper's cause was not helped by an open letter to Obama from nine prominent world figures, including Desmond Tutu and the Dalai Lama, urging him to reject the project. By late November 2011, Obama had approved only the southern portion of the proposed pipeline, but he did indicate that TransCanada could reapply for a permit for the northern half if it was able to propose an alternate route that would avoid the Nebraska Sandhills, an environmentally sensitive area. Then the exigencies of a presidential election intervened in 2012, delaying any decision until at least 2013.

When Obama was returned to office, however, he reiterated his concerns about climate change in his State of the Union address and identified the Keystone project as one with international implications for the environment. Thrown into disarray by this apparent resistance to something he had once described as a "no brainer,"

Harper organized an unprecedented high-pressure sales campaign over the next few months. Western provincial premiers, federal ministers, and Canada's ambassador to the US, Gary Doer, all attempted to convince Washington of the necessity of the plan, as well as the sincerity of Canada's emission-reduction plans. Since the US was on track to meet its 2020 Copenhagen commitments, while Canada (which had made the same commitment as the Americans at the 2009 Copenhagen Summit) at that point was already heading for a 50-per-cent overrun due primarily to oil-sands production, this line of argumentation was less than persuasive. After another aggressive visit by John Baird, Secretary of State John Kerry testily informed him that the United States government would make up its mind when it was ready, and not before.

Evidently sensing that the plan might actually be rejected, Harper delivered a pointed message to Obama during a speech to 150 businessmen in New York in September. He maintained the arguments in favour of the deal were "overwhelming" and it was "so clearly in everybody's interest." Then, to the amazement of the media present, he declared that, if the deal were to be rejected by the president, "My view is that you don't take 'no' for an answer ... This won't be final until it's approved and we will keep pushing forward." Harper made matters worse by describing the delay as "just politics" and a potential rejection as "bad policy. And I believe that in strong, advanced countries and economies like ours, bad policies ultimately get reversed."[66] Although Obama did not comment on the remarks, key opponents of the deal in Washington described Harper's speech as "disrespectful" and "unhelpful." When Obama later announced that no decision would be taken until 2015, most observers concluded the pipeline was history.

But even the rejection of this key foreign-policy initiative would be unlikely to deter the Conservatives from their chosen course in foreign policy. Lacking the constraints found in domestic policy, which often required them to be pragmatic and to put aside their ideological preferences, their views here have had free rein. Basing their policies on moral judgments and rejecting "relativism," the Conservatives' approach to foreign policy has been little short of revolutionary. According to Joe Clark, it has also been "almost adolescent – forceful, certain, enthusiastic, combative, full of sound and fury." To Clark's dismay, they have transformed Canada into "the country that lectures and leaves."[67] Certainly their tendency to see the world as black hats and white hats was always too simplistic, but it has been even more counterproductive in an era of rapidly developing global transportation, communications, and information technologies. Yet the Harper Conservatives fail to recognize this, and appear to be mired in a 1950s Cold War version of world politics which is not only inaccurate but dangerous.

Moreover, although Harper and many of his cabinet had travelled very little before assuming political office, their lack of interest in the rest of the world apparently continued to hinder their ability to learn about or appreciate differences once they did. Even more significant is the fact that Canada under the Harper Conservatives has appeared to stick its head in the sand on some issues, and stick its neck out on others. And, as both their trade and natural resource efforts have demonstrated, their concerns reflect primarily the concerns of the private sector and western Canada, positions which put them at odds with other regions of the country – especially Ontario and Quebec. As noted historian J.L. Granatstein put it, theirs is "a very Albertan foreign policy."[68] As we will see, these foreign-policy priorities have also had a negative impact on federal-provincial relations and on national unity.

9

Dismantling the Welfare State: The Open Federalism Agenda

Canada is a Northern European welfare state in the worst sense of the term, and very proud of it.

Stephen Harper, Speech to National Council on Policy, 1997

What we clearly need is experimentation with market reforms and private delivery options in health care.

Stephen Harper, 2002

We need to re-establish a strong central government that focuses on genuine national priorities like defence and the economic union.

Stephen Harper, "My Plan for Open Federalism," 2004

We will ensure the use of federal spending power in provincial jurisdiction is limited … authorize the provinces to use the opting out formula with full compensation … [and]) limit the federal role to complementing and supporting provincial actions.

Conservative Party Platform 2006

Few Canadian prime ministers have put down in writing their views on the role of government, or their philosophical approach to policy development and democratic institutions, before running for public office. Even fewer have written in detail about their understanding of Canadian federalism. Not since Pierre Trudeau has a future Canadian prime minister devoted so much time and energy to the fundamental concerns surrounding the operation of the federation, or laid out his prescription for those concerns so clearly. Yet long before he became prime minister, Stephen Harper did precisely that. He also made it clear that he had a much different vision of Canadian federalism than the Liberals, and especially of former prime minister Pierre Trudeau. Not for him the sentiments expressed in Trudeau's seminal *Federalism and the French Canadians.*[1] For Harper, Trudeau's pan-Canadian vision, in which Canada, not Quebec, is the distinct society, was a snare and a delusion, and Trudeau himself a dangerous influence, whose policies, in addition, wreaked havoc on western Canada.[2]

But Harper's federal vision was also different from those of any other federal leader, including his Progressive Conservative predecessors. On the one hand, Harper's approach to federalism originally seemed classically decentralist, like the approaches of Robert Stanfield, Joe Clark, and Brian Mulroney. It gave priority to provincial autonomy and interpreted Confederation in terms of the compact theory. This decentralist approach was epitomized by the Mulroney government's failed Meech Lake Accord, a constitutional reform package diametrically opposed to the Trudeau vision of a strong national government and the supremacy of individual rights.[3]

On the other hand, over time several new aspects of Harper's federal vision emerged which were more extreme and inflexible than the traditional Tory approach. Progressive Conservatives may have been in favour of more provincial autonomy than Liberals, but their parameters of acceptable federal government involvement were much greater than what Harper was proposing. Harper himself recognized this fact by introducing a new term, "open federalism," to better reflect his views and distinguish them from those of the Tories.

Like Pierre Trudeau, Harper's actions in power have reflected his vision. Harper's views were spelled out in statements he made as a Reform MP, president of the National Citizens Coalition, and leader of the Alliance Party and the new Conservative Party, all before taking office in 2006. With each new pronouncement, it became increasingly clear that, if his new Conservative Party formed a government, the operation of the federation would change dramatically. At the same time it also became clear that Harper's stated rationale for open federalism was at odds with the facts. Although his arguments were couched in terms of seemingly objective academic theories, his proposals flew in the face of Canada's constitutional realities and the historical record. Yet he persisted in his controversial interpretation of the constitution. The obvious question is why.

Once again the answer can be found in Harper's right-wing conservative ideology. His vision of open federalism is, above all, one in which provinces have far more discretion in their implementation of the shared-cost programs that make up the welfare state, while the federal government's role is sharply reduced or eliminated entirely. The only rational explanation for Stephen Harper's vision of Canadian federalism is one based not on academic theories and history but on his desire to implement major policy change by stealth. Indeed, his approach to federalism appears designed with the express purpose of dismantling the welfare state, through a policy of disengagement rather than direct intervention.

The path to this objective has not always been easy. As prime minister, Harper has been confronted with a number of unanticipated policy dilemmas that have challenged his federal vision. On some occasions, his determination to chart his own course, regardless of difficulties, is evident. On others, Mr Harper has been obliged to temper his views with the pragmatism born of political necessity that he has demonstrated so often elsewhere. And here, too, he has been forced to confront the reality of Canada's liberal political culture, as well as the unique challenges posed by the existence of Quebec.

His ability to implement his open federalism agenda was also severely hampered for years by his government's minority status. However, with the May 2011 majority secured, he moved quickly. As the funding agreements for the various social programs that make up the welfare state came up for renewal, significant changes were imposed by his government, with little discussion or negotiation with the provinces. In many cases these changes also occurred with little or no public recognition of the changes or their consequences.

OPEN FEDERALISM IN THEORY

An early indication of Stephen Harper's federal vision came in 1992, when he was serving as the Reform Party's policy adviser. Harper was instrumental in convincing Reform leader Preston Manning to oppose the Charlottetown Accord, primarily because of the special status it offered to Quebec. In one of the greatest ironies of Canadian politics, Harper's emphatic rejection of the special status offered to

Quebec in the accord placed him squarely on the No side, with none other than Pierre Trudeau, albeit for very different reasons. The subsequent failure of the Charlottetown deal played a major role in bringing down the Progressive Conservative government of Brian Mulroney and his successor, Kim Campbell, paving the way for the Reform Party in the 1993 federal election. Although the Chrétien Liberals were returned to power with a majority, Reform came close to forming the official opposition, falling just two seats short of the Bloc Québécois.

Harper was among the Reform MPs elected in the party's 1993 sweep of western Canada, and Manning appointed him as the party's intergovernmental affairs critic. Consequently, when the PQ government in Quebec launched the 1995 sovereignty referendum, it was Harper who drafted a comprehensive package of reforms that he argued would strengthen national unity by reducing the role of the federal government. The changes, he said, "will assert the autonomy of the provinces and the power of the people well into the future."[4] When critics asked how national unity could be reinforced by such measures when Canada was already among the most decentralized federations in the world, Harper responded that stronger provinces would create a stronger country. He categorically denied that his position was inconsistent with his earlier rejection of special status for Quebec, arguing that all provinces would benefit equally from the decentralization of power. No doubt influenced by Brian Mulroney's two failed attempts at constitutional reform, Harper also stressed that his plan could be implemented without constitutional amendments, since the changes he proposed were "administrative" in nature and "simply require a federal government that is willing to act."[5]

Still, at this point Harper's views on Canadian federalism had not diverged significantly from traditional Tory positions. Over the next decade, however, as his views on the appropriate functioning of the federal system were elaborated, Harper's concept of Canadian federalism could clearly be seen to be far more extreme, and it differed from the traditional Progressive Conservative approach in several very important ways.

First of all, he argued for the total withdrawal of the federal government from areas of provincial – or even shared – responsibility, instead of a more "collaborative" approach in which the provinces and the federal government shared equal billing. The 2006 Conservative

Party platform included a predictable commitment to "the federal principle and the notion of strong provinces within Canada," but also a pledge to "ensure the use of the federal spending power in areas of provincial jurisdiction is limited" and another to "authorize the provinces to use the opting-out formula with full compensation if they want to opt out of any new or modified program" in areas of exclusive provincial or shared jurisdiction. (It is perhaps not a surprise that this approach mirrors the language found in the ill-fated 1999 Social Union Framework Agreement, or SUFA, promoted by Alberta's Ralph Klein and Mike Harris of Ontario, two right-wing premiers who shared Harper's extreme decentralist views and ideology.)

Harper expanded on his platform pledges in a speech in Quebec City during the 2006 election. He suggested the provinces should take the lead on social policy and the social union, and declared that any government he led would limit the federal role to "complementing and supporting" the activities of the provinces, an unprecedented ceding of federal involvement.[6]

Not surprisingly, the Liberals criticized this voluntary retrenchment as an abdication of federal responsibility and a threat to national unity. More revealing was the criticism by well-known Tories. Former Progressive Conservative prime minister Joe Clark declared he would vote for the Martin Liberals as the lesser of two evils. His views were echoed by his former intergovernmental affairs minister, Senator Lowell Murray, who declared the new party was "fundamentally different" and "incompatible" with Progressive Conservative values. Several former Mulroney cabinet ministers also declined to be identified with Harper's new Conservative Party and one, Sinclair Stevens, specifically criticized the new party and its leader for their radical views on the federation. "This is the first time in Canadian history that a national political party has embraced a provincial rights agenda," he wrote.[7]

Nevertheless, shortly after Harper secured a minority victory for his new party in the 2006 election, he declared boldly that he would consider his time in office a success if he was able to limit federal activities to defence, foreign policy, and the economic union.[8] One commentator described Harper's approach as more American than Canadian, promoting a mere "night watchman" role for the federal government.[9] This analysis was confirmed when Harper made additional concessions to the provinces during the 2008 election. Not content with simply allowing provinces to opt out of federal programs. Harper now declared that no new programs would be introduced unless the majority of provinces agreed to them.

Harper defended his plan to withdraw from the social union by citing academic theory, and specifically the need to "return" to a classic form of federalism. Many Progressive Conservatives before him had argued that Canadian federalism in practice did not adequately respect the formal allocation of responsibilities between the two levels of government. But Harper went much further, criticizing Ottawa for "sticking its nose into provincial and local matters," while "neglecting what it had to do."[10] Harper considered British scholar K.C. Wheare's "watertight compartments" principle to be an accurate reflection of the constitution and the intentions of the Fathers of Confederation.[11] He made this point explicitly during the 2008 election, declaring that it was time "to return to the original principles of the constitution."[12]

Yet Mr Harper's insistence on this strict "originalist" interpretation of the Canadian constitution is incorrect, as historian Michael Behiels, among others, has noted.[13] The BNA Act, 1867 did *not* meet the "watertight compartment" criteria of Wheare on several grounds. First, it provided for areas of shared jurisdiction, such as agriculture and immigration. Second, it conferred on the federal government several tools – such as the Peace, Order and Good Government (POGG) clause, the federal spending power, the disallowance provision, and the assignment of residual powers – that were designed to ensure the supremacy of the federal government. Wheare himself referred to Canada as only a "quasi-federal" system for these very reasons. Moreover, Harper implicitly recognized the importance of these provisions, and the true intent of the drafters, when he criticized "this outrageous spending power" which he saw as "giving rise to a domineering and paternalistic federalism," despite the fact this power was not only constitutional but deliberately unrestrained.[14]

Harper's proposed "return to classic federalism" also ignored much of the history of Canadian intergovernmental relations, which has led to a high degree of federal-provincial cooperation. Although the notion of watertight compartments was never accurate, such a system could only ever have been possible in the early years of Confederation, when little was expected of a government, other than providing for basic services and facilities such as defence, transportation, currency, and a postal service. But after two world wars and a global depression, citizens demanded that liberal democracies everywhere take on more responsibilities, resulting in the programs that collectively came to be known as the welfare state.

Creating the welfare state proved a constitutional conundrum for Canada. While the provinces had jurisdictional responsibility for most of the policy areas involved, they were unable to fund such programs, because of their limited capacity to raise revenues. Since there was no constitutional amending formula, the federal government and the provinces were forced to search for administrative solutions. In the end, the federal government agreed to use its spending power to share the cost of such programs, in exchange for provincial agreement that these programs would meet minimum national standards. This practical approach led to what many observers have described as a sort of golden age of Canadian federalism, in which much was achieved and everyone benefited.

For Mr Harper, however, the era of "cooperative federalism" represented the unwarranted intrusion of the federal government into exclusive areas of provincial jurisdiction. But here, as well, his interpretation of history was problematic. As Tom Kent, a senior official involved in the early medicare and pension-plan negotiations, pointed out, "it is difficult to believe that … Stephen Harper is a true believer in such a myth-based misreading of federal-provincial bargaining … Ottawa did not barge in. Initially it was dragged in."[15] Kent's views are reinforced by the federal government's adoption of the Quebec model for the Canada Pension Plan, and of Saskatchewan's medicare plan to form the basis of the Canada Health Act, underlining the importance of provincial governments in serving as incubators for national policies, a point emphasized by American president Bill Clinton in a speech at the first Forum of the Federations conference at Mont Tremblant in 1999.

Over time, the range and scope of such federal-provincial cost-sharing arrangements greatly expanded under both Liberal and Tory governments, highlighting the common elements of their philosophical approach. As a result, any serious attempt to rein in the federal spending power and "return to classic federalism" as proposed by Harper, would represent a major break with his PC predecessors, as well as with the Liberals, and would inevitably have significant implications for the operation of the social union.

However, Stephen Harper's federal vision is not exclusively decentralist. On the contrary, he has repeatedly outlined his plans to expand the role of the federal government in areas of exclusive federal jurisdiction related to the economic union. In a 2004 *National Post* article entitled "My Plan for Open Federalism," he underlined "the need to re-establish a strong central government that focuses on genuine national priorities like defence and the economic union."[16] Conversely, he saw little or no role for the provinces in the economic union, and little need for federal-provincial dialogue.

At first glance, his emphasis on a strong central government with respect to the economic union might seem to contradict the overwhelmingly decentralist thrust of his stated federal vision, but this apparent contradiction can be resolved fairly easily by taking into account Harper's new conservative ideology.

IDEOLOGY AND OPEN FEDERALISM

The importance that Stephen Harper has assigned to his plan for "open federalism" can only be explained by his determination to implement an extreme right-wing agenda in areas where he can not do so directly, because of public opinion and lack of constitutional jurisdiction. His plan, therefore, seems to be to effect significant change by acts of omission on the part of the federal government. Since the programs of the welfare state comprise the only major area involving formal federal-provincial cooperation, and the use of the "outrageous" federal spending power is essential for provinces to maintain those programs, it follows that the welfare state is the real target of this plan.

There can be little doubt about Stephen Harper's true opinions concerning the welfare state, although, not surprisingly, his most revealing comments were made when he was not in power. While working for the National Citizens Coalition (NCC), the right-wing advocacy group whose motto is "more freedom through less government," he delivered the infamous speech to the American Council for National Policy mentioned earlier, in which he referred to Canada disparagingly as "a Northern European welfare state in the worst sense of the term, and very proud of it." He went on to urge his audience not to "feel bad" about Canada's unemployed, because "they don't feel bad about it themselves, as long as they're receiving generous social assistance and unemployment insurance." He also criticized the Progressive Conservative party, whose membership he described in unflattering tones as "officially in favour of the entrenchment of our universal, collectivized health care system and multicultural policies in the constitution of this country."[17]

In 2001, Harper signed the infamous "Firewall Letter," which defended Alberta premier Ralph Klein's health-care policies, including his controversial creation of "truth squads" to promote the benefits of privatization and demands that no conditions be attached to federal funding for health care. The letter called for Klein to adopt an Alberta Agenda that would isolate the province from the federal government as much as possible. Among its recommendations were provincial withdrawal from the Canada Pension Plan and "resuming provincial responsibility for health-care policy." It argued that "each province should raise its own revenue for health care," thereby dismissing the problems of poorer provinces that relied on equalization, from which the province would also withdraw. (In practice this recommendation made little sense, since equalization is an exclusively federal program.) The authors also urged the premier to fight any federal attempt to challenge the legality of these moves, especially concerning the Canada Health Act. "If we lose, we can afford the financial penalties that Ottawa may try to impose," they wrote.[18]

In a similar vein, Harper dismissed the efforts of the newly created Romanow Commission on health care, appointed by Prime Minister Chrétien, as "not only useless but dangerous." His position, summarized by the *Globe and Mail*, was that "a fully socialized system is incapable of generating or efficiently allocating the funds to meet growing health-care demands." In his view, the solution was "provincial experimentation with market reforms and private delivery options."[19]

In short, Stephen Harper has repeatedly demonstrated a profound dislike for the welfare state. Such social policies are not valued as creating equality of opportunity and demonstrating a positive role for the state, but as providing unfair and unacceptable "entitlements" for some, entitlements which encourage citizens to relinquish responsibility for their own well-being. Harper mirrors Margaret Thatcher's view that "there is no such thing as society," only individuals, and the state's role should be as minimalist as possible. Moreover, in creating the concept of "open federalism," he appears to have been mirroring the "states' rights" approach of Ronald Reagan and the New Right. For decades, the two overarching themes of American conservatives have been "states' rights" and "small government," both of which have important implications for conservatives' views about the correct functioning of a federal system.

As discussed in an earlier chapter, the American term "states' rights" has served as a code for the dismantling of liberal policies and programs introduced by the federal government, doing so on a state-by-state basis. The second, equally important theme – the need to reduce "big government" – is also one in which federalism has an important role to play. The Republican New Right has demonstrated that liberal initiatives can be minimized or eliminated not only by reducing the size of the federal government but by diffusing its power. One classic right-wing manoeuvre has been to eliminate federal regulations and standards, if necessary by having them declared unconstitutional because they exceed federal jurisdiction. This strategy allowed the development of "market-preserving federalism," or, as one of its critics describes it, the promotion of an unfettered competition among the subnational units to force a race to the bottom.[20]

As we have already seen, Stephen Harper's insistence on the "watertight compartments" interpretation of the Canadian constitution, and his withdrawal of the federal government from areas of provincial jurisdiction, lies at the heart of his concept of open federalism.

It is this "originalist" interpretation that allows him to utilize the states'-rights argument to deconstruct the social union. Conversely, Mr Harper's determination to further centralize some powers at the federal level can be explained in terms of his economic agenda. As Canadian economist Adam Harmes has demonstrated, there are many tools available to the federal government to implement this right-wing agenda nationwide if the federal government chooses, including voluntary deregulation and the elimination of national standards.[21] And there is considerable evidence to demonstrate that Mr Harper was always aware of this. Shortly after winning the federal election, the new prime minister gave a speech to the Montreal Board of Trade in which he declared that tax reduction is "the ultimate decentralization," promising significant tax cuts and offering tax room rather than any increase in transfer payments to the provinces. Columnist John Ibbitson described this commitment as "Mr Harper's most important neoliberal initiative."[22]

This unprecedented approach has serious implications. At a conference in Kingston to discuss the real meaning of open federalism, political scientist Peter Leslie described Harper's stated objectives of "developing" the social and economic unions in opposite directions (decentralized for the former and highly centralized for the latter) as entirely consistent with a world view of the role of the state which is both minimalist and assertive. Such objectives, Leslie argued, "not only call for a review of the conduct of intergovernmental relations, but open up questions of broad scale political design … At stake is the kind of country that Canada is and should become."[23]

An examination of the Harper government's approach to federalism since taking power in 2006 not only confirms Leslie's hypothesis, but demonstrates the degree to which Harper has succeeded in implementing his new federal vision.

OPEN FEDERALISM IN PRACTICE: DISMANTLING THE SOCIAL UNION

No sooner had Harper been elected than he began to act on his commitment to withdraw the federal government from areas of provincial jurisdiction. This retrenching involved significant deconstruction of the social union, and ultimately had serious repercussions for the conduct of intergovernmental relations.

To begin with, Harper immediately killed the national child-care strategy established by the Chrétien and Martin governments. This strategy was part of the National Children's Agenda, developed over a decade of negotiations with the provinces, an agenda that had been praised by the premiers for the flexibility and discretion it offered to provinces. (Interestingly, two components of the agenda, the National Child Benefit and the Early Childhood Development Initiative, were criticized by the National Council of Welfare because low-income families across the country received very uneven benefits as a result of this very provincial discretion.)

The Multilevel Framework on Early Learning and Child Care, the primary objective of which was to increase the total number of child-care spaces, was the most significant element of this plan. It was agreed to in late 2003 by the first ministers of all provinces except Quebec, which had already set up its own child-care program and would therefore receive funding automatically. Martin's 2005 federal budget committed $5 billion over five years to the program, but the funding could be spent only on non-profit child care. His government signed bilateral agreements in principle with nine provinces.

Manitoba and Ontario also released detailed Action Plans and signed final funding agreements with the federal government.

Nevertheless, in early 2006 the Harper government gave notice that it was invoking the one-year termination clause found in the umbrella Social Union Framework Agreement (SUFA). Shortly afterwards, the Speech from the Throne introduced alternative measures, which led many observers to conclude that the decision to cancel the child-care deal was motivated by ideology rather than any concern for constitutionally watertight compartments. As we have seen, the government first established a new $1,200-per-year Choice in Child Care Allowance, a non-targeted tax credit that went directly to families for each child under the age of six. As Harper himself said, it ignored the advice of academics and other so-called experts, and "delivers expanding resources to the real child-care experts. Their names are mom and dad."[24]

Experts called the allowance counterproductive, and concluded it would do nothing to encourage the use of quality child care or increase the number of spaces. But it did much to placate the Conservative base, as did the Harper government's eventual response to growing public pressure concerning the lack of spaces. Its solution was a 25-per-cent tax credit for businesses that created child-care spaces in the workplace and provided $250 million as incentives for those businesses. Despite this, most of the funding earmarked by the Martin government for the child-care strategy was never spent.

For a variety of reasons, social housing was handled differently, and again demonstrated Mr Harper's pragmatism. Initially Harper had said his government was planning to pull out of the social-housing field as well, despite the existence of a number of multi-year federal-provincial agreements. He even considered the possibility of shutting down the federal government's window on the industry – the Canada Mortgage and Housing Corporation (CMHC) – since it represented an "unacceptable" intrusion into both provincial jurisdiction and the private sector.[25]

However, the advent of the 2008 world recession less than a year later forced Harper's government to adapt. They left the social-housing agreements in place, and then moved to avoid the appearance of a looming housing crisis for which Harper feared his minority government would shoulder the responsibility. He directed CMHC to offer more guaranteed mortgages, and at 0-per-cent interest over forty years. The American subprime disaster of mid-2008 effectively forced Finance Minister Flaherty to order a return to 5-per-cent interest and a thirty-five-year amortization, but even this remained an exceptionally favourable (or risky) situation for Canadian borrowers.

The government also ordered CMHC to approve high-risk borrowers in order to keep credit levels up. According to CMHC records, the approval rate for risky loans rose from 33 per cent in 2007 to 42 per cent in 2008 alone, resulting in a 9.3-per-cent increase in Canadian household debt between June 2008 and 2009. As economist Murray Dobbin has noted, "Every single US lender specializing in sub-prime has gone bankrupt. The largest subprime lender in the world is now the Canadian government."[26]

Without doubt, the area of the social union in which the Harper government trod most carefully was health care. Aware of the difficulties Stockwell Day had encountered, Harper stressed that his government would respect the primacy of a publicly funded health-care system, ignoring entirely his earlier comments to the contrary. Given the Martin government's 2004 negotiation of a ten-year, $41-billion agreement with the provinces to "fix health care for a generation," (which was not only signed but, exceptionally, would run until April 2014 under the Canada Health Transfer, or CHT), he was left with few options.

Countless public-opinion polls showed that health care remained the top priority of Canadians, and Harper paid attention. Consequently, in the May 2011 election, with the prospect of a majority government looming large, Harper repeatedly assured voters (and provincial premiers) that his government would continue the 6-per-cent annual health-transfer payments guaranteed in the 2004 agreement. He also promised his government would begin negotiations with the provinces for a new health deal "sooner rather than later."[27]

The day after the election, Harper repeated the 6-per-cent commitment, but added "we do want to sit down as we renegotiate to look at how to ensure better and clearer results," a reference to the fact many provinces failed to follow through on promises made in the 2004 accord.[28] The next day, he agreed that provinces were experimenting with alternative service delivery, and said they should be encouraged. While he was careful not to contradict his promised support for a "universal public health-care insurance system," he also warned that Ottawa would not impose solutions on provinces. "This is a discussion that will be collaborative," he declared.[29] He also made it clear that no new initiatives, such as a national pharmacare plan or home-care plan, would be on the table, to the dismay of social-policy experts, who argued these measures were long overdue, and could serve to reduce some elements of health-care costing if properly implemented.

Then, in August 2011, Ontario premier Dalton McGuinty delivered a speech to the Ottawa Chamber of Commerce, urging Harper to begin negotiations to renew the health-care agreement immediately, as more than two years were usually necessary to reach agreement on the details. There was no response until the November 2011 fiscal update, when the federal government's financial situation was deteriorating rapidly in light of the fallout from the global recession. At that point, Finance Minister Flaherty declared the 6-per-cent annual CHT escalator could not be guaranteed for more than two years after the end of the existing health accord in fiscal 2013–14. A First Ministers Conference on health-care issues still had not been scheduled by December 2011. Tired of waiting, the premiers announced they would hold their own special conference on the issue in early January. Most observers concluded that Harper was delaying in order to better position his government for the negotiations. Many health-care experts expressed serious concern that a frank dialogue on the underlying issues affecting public health-care delivery might not take place if the negotiations were rushed. This concern was heightened when one prominent economist – former senior Finance bureaucrat Don Drummond – predicted that, if unchecked, health-care costs in Ontario would consume nearly 100 per cent of that province's budget within twenty years.[30] As a result, it was the economic viability of a publicly funded health-care system – rather than its merits, delivery options, or best practices – that was rapidly becoming the primary focus of political debate.

However, the experts' concerns were seriously misplaced. The real purpose of Harper's silence became clear when Finance Minister Flaherty appeared briefly at a meeting of provincial health ministers in December and laid a unilateral "take it or leave it" offer on the table. He announced that there would be no federal-provincial negotiations after all, an unprecedented development. Instead, he informed them that, after 2014, the funding formula for federal transfers would not be tied to income, but rather to population. The move to an equal per-capita allowance of the CHT in 2014–15 would uniquely benefit the province of Alberta. Indeed, with income removed from the equation, it was estimated that Alberta would receive more than 50 per cent of the new federal funding, or more than $1 billion of the $1.8 billion in new money that Ottawa would provide in 2014–15.[31] In an apparent attempt to assuage irate premiers, Flaherty also confirmed there would be no more "strings" attached. Provinces were free to experiment, a clear signal that the minimum national standards so fundamental to the original agreement were at risk.

As journalist Frances Russell warned, if unchecked this withdrawal of a federal leadership role will likely lead to the very "checkerboard Canada" Pierre Trudeau had talked about under Meech Lake, in which there would be "thirteen kinds of citizens" and only those Canadians living in wealthy provinces would have reasonable access to health care and social services. Pointing to sections of the Constitution Act, 1982, which guarantee the principle of equalization and "reasonably comparable levels of public services at reasonably comparable rates of taxation," Russell specifically noted that these sections "contradict the Harper Conservatives' 'strict constructionist' stance,"[32] and make a mockery of his stated rationale for open federalism.

The premiers claimed the government's new plan would reduce their funding by $36 billion over ten years. In addition, they signalled their concerns over the fate of equalization, since those agreements were set to expire in 2014 as well. Adding to their concerns, the Parliamentary Budget Office predicted the federal share of health-care funding will fall from 20 per cent to 12 per cent in less than twenty years if all of the Harper government's new measures are implemented.

Then, in the 2012 budget, the federal government took an axe to its own health-related programs and services. It reduced funding for Health Canada by more than $200 million and cut the budget of the Public Health Agency by $68 million and the Institutes of Health Research by $45 million. And in the 2014 budget, Harper followed through on the plan to eliminate the equalization portion of health-care transfers in favour of the per-capita transfer – once more benefiting only Alberta, and leaving have-not provinces with an insurmountable gap of $16.5 billion over the next five years.

Taken together, the consequences of the Harper government's actions on medicare are potentially life-threatening. As Mike McBane, director of the Canadian Health Coalition, concluded, if nothing is done to alter the Harper government's course, "National medicare will not survive this 'cut and run' course. Instead, it will fragment into fourteen separate pieces where access to essential care will depend on where you live and your ability to pay."[33] And, as McBane noted, "All Harper has to do is nothing." Yet few Canadians appear to realize how effective, and how comprehensive, those actions have been, largely because he has effected the changes as unobtrusively and/or indirectly as possible, leaving the provinces to pick up the pieces. In short, Harper's acts of omission appear to have served their purpose. Many elements and underlying principles of the most important program of the welfare state have been effectively gutted, and most Canadians are oblivious.

Not surprisingly, given their apparent success on medicare, in short order the federal government's unilateral approach of withdrawal was repeated on several other established social programs. A number of arbitrary and unilateral federal decisions were announced, leading to even more federal-provincial conflicts, which the Harper government appeared to relish, as various ministers took on provincial premiers in unexpectedly partisan attacks, particularly after their majority victory in 2011. In addition, as political scientist David McGrane has demonstrated, the Harper government increasingly adopted the mechanism of bilateral agreements, which not only allowed for a degree of asymmetry in the various arrangements it struck, particularly with respect to Quebec, but also were concluded out of the public eye, heightening the lack of accountability and transparency. Referring to this trend as "one-off" federalism, McGrane concludes:

> The Harper government's use of one-off federalism is reflective of its embrace of decentralization, bilateralism and asymmetry in managing the Canadian federation ... As such, the Conservatives may ensure national unity, but at the expense of accountability and transparency within the federation, and through excusing themselves from a leadership role in the realm of social policy.[34]

At the same time, the Conservatives did not hesitate to act unilaterally to impose their views on the provinces, particularly if they believed economic issues were involved rather than purely social-policy issues, even in areas of provincial jurisdiction, thereby demonstrating the other side of open federalism. A case in point was their proposed new Canada Job Grants Plan.

OPEN FEDERALISM IN PRACTICE: THE CANADA JOB GRANTS PLAN REVERSAL

The federal Canada Job Grants Plan was announced in the March 2013 budget, without any consultation with the provinces. The premiers were taken aback by the proposal, which they considered a blatant attempt to claw back what had been mandated by the same government only a few years before. Even more surprising was the fact that the move was in direct opposition to what they saw as the "decentralist" principles of open federalism, as spelled out repeatedly by the Harper government. Their mistake was to assume that such programs were seen as intiatives related to the social union, and therefore something the federal government could safely leave, or even abandon, to the provinces. Once the Conservatives became concerned about the economic consequences of such programs, particularly in western Canada, they imposed their "centralist" view of open federalism, in which the federal level has responsibility, and can act unilaterally, on issues relating to the economic union.

The Job Grants Plan appeared to be a spur-of-the-moment response to several reports indicating that a serious mismatch existed between worker skills and employers' job requirements. To remedy the situation, the government first proposed to eliminate 60 per cent of federal funding for existing provincial training programs introduced in 2007 by Harper, programs which many experts viewed as one of the most successful of the government's initiatives. Instead, the Conservatives indicated they were now planning to introduce their own, business-oriented, replacement program for short-term training. Worse still, the provinces would have to contribute an equal amount of their own money, along with the business sector, in a three-way shared-cost approach.

As labour-market experts, union spokespersons, and even the Canadian Federation of Independent Business pointed out, six months after the program was announced in haste, many questions were still unanswered about the proposal, which was to come into effect in April 2014. Even more troubling was the distinct possibility that big business would benefit at the expense of small and medium-sized businesses, which were most likely to create jobs. Equally concerning was the finding of numerous studies that the "crisis" of labour shortages caused by a mismatch in short-term training was a myth. On the contrary, in those few areas where a shortage could be demonstrated, such as engineering, more than two years of formal training would be required, so that the proposed new program would be irrelevant.[35]

Apart from the many technical and practical problems, the most striking element of the proposal was the complete lack of consultation with the provinces, either before it was announced or subsequently. Premiers were unhappy with what they perceived to be an unwarranted federal intrusion, particularly since their existing programs were tailored to specific local and regional concerns and for the most part were considered to be working well. Nor could the provinces afford to maintain those programs on their own, since the federal proposal not only removed federal funding for those programs, but required them to dedicate new money from their already strained budgets for the unproven new plan.

Yet, despite numerous requests for a meeting with the minister responsible, Jason Kenney, the premiers met in late July 2013 in Niagara-on-the-Lake for their annual Council of the Federation summit without any federal feedback or communication. They emerged from that meeting demonstrating a united front. They announced bluntly that none of them would participate in the program. As one editorial put it, "It's an offer the provinces ought to and most certainly will refuse." Its rationale was succinct:

> It's no wonder the premiers want nothing to do with it. The Harper Government announced earlier this year that it would claw back 60 per cent of provincial transfers for skills training, effectively killing many well-established jobs programs across the country. In their place, the feds vowed to create a $900-million grant program for employers looking to train people for particular jobs, which would be funded in equal parts by Ottawa, the provinces, and the private sector.[36]

Still, the newly minted employment minister ignored their concerns until a gauntlet was thrown down by BC premier Christy Clark and New Brunswick premier David Alward in October. They were meeting in Toronto with national business groups, in an effort to develop an alternative to the Canada Jobs Grant. Clark stated, "All premiers have agreed that the program as it stands will not go ahead in any province in the country. It needs to be changed or that 2014 date isn't going to go ahead."[37] Moreover, she and other premiers noted that the federal proposal would take money from provincial programs designed to help the most vulnerable receive training and find jobs, in order for the Harper government to pay for its share of the new plan, which would only benefit those eligible for EI. Since the government's earlier changes to the EI program – which eliminated thousands from eligibility for the benefit and required others to travel great distances for work – were widely criticized by many premiers, this additional decision to create a two-tiered system for workers was viewed as particularly mean-spirited.

Evidently worried that their plan might not go ahead after all, Kenney belatedly offered an olive branch a week after Clark's comments. He told journalists that he was prepared to be "flexible" in his approach, and provinces could use money from another federal program to pay for the new one. Given Kenney's previous "bull in a china shop" approach when clawing back immigration settlement programs from Manitoba and British Columbia, as discussed in Chapter 7, this was perhaps a major concession from his point of view. However Ontario's minister for training, colleges and universities, Brad Duguid, described the offer as "a figleaf," a move akin to robbing Peter to pay Paul, and said Ontario would not back the new plan unless major changes were made.[38] Premier Robert Ghiz of PEI was also unimpressed and told reporters that "Stephen Harper's Conservatives better start listening to the provinces." Then he added, "The part that is most disturbing is the federal government is actually taking a program that is working and saying even though it works, 'we don't care, it doesn't fit with us ideologically.'"[39]

Adding to the drama, the release of a research document prepared by Kenney's own department confirmed that the provincial training programs were effective. Unfazed, Kenney told reporters the government would still proceed with its plan. He suggested provinces should "tweak" their programs in order to find the money to participate, but added that his department was working on alternative strategies to deliver his program in any province that did not choose to participate.

The Conservatives' apparent determination to go to war with the provinces can only be explained by their commitment to their right-wing economic agenda. As one economist noted,

> This is the same Conservative government that preaches the importance of tending to its own areas of responsibility, such as

> defence and foreign policy, and leaving the provinces to theirs. Conservatives would never dream of rejigging their transfer payments for health care to take control over, say, emergency ward operations. But that's exactly what Kenney is doing with funding for skills training, to further the Conservatives' economic agenda.[40]

That agenda, as noted earlier, is dedicated to promoting natural-resource development to the exclusion of almost all other options. And, as numerous observers commented, the mining, oil, and gas industries of Alberta and western Canada were precisely those which would benefit most from such a short-term training program. Professional and/or highly skilled workers require years, not weeks, of education, but many jobs involved in the resource industries were a perfect fit for this approach.

OPEN FEDERALISM IN PRACTICE: DOWNLOADING COSTS TO PROVINCES

Interestingly, the Harper government's reluctance to participate in shared-cost programs with the provinces has also been accompanied by a willingness to act unilaterally to promote an *alternative* social-policy agenda in areas it considers exclusive federal jurisdiction. For example, it eliminated several long-standing federal social programs and regulatory regimes of which it disapproved, as discussed in Chapter 6, but it also created several new federal programs to promote family values and the missionary work of fundamentalist religious groups.[41] While most of these initiatives did not affect provinces directly, the clear exception was the Harper Conservatives' law-and-order agenda, the financial implications of which once again provoked widespread anger among provincial premiers. Moreover, as with other social-conservative initiatives of this nature, the changes were introduced as unobtrusively as possible and were frequently buried in larger legislative packages. Nor was there any consultation with provinces, which were once again blindsided by the changes. Also, as PBO Kevin Page revealed, claims that the measures would not increase *federal* expenditures were undoubtedly deliberately disingenuous, since the costs to provincial coffers would be significant but were never mentioned.

A case in point was the omnibus crime bill introduced by the Conservatives in October 2011, just months after they obtained their May 2011 majority. The Safe Streets and Communities Act combined nine separate bills that died on the order paper before the election. The Liberals and NDP both opposed specific measures, but, as in the case of other omnibus bills, Justice Minister Rob Nicholson refused to separate out any portions of the bill, and the entire package was pushed through without amendments by March 2012.

One of the measures it contained was the removal of conditional sentences as an option for a number of offences. Since conditional sentences can only be granted for offences that require a penalty of less than two years in jail (most often property crimes), this meant that those denied such conditional sentences in future would automatically serve time in a provincial jail as a result of the change. Charts tabled with the bill in October indicated there would be no additional cost to the federal government, but they were silent on the implications for provinces. However, a detailed, hundred-page study by the PBO found that the added cost for provinces would be more than $140 million per year. Using Statistics Canada data, the PBO predicted an additional 3,800 offenders would serve time in a provincial jail, at a cost to the Canadian taxpayer of $41,000 per individual, as opposed to the $2,600 involved in supervising a conditional sentence. Other provincial costs would result from more court hearings, since more defendants would likely elect to go to trial if the alternative was the certainty of jail time. In addition, the PBO predicted there would actually be increased costs of $8 million for the federal government, as incarcerated offenders would be subject to Parole Board hearings. The report also stressed that the bill ignored the real possibility of additional provincial costs for the construction of new prisons.

Criticism of the omnibus bill came not simply from experts who insisted the bill would do nothing to reduce crime or enhance public safety, but from premiers livid about the addition to their bottom line. Nicholson promised to space out implementation of some of the measures over a period of time to alleviate the burden, but premiers were not placated. All provinces were unhappy, but Ontario and Quebec responded most aggressively to the federal government's decision to push ahead with the change, since they were the provinces most likely to be significantly affected. Ontario's minister responsible, Madeleine Meilleur, noted that Ontario had already invested significant sums in the building of two new prison facilities to replace older jails, but had not anticipated the added strain on the system from the omnibus crime bill. "Ontario taxpayers cannot be expected to pay the full costs for federal anti-crime initiatives," she declared, adding that she anticipated the construction of another thousand-bed facility would be necessary to accommodate the conditional-sentence change. "We expect Ottawa to do what's right and provide additional funding," she warned. Similar criticism came from her Quebec counterpart, Jean-Marc Fournier, who noted that his government estimated the additional cost at $60 million and insisted they would refuse to pay for it at all.[42]

Their concerns were reinforced by a second PBO study, issued in March 2013, which revealed that the overall cost of jails, policing, and courts had risen 23 per cent in the past decade (almost entirely since the arrival of the Harper government in 2006), despite the continuously declining crime rate. The report placed the overall cost of criminal justice at $20.3 billion in 2011–12 alone, and indicated that 73 per cent, or almost $15 billion, was paid for by provinces and municipalities. The report also noted that, unlike the United States, the federal government in Canada has the exclusive jurisdiction to make criminal law, but the administration of justice is a provincial matter. This allows the federal government to pass laws for which provinces will be responsible, with little or no direct cost to itself, and for which it can claim credit.[43]

These actions again suggested that open federalism was more of a political tool than a serious commitment to "respect" provinces and work with them "collaboratively," as promised. The combination of initial neglect, followed by belligerence, which Harper's government demonstrated repeatedly in its relationship with the premiers, was also in evidence with respect to its dealings with aboriginal Canadians. Indeed, the relationship between the Conservatives and aboriginal leadership deteriorated to such a degree that the Idle No More movement was launched in December 2012 to draw public attention to a number of ongoing conflicts with Ottawa. Here again, Harper's willingness to divest the federal government of as much responsibility as possible was not seen as being motivated by a desire to further the cause of aboriginal self-government. Instead, most critics attributed his indifference to his determination to reduce federal expenditures and the size of government (including the possibility of eliminating the Department of Aboriginal Affairs and Northern Development entirely) and also to his desire to provide assistance to the private sector for their various natural-resource projects.

OPEN FEDERALISM IN PRACTICE: IGNORING ABORIGINAL CANADIANS

Almost immediately after the Harper government was elected in January 2006, it announced that it would not implement the Kelowna Accord. This refusal to honour the landmark agreement reached in November 2005 was particularly stunning, since the federal government's constitutional responsibility for First Nations aboriginal peoples under the Indian Act is unquestioned. Moreover, the accord was the result of months of negotiations, involving federal, provincial, territorial, and aboriginal leadership.

The participants made a ten-year commitment to improve the situation of *all* aboriginal Canadians in four key areas: education, housing, health, and a new relationship. Leaders of the federal government, ten provincial governments, three territorial governments, and four national aboriginal organizations participated in the discussions, which included three earlier sets of meetings in September 2004, May 2005, and November 2005. The Kelowna Accord committed $5.1 billion over the first five years for the various programs announced in the deal. A detailed set of tables was included, outlining the breakdown of funding, along with specific commitments in all four subject areas. The federal government, the government of British Columbia, and the Leadership Council of First Nations in British Columbia provided an additional document, detailing how the Accord would be implemented in that province.

BC premier Gordon Campbell said the "historic" meeting offered "a seat at the Table of Confederation" for aboriginal Canadians. "We have an obligation to build on the legal framework of our Constitution," he said, "to extend the same rights, entitlements, and opportunities to aboriginal Canadians, on and off reserve or treaty lands."[44] Likewise, PEI premier, Pat Binns, declared the Accord "will be the test of our nationhood and its federalist underpinnings."[45] Phil Fontaine of the Assembly of First Nations (AFN) shared their enthusiasm. "We are making history by taking the first steps towards creating a new Canada and a new federation; a federation where first peoples of this land enjoy the same quality of life as other Canadians, and where we control the decisions that affect our lives."

The Martin Liberals highlighted the agreement as one of their accomplishments during the 2005–06 election. Initially it appeared that the opposition agreed. Conservative candidate Jim Prentice stated during the campaign that the terms of the Kelowna Accord would be followed if the Conservatives won.[46] Yet soon after the Conservative victory, the Kelowna Accord was shelved. The government provided various explanations for its refusal to honour the Accord. The most frequent objections raised were, first, that the Accord had not actually been signed and therefore was not legally binding and, secondly, that it did not represent a meaningful consensus, because aboriginal leaders from Quebec were not in attendance. This latter argument, surprisingly, was made by the new minister of Indian affairs and northern development, Jim Prentice.[47]

Virtually all the participants at the Kelowna meetings disagreed. The degree of detail provided, the financial commitments, the existence of the signed tripartite agreement with BC, and the statements of the various participants at the time, were all seen as concrete proof that the deal was considered binding. Inuit Tapirisat leader Mary Simon further noted that "the Kelowna Accord committed to … targeted outcomes and allowed for a high level of accountability to the public in the measurement of progress towards those outcomes." Quebec premier Jean Charest noted that he had specifically addressed the absence of his province's aboriginal leaders in his opening remarks in Kelowna, pointing out that, while choosing not to attend for political reasons, they had already been consulted in detail, and their views were effectively represented.

Several academic studies examined the Accord to determine its legal and constitutional status. Many concluded the agreement was not legally binding, but they also argued that it should be treated as such. Most also found that it should be considered a political convention, and said the Harper government's decision to renege on the deal constituted a violation of that convention.[48] Others warned presciently that, if the federal government could renege on this deal with impunity, it would likely feel free to do so on a number of other federal-provincial agreements.

Despite these objections, the Throne Speech and later budgets made no mention of the Accord. Paul Martin's private member's bill calling on the federal government to implement the Accord (which unsettled the government by receiving support and passing the House of Commons as well as the Senate), were simply ignored. So were the objections of the premiers. In June 2006, Premier Ralph Klein of Alberta chaired a meeting of western premiers, which collectively called on the Harper government to fulfil its obligations under the Kelowna Accord. Nor did provincial anger subside. Quebec's Jean Charest, the chair of the Council of the Federation's annual meeting in July 2008, told reporters, "We are doing everything in our power to offer the federal government an opportunity to sit down with us."[49]

This did not happen. Indeed, after the "emergency" meeting of First Ministers in early 2009 brought about by the crisis of the global economic recession, Stephen Harper did not meet with his provincial counterparts again for any reason, and certainly not for a discussion of aboriginal issues. Instead, in a similar vein to his other symbolic gestures – such as the Quebec nation motion in Parliament – Harper made much of a formal apology he offered for the federal government's earlier residential-schools policy. The apology, offered in a moving statement by Harper in the House of Commons, was well-received by virtually everyone involved in the issue. Many hoped it would lead to concrete action by the federal government on a number of outstanding files concerning the dismal state of housing, lack of potable water on reserves, and the need for greater consultation with aboriginal Canadians about resource development on their lands, to say nothing of the need to ensure a prompt settlement of the growing land-claims backlog.

The election of a new leader of the Assembly of First Nations in 2009 also seemed to offer real potential for progress. Shawn Atleo was widely viewed as progressive and conciliatory, and he made it clear in his early speeches that he felt he could work with Harper and his government to bring about positive change. Yet after more than three years, Atleo had little to show for his efforts. Instead, he found himself confronted with a parliamentary committee on aboriginal affairs that was intent on pursuing an idea long promoted by former Harper mentor and adviser Tom Flanagan: the private ownership of reserve lands.

According to the government, it was planning to explore this option as a means of encouraging aboriginal economic development. However, many aboriginal communities were concerned that they would be taken over by large corporations and industries, and would not even benefit from the economic development that resulted. There was nearly universal rejection of the idea among native leadership. Westbank, BC, Chief Robert Louie, chair of the First Nations Land Advisory Board, declared "there's going to be such a huge outcry against this" if the federal government tried to proceed unilaterally. He noted that his own reserve's economic prosperity had been developed without sacrificing ownership of reserve land, through the use of long-term leases for business interests. The AFN also disagreed with the proposal, indicating in a detailed report that there were many options available, not simply the status quo or privatization as suggested by the government.

Then the government's March 2012 budget, intent on making major program cuts to achieve a balanced budget before the next federal election, dropped a series of bombshells on aboriginal communities. First, in an announcement on the Friday afternoon of a long weekend, the highly regarded National Aboriginal Health Organization learned that Health Canada had cut off its funding and it would be shut down by June 30. An incensed André Picard, award-winning medical journalist, took devastating aim at the government in an article which spelled out the desperate state of aboriginal health in Canada and argued against "this travesty of public policy decision-making." Picard added "one cannot help but see this as part of the continuing attack this government has waged on information," and concluded the government was actually "at war with aboriginal peoples.[50]

This action paled, however, in comparison with the government's subsequent decision to modify the venerable Navigable Waters Protection Act (NWPA) of 1882, as discussed earlier. Many of the newly deregulated waterways passed through traditional First Nations land. While the NWPA had originally been intended to facilitate actual navigation, the modern impact of the bill had been to provide strong environmental protection by preventing industrial development, especially to projects such as pipelines which crossed many rivers. Since the Harper government was also heavily involved in promoting the Enbridge Northern Gateway Pipelines Project (a proposal to build a pipeline connecting the Athabasca tar sands with the Pacific Ocean), aboriginal communities – especially in British Columbia – feared the worst. Yet the government refused to meet with aboriginal leaders or reconsider its legislation.

The result was an internationally reported nation-wide protest by aboriginal peoples, the Idle No More movement, involving individual fasts, blockades of roads and train tracks, and physical violence. The AFN was split on the issue of support for the movement. Atleo was subsequently re-elected to a second term as AFN chief in early 2013, but after considerable opposition. Many aboriginal leaders argued it was time for more aggressive action, rather than making any further attempts to reason with the Harper government. Relations between aboriginal leadership and the Harper government deteriorated further in the absence of any meaningful consultation or progress on important policy issues, such as substandard housing and poverty, to say nothing of resource development on aboriginal lands. In a stunning rebuke, Jim Prentice, Harper's former minister of Indian Affairs, who had retired from public life, stated in a public address that it was essential for the federal government to engage aboriginal peoples in meaningful negotiations on the Northern Gateway Pipeline proposal, not only for practical or economic reasons but because it was the federal government's constitutional obligation. A Supreme Court ruling in June 2014 that gave legitimacy to the concept of aboriginal title reinforced Prentice's argument, and left the pipeline project, as well as many other resource-development proposals, in limbo. As a result, many senior corporate spokesmen took up the call for the federal government to assume its responsibility to negotiate. When Prentice subsequently assumed the role of premier of Alberta after the resignation of Alison Redford, analysts predicted the issue would come to a head. Certainly the new premier could be expected to urge Harper to negotiate, and to meet with the various stakeholders.

This, however, was something that Stephen Harper was unwilling to undertake. Having given the green light to the Enbridge Gateway project, he then washed his government's hands of the issue and made it clear that it was up to the private sector to complete negotiations with stakeholders. This ambivalence once again reflected the inherent conflict he faced between ideological commitment and political pragmatism. Public-opinion polls increasingly demonstrated that the federal Conservatives' future electoral prospects could be seriously damaged by their unqualified support for a project opposed by far more voters in western Canada, and especially British Columbia, than merely environmentalists or aboriginal leadership. Having done what he could to help the private sector, Harper pulled back to try to ensure the support of his western base and his government's survival.

Conversely, the particular concerns of Quebec were also increasingly of no interest to Harper, since his 2011 majority eliminated the need for him to view that province as an essential element of his electoral strategy. Instead, he continued to engage in outright battles with the province on both the social and economic-union fronts, a battle which potentially could have serious implications for national unity.

10

Abandoning Quebec: The National-Unity Agenda

Whether Canada ends up as one national government or two national governments or several national governments, or some other kind of arrangement is, quite frankly, secondary in my opinion ... And whether Canada ends up with one national government or two governments or ten governments, the Canadian people will require less government no matter what the constitutional status or arrangement of any future country may be.

Stephen Harper, Speech at the Colin
Brown Memorial Dinner,
National Citizens Coalition, 1994

Quebec separatists are the problem and they need to be fixed.

Stephen Harper, 1997

When one is part of a nation, it is perfectly normal to be nationalist. It is perfectly normal to want to preserve one's history, one's language, one's culture and one's institutions. Not only do I understand and respect this sentiment, I want to help you achieve it.

Prime Minister Stephen Harper, 2006

Soon after taking office in January 2006, Stephen Harper confounded supporters and critics alike with a series of policy decisions that at times delighted Quebec nationalists and at others infuriated them. From the "highs" of his resolution in the House of Commons recognizing the existence of a Quebec "nation," and his willingness to allow the province to attend UNESCO meetings independent of the federal government, to the "lows" of pushing for a federal securities regulator, cutting funding for cultural programs, and refusing to provide gun-registry data to the province, the Harper Conservatives appeared almost schizophrenic in their approach to Quebec.

Conventional wisdom attributed their contradictory policies to political incompetence. It was widely believed their lack of experience in government and, more importantly, their collective lack of understanding of Quebec, were the culprits. Certainly there was widespread agreement that these contradictions were the primary reason why Harper's government – once hopeful of replacing the Liberals as the federalist option in Quebec – soon found themselves hopelessly out of contention and looking elsewhere for the votes to obtain their coveted majority.

However, there is an alternative explanation for the apparent incoherence of the Conservatives' approach to the province. Instead of simple incompetence, their janus-like behaviour once again can be seen as the result of the genuine and deep-seated conflict between two well-defined objectives, namely, their ideological desire to pursue a right-wing agenda and their pragmatic desire to win a majority.

In many cases the first objective took precedence with respect to Quebec, with predictable results in such a predominantly liberal province. This suggests that Harper's strategy of using Quebec to form the third pillar of his majority, as discussed earlier, was doomed to failure from the beginning.

Unfortunately, it also suggests that his approach has been counterproductive in terms of national unity. With separatism having fallen into disfavour after the 1995 referendum, particularly after the Chrétien government's introduction of the Clarity Act (which ensured any future vote would be governed by a clear set of rules and procedures), many would argue that only the consistently right-wing policies of the Harper government could have allowed Pauline Marois and the PQ to succeed in forming a government by positioning themselves as the defenders of a liberal society. That she was not re-elected in 2014 is, conversely, the result of her own political incompetence, for which Harper can take no credit. Indeed, the general deterioration in federal-provincial relations discussed in the preceding chapter pales in comparison with the open conflict that developed with Quebec under Harper, especially after his 2011 majority win.

THE DISTINCT SOCIETY: HARPER'S ABOUT-FACE

When Stephen Harper introduced a resolution in the House of Commons in November 2006, recognizing the existence of a Quebec "nation," those who recalled his staunch opposition to the distinct-society clause in the Charlottetown Accord could hardly contain their astonishment. As someone who had vigorously opposed the Accord's offer of special status to Quebec, Harper's seemingly sudden change of heart was not only unexpected but appeared blatantly opportunistic.

Yet several of his closest advisers were not surprised. As his former chief of staff and academic mentor, Tom Flanagan, stressed, the new prime minister had learned many lessons – including the importance of pragmatism – since his second-place finish in the 2004 election.[1] These developments led Flanagan, a key Conservative campaign organizer and policy adviser throughout this period, to develop a concrete strategy for turning a Conservative minority into a majority. The strategy called for the Conservatives to become the federalist alternative in Quebec, replacing the Liberals. In theory, the Quebec vote would be garnered from Quebec nationalists, who would find Harper's support for a greatly decentralized federation to be far more appealing than the centralist thrust of the federal Liberals. Hence Flanagan publicly praised Harper's pragmatism in introducing the resolution in Parliament and describing Quebec as a nation, even though he too had vociferously opposed the distinct-society clause in the Charlottetown Accord.[2]

Yet in the 2008 election, despite considerable help from the Liberals – who ran one of the most incompetent political campaigns in living memory, with one of the least politically astute leaders – Harper was still only able to achieve a slightly larger minority.[3] Moreover the importance of the Conservatives' ideological agenda was often ignored by analysts when attempting to explain the government's failure to make inroads in Quebec. Yet it was this innate conflict between the new Conservative agenda (which guided many of their policy decisions) and their strategy of political pragmatism to gain support from the Quebec nationalists (which guided several other policies), that was primarily responsible for the seemingly mixed messages coming from the Harper government, and for the ultimate failure of their Quebec strategy.

In order to fully appreciate the significance of these two competing forces, it is important to first situate the relevant policy initiatives within the context of Harper's principal tool for achieving his objectives: namely, "open federalism." Indeed, as the previous chapter demonstrated, long before he became leader of the Conservative Party, Stephen Harper had been developing his "new" approach to

Canadian federalism, one that would allow him to pursue his conservative agenda through administrative rather than constitutional reform and, coincidentally, appeal to Quebec nationalists.

In the 2005 Conservative Party platform, which devoted three full sections to "federalism," "reform of the federation," and "the fiscal imbalance," the party promised to "ensure that the use of the federal spending power in provincial jurisdictions is limited," and "authorize the provinces to use the opting-out formula with full compensation if they want to opt out of any new or modified federal program in areas of shared or exclusive jurisdiction."[4]

Harper went further in a speech he deliberately chose to give in Quebec City on 19 December 2005. There he said that his approach to federalism would involve "expanding" or "developing" the social union by allowing the *provinces* to play the lead role. The federal government's actions, he promised, would be limited to "complementing and supporting" those of the provinces.[5] Although this would apply to all provinces, he knew the pledge would have special appeal for Quebec.

Soon after the party obtained a minority in that election, Harper reiterated his promise. His letter to the Council of the Federation on 13 January 2006 specifically underlined his determination "to initiate a new style of open federalism which would involve working more closely and collaboratively with the provinces." This commitment was reinforced in another speech in Quebec in April of the same year, to the Montreal Board of Trade, where he declared "the time has come to establish a new relationship with the provinces, a relationship that is open, honest and respectful."[6]

By 2008, hoping for a majority government, the Harper Conservatives' platform reiterated these commitments, with some important additions. One section on open federalism was entitled "respecting the provinces and territories" and promised, somewhat paradoxically, that a re-elected Harper government would recognize provincial jurisdiction, "as spelled out in the *Constitution Act, 1867*," by "enshrining our principles of federalism in a new Charter of Open Federalism." Further voluntary limitations on the federal spending power were also promised. Now, any new shared-cost program would not even proceed without the consent of the majority of provinces, and provinces could still choose to opt out with compensation "so long as the province offers a similar program with similar accountability structures."[7]

It is noteworthy that Harper did not single out Quebec in *any* of his three stated rationales. On the one hand, Quebec was viewed as a province like the others. As such, it would benefit from open federalism in the same way as any other province. On the other hand, Harper was prepared to use the "open federalism" argument quite aggressively to appeal to Quebec nationalists. At one point during the 2008 campaign, he even told an audience in Montreal that open federalism demonstrated *the Conservatives* were the "true" Quebec nationalists.

HARPER'S RECORD ON QUEBEC: A CASE OF DUELLING OBJECTIVES

As demonstrated in the previous chapter, after taking office in January 2006 the Harper government proceeded to implement some of its decentralist commitments regarding open federalism quite aggressively. In other policy fields, it took strong federal initiatives that, to the uninitiated, appeared to fly in the face of its decentralist vision. This apparent mixed message led some observers, including Norman Spector, former clerk of the Privy Council, to conclude that Harper was more opportunistic and less ideologically driven than previously believed.[8]

No doubt Harper's stunning introduction of the Quebec nation resolution in the House of Commons played a part in that analysis. However his government's record suggests Harper did not succumb to pragmatism as often as Spector might have predicted. Instead, the evidence suggests a constant tension between Harper's genuine commitment to the new conservative agenda, which prevailed much of the time, and the need to practise pragmatic politics in order to survive, particularly in a minority situation, which was a motivating factor on many other occasions. Equally significant, the findings demonstrate that Harper adopted centralizing measures to pursue his market-oriented economic agenda as frequently as he pursued decentralizing measures on social-policy issues. Both were often an extreme irritant for Quebec.

Evidence of Harper's two-pronged approach to federalism could most clearly be found in the October 2008 Throne Speech, where the dual concepts of aggressive federal intervention on the economic union, coupled with an abdication of the federal role in the social union, were both strongly reinforced. The Harper government's commitment to legislate limits to the federal spending power, and to allow provinces to opt out of existing national schemes with full compensation if they set up their own, combined with his determination to impose a national securities regulator, served notice that the underlying rationale for open federalism was alive and well.

Nevertheless Harper's early acts of political pragmatism were frequent and high-profile, and they were almost entirely focused on Quebec. This aspect of his government's agenda drew far more attention, and was clearly designed to garner support among Quebec nationalists in preparation for another election. Given the concerns expressed by his western base, it was evident that he persevered in spite of those concerns, because he believed the political gains would be worth it in the end. Even before the "Quebec nation" resolution of December 2006, Harper had made good on his election promise to allow Quebec a seat at the table alongside the Canadian delegation to UNESCO. Announcing the agreement in May 2006, he also reiterated his willingness to allow provincial input on federal matters when he declared "le fédéralisme d'ouverture de notre nouveau gouvernement consiste a tirer parti de l'expérience et de l'expertise que les provinces peuvent apporter au dialogue national." ("The open federalism of our new government takes advantage of the experience and expertise which the provinces can bring to a national dialogue.")[9]

This move was followed by a series of announcements indicating support for Quebec's ongoing negotiations with the government of France concerning the recognition of professional credentials. Stressing that their open-federalism approach allowed Premier Charest to undertake this initiative without federal interference, Harper emphasized his government's respect for the fact that labour matters fell under provincial jurisdiction. Even here, though, Transport Minister Lawrence Cannon also underlined that the Conservatives would be prepared to indirectly support any other province wishing to engage in bilateral negotiations at the international level, making it clear that the concept of provincial equality was still an important principle.[10]

During the 2008 election, Harper enthusiastically committed his government to the concept of asymmetrical federalism, and to offering provinces a say in matters of federal jurisdiction. When a proposed "tough on crime" measure in the Conservative platform (decreasing the age of majority from sixteen to fourteen for serious crimes) came under fire in Quebec, Harper simply suggested that provinces could "opt out" of federal sentencing rules and introduce a higher age limit if they preferred.[11] This remarkable, and remarkably nonchalant, approach to the criminal code was seen by some as a strictly political move to placate Quebec voters during an election. But a close reading of Harper's earlier statements and party platforms makes clear that this approach is entirely consistent with his broad vision for the federation.

Then there was Harper's decision to recognize the existence of a fiscal imbalance vis-à-vis Quebec, something neither he nor any other federal politician had been prepared to do until then. Unlike virtually all of the previous pragmatic political gestures towards the province, this move would end up costing the government a considerable amount of money. And, as several commentators were quick to note, in the end it was judged insufficient by Jean Charest, who viewed it as a down payment rather than a settling of accounts.[12]

Yet another example was the strikingly symbolic gesture of transferring ownership of the lands surrounding the National Assembly buildings to the provincial government. But none of these measures appeared to have moved public opinion in Quebec about the Conservatives. And while the gestures may have been appreciated by the Charest government at the time, they had no lasting impact with them either, as the ensuing public battles between Harper and Charest demonstrated.

HARPER'S SOCIAL UNION AND QUEBEC

The primary reason for the failure of its Quebec strategy lay in the Harper government's social and economic policy initiatives, many of which ran directly counter to the political culture of the province. As one Quebec commentator noted of Harper's gesture in ceding ownership of federal lands, "Les Québécois lui sauront gré de corriger cette anomalie. C'est toutefois dans un dossier plus substantiel qu'on jugera si le gouvernement conservateur croit toujours au fédéralisme d'ouverture." ("Quebecers will thank him for correcting that anomaly, but it is only on a more substantial file that we will be able to judge if the conservative government still believes in open federalism.")[13]

In the crucial area of social union, for example, it soon became evident that the Conservatives' right-wing agenda and social conservatism had fallen afoul of one of the most left-wing societies in the country. From their determination to eliminate the gun registry to their cuts in funding for women's groups, opposition to gay marriage, and serial problems with women's-rights issues, the Conservatives consistently demonstrated that they did not share the same values as most Quebecers.

Another dramatic example of this dilemma emerged over the Conservatives' refusal to include funding for abortion in their own G8 initiative on maternal and child health in Africa. In what was described as a "concerted broadside" against Harper's position, Quebec legislators unanimously passed a private member's motion supporting a woman's right to choose. Premier Jean Charest supported the motion, declaring "Abortion is an inalienable right and the consensus expressed in the National Assembly reflects the consensus on this issue in Quebec society."[14]

As we have seen, Harper's early fiscal measures to "starve the beast" included a significant reduction in the GST and a variety of tax cuts for individuals and businesses. These turned Paul Martin's legacy surplus into a deficit, and left the government vulnerable to the advent of the 2008 economic crisis. To counter this, Harper then reduced funding for a variety of federally funded social programs, such as youth employment and workplace-skills training, adult literacy programs, and social-development partnership programs, all of which infuriated the Charest government. Although many of the Harper Conservatives' specific actions may have remained below the radar screen of the average Quebecer, the cumulative effect of these cuts was outlined repeatedly in the Quebec media, with negative consequences for his government's image in that province.

Another key problem area for Harper's Conservatives was, of course, transfer payments in support of the welfare state. As Harper learned to his dismay, transferring power to Quebec could not compensate for money. With a string of federalist premiers from Robert Bourassa to Jean Charest adopting the "fédéralisme rentable" defence of the federation, they simply could not be seen to accept less from a federal government, and certainly not with respect to fundamental elements of the welfare state such as equalization. Yet Harper persisted in defending what Jean Charest loudly and repeatedly described as a $1-billion reduction in equalization payments for Quebec, and his recalcitrance was widely reported in the province. "Meme si Québec lui avait fait part publiquement de ses inquiétudes a l'approche de dépôt de son budget," one journalist wrote critically, "le gouvernement fédéral a dépose un document qui n'a rien pour rassurer la province." ("Even though Quebec expressed its concerns publicly before the budget was tabled, the federal government brought down a budget that did nothing to reassure that province.")[15] This led a furious Jean Charest to denounce "l'unilateralisme" of the Harper government, insisting that consultation with provinces must be part of any concept of open federalism, even in areas of federal jurisdiction.[16]

The "cold war that refuses to thaw"[17] continued with the Harper government's initiatives – or rather lack of initiatives – in environmental policy, another area of great concern to ordinary Quebecers. Interestingly, the equalization debate focused on the new formula's treatment of oil revenue, and Jean Charest's determination to portray Quebec as the greenest province in the country, a position that Harper mocked. As Quebecers watched aghast, Charest and Harper publicly and heatedly criticized each other's policies for several months leading up to the United Nations Copenhagen Summit on climate change. Even from India, Jean Charest derided Ottawa's plan to link its eventual climate-change emissions policy to that of the United States.[18] Ottawa responded by deriding Charest's plan to impose his own higher standards in concert with Ontario. At the conference itself, the two men took repeated swipes at each other's approaches, to the amazement of ordinary Quebecers.[19]

The Conservatives' law-and-order agenda was another key bone of contention, as the issue of young offenders during the 2008 election demonstrated. Although there were several more disagreements over the next three years, it was the move to impose mandatory minimum sentences contained in the Harper government's 2012 omnibus crime bill (described in detail in Chapter 7), that was the next major flashpoint in Quebec. Opposition to the move was found across the country, but it was the Quebec government that took the most aggressive tone, promising to introduce its own measures to deliberately "soften" the intent and the impact of the new rules. It was also clear that the provincial government had the support of stakeholders and citizens. The Quebec Bar Association was so incensed by the proposals that they filed a formal complaint with the Quebec Superior Court, while a small group of defence lawyers warned that they were considering a constitutional challenge to the legislation.

However nothing compared with the knock-down drag-out battle that ensued over the Harper government's plans to abolish the long-gun registry. Since it was a perennial platform commitment of the

Conservatives, designed to satisfy one of their most important social-action support groups, no one was surprised when Harper's government moved swiftly after their 2011 majority victory to follow through on their pledge. However virtually everyone was caught unaware by Public Safety Minister Vic Toews's announcement that, in addition, the government would destroy all the data that had been collected. Quebec's Liberal government objected immediately. "The federal government said during the campaign that it would abolish the long gun registry," provincial Public Security Minister Robert Dutil acknowledged, "but it never said anything about destroying the database. We are strongly and ferociously against that."[20]

The issue was crucial for Quebec, since the provincial Liberal government and its PQ successor had both pledged to maintain an independent registry if the Conservatives did abolish the long-gun registry. However, they had also assumed that it would cost only a few million dollars to do so, because they did not expect to lose the existing data. In addition, Quebec was home to the original movement to establish the registry, prompted by the École Polytechnique massacre, and public support for the program was therefore especially strong.

Quebec Intergovernmental Affairs Minister Yvon Vallières attempted to negotiate with his federal counterpart to amend the federal legislation, and Robert Dutil appeared at a House of Commons committee hearing on the legislation, Bill C-19, to plead for an exception. But Toews and the Conservatives were adamant. As a result, on 11 December 2011, Dutil announced that Quebec was launching a court challenge of Bill C-19 to obtain the data for Quebec. The press conference for the announcement was attended by representatives of police forces, police unions, crime experts, and victims, and was widely and favourably covered by the Quebec media. The same day, in a unanimous vote in the National Assembly, a motion was passed instructing the provincial firearms officer to ignore Ottawa's demands and do whatever was necessary to protect the relevant data. As Justice Minister Jean-Marc Fournier declared, "Here [in the National Assembly] you have people with very different views on a number of issues. But on this one we have unanimity. It truly represents what Quebecers think."[21]

The Quebec government won an early round by obtaining an injunction against the federal government from the Quebec Superior Court, preventing it from destroying the data immediately after the passage of Bill C-19, as it had originally planned. However, in June 2013, Quebec's Court of Appeal sided with the Harper government, stating that the province had no property right to the data. Then in September the Federal Court refused to stay the injunction, as requested by the federal government, noting that the province had filed a request to appeal to the Supreme Court. As a result, the data remained in limbo, and in November 2013 the Supreme Court announced that it would agree to hear the appeal, suggesting that the battle between the two governments over the eventual fate of the data would continue for some time.

Nevertheless, probably the most embarrassing example of the growing divide between Quebec and Ottawa came in the area of foreign affairs. Harper's willingness to allow "symbolic" gestures, such as the Quebec seat at UNESCO, appeared to have opened the floodgates, particularly after the election of a PQ government. Having won the provincial election in part due to her ability to position the PQ as the guardian of "Quebec values" in the face of the social conservative thrust of the Harper Conservatives, Premier Pauline Marois wasted little time in exploiting these differences wherever she found them. On an official visit to France to meet with French Prime Minister Jean-Marc Ayrault, Marois stated, "Quebecers no longer recognize themselves in Canada's foreign policy, which has turned its back on a tradition of openness, mediation, and multilateralism."[22] In a fascinating interview with Quebec media accompanying her tour, the separatist premier spent considerable time praising former Liberal prime minister Lester Pearson, whom she noted had won a Nobel Prize for the "liberal values" that had aided the peace process in Suez. Reporters were quick to note the irony of this recognition of Pearson and of liberal values, which had also been spelled out expressly in the 2011 federal leaders' debates by none other than Bloc leader Gilles Duceppe.

A few months later, another gauntlet was thrown down by the PQ when Intergovernmental Affairs Minister Alexandre Cloutier announced his government was setting up a committee to examine the possibility of Quebec developing its own foreign-aid agency. In unveiling the plan, Cloutier indicated one item under review was to take back that portion of CIDA monies funded by his province's contribution to federal tax revenues. He claimed this was because CIDA had become "tainted" by Conservative ideology and a commitment to aid Canadian businesses abroad (and particularly mining operations), rather than supporting humanitarian concerns. "When CIDA was founded it was founded on Quebec values that were shared by many Canadians," Cloutier declared. "Now, the notion of international solidarity [under Harper] appears more and more marginalized."[23]

HARPER'S ECONOMIC UNION AND QUEBEC

As if this were not sufficient, the Harper Conservatives' approach to the economic union led to further conflict with Quebec. Here again, Stephen Harper remained remarkably committed to his vision of strong unilateral federal initiatives, even during a period of economic turmoil and recession. Indeed, as early indications of the global recession developed during the 2008 election campaign, Harper made it clear that his preference was to do little, but, if necessary, to act alone. As Michael Behiels has demonstrated, only when it became abundantly clear that this approach would be politically devastating in a federal election did Harper give in and involve the provinces in a joint action plan for recovery.[24]

Despite this, however, it should be noted that Quebec's repeated calls for federal investment in social infrastructure (such as a national child-care plan), environmental technology, or even EI reform to be included as part of a federal stimulus package, all fell on deaf ears. Meanwhile, Harper had virtually removed environmental and aboriginal issues from the national agenda by refusing to deal with them in the intergovernmental forum, arbitrarily relegating them to obscurity or to the sole domain of the provincial arena.

Harper's emphasis on the economic union also translated quickly into a concern with the removal of internal trade barriers and the push for a national securities regulator. Former Mulroney cabinet minister Tom Hockin, the man appointed by Finance Minister Jim Flaherty to examine the securities issue, produced a report that defended the creation of such a national regulator on constitutional grounds. "The federal government has a 'constitutional' right to impose a regulator that would have authority to pre-empt existing provincial agencies," the report said. In his forward to the report, Hockin himself stressed "Canadians are ill-served by such a Balkanized system ... and we are assured by our constitutional advisor that the federal Parliament has the constitutional authority to enact legislation that would provide for comprehensive capital markets regulations in Canada."

Harper's determination to pursue this issue in the face of staunch opposition from Quebec – not simply Jean Charest's government but many of Quebec's business and media elites – suggested his commitment to this belief was far stronger than his concern about political gain in the province. Not only did Harper and his minister insist on their right to establish a national securities regulator, they took the issue to the Supreme Court for an opinion, rather than attempt any form of negotiation or compromise. As prominent Quebec journalist André Pratte noted, "MM Harper et Flaherty doivent savoir que leur projet inquiéte non seulement le Bloc Québécois, non seulement l'Assemblée nationale au grand complet; la majorité des gens d'affaires et des professionales de la métropole québécoise s'y oppose." ("Messrs Harper and Flaherty must know that their plan upsets not only the Bloc Québécois and the whole National Assembly; the majority of business people and professionals in urban Quebec oppose it.")[25] Journalist Chantal Hébert went further, declaring that "Ottawa et Québec s'en vont en guerre." ("Ottawa and Quebec are going to war.")[26]

A similar situation emerged with respect to the proposed harmonization of the sales tax. Noting that the federal government had already compensated Ontario and BC for associated costs, while remaining silent on the situation for Quebec (that province had already harmonized its sales tax in 1997), Quebec Finance Minister Raymond Bachand declared it was an essential measure and a simple matter of "justice." But Ottawa remained intractable for some time in the face of Quebec's resistance to becoming a fully integrated partner in a national plan. Although harmonization had been introduced in 1997, Quebec remained responsible for administering the system, a situation about which open federalism technically should have been sanguine. In the end, Harper and Charest finally reached an agreement on the issue in 2011, after more than five years of squabbling, but the damage to the Conservatives' image had been done.

The level of conflict escalated again with Harper's announcement of the Canada Job Grant program discussed in the preceding chapter. Premier Marois added a new wrinkle to provincial opposition to this program, claiming that Quebec should be allowed to opt out of the program with full compensation, a position that other premiers supported unanimously and Jason Kenney rejected out of hand. Equally damaging was the Harper government's package of proposals to tighten conditions in the EI program, which they had introduced in the fall of 2012. The package was criticized by experts because of its likely negative impact on seasonal workers. Not surprisingly, Quebec, home to more than 40 per cent of all seasonal workers in the country, was viscerally opposed to the planned changes. Yet here too, Harper remained adamant. Before a planned meeting with Pauline Marois in early 2013, Harper "categorically" rejected any changes to the plan and told reporters, "As you know all too well, employment insurance is clearly a federal jurisdiction according to the Canadian constitution. Obviously, we have every intention of respecting jurisdictions."[27]

Meanwhile, in the area of the environment, which is undeniably a shared area of jurisdiction, but one in which the federal government has the constitutional authority to act and has historically shown leadership, the situation deteriorated still further. In the face of the federal government reneging on Canada's Kyoto commitment and refusing to take concrete, mandatory measures to reduce emissions, all the while promoting the oil sands as the "ethical" solution to energy shortages, the newly elected PQ government picked up where the Charest government had left off. Environment Minister Pierre Arcand announced that his government would be the first provincially to take independent action by introducing a cap-and-trade policy for carbon emissions, based on the widely recognized California model. Providing a one-year phasing-in period for business, the new system was to come into effect in January 2013. Arcand's rationale by now was becoming familiar. "I think Canada should absolutely be showing more leadership," he declared. He noted that the Conservatives' excuse for failing to act had been based on a need to work hand-in-hand with the Americans, and then added sarcastically that California was in America, and that President Barack Obama had already announced several progressive measures. Arcand concluded, "I find it altogether unacceptable that the Canadian position is still to be 'tied' to the American position."[28] Harper's reply was equally familiar: the federal government would respect jurisdictions, and had no intention of taking further action which could jeopardize Canada's economic advantage.

In short, it would seem that the Harper government was determined to implement as much of its economic agenda as possible, regardless of the consequences in terms of its relationship with Quebec or its image with Quebec voters. And, as Chantal Hebert predicted, in addition to turbulence at the federal level, many of Harper's proposed measures in both economic and social policy "would amount to a substantial rebalancing of the federation" which "may not involve constitutional change but [are] bound to trigger massive federal-provincial debate."[29] This was nowhere more true than in the case of Quebec, which watched its economic status and political influence deteriorate dramatically as the Alberta economic agenda and drive for Senate reform came to dominate the national stage.

HARPER'S UNILATERAL CONSTITUTIONAL APPROACH AND QUEBEC

Despite Harper's well-known preference for administrative change over constitutional reform, the constitution did enter the agenda as well, notably with respect to reform of the Senate and the appointment of a judge to the Supreme Court. In both cases, Quebec opposed the government's plans and its unilateral process, and challenged their constitutionality in court.

When the Supreme Court appointment of supernumerary Federal Court justice Marc Nadon was announced, it immediately became controversial. It was soon learned that such a controversy had actually been anticipated by the Harper government. In fact, Justice Minister Peter MacKay had gone to the trouble of requesting legal opinions from two former judges, both of whom had indicated that in their view the appointment, although unusual, was constitutional. This was especially significant, since appointments to the Supreme Court from Quebec are guaranteed in the constitution, something that is not the case for the rest of Canada. While convention or tradition may suggest that a specific vacancy should be filled with a candidate from other provinces or regions, this is an informal arrangement that need not be respected. But Quebec is entitled to three seats.

As a result, when Nadon's appointment was announced, Quebec immediately took issue, noting that the Federal Court is not specifically named as a potential source of Quebec candidates for the Supreme Court. Quebec's justice minister protested the appointment, adding that Nadon had neither lived nor practised law in Quebec for decades. Intergovernmental Affairs Minister Alexandre

Cloutier quickly followed up by announcing that Quebec would challenge the appointment in the Supreme Court, a first in the court's history. "It is certain we will make sure Quebec's voice is heard on the Court," Cloutier said. "We have the right to three judges and we will demand it."[30] With Nadon obliged to step aside before ever taking his seat, the Court was left short-handed at a busy time and Nadon was left with a lame-duck image, even if his appointment eventually was to be confirmed. But in the end, the Court delivered another stinging rebuke to Harper, stating in a 6–1 decision that Nadon was not eligible to sit, and that Harper's last-ditch effort to change the rules on appointments, contained as part of his latest omnibus budget bill, was unconstitutional. Harper's attempts to salvage the situation by accepting a short list proposed by the newly elected government of Philippe Couillard may have gone some way towards reducing the level of hostility. However as discussed in an earlier chapter, Peter MacKay's subsequent decision to appoint another Federal Court justice to the Quebec Superior Court, in an obvious move to position this second appointment in advance of Supreme Court Justice Louis LeBel's resignation in December 2014, clouded the issue and again raised concerns about the Harper government's intentions.

Meanwhile the Senate reference was a last-ditch effort by Harper's government to demonstrate that it was following through on earlier election commitments to reform and "democratize" the Senate. But the reference the government sent to the Supreme Court in late 2012, asking for clarification on Ottawa's powers to act alone in that reform, was not expected to provide the answers that the Conservatives hoped for. Despite Harper's earlier assurance that political will could achieve his objectives through administrative rather than constitutional means, virtually everyone following the Senate reference case had concluded that the Court would indicate a constitutional amendment process involving the provinces, and especially including Quebec, would be an essential component of any future attempts by Harper to tackle the contentious issue of Senate reform. Quebec, meanwhile, was further incensed by the decision of the Court to hear the reference without the presence of a third Quebec justice. As a result, Quebec launched its own reference to the Quebec Court of Appeal, which did indeed find in October 2013 that the federal government's Senate-reform plan was unconstitutional.

THE HARPER MAJORITY AND QUEBEC'S FADING INFLUENCE

The Harper government's failure to make further gains in Quebec in the 2008 election caused them to rethink their coalition pillar strategy. Their attempts to secure the support of Quebec nationalists through symbolic gestures and the decentralist thrust of open federalism had clearly been insufficient, largely because of their actions on the left-right axis. The Conservatives' had assumed they could win on the federalist axis, which dominates Quebec politics in many respects, and therefore did not need to worry about their positions on the left-right axis. They were wrong. In fact, the importance of the left-right axis was amplified by the left-wing positions taken by the Bloc in parliament, and by Harper's own brief dalliance with the right-wing Action démocratique du Québec (ADQ).

As well, Harper's government was dependent on its core support in western Canada, support that was predicated on the new conservative agenda. This agenda therefore could hardly continue to take a back seat to further political pragmatism vis-à-vis Quebec. Having cajoled both his hardline grassroots supporters and his caucus into accepting his pragmatic Quebec initiatives in order to gain a majority, and having reaped no benefits from that strategy, Harper could not go to that well again.

Instead, by the 2011 election he had decided to move on, a move which in itself demonstrated his decreasing concern about the province. While he may have been unable to replace the Liberals as the federalist option in Quebec, it also was evident that the Liberals were nowhere near regaining their former status with Quebec voters. As long as the Bloc continued to dominate the political scene in the province, Harper could effectively ignore Quebec and seek his majority elsewhere. As it happened, it was the NDP that reaped the benefits of the Quebec vacuum in 2011, but this too was of no concern to Harper, who in fact could view the presence of a socialist party as the Official Opposition with delight.

Tom Flanagan outlined the new strategy of end-running Quebec in detail. Returning once again to the "three pillar" concept, Flanagan pointed to the successful capture of formerly Liberal "ethnic" voters in Ontario. In a plan reminiscent of the "Reagan Democrats" strategy of the Republicans (in which they targeted certain groups who normally supported the Democrats), Flanagan argued, "The role of a third and essential pillar to complement the western populists and traditional Tories would be played by ethnic voters, new Canadians, mostly in Ontario rather than Quebec." In the Canadian context, this involved "a direct assault on the Liberals' ethnic fortress of Toronto rather than on the BQ's hegemonic hold over francophones in Quebec."[31] Moreover, Flanagan argued that this new ethnic pillar would be more stable than the always "difficult" voting bloc of francophones in Quebec.

The success of this strategy had significant consequences for the place of Quebec in the federation. For the first time, a federal government had obtained a majority without support from that province, leading almost immediately to its decreased relevance in federal calculations. An example of the declining influence of Quebec in Harper's thinking emerged shortly after the majority was obtained, with his appointment of Angelo Persichilli as his new director of communications in September 2011. The appointment was immediately criticized in many quarters, primarily because Persichilli, a Toronto journalist and editor of *Corriere Canadense*, whom Jason Kenney once described as the "eminence grise" of Toronto's 905 ethnic community, was not bilingual. Little effort was made by the PMO to explain this development or offer a fig leaf to Quebec French-language reporters. The already tense situation escalated when it was learned that Persichilli had recently written an article for the *Toronto Star* in which he had not only praised Harper, comparing him to Pierre Trudeau, but attacked Quebec. "Many are tired of the annoying lament from a province that keeps yelling at those that pay part of its bills," Persichilli wrote, "and are concerned by the over-representation of francophones in our bureaucracy, our Parliament, and our institutions."[32]

Even more revealing of the turning away from Quebec was Harper's subsequent introduction of legislation to implement changes to the distribution of seats in the House of Commons, which would see Quebec's proportion of seats drop below 25 per cent. As a furious Bloc Québécois House Leader, Pierre Paquette, demonstrated in an opinion piece, this move was not only widely seen in Quebec as a rejection of all of Harper's symbolic gestures, but a clear indication that open federalism meant very little for Quebec. Paquette wrote, "Il y a un test fondamental pour Stephen Harper ...

le fédéralism d'ouverture de Stephen Harper est-il sincère et vrai, ou n'est-ce qu'un fédéralisme de pacotille?" ("This is a fundamental test for Stephen Harper – is his open federalism sincere and real, or is it nothing but junk federalism?")[33]

By April 2012, Harper's lack of attention to Quebec, and his heightened pursuit of the social-conservative agenda – including the gun-registry battle with Quebec – were being seen by all Quebec federalists, including Quebec Conservatives, as a gift to the separatist Parti Québécois. As former Progressive Conservative power broker and Mulroney aide Peter White, head of an eastern township Conservative riding association, complained, "Every time Pauline Marois attacks Harper she goes up in the polls ... Harper is giving her all these targets."[34] Similarly, Harper's pursuit of Alberta-centric economic policies did little to endear him to Quebecers, and in fact led some critics to suggest that he was helping to create the so-called "winning conditions" that Lucien Bouchard had argued were necessary before another referendum could reasonably be launched by a separatist government. White, who urged Harper to engage in a charm offensive and tour the province with his small band of Quebec MPs to change perceptions, could hardly have been more blunt. "People hate the guy," he said, "they really hate him. They think he has horns and a tail and eats babies, and I'm sure he has no idea that this is the case."[35]

National columnist Jeffrey Simpson's analysis of the situation was equally blunt. "Not since the first Diefenbaker government of 1957 has a federal government been weaker in Quebec and apparently cared so little for the province," he wrote. At the same time, public-opinion polls demonstrated two even more ominous developments. On the one hand, Canadians outside of Quebec were less inclined to worry about the consequences of Quebec separation. On the other hand, Quebecers were less inclined to think about the rest of Canada at all.[36]

Despite this growing divide, public-opinion polls also continued to demonstrate a low level of support for separation. For the most part, this situation was attributed to the economic and social crises taking place in Quebec, which had seen widespread civil unrest, including a student revolt, over issues such as tuition fees and the growing gap between rich and poor. Focused on their internal problems, it was not surprising that no political elites felt capable of raising the issue of Quebec's place in Confederation. Nevertheless, numerous observers pointed to the growing alienation from Ottawa and the rest of Canada as a potentially damaging development in the medium to longer term, and one that needed to be addressed to prevent a resurgence in Quebec nationalism.

Instead, with Pauline Marois's defeat in the 2014 provincial election that she had originally called in the hopes of obtaining her own majority, it was Harper who was handed a gift. As the election unexpectedly developed into an unofficial third referendum on sovereignty, the Quebec Liberals, under new leader Philippe Couillard, took a commanding lead and coasted to a majority victory themselves. An ardent federalist, Couillard is perhaps the most articulate and committed provincial leader to represent the province in decades. As a result, the very real possibility that the highly unpopular Harper might be forced to face off against a majority separatist government was averted, again through no fault of his own. However, while Couillard may be a committed federalist, he also has demonstrated considerable distaste for various social policies of the federal government, and especially their approach to health care, a situation which would suggest the battle between Harper and Quebec will continue. Nor do these developments bode well for the progress of Harper's long-term agenda to develop a conservative political culture and entrench the federal Conservative Party as the natural governing party.

Still, it appears that Harper has not given up entirely on that strategy. Despite his party's falling standings in public-opinion polls, several of his spokespersons stressed that the Conservatives hope to retake at least five seats in Quebec in the 2015 election, thanks to the PQ provincial defeat and the declining fortunes of the federal NDP and it's so-called Orange Wave. In June 2014, Harper gave a speech at the Calgary Stampede in which he made an unlikely reference to George-Étienne Cartier, a Quebec Father of Confederation, praising his "Conservative vision of a strong Quebec in a united Canada."[37] Then, in early September 2014, he attended an event in Quebec City related to the celebration of the 150th anniversary of the 1864 Quebec Conference, the meeting which paved the way for the Charlottetown Conference and Confederation. At that event, the prime minister unveiled a plaque honouring Cartier, and stressed in his remarks that Cartier was a "Bleu" (conservative) who had protected francophone culture and language in the confederation agreement, suggesting that his own government had done the same. Then he took credit for the gradual decline in support for separation, which in fact had occurred long before he took office. However, as opinion polls demonstrated, few Quebecers appear to be moved by those arguments, and increasingly view Ottawa and the federal government as irrelevant to their concerns and aspirations.

11

Rebranding Canada: The Real Conservative Agenda

This political party stands for values that are eternal ... this country will either adopt our values or it will fail.

Stephen Harper, 20 December 2001

There is a continental culture. There is a Canadian culture that is in some ways unique to Canada, but I don't think Canadian culture coincides neatly with borders.

Stephen Harper, *Report* newsmagazine, 7 January 2002

When Stephen Harper became prime minister in 2006, he was unique among Canadian politicians. A man of many firsts, he was not only the first leader of the new Conservative Party but the first conservative prime minister to come from a Reform/Alliance background. Mr Harper's stated objectives were unique as well. Not content to win power and implement his party's campaign platform, he was the first Canadian leader whose self-proclaimed long-term plans included the destruction of his principal adversary (the Liberal Party of Canada), and the rebranding of Canada's political culture. Perhaps most striking of all, Harper was the first federal leader to express his deep-seated disdain for the country he was about to govern.

Harper's views were made crystal clear long before 2006. His 1997 speech to the American Council for National Policy provided first-hand evidence of this disdain, outlining important "facts" about Canada for his visitors. As we saw earlier, the first was that Canada is "a Northern European welfare state in the worst sense of the term, and very proud of it." However there was more to come. The second was that "Canada is basically an English-speaking country, just as

English-speaking as, I would guess, the northern part of the United States." Harper's third fact was that "many Canadians fancy [Canada] as some kind of a third force ... that's where you get the strong support for the United Nations. Canada contributes a great deal to the UN relatively, and takes a great deal of pride over always being praised by UN bodies. This distresses conservatives like myself quite profoundly."[1]

His frustration with Canadians' respect for peacekeeping and the United Nations surfaced again when he criticized the Chrétien government's popular decision to stay out of the 2003 Iraq War. He denounced the government's position as "gutless and juvenile" in the Commons. Then he co-authored an article in the *Wall Street Journal* with his party's shadow critic for foreign affairs, Stockwell Day, entitled "Canadians Stands with You," apparently unconcerned that, as leader of the Official Opposition he was undermining Canadian foreign policy abroad.[2]

At various points in his career, Harper has disparaged such revered political icons as medicare, the Canada Pension Plan, and equalization, his opinions epitomized in the 2001 Firewall Letter to Alberta premier Ralph Klein. He has also denounced important symbols of Canadian identity, such as the Charter of Rights and Freedoms, official bilingualism, and multiculturalism. He even criticized regions of the country, as evidenced in his controversial description of Atlantic Canada's "Culture of Defeat."[3]

In their place, Harper has attempted to create a new set of myths and symbols that reflect the conservative vision of Canada. For many Canadians, however, this vision of Canada is unrecognizable. It appears frozen in a 1950s time warp, based on mythical images of happy middle-class families living in leafy suburbs with low crime rates and no immigrants. It also appears to be intensely pro-American, reflecting well-known arts-and-culture critic Robert Fulford's famous comment that some Canadians hope they will become Americans when they grow up. Moreover, it is based on a Darwinian view of society and individual responsibility, and, as Harper himself has said, the belief that the country's economic destiny is to be nothing more than a hewer of wood and drawer of water, relying on natural resources for continued prosperity.

As the preceding chapters have demonstrated, Harper knew full well that his political vision of Canada was not shared by most Canadians. Consequently he attempted to implement much of his policy agenda slowly and incrementally, and even by stealth. Given the widespread opposition to his agenda, he also believed he must ignore existing conventions, rules, and regulations in order to achieve his objectives, and he unapologetically did so. As a result, in December 2008, he became the first Canadian prime minister to prorogue parliament twice in less than two years, creating a constitutional crisis unlike anything seen since the King–Byng affair of the 1920s. In 2011, his government became the first in the Commonwealth to be cited for contempt of Parliament by a Speaker. Internationally, the Harper government became the first Canadian government to withdraw from a United Nations convention, the first to lose a bid for a seat on the Security Council, and the first to boycott a Commonwealth Heads of State conference.

These developments did not go unnoticed by our traditional friends and allies. More than one Canadian diplomat overseas was confronted with the question "What has happened to Canada?" Or, as one veteran ambassador to Canada mused, "How can this be the same country that Pierre Trudeau led?" Closer to home, former Progressive Conservative prime minister Joe Clark once remarked that Harper's vision was "not my Canada." But what does this mean? What defines Canadian political culture and how does Harper's vision differ? As we have seen, Stephen Harper's new right-wing conservative philosophy emphasizes a different set of underlying values and beliefs from those of the modern liberalism shared by the majority of Canadians. In the same way, Harper's vision of Canada is based on an equally out-of-step emphasis on symbols and institutions that hold little or no relevance for many of his fellow citizens, and a rejection of many others that most Canadians cherish and consider fundamental to their definition of themselves and their country.

TRADITIONAL VIEWS OF CANADIAN POLITICAL CULTURE

The term "political culture" is an admittedly vague one, which, not surprisingly, has led to a number of different definitions. The classic one, offered by political scientist Sidney Verba,[4] describes political culture as "the system of empirical beliefs, expressive symbols, and values which defines the situation in which political action takes place." Authors Gabriel Almond and Bingham Powell expanded on this definition to include "individual attitudes and orientations towards politics" among citizens in a given political system.[5] Finally, Carleton political science professor Robert Jackson provided a further useful explanation in the Canadian context, noting that such values and attitudes may be reflected in "concrete objects such as government institutions or national symbols such as the flag, but they may also be intangibles like power."[6] Equally important in an artificially constructed New World country like Canada, the political culture, and especially the symbols and myths that express it, typically play a major role in defining national identity and promoting national unity.

All of these definitions are relevant to the Canadian context. First and foremost, Canadian political culture has always been seen as significantly different from that of the United States, even though the US is another New World country and arguably could have evolved along similar lines. Instead, as political sociologist Seymour Lipset conclusively demonstrated, the Canadian and American political cultures diverged dramatically from their earliest days, a development he attributed to differing "formative events," such as the way in which the Canadian state was founded (evolution rather than revolution), the settlement of the West (orderly versus chaotic), and the religions of the original settlers (mainstream Catholic and Anglican versus Calvinist, evangelical, and fundamentalist).[7]

Secondly, in terms of political myths and symbols, Canada's identity lagged far behind. The United States acquired the trappings of nationhood almost immediately and in full force. From their militaristic national anthem, ubiquitous portraits of the president, and reverential treatment of their flag, to the use of powerful symbols, ranging from the eagle and the White House to Air Force One, Americans were never in any doubt as to what images epitomized their country. Nor did they lack national heroes, from the martyrs of the War of Independence and early American presidents like Washington and Jefferson, to pioneer adventurers of the "wild west" such as Davy Crockett and Wyatt Earp, the robber barons, and even the 'anyone can make-it-rich and become president' novels of Horatio Alger. By contrast, it would take more than one hundred years after Confederation for Canada to acquire its own version of even the most basic national symbols such as a flag (1965), an anthem (1980), and a coat of arms (1921). Moreover there was a distinct lack of heroic national figures, courtesy of a calmly negotiated separation from Britain rather than a War of Independence, and western settlement organized by the federal government and supervised by the North-West Mounted Police (later the RCMP).

Into this unusual cultural void came the state itself. For Canadians, government institutions and programs were substituted for such symbols, and became an integral part of national identity. From the building of the national railroad (later eulogized by Pierre Berton and Gordon Lightfoot) to the creation of the Canadian Broadcasting Corporation and Air Canada, the transportation and communications infrastructure of the country served as a crucial element of nation-building. Nothing, however, could compete in importance with the creation of the welfare state and, in particular, the implementation of medicare, as important elements of Canadian identity.

As Harper himself noted, this identity also included the country's role in peacekeeping and foreign aid, a narrative in which Canadians proudly saw themselves as a New World version of Switzerland. Then came the introduction of official bilingualism, multiculturalism, and, ultimately, the 1982 Charter of Rights and Freedoms. In fact the Charter soon surpassed even medicare in public-opinion polls as a fundamental symbol of Canadian identity.

This rather unusual emphasis on the role of government programs and institutions in political culture is one that has been explored in detail. And, as Allan Gregg and Michael Posner demonstrated in their book *The Big Picture*, citizen attachment to the welfare state, bilingualism, and multiculturalism remained extremely high at the end of the twentieth century across all regions of the country. Even after a lengthy and severe recession, some 93 per cent of Canadians declared Canada was "the best country in the world in which to live." The reasons they gave included medicare (90 per cent), access to post-secondary education (78 per cent), a clean environment (76 per cent), immigration and multiculturalism (74 per cent), the parliamentary system of government (63 per cent), and bilingualism (57 per cent).[8]

The role of government programs and institutions was especially important in terms of national identity, because it provided citizens with a narrative to distinguish their country from that of their powerful neighbour to the south. Canadians had medicare; Americans did not. Canadians had two official languages; Americans did not.

Canada was a mosaic; America was a melting pot. And Canadians were peacekeepers, while Americans fought wars.

Not surprisingly, then, Canadians collectively saw themselves as peaceful, tolerant, and compassionate, while they regarded Americans as violent, prejudiced, and Darwinian. Canadians also valued the clear separation between church and state, and increasingly rejected government intervention in areas they considered to involve personal morality rather than criminal behaviour (such as abortion, prostitution, pornography, drug use, and sexual preference), a trend clearly at odds with the typical American outlook.

As a result, while Canadians found much to admire in their southern neighbour, another important element of Canadian identity was the insistence on a unique Canadian culture and a firm desire to keep the relationship between Canadian and American politicians cordial but not overly friendly. Prime Minister Trudeau's groundbreaking trip to China and subsequent visit to Cuba were therefore widely viewed with pride, while Prime Minister Mulroney's apparently close friendship with President Reagan was viewed with skepticism.

In 1989 nearly three-quarters of Canadians believed their culture was "significantly different" from that of the United States.[9] As author Richard Gwyn concluded:

> Canadians are no longer simply not Americans. We have evolved into a people who are as fully North American as Americans, and yet who, because of our political culture, are now a quite distinct kind of North American ... Here, two nations have evolved that are very much alike in almost all of their externals, and yet are utterly unalike in their political cultures, so that they are as distinct from each other as the Germans from the French.[10]

THE NATURAL GOVERNING PARTY

Despite this initial reliance on the government institutions, when national symbols like the flag and anthem were finally adopted, they quickly became important elements of national identity. Robert Fulford has described the period in which these outward and visible trappings of the state were created as a sort of nation-building golden era, epitomized by a "coming out" party for the country at Expo 67.[11]

That golden era culminated in the election of a charismatic new political leader, Pierre Elliott Trudeau, as prime minister. It ushered in a period of patriotic excitement and high expectations, which led journalist Allan Fotheringham to describe Ottawa as "Camelot North," revealing the Canadian preference for Democrats and the charismatic John F. Kennedy, whose White House administration was seen as youthful, glamorous and, most important, reflecting hope for the future, rather than the tired Republican Richard Nixon.

For many voters, the self-assured intellectual and cosmopolitan Trudeau represented the ideal image of a Canadian leader. Although often controversial, Trudeau's "heroic" image as the defender of Canada from the separatist threat, and his introduction of the Charter of Rights and Freedoms, subsequently served to cement his place in history. That heroic image was captured perfectly during the 1992 referendum by his declaration that Canada, not Quebec, was the distinct society. As *Globe and Mail* columnist Jeffrey Simpson declared bluntly the morning after the defeat of the Charlottetown Accord – an initiative of the Mulroney government which Trudeau vigorously opposed – "the Trudeau vision won."

According to numerous public-opinion polls, Trudeau remains one of the most highly regarded Canadian leaders. His ongoing popularity is particularly significant, since he was not only a long-serving prime minister but the leader of the Liberal Party of Canada for nearly two decades. As all conservatives, and especially Mr Harper, are only too well aware, the Liberal Party has been so dominant in Canadian electoral politics that it was often referred to as the "natural governing party." As late as 2005, even after several humiliating defeats, the party could still claim to be the most successful political party in the western democratic world.

One widely recognized reason for the party's success was its ability to position itself as the defender of national unity, under leaders such as Laurier, Pearson, Trudeau, and Chrétien. Another was its ability to frame Canadian values as Liberal values. Such a combination was virtually unbeatable most of the time, so much so that noted Canadian scholar John Meisel once said, "the line between the government and the Liberal Party has become tenuous."[12]

It is not difficult to understand why this would be the case. Liberal governments created the welfare state and much of the national infrastructure. They also introduced the new flag, the national anthem, Canada Day, official bilingualism and multiculturalism, and the

Charter of Rights and Freedoms. They promoted Canadian identity through government agencies and granting councils, and the Canadian-content provisions of the CRTC. Liberal governments promoted the separation of church and state by decriminalizing a variety of "private" activities, a trend summed up by then Justice Minister Trudeau's comment "the state has no place in the bedrooms of the nation." And, finally, Liberal governments emphasized foreign aid and Canada's peacekeeping role in the world, for which Liberal prime minister Lester Pearson received a Nobel Prize long before Barack Obama.

Under Liberal prime minister Jean Chrétien, yet another Liberal decade saw the introduction of programs such as the National Child Benefit, Millennium Scholarships, and Canada Research Chairs. On the national-unity front, it saw the prime minister introduce the popular Clarity Act. Internationally, it also saw the ratification of the Kyoto Accord, the government's refusal to participate in the American-led Iraq War, and the international community's enthusiastic adoption of two major Canadian initiatives, the International Criminal Court and the Land Mines Agreement.

In short, many of the activities and programs of Liberal governments throughout the twentieth and early twenty-first century clearly reflected the values, beliefs, and attitudes foremost in Canadian political culture. The synergy between Liberal platforms and Canadian identity served to deliver a steady stream of electoral victories for the party, including Trudeau's nearly sixteen years in office and Jean Chrétien's record three majority governments.

It was in this context, then, that a frustrated Stephen Harper as Canadian Alliance leader declared during the 2000 election campaign, "You can be a good Canadian and not vote Liberal!" For Harper – an economic conservative opposed to state intervention in the marketplace, a social conservative who disliked publicly funded welfare programs and preferred retribution to rehabilitation, and a moral conservative who viewed many so-called private issues as criminal activities falling squarely within the purview of the state, as well as an ardent admirer of American political culture and the Republican Party – the disconnect between mainstream Canadian political culture and his own world view posed an enormous challenge.

While his interim strategy to achieve power was based on the pragmatic targeting of voter support, and his government adopted many short-term policies as quietly and unobtrusively as possible, his stated long-term objective – to change the political culture so that the Conservative Party could replace the Liberals as the natural governing party – would require a more complex and comprehensive approach. In addition to the concrete policy measures discussed in earlier chapters, therefore, Harper introduced a number of initiatives specifically designed to help the Conservatives become the natural governing party. He created an extensive narrative about his new party, introduced several new "national" myths, and even appropriated various existing national symbols and icons for his own party. He has also attempted to eliminate much of the Liberal legacy – either through inaction or neglect – and actively worked to undermine the Liberal Party in order to create a polarized two-party system in which the Conservatives would become the only party capable of forming a national government.

CREATING THE FOUNDATIONAL MYTHS OF THE NEW CONSERVATIVE PARTY

There are at least three "founding narratives" of the new party, all of which are at odds with the facts. Nevertheless, at least two of them appear to have found some resonance with ordinary Canadians.

The first is the claim that *the new Conservatives are simply Tories by another name*. Former prime minister Joe Clark and several former Clark- and Mulroney-era cabinet ministers have repeatedly denounced this, but their protests have fallen on deaf ears. The media continue to use the two terms interchangeably, as do ordinary Canadians. Even traditional Progressive Conservative voters, while they may well feel that their party has been captured by the Reform/Alliance "wing," overwhelmingly view the differences of opinion between Tories and new Conservatives as an internal family quarrel, rather than a battle between two competing ideologies.

Harper has taken many symbolic steps to reinforce this view. For example, shortly after obtaining their majority, the Conservatives began making aggressive use of their authority over the National Capital Commission. Without consulting either the City of Ottawa or other stakeholders, they introduced a series of name changes at various landmarks around the capital. First they renamed the Old City Hall building the John G. Diefenbaker Building. Then, in January 2012, the heritage Bank of Montreal building, across from the Parliament Buildings, was renamed the Sir John A. Macdonald

Building. Then, in late summer 2012, Foreign Affairs Minister John Baird announced that the Ottawa River Parkway would henceforth be known as the Sir John A Macdonald Parkway to commemorate the two-hundredth anniversary of Macdonald's birth.

Given their rejection of Macdonald's National Policy, the Conservatives' efforts to link themselves with him – and to the Progressive Conservative Party they took over – have raised a few eyebrows. This narrative is all the more perverse when contrasted with their second foundational myth, namely that *they are outsiders and anti-politicians* who reluctantly agreed to go to the capital to root out waste and corruption. Given the electoral success of the Progressive Conservative Party over time, this portrayal would hardly make sense if the new Conservatives were really "just the Tories by another name." Only as westerners with Reform/Alliance roots could the new Conservatives realistically make such a claim, distancing themselves from the Progressive Conservatives as much as the Liberals.

It is worth noting that this outsider myth is imported from the New Right Republicans, where its success was all the more noteworthy, since Newt Gingrich and his colleagues had already been sitting in Congress for some time before their 1994 congressional breakthrough. Gingrich himself had first been elected to the House of Representatives in 1978, and served as Minority House Leader from 1988 to 1995. Yet he was able to utilize his party's minority status in Congress to portray himself and the Republicans as "underdogs" or "outsiders," pitted against the "establishment" Democrats. For the Harper Conservatives, this outsider theme began with the Reform/Alliance slogan "the West wants in," although this argument was severely hampered by the fact that both Joe Clark and John Diefenbaker had been western prime ministers. Even more difficult to overlook was the fact that the Mulroney government had boasted a western finance minister and deputy prime minister (Albertan Don Mazankowski), energy minister (Pat Carney), fisheries minister (Tom Siddon), and intergovernmental affairs minister (Joe Clark). Harper's solution to this latter dilemma was to argue that Mulroney's government had been captured by eastern elites and Quebec, the focus of his constitutional reform efforts.

Eventually the new Conservatives formed a government, just as the New Right took control of Congress, but this did not stop either of them from continuing to paint themselves as outsiders and anti-politicians. After more than seven years in power, Harper's keynote address to party faithful at the Calgary convention in fall 2013 actually included the following lines: "In our party, public service must mean private sacrifice. That's why Laureen and I first left our home here in Calgary. We didn't go to Ottawa to join private clubs or become part of some elite. That's not who you are; it's not who we are." Meanwhile his government's minority status allowed Harper to explain policy setbacks and delays to his core supporters. Hence his emphasis in the 2011 election on the need for "a strong, stable, majority government" in order to complete the implementation of his agenda. Yet nearly three years after achieving that majority, Harper was still blaming the courts, academics, lobbyists, so-called experts, and rogue senators for his inability to go much further or faster. By then, opinion polls suggested that a growing number of Canadians, even among his "base," were beginning to question those claims.

Nowhere was this more likely to be true than with respect to the party's third foundational myth, namely that *the new Conservatives are good economic managers*. Just as their other founding myths emphasized that they were not Tories or eastern elites, so this one claimed they were not "tax and spend" Liberals who ran deficits. The sheer audacity of that claim astonished experts. If Harper was intent on hitching his party's star to the Progressive Conservatives, then logically he should have had to justify the Mulroney government's ruinous fiscal policies and responsibility for doubling the national debt. Similarly, he normally would have had to acknowledge the importance of long-standing Liberal policies, such as the regulation of banks and restrictions on foreign ownership, in protecting Canada from the lion's share of the fallout from the disastrous 2008 global recession. But Harper's impressive discourse, in the patter of Karl Rove, stood reality on its head. He simply ignored his past criticism of many of those Liberal programs, and then took credit for the fact that Canada's economy emerged largely unscathed. Surprisingly, his claim was aided by the inability or unwillingness of the Liberals to challenge his rewriting of history.

Nevertheless, by the time Harper addressed the 2013 party convention, various opinion polls suggested that Canadians were becoming aware that all was not well. The never-ending sales pitch of the Economic Action Plan ads led to the growing realization that the party had single-handedly turned Paul Martin's surplus into a deficit. This inconvenient truth was reinforced by a series of revelations by the parliamentary budget officer, Kevin Page, over government spending, which rose despite the Conservatives' tough talk about public-service cuts, just as the total number of public servants increased significantly, despite their downsizing rhetoric. These contradictions were also highlighted by the opposition parties in parliament, and reports of the auditor generals that identified important cases of government mismanagement related to defence contracts, infrastructure spending, and the G8 summit.[13]

Not surprisingly, Harper ignored these problems and emphasized other achievements at his party's convention, such as the litany of tough-on-crime measures he had implemented and the elimination of the gun registry and the Wheat Board. He also made frequent reference to the two new "national" myths he had been promoting to cement the party's image as the natural governing party, claiming that considerable progress had been made.

CREATING ALTERNATIVE NATIONAL MYTHS

For his own take on nation-building, Stephen Harper first reached into the past and attempted to recreate a story line originally proposed by John Diefenbaker. The former Progressive Conservative prime minister had argued that Canada's destiny was inextricably tied to the North, and to Arctic sovereignty. In a speech entitled "The New Vision," delivered in Winnipeg in 1958, Diefenbaker declared "I see a new Canada – a Canada of the North. That is the vision." He spelled out a plan that emphasized military occupation and economic development of Arctic resources as a means of ensuring Canadian sovereignty. "We will aid in projects which ... will lead to the development of the national resources for the opening of Canada's northland. We will open that northland for development by improving transportation and communication and by the development of power," he declared.

However Diefenbaker's northern vision was considered to be a failure, due partly to his underestimation of the massive costs involved (which rapidly diminished his interest), and partly to several political crises, including the Bomarc missile and Avro Arrow debacles (which diverted his attention). Moreover, Diefenbaker's northern policy was primarily an economic one that "ignored critical human elements." Even if it had succeeded, historians agree that it would have benefited commercial interests in the private sector, "rather than northern residents, and especially indigenous peoples."[14]

Liberal successors did not emphasize Canada's northern identity in the same way. Instead they focused on promoting the social welfare and cultural development of indigenous peoples (leading to the creation of Nunavut and agreements such as the Yukon Indian claim settlement), environmental protection (which led to the development of Arctic research institutes), and international cooperation (which led to the creation of the Arctic Council). Nevertheless, Liberal prime minister Pierre Trudeau's annual canoe trips in the north became the stuff of popular legend, and the Liberal Party maintained a hold on Canadians' images of Canada's wilderness areas, even without such an agenda. It was only with the advent of the Mulroney Progressive Conservatives that a concern with Canada's northern identity returned. In Mulroney's case it was not a campaign pledge but a sovereignty "crisis" involving an American icebreaker's unauthorized voyage through the northern passage that prompted the response, and here again it was a military one. Defence Minister Perrin Beatty quickly committed the government to building the "world's largest icebreaker" and purchasing twelve nuclear submarines, a commitment that was cancelled less than three years later due to lack of funds.

In this sense, then, Stephen Harper's 2008 "Northern Vision" speech in Inuvik was simply a continuation of the conservative narrative of Canadian identity. But it was one he pursued far more aggressively than Mulroney, at least in terms of rhetoric. "We are a northern country," he declared. "The True North is our destiny – for our explorers, for our entrepreneurs, for our artists. To not embrace the promise of the True North, now, at the dawn of its ascendency, would be to turn our backs on what it is to be Canadian." His government's response to another sovereignty "crisis" was also military, this time brought about by Russian scientists in a mini-submarine planting a flag in the Arctic basin. Foreign Affairs Minister Peter MacKay bristled at the invasion of Canadian sovereignty and declared, "You can't go around the world these days dropping flags somewhere. This isn't the fourteenth or fifteenth century." Harper went much further, announcing an ambitious plan to acquire three Arctic icebreakers and beef up Canada's military presence North of 60. "You don't defend national sovereignty with flags, cheap election rhetoric, and advertising campaigns," he exclaimed. "You need forces on the ground, ships in the sea, and proper surveillance."[15] Perhaps equally predictable was Harper's announcement that the first new icebreaker would be named the *John G. Diefenbaker.*

Yet by 2013 Harper's northern vision had become suspect. As outlined earlier, most of his efforts to promote sovereignty were abandoned, delayed, or significantly reduced. Three icebreakers were reduced to one. Arctic research stations and other federal facilities were shut down, and the Arctic Council – chaired once again by Canada in 2013 – was used to further a resource-based exploration and a commercial development agenda, rather than environmental protection, or education, training, and social-welfare programs for aboriginal communities. Indeed, the Conservatives made it clear that they expected social benefits for northerners to emerge from the economic development they were eagerly encouraging the private sector to launch, rather than from any direct federal assistance.

It was also becoming increasingly clear that lip service was being paid to even the military-occupation theme, for example when it was revealed that the Canadian Rangers accompanying Harper for a photo opportunity were using sixty-year-old rifles. Not surprisingly, only three in ten Canadians polled at the time agreed that "protecting Canada's Arctic sovereignty" should be a priority of the federal government. Nevertheless, Harper persisted with his personal annual visits to the North, an important part of his summer agenda. At the beginning of 2014, he again travelled north for a photo opportunity cutting the ribbon for the all-weather road to the Arctic Coast that his government was promoting from Inuvik to Tuktoyaktuk.

He also made much of the discovery of one of the ships of the doomed Franklin expedition, which had been lost in the Arctic for more than 170 years. Although Parks Canada had already assembled a team for this purpose, Harper associated himself with it and championed the cause, taking it upon himself to make the announcement of the find in September 2014, a discovery he termed a "historic moment" for Canada. Critics noted that the lost ships and crew were British, and had perished long before Canada was born, but Harper continued to promote the find as another example of Canada's military occupation of the North.

Often during his Arctic trips Harper was accompanied by a media corps, whose primary role was to take photographs of the prime minister with various groups. One widely distributed photo showed the prime minister wearing desert camouflage, perched on the strut of a military helicopter. Another showed him practising at a rifle range with Defence Minister Rob Nicholson and Canadian Rangers. As conservative journalist Michael den Tandt wrote of that summer trip:

> Gjoa Haven, 2,000 kilometres north of Winnipeg as the crow flies, may be the most alien environment any southern-raised Canadian will ever encounter within this country's borders. The people who live here, the Nattilik Inuit … form the backbone of the Rangers, a mainly aboriginal force serving as a northern patrol for the Canadian Forces. And they have become, this year, the latest instrument of the Harper government's long-standing, often-frustrated desire to cast itself as a champion of Arctic sovereignty, and thus inherit beloved national imagery that used to be exclusive Liberal property.[16]

This emphasis on military occupation of the North to protect Canadian sovereignty is in fact a logical outcome of the second "national" myth that the Harper Conservatives have attempted to lay down, namely the existence of a patriotic militarism.

Harper's emphasis on patriotic militarism is also the continuation of a trend begun under the Mulroney government. Furious with the unification that took place under Trudeau, Mulroney promptly reintroduced separate uniforms for the three branches of the Canadian Armed Forces, although he did not attempt to undo unification itself. His initial Throne Speech emphasized a determination to "fulfil our NATO commitments" and to increase defence spending. In keeping with Mulroney's pro-American sentiments, his party's platform also promised an "excellent" relationship with the United States, and he was an enthusiastic supporter of the US-led Persian Gulf War. Nevertheless, opinion polls continued to demonstrate Canadians' preference for peacekeeping and development assistance. The Chrétien government's subsequent policy initiatives reflected that preference when it promoted the International Criminal Court and the Land Mines Initiative, and refused to participate in the Iraq War.

But with the arrival of the Harper Conservatives, a much greater effort was made to promote patriotic militarism as an important element of Canadian political culture. Here again, Harper had deliberately chosen something that could not be linked to the dominant Liberals, a point David Bercuson, director of the Centre for Military and Strategic Studies at the University of Calgary, stressed in a speech to the Canadian International Council in 2011.[17] And in the short term, the plan met with considerable success.

As author Lawrence Martin has noted, Harper's far-more-hawkish stance benefited greatly from the events of 9/11.[18] While the Chrétien government had quietly focused its response to those events on enhanced border and transportation security measures and greater intelligence-gathering capacity, the Harper Conservatives first responded in 2006 with a communications strategy using Cold War–style rhetoric about potential dangers to Canadians from various external enemies. The "enemy" had merely changed from the Soviet Union to terrorism, extreme Muslim sects, and marine pirates. This rhetoric echoed developments south of the border, as Harper adopted the "war on terrorism" discourse of another right-wing conservative Harper admired, George W. Bush.

Secondly, the Conservatives enthusiastically committed Canada to military action. As outlined in Chapter 8, Harper was particularly intent on extending and expanding Canadian participation in Afghanistan. In his first mandate, the prime minister himself visited the troops, along with Foreign Affairs Minister Peter MacKay and Defence Minister Gordon O'Connor (a former Brigadier General), as did Chief of Defence Staff Rick Hillier. Governor General Michaëlle Jean also visited Afghanistan, and sported a military uniform at November 11 ceremonies in Ottawa. Indeed, the outward and visible symbols of the new militarism were ubiquitous in the early years of the Harper mandate. Military personnel were introduced at sporting events ranging from the Grey Cup to Raptors basketball and NHL games. "We support our troops" slogans for bumper stickers emerged, and a ribbon campaign soon followed. A leaked memo revealed that military personnel were to be given prominent positions at all citizenship ceremonies.

In addition, early budgets committed the government to massive increases in defence-related spending, primarily for new equipment, to counter what Hillier and Harper both referred to as the "decade of darkness" that had seen such spending decline under the Chrétien Liberals. Even in deficit territory, the government stubbornly clung to some of those commitments, including the controversial F-35 purchase.

But the hoped-for change in Canadians' perspective did not materialize. By September 2008, an Angus Reid poll reported that

"Opposition to the Afghan mission is persistently high in Quebec (77%), followed by Atlantic Canada and Ontario (both at 58%), and British Columbia (53%)." That same month CTV reported a Canadian Press–Decima survey found "61 per cent of respondents believe the cost of the country's mission in terms of lives and expense has been unacceptable, while only one in three said it was acceptable."

Nevertheless, the Harper government persisted. Canadian participation in the Libyan expedition was expanded at Harper's request. Canadian fighter pilots flew more than 10 per cent of the total NATO missions. Foreign Affairs Minister John Baird even visited a rebel outpost in Benghazi, where he signed a Canadian bomb destined for Muammar Gaddafi's infrastructure with the message "Free Libya. Democracy." And, despite controversy during major cost-cutting efforts, the government remained adamant about its decision to purchase F-35 fighter jets, apparently regardless of the cost.

Inevitably those military expeditions faded from public consciousness with the eventual return of troops from Afghanistan in 2011, just as the public's initial fears in the post-9/11 era diminished with time. For some foreign-policy and defence experts, such as J.L. Granatstein, this may explain the Harper government's subsequent and largely mystifying decision to promote the War of 1812 as a major element of Canadian history. Certainly the event was of little interest to most Canadians, particularly since almost all of the action occurred in what later became the provinces of Ontario and Quebec. The choice appeared even more puzzling since the war involved British rather than Canadian troops (because it predated Confederation), and it was waged against Harper's idol, the United States. Most academic analyses of the conflict, such as the account of historian Alan Taylor, conclude that it was a politically divisive and militarily inept folly rather than an event worth celebrating.[19] In fact, many critics have argued that the two-hundred-year history of peaceful coexistence between the two countries, and claim to the world's longest undefended border, is far more worthy of celebration.

Still, the Harper government allocated some $30 million to mark the two-hundred-year anniversary of the war, including television ads and community events sponsored by local MPs. The importance the Conservatives placed on this forgotten conflict was underlined when correspondence between Heritage officials and the PMO over the content of the ads revealed a degree of micromanagement resembling that in the satirical American movie *Wag the Dog*. ("The Centre asks if Laura Secord's costume could have a little more colour.")[20] Heritage Minister James Moore actually issued a press release on 2 August 2012, announcing federal funding to commemorate a single incident, the Battle of Chrysler's Farm, in which he declared, "The commemoration of this battle and its importance in the outcome of the War of 1812 reminds us how people of different backgrounds and various regions came together to fight for Canada and defend our land, ensuring the independent destiny of our country." Providing no evidence to support this remarkable claim, he concluded hopefully, "The project will provide a great opportunity for Canadians to learn more about our collective past and strengthen our national pride."

Sadly, public-opinion polls did not demonstrate any appreciable increase in public knowledge or interest in the conflict, let alone a strengthening of national pride. Even a study prepared for the government concluded "Respondents may be aware of the war," it said, "but their knowledge of key countries, historical figures and sites involved is very limited." Moreover, it found that interest in the war decreased dramatically outside of Ontario, where most of the battles were fought, and among those below age fifty.

The government's decision to broadcast advertisements about the war during the Olympic Games *did* capture the public's attention, but only in a negative sense. Similar public disapproval surfaced after the announcement that the government had commissioned a new monument to commemorate the war, at a cost of $1 million, and planned to locate it on Parliament Hill, overshadowing an existing statue of Liberal prime minister Wilfrid Laurier.

Undeterred, the Harper government proceeded with commemorative coins, special documentaries, and staged re-enactments. In October 2012, three federal buildings were renamed to commemorate heroes of the war – Laura Secord, Sir Isaac Brock, and Dominique Ducharme – followed in February 2013 by the renaming of three additional buildings, including the Tecumseh Building in Chatham–Kent, Ontario.

Meanwhile the Conservatives' ongoing efforts to appropriate existing national symbols and icons, always a priority, were also beginning to produce results.

APPROPRIATING NATIONAL SYMBOLS AND ICONS

In the second half of the twentieth century, the Tory strand of the Progressive Conservative Party surfaced during several national debates on cultural symbols. Opposition leader John Diefenbaker campaigned against the new Canadian flag as well as unification of the armed forces, emphasizing the importance of a strong ongoing connection with Britain and the monarchy. Stephen Harper paid close attention to history, and saw an opportunity to appeal to the Tory third pillar of his coalition through symbolic efforts to revisit these debates, with little or no cost. This, then, is the explanation for such otherwise mystifying initiatives as the re-introduction of the term "royal" to the Canadian navy and air force.

Harper's enthusiasm for the monarchy was evident from the beginning, in April 2006, when he delivered his first speech in parliament as prime minister. He began by recognizing "our head of state, Her Majesty Queen Elizabeth II, whose lifelong dedication to duty and self-sacrifice have been a source of inspiration and encouragement to many countries that make up the commonwealth, and to the people of Canada." Not long after, Harper publicly chastised Governor General Michaëlle Jean for referring to herself as the head of state. (Yet in 2014 he caused a major protocol furor when he insisted on replacing the governor general – the constitutionally recognized commander-in-chief of the armed forces – to receive the flag brought home with the last of the returning soldiers in Afghanistan.)

This promotion of the monarchy naturally received support from long-standing Tories and groups such as the Monarchist League, but was widely regarded with amusement or mild objection by most Canadians. Not so in Quebec, however, where this sudden resurrection of the British monarchy was poorly received for obvious reasons. As one Quebec columnist declared, "seen from Quebec, the 'royalization' of Canada so actively pursued by the Harper government looks like something from Mars."[21]

Such comments did not deter him. Soon outward and visible symbols of the monarchy began to surface throughout government, beginning with Foreign Affairs Minister John Baird's order to replace a painting by famed Canadian artist Alfred Pellan, which was hanging in the lobby of his building, with a portrait of the Queen. By early September 2011, the order to hang portraits of the Queen in public areas was expanded to include all 260 foreign embassies, high commissions, and consulates. Retired diplomats were quick to criticize the move as counterproductive, noting that foreign-service officers had spent the decades since the Second World War attempting to create a unique and independent image of Canada abroad. Paul Heinbecker, Canada's former ambassador to the UN, told journalists the "sudden appearance of the Queen will confuse the hell out of people," who find Canada's linkages to the British monarchy "kind of bizarre and certainly they find it anachronistic. And, except perhaps for the United Kingdom, I don't see how this will advance our interests in any other country in the world."[22]

This move was particularly concerning, given the government's earlier decision to cancel outright the thirty-five-year-old Understanding Canada program, which had included support for Canadian Studies programs in universities abroad. As one retired diplomat noted, "All the work we've done for years trying to convince people we aren't some backward wilderness with moose, beavers, and Mounties will be down the drain."

The Harper Conservatives' fascination with the monarchy was evident in many other actions. They hosted the highest number of royal tours in decades, a significant development considering the high cost to the federal government of such tours and the fact that royal tours only take place after an official invitation has been issued by the host government. Nevertheless, the tours paled in comparison with the activities generated by the Queen's Diamond Jubilee. Although the Queen had no plans to come to Canada, and the actual event would be celebrated in London in June 2012, the Conservatives ordered five-hundred-thousand special flags to be used at ceremonies across the country planned for February 2012, the actual date of accession. In October 2011, Heritage Minister James Moore said $7.5 million had been allocated for the Jubilee, including nearly $1 million for such community ceremonies. Plans were announced to revise and republish *A Crown of Maples*, the document provided for education purposes on the role of the monarchy in Canada. There was also a commitment to produce a series of commemorative coins and stamps. Moore's press release declared "By supporting this most historic and significant anniversary, our government is delivering on its commitment to reinforce our heritage through active celebration of the institutions that define us as Canadians."

The most important element of the government's plan was the creation and distribution of some sixty-thousand Diamond Jubilee

Medals, which were to be awarded to "civic-minded" Canadians who had made a "significant contribution" to their communities. This aspect of the Conservatives' initiative did not unfold as planned, however, primarily because it lacked the normal structure of such award programs, including clearly defined criteria and independent selection panels. Instead, the government arbitrarily selected a number of non-governmental organizations (NGOs) and asked them to nominate individuals. It then left the selection of other recipients to individual MPs and senators. It soon became evident that many of the NGOs selected were Conservative supporters, such as REAL Women, while counterparts such as Status of Women or EGALE Canada were not included. Moreover, individual MPs were not provided with guidelines, and several made controversial choices. Saskatchewan MP Maurice Vellacott, a strident opponent of legal abortions, actually awarded one of the medals to an anti-abortion activist who was serving time in jail for her refusal to comply with court orders.

Not content with this one-time distribution of honours, the Conservatives announced the prime minister would henceforth distribute many honours normally handed out by the head of state. In the fall of 2012, Harper's office announced they were conducting a full-scale review of such honours to determine which ones (such as the Order of Canada) might be transformed into "the Prime Minister's Awards." As columnist Jeffrey Simpson noted, "for decades the office of the Governor General has been the place where honours and awards are organized and distributed. Why? Because the office is above politics, represents the entire country, and can't be accused of having ulterior motives, let alone political ones."[23]

Their approach to other established national symbols varied. In the case of the flag, for example, they decided to aggressively wrap themselves in it and promote its "protection." They held a press conference in the lobby of the House of Commons to announce government support for a private member's bill, in which Heritage Minister James Moore stood side by side with backbench Conservative MP John Carmichael to promote An Act Respecting the National Flag of Canada, an act to "protect the rights of Canadians to fly their national flag where they live and encourage Canadians across the country to display the national flag not just on Canada Day or Flag Day, but every day of the year."

At the same time Mr Harper diligently ignored, dismissed, or dismantled a number of other pre-existing symbols of Canadian identity that he could not appropriate. For example, he never referred to official bilingualism or multiculturalism, much less promoted them. He deliberately ignored both the twenty-fifth and the thirtieth anniversaries of the adoption of the Canadian Charter of Rights and Freedoms, even though public-opinion polls showed that Canadians viewed this event as the second-most-important date in Canadian history after Confederation. Former prime minister Jean Chrétien, who had served as justice minister in 1982, declared that he was "shocked" by the government's deliberate snub, and added "The first of July, I never refused to celebrate it because John A. Macdonald was prime minister at the time. It would be ridiculous to say no, he was not a Liberal."[24]

Chrétien missed a crucial point. As the first chapter demonstrated, the Harper Conservatives profoundly dislike the content of these initiatives, not merely the fact that they were introduced by Liberals. They would eliminate them if they could, but because they are entrenched in the constitution, they cannot. According to several senior bureaucrats, speaking off the record, the government's reasoning was similar when they refused to implement the Kelowna Accord, eliminated the Court Challenges Program, and "de-funded" the Forum of the Federations. True, they were all seen as Liberal achievements, but most of them also were offensive to the Conservatives' core values and beliefs.

Finally, the third aspect of their long-term strategy to influence the hearts and minds of Canadians involved the use of government institutions to promote their own values and vision. This effort to identify the Conservative Party with the government was referred to by distinguished political scientist John Meisel as "Harperizing Our Minds."[25]

HARPERIZING CANADIAN INSTITUTIONS

The top-down influence of political elites in defining values and determining political issues, a well-known theoretical concept which Meisel discussed in his seminal piece, was already the subject of academic interest in terms of the Harper Conservatives long before the May 2011 election that delivered their majority. Indeed, the Harper government's use of federal funds for the purpose of promoting the

Conservatives' image had been widely questioned. Of course Harper was not the first to make use of such funds for partisan purposes, but he certainly took the practice to a much higher level than even his PC predecessor, Brian Mulroney.

Mr Mulroney's government was known in the early years for such minor fiddles as changing the flag on federal letterhead from red to blue, and for using blue bulbs on the Christmas trees in the parliamentary precinct. While Mr Harper was not above such measures, his more significant efforts were directed at government websites, where blue predominated and the slogan of the federal government became "the true north strong and free." Similarly, the Canadian Mint's plan to use human-rights motifs, such as the UN and the Famous Five (Canadian pioneers of women's rights) on new $50 bills was scuttled by the Conservatives in favour of an image of Arctic icebreaker the *John G. Diefenbaker*.

Harper also tackled the issue of prime-ministerial trappings and travel arrangements. But where Mulroney had limited himself to a much-mocked portable podium and RCMP honour guard, Harper took on the use of military airplanes for prime-ministerial travel. The auditor general's controversial criticism of the practice under Jean Chrétien was dismissed by most observers as unwarranted, but Harper, as leader of the Opposition, had been vocally critical. Nevertheless in 2013 he proceeded to have a Polaris Airbus painted a highly visible blue, white, and red, at a cost of $50 million. The design bore more than a passing resemblance to the Conservative Party logo, and the ubiquitous slogan "the true north strong and free" was also added. As Department of Defence officials noted anonymously, this meant the plane could no longer be used for any other purposes and was obliged to remain idle when not in prime-ministerial use. Yet apart from some minor media commentary about Harper's apparent desire to emulate the American president's Air Force One, the move surprisingly occasioned little comment.

More troubling was the Conservatives' insistence, mentioned earlier, that bureaucrats refer to "the Harper government," rather than "the government of Canada" in all press releases and correspondence. According to Jonathan Rose "such language is expressly forbidden under an Ontario law that prohibits partisanship in government messaging. The effect of this subtle framing is to equate government with Harper." Rose confirmed Harper's expectations by concluding, "It creates a perception of a natural affinity between one party's leader and the act of governing."[26]

New concerns soon emerged regarding the role that the government appeared to be playing in the indoctrination of newcomers to Canada, particularly through its preparation of a new handbook that is required reading for immigrants before applying for citizenship. The text of *Discover Canada* (approved by Minister Jason Kenney) makes frequent reference to Canada's military past and the role of the monarchy, as well as former prime ministers John A. Macdonald and John Diefenbaker. However there is no reference to long-serving Liberal prime ministers Mackenzie King and Pierre Trudeau, nor to Canada's peacekeeping role and the Nobel Prize of Prime Minister Pearson, and only a brief, negative mention of the Constitution Act, 1982.

Similar concerns were raised over the government's 2013 decision to significantly reduce the role of the independent National Capital Commission. Many of the NCC's most visible and symbolic activities – such as the organization of Canada Day festivities and Winterlude – were to be taken over directly by the Department of Canadian Heritage. However it was the subsequent decision to rename and re-orient the Canadian Museum of Civilization that stunned many observers and prompted the greatest outcry. The planned name change to the Canadian Museum of History was indicative of a new focus for the largest and most popular of all national museums, which contained among other things a world-class collection of Canadian and foreign aboriginal artifacts. According to press reports, the Harper government intended to change the focus to one that exclusively reflected "important" developments in Canadian history, and notably those related to the military and the monarchy, despite the existence of the Canadian War Museum.[27]

This selective use of history, and the politicization of many traditional symbols and icons of Canadian political culture, has been accompanied by an intensive campaign to develop an alternative world view to present to Canadians on a daily basis. Here the Conservatives have relied heavily on the lessons learned from the New Right Republicans, who created their own think tanks to challenge scientific and academic views on major policy issues, and launched their own alternative media to communicate the findings to the broader public.

MAKING THE NEWS: THE ROLE OF ALTERNATIVE MEDIA

The American Right has long opposed government funding for public broadcasting, which it considers biased in favour of liberal values. The Reagan and Bush administrations significantly cut public funding, but in 2012 US Senator Jim DeMint, a Tea Party supporter, called for total "defunding." His cause was taken up by Republican presidential nominee Mitt Romney, who pledged to eliminate federal funding for public television and radio as part of his plan to reduce the massive US deficit.

Distrust of public broadcasting, and indeed of all mainstream commercial broadcasters and newspapers, led the New Right to develop their own alternative right-wing media. Their purpose was to disseminate the positions of their right-wing politicians, along with the ideas being churned out by the conservative think tanks they had created. Originally they were limited to talk-show hosts, such as Rush Limbaugh, and online publications. But through the concerted efforts of a number of conservative journalists, and massive financial contributions by wealthy individuals, the conservatives eventually gained the upper hand. Mainstream, or "liberal," media in the United States are now outnumbered, even in conventional areas such as print media and television, and their influence is declining dramatically.

As David Brock and Ari Rabin-Havt demonstrate in *The Fox Effect*, media mogul Rupert Murdoch's decision to hire Roger Ailes as the president of Murdoch's new American cable news network was the crucial turning point. Ailes, a former communications adviser to Richard Nixon, Ronald Reagan, and George Bush Sr, was hired in 1996 specifically to bring his political operative's perspective to the network. As the authors conclude, "Ailes used his extraordinary power and influence to spread a partisan political agenda that is at odds with long-established, widely held standards of fairness and objectivity in news reporting."[28] Their book chronicles numerous examples of slanted reporting, the coverage of marginal stories, and the outright neglect of other – more important – ones, as well as the "manipulation" of established facts. When challenged, Fox argued for constitutional freedom of the press, and two key Supreme Court rulings upheld their argument, to the dismay of liberals and many professional journalists, who once again lamented the bias of a Supreme Court loaded with Reagan appointees.

Confirmation of this deliberate strategy came from an unexpected quarter, with the publication of a book by well-known conservatives Richard Viguerie and David Franke entitled *America's Right Turn: How Conservatives Used New and Alternative Media to Take Power*. As the authors make abundantly clear, the recent purchase of mainline newspapers by ultraconservative billionaires such as the Koch brothers is only the latest in a long line of tactics to take control of information dissemination. As of 2008, they confidently announced that some 60 per cent of Americans received their news from one of the conservatives' media. "Put the four alternative media together – direct mail, talk radio, cable news TV, and the Internet – and you can appreciate why the liberals are on the run. They have seen the four horsemen of the conservative apocalypse."[29]

A few facts serve to underline the significance of this development. To begin with, under new ownership, even the venerable *Wall Street Journal* is now routinely viewed as a conservative organ. Second, roughly four times more viewers tune in to Fox News than CNN. Third, local and regional news stations, including Christian radio programming, have even higher numbers. Fourth, with the sale of the formerly progressive *Huffington Post* to AOL and its quixotic conservative CEO, former Google president Tim Armstrong, the Internet is now without any major liberal voice.

According to a 2013 Gallup poll, more than 50 per cent of Americans consider television their principal news source, roughly 20 per cent cite the Internet, and fewer than 1 per cent cite newspapers. This situation has proven an invaluable aid to the conservatives in shaping and even defining public discourse, as the Weapons of Mass Destruction campaign demonstrated. In 2013, a majority of Americans still believed those weapons had been found in Saddam Hussein's arsenal, just as a significant minority believed that Barack Obama is a Muslim born in Africa. This point was reinforced by progressive media commentator Don Hazen (the former editor of award-winning left-wing magazine *Mother Jones*), who decried the almost total absence of liberal-minded financial backers with deep pockets who were willing to support conventional professional media. "The relentless conservative propaganda machine dominates the public discourse more than ever," he warned.[30]

Admittedly the situation in Canada is much less dramatic, but the arrival of the Harper Conservatives unquestionably saw an increase in the presence of alternative right-wing media, a trend begun modestly under Brian Mulroney with the introduction of the *National Post* by Conrad Black. The most obvious example of the new conservative emphasis on alternative media is Sun TV, the creation of Pierre Karl Péladeau, former president and CEO of Quebecor and owner of the Sun newspaper chain. Although Peladeau has objected to the right-wing label, and this may be seen as a moot point by some, a widespread consensus exists regarding its extreme content and lack of professional standards.[31]

Often referred to by critics as "Fox News North," the new television network was launched in April 2011 under a Category 2 licence from the CRTC. The launch had actually been delayed while the network fought a highly publicized battle with the CRTC to obtain a Category 1 licence, which would have meant its mandatory inclusion in cable and satellite providers' menus. Such an award would have set a precedent, since other new channels require several years of successful production before being granted the top-level licence. Yet Péladeau implied his application was being treated in a discriminatory fashion. The application was opposed by the international media watchdog organization, Avaaz, which claimed the Harper government was supporting the application in an attempt to "put American-style hate media onto Canadian airwaves." An online petition was signed by thirty-thousand individuals. In the end, Péladeau abandoned his fight and the network launched under Category 2.

Even before that launch, the network was involved in a series of controversies. Like Roger Ailes, the prime minister's former director of communications Kory Teneycke was hired by Sun News to help steer the application through the CRTC. A public outcry followed, focused on the apparent lack of teeth in Harper's new conflict-of-interest rules for former public-sector employees. As a result, Teneycke was named vice-president of Quebecor, which he claimed allowed him to avoid the two-year cooling-off period required by the rules. However, when questions arose as a result of his accusations that the Avaaz petition contained false signatures, he abruptly resigned. A few months later, he was rehired, this time as vice-president of the Sun News Network. Shortly thereafter another PMO staffer, Matt Wolf, joined Sun TV News as an editorial producer in Toronto. Other Conservatives involved with the network included on-air personnel such as Ezra Levant, a former Reform staffer and author, and director of programming Luc Lavoie, a former press aide to Brian Mulroney.

Meanwhile the CRTC was considering an amendment to its "false and misleading" news provision, which guarantees truth in reporting. This was a result of concerns raised by a Conservative-dominated parliamentary committee that the provision might infringe on freedom of the press and freedom of expression as guaranteed in the Charter. However, after soliciting public input about its plans to soften the language in the provision (input which overwhelmingly urged the CRTC not to do so), and a court ruling that found the provision was not in contravention of the Charter, the CRTC announced it would not alter the section. Subsequently Sun News was involved in the fake citizenship ceremony described in Chapter 5. Meanwhile on-air commentator Ezra Levant was the object of several public complaints and libel lawsuits.[32]

Several surveys revealed the network regularly finished a distant fourth in most categories of viewership. One snapshot placed 11,000 viewers with Sun News at 7 p.m., compared with 263,000 for the CBC. This result was particularly galling for Péladeau, since on-air commentators such as Levant regularly attacked the public broadcaster, as did Péladeau himself in testimony before the parliamentary committee. Péladeau also filed numerous Access to Information requests in a failed attempt to determine individual salaries of on-air CBC personalities. He was aided in his ongoing battle with the public broadcaster by various backbench Conservative MPs, who filed questions in the House of Commons that resulted in the responsible minister, James Moore, tabling information on the number of CBC employees earning more than $100,000 annually. This in turn was used by interest groups such as the Canadian Taxpayers Federation to loudly demand further cuts to the public broadcaster, whose greatly reduced annual budget had already diminished its range and influence.

Certainly Péladeau showed no sign of backing off on his ambitious project, and expressed the view that he was in it for the long haul, although his subsequent unsuccessful entry into Quebec politics cast some doubt on that assertion.

CREATING A PARALLEL UNIVERSE: THE RISE OF RIGHT-WING THINK TANKS

Another long-term strategy of the Republican New Right has been to create right-wing think tanks, prompted by their distrust of conventional academic research. Although they started slowly in the 1970s, these centres mushroomed by the 1990s and, like the alternative conservative media, are now the dominant source of public thinking about many current American issues. The activist group Right Wing Watch provides a list of more than seventy such organizations, many of which it claims "masquerade" as think tanks, without credible academic credentials or peer-review processes, and often while performing lobbying and training functions.

Much has been written about their ascendancy, but the pre-eminent work on this strategy of building a parallel universe of ideas was conducted by two academics from Temple University, whose findings are contained in *No Mercy: How Conservative Think Tanks and Foundations Changed America's Social Agenda*. In their book, Jean Stefancic and Richard Delgado identify three main reasons for the success of these organizations. First, they are ideologically motivated. As a result, their material always promotes their values and objectives, while traditional think tanks produce neutral material with carefully worded, balanced findings that are less convincing for ordinary citizens and the media. (Even anecdotal evidence may be used in conservative publications, while academic material will rely on less appealing and less well-understood but more accurate statistical evidence.) Second, the right-wing think tanks focus very narrowly on one or two subject areas, unlike traditional academic think tanks, which tend to cover a wide range of issues. Consequently, the publications of traditional think tanks are diffuse, and a particular subject will be infrequently addressed. Meanwhile a think tank devoted exclusively to, for example, opposition to affirmative action, global warming, or immigration can produce much more material much more frequently. Thirdly, and again unlike traditional think tanks, the conservative organizations do not move on to another issue. Instead, they continue to promote their case, rather than concluding that, having produced a convincing document, they can assume it has succeeded in changing minds and proceed to other subjects.[33]

Several of these organizations have the confidence of Republican politicians of the New Right; many were highly influential during the Reagan and Bush administrations, since their self-described "independent" and "non-partisan" research promoted the very policies the politicians planned to undertake. As a result, their studies are frequently cited in testimonials by those politicians, lending apparent credibility. In exchange, several prominent politicians are employed by the think tanks after their departure from public life, confirming the symbiotic relationship.

One of the reasons why these think tanks have the luxury of time and focus is that there are so many of them. This, in turn, is due to the fact that they receive nearly unlimited financial support from fabulously wealthy individuals and corporations. Unlike grassroots movements, they do not need to raise money from ordinary citizens through direct mail. Their source of funding is secure for lengthy periods of time through a small number of fixed-term donations. This allows them to hire permanent staff and create a long-term work plan. According to Right Wing Watch, the American conservative think-tank industry is funded to the tune of more than $1 billion annually, an amount liberal organizations cannot hope to match. This is hardly surprising since, apart from George Soros – the exception that proves the rule – the wealthy individuals supporting such organizations are predominantly self-made capitalists who fail to recognize the contribution that the institutions of liberal democracy made to their success. Consequently, they have a limited attachment to the state, a phenomenon both philosopher Christopher Lasch and economist John Kenneth Galbraith foresaw and warned against several decades earlier.[34]

Among these organizations, the Heritage Foundation is the clear frontrunner, with $52 million in annual revenue in 2004 alone. Founded by Paul Weyrich, with support from the Coors family, it employs 173 individuals and produces an average of ten "policy" papers a month, distributed widely to members of Congress and to journalists. Its publicly declared mandate is to "formulate and promote conservative public policies based on the principles of free enterprise, limited government, individual freedom, traditional American values, and a strong national defence."

Other prominent think tanks widely cited in the media and considered very influential in shaping American public-policy discourse include the Cato Institute (a self-described "libertarian" organization, with a budget of nearly $15 million, ninety permanent staff, and sixty "adjunct" scholars, supported by, among others, the Koch family) and the Galen Institute, whose mandate more typically is focused on one issue, namely "advancing free-market issues in health policy and ... promoting innovation, individual freedom, consumer choice, and competition in the health sector."

Although most of these large organizations are quite transparent about their mandate and supporters, there are a significant number of smaller think tanks whose names and purpose appear to be deliberately obscure. A classic example is the American Civil Rights Institute, an organization frequently confounded with the American Civil Liberties Association. Its newsletter, the *Egalitarian*, also suggests the opposite of its actual mandate, which is to *oppose* affirmative action. With a budget of more than $2 million annually, it has proven extremely effective, beginning with its successful 1997 campaign to eliminate affirmative-action programs in California. The Center for Media and Democracy (CMD) published twelve detailed reports exposing what it referred to as a massive organization of "pressure groups masquerading as think tanks" under the umbrella title of the State Policy Network, an organization with an annual budget of more than $83 million. According to CMD executive director Lisa Graves:

> SPN and its State affiliates are major drivers of the American Legislative Exchange Council-backed corporate agenda in state houses nationwide, with deep ties to the Koch brothers and the national right-wing network of wealthy funders ... The "experts" of State Policy Network groups get quoted on TV and in the papers, or in the legislature, as if they were neutral, non-partisan, and objective scholars on issues of public policy. But in reality, SPN is a front for corporate interests with an extreme national policy agenda.[35]

A final category of such think tanks is the training institute. The Leadership Institute, founded by New Right legend Morton Blackwell, is the pre-eminent example of this category. With a budget of more than $8 million annually in 2000, the institute has "graduated" more than ninety thousand individuals, several of whom are prominent Canadian conservatives and some of whom have become ministers in the Harper cabinet.

The strategy of creating right-wing think tanks to challenge conventional academic research appears to be finding much more traction in

Canada than the alternative-media strategy. The pre-eminent example is the Fraser Institute, which has been a presence since the early days of Reform. Founded in 1974 by economist Michael Walker (a co-founder with Reagan adviser Milton Friedman of the Economic Freedom of the World project) and MacMillan Bloedel's vice-president Patrick Boyle, its mission statement describes it as "an international independent research organization [dedicated to] a free and prosperous world where individuals benefit from greater choice, competitive markets, and personal responsibility." The influential *Forbes* magazine and the *New York Times* have both described the institute as "libertarian," and even the *Calgary Herald* referred to it as "right-of-centre conservative." Its 2012 budget exceeded $12 million, with reported donations from the Canadian Donner Foundation, the American Koch brothers, and Exxon Oil. In its early years it was also heavily supported by the tobacco industry, which led to numerous controversies, as the Institute published reports and organized events to counter what it described as the "junk science" of health threats posed by smoking. Its 2013 staff comprised fifty-seven permanent employees as well as sixty-four associated "scholars," who have included at various times several former Reform MPs, such as economist Herb Grubel and Preston Manning himself, as well as former conservative premiers Ralph Klein and Mike Harris.

One factor which undoubtedly aided the Fraser Institute's rise to prominence was the gradual elimination of pre-existing independent, neutral, and academic-research-based organizations across the country. Successive Liberal and Progressive Conservative governments had established a number of research institutions to assist with policy development, and provided significant funding for other independent academic research. The Pearson, Trudeau, and Chrétien governments established the Economic Council of Canada (1963); the Science Council of Canada (1966); the National Welfare Council (1968); the Law Reform Commission of Canada (1970); the Institute for Research on Public Policy (1972); the Canadian Institute for International Peace and Security (1984); the Canadian Policy Research Networks (1994); the North-South Institute (1976); and the Forum of the Federations (1997). However the Mulroney and Harper governments wound up virtually all of this government-supported independent research, leaving a vacuum that the Fraser Institute was quick to fill.

With the arrival of the Harper Conservatives, the number of right-wing think tanks increased significantly. Several, such as the

Ottawa-based Institute for Marriage and Family and the Institute for Canadian Values, are social-conservative organizations with religious concerns and close ties with American counterparts. Many also employ former Reform/Alliance MPs, candidates, and staffers. Another, the oddly named Work Research Foundation (WRF), describes itself as a "Christian-inspired think tank" that seeks to provide alternative models for industrial-relations policy, but is often viewed as anti-union. An equally impressive number of new economic think tanks whose concerns are the free market and a libertarian approach to government have proliferated in the past fifteen years as well. They include the Frontier Centre for Public Policy (a vigorous opponent of conventional climate-change theory) the Montreal Economic Institute, and the Atlantic Institute for Market Studies.

In addition, former Reform leader Preston Manning has created the equivalent of Morton Blackwell's Leadership Institute, the Manning Centre for Building Democracy. Its stated mandate is to train the next generation of Canadian conservative party workers, staffers, and politicians. According to several sources, it was started with a donation of $10 million. And, despite its surprising eligibility for charitable status, a number of controversies have unfolded over the years surrounding the alleged involvement of its employees in election activities and support for conservative candidates, most notably during the Calgary municipal election in which progressive candidate Naheed Nenshi was chosen mayor.

Another particularly striking development in Canada has been the close relationship between some members of the media and these right-wing think tanks. For example, the WRF employs a former *Calgary Herald* publisher, Peter Menzies, as a senior fellow, as does the Fraser Institute. Meanwhile former *Ottawa Citizen* Opinion editor David Walker found employment at the Macdonald–Laurier Institute as director of communications and managing editor.

These linkages go some way towards explaining the findings of the Stafford Study on Media Coverage of Think Tanks in Canada, which concluded as early as 1997 that these right-wing think tanks were winning the battle for "positioning their ideological stances within the mainstream culture." The study followed fourteen mainstream daily newspapers, as well as CBC and CTV news broadcasts, over a six-month period. It found "right-wing think tanks received 68 per cent of all references, while left-wing think tanks received 19.5 per cent." (Academic studies and research institutes received the balance of roughly 12 per cent.) Moreover, the study found that, on any given subject, "no news organization gave equal coverage to right- and left-wing think tanks, although some were more balanced than others."[36] The Fraser Institute alone received five times more mentions than the Centre for Policy Alternatives, and indeed more coverage than all other Canadian think tanks combined. These findings were particularly significant given the results of another independent survey – on accuracy in conservative think tank research reports – which revealed a widespread pattern of selective reporting.[37]

Of even more significance is the fact that this study was conducted before the arrival on the scene of another influential and well-funded right-wing think tank, the misleadingly-named Macdonald–Laurier Institute, mentioned above. Although it claims to be a "non-partisan" and "independent" research organization, its ties to the new conservative movement in Canada, and to the Harper government, are extensive.[38] Its chair is Rob Wildeboer, a wealthy evangelical Christian who is also the principal backer of the ECP (Equipping Christians for the Public-Square) Centre, an organization apparently devoted to the elimination of human-rights commissions. Its managing director and senior researcher are former advisers to ministers in the Harper government. But, much like the American Civil Rights Institute, the MLI appears intent on claiming independence and lack of partisan bias.

The biography of its managing director, Brian Lee Crowley, provides a different picture. He has been a visiting scholar or senior fellow at two American think tanks described above, the Heritage Foundation and Galen Institute. He is a member of the Civitas Society, and was twice the recipient of the Sir Antony Fisher Award, a British prize named after its wealthy financier backer, which rewards publications promoting "public understanding of a free market and society." Crowley was appointed Clifford Clark economist-in-residence in the finance department in Ottawa by Finance Minister Jim Flaherty, and Flaherty supported the creation of the Institute by hosting a fundraiser in Toronto and sending a letter to potential donors encouraging them to contribute. At the time, concerns were raised publicly about potential conflict of interest, notably by Toronto columnist Linda McQuaig and Simon Fraser communications professor Donald Gutstein, who also highlighted the similarity between the Institute's motto, "the true north in Canadian public policy," and the official Harper government slogan "Canada's true north strong and free."[39]

Like some of its prominent American counterparts, the MLI has proved a stalking horse for a number of controversial policies the government was intending to implement. These have included highly controversial publications on law-and-order issues, some of which were produced by MLI senior researcher Scott Newark, a former aide to Public Safety Minister Stockwell Day.[40] A classic example of government use of its studies to justify policy decisions occurred when Day cited the existence of "unreported crimes," a theme in one of Newark's reports, when defending the elimination of the long-form census.

Many of these Canadian organizations are also funded privately by wealthy individuals, and hence do not need to obtain charitable status for income-tax purposes. As a result, the source of much of their funding remains a mystery. Nevertheless, the information available on the public record is instructive. Specifically, it demonstrates the importance of a few wealthy entrepreneurs, such as Barrick Gold chair Peter Munk, who donated more than $1 million to various think tanks, including the MLI, in 2009 alone. Other major donors include the Weston family (Loblaws), the Donner Family, the Zeller Family Foundation, the Max Bell Foundation and the John Dobson Foundation, the Pirie Foundation (Sabre Energy), and the Carthy Foundation (Mannix Energy).

According to the Canada Revenue Agency the only left-wing/socialist think tank in the country, the Canadian Centre for Policy Alternatives, ran a deficit of $200,000 in 2010 on revenues of $4.2 million, raised through direct-mail campaigns and from unions, while its expenses amounted to $4.4 million. Perhaps even more significant, numerous attempts to establish a liberal think tank in Canada have *never* succeeded, due to the lack of private financing, a point underlined by several journalists and academics.[41]

In the end, however, the Harper government's concerted efforts to entrench a conservative political culture are problematic. One reason is undoubtedly their failure to decisively eliminate the Liberal Party of Canada. Instead, as the federal election of 2015 approaches, it is the Liberal Party and not the NDP which appears to be resurgent, no doubt much to Harper's chagrin.[42]

THE LONG GAME: ELIMINATING THE LIBERALS?

Originally the Conservatives were reasonably successful at hobbling the Liberal Party. They began by altering the party-financing legislation introduced by the Chrétien government, lowering individual contributions from $5,000 to $1,000 at a time when the Liberals had recently lost an election and were in the process of selecting a new leader. Consequently, the party found itself in serious financial difficulty and individual leadership candidates were placed in a Catch-22 situation, unable to retire their campaign debts.

After May 2011, Harper inflicted further financial damage on the Liberals, withdrawing long-standing public funding for all political parties. This move was widely criticized, even by conservative stalwarts Tom Flanagan and Gerry Nichols. Nichols argued the move was motivated by partisan considerations, and described it as a mean-spirited initiative, which would damage the democratic process.[43] Certainly it affected the opposition parties disproportionately, as many experts noted. However the Conservatives seemingly won the public debate, arguing they were motivated by fairness (the measures would be applied to all parties) and fiscal prudence (taxpayers should not be expected to foot the bill).

Nevertheless, with Justin Trudeau as party leader, the Liberals gained ground on the fundraising side as well as in popular opinion. By fall 2013 the party outdid the Conservatives in the number of contributors, at thirty thousand versus fewer than twenty-nine thousand. However the total amounts raised were still one-sided. Even in political difficulty the Conservatives raised $13 million in the first three-quarters, or nearly twice as much as the Liberals, at $6.8 million.

The Conservatives' assault on the Liberal Party also included targeted attacks on individuals. But while the attack ads against Stéphane Dion and Michael Ignatieff were unquestionably effective, similar efforts directed at Trudeau proved counterproductive, leading former adviser Tom Flanagan to declare they were "not working," and a different approach was needed. There were also attempts to discredit individual MPs, such as the ploy to convince Montreal MP Irwin Cotler's constituents that he had resigned when he had not. As Cotler argued in a December 2011 OpEd in the *National Post*, "damage was done that must be remedied ... Spreading false and misleading information on something so fundamental as whether an MP has resigned and a riding is now in a by-election is simply unacceptable. Allowing such practices only furthers – as the Speaker himself said – the cynicism and contempt people feel towards politics and politicians." Although forced to admit guilt, Conservative MPs still refused to apologize for actions the Speaker described as "reprehensible" and deliberately "attempting to sow the seeds of confusion" for partisan gain. Instead they launched a counter-attack, defending their actions on the basis of free speech, and the matter soon faded from public consciousness.

The Conservatives' efforts in co-opting the legacy of the Liberal Party also initially appeared successful in several cases, notably on immigration and foreign policy vis-à-vis Israel. Nevertheless, Harper's efforts were most rewarding on fiscal policy, where his government was regularly considered the most competent in opinion polls, despite the superior record of the Chrétien/Martin government in eliminating the Mulroney deficit and maintaining a surplus for a decade. According to these polls, this image of the Conservatives as solid economic managers prevailed, although most economists argued they had mishandled the economy and increased government debt unnecessarily, if not recklessly.

Despite Harper's disdain for the premiers and their concerns, it appeared the lack of outright conflict in the federation had even deprived the Liberals of their traditional advantage with Canadians on the national-unity issue. However, when the PQ government of Pauline Marois introduced the Secular Charter, Justin Trudeau's immediate denunciation of it seemingly secured his image as "Captain Canada" within the province and across the country,[44] further resurrecting Liberal fortunes. By 2014 the Liberals had pulled ahead of the Conservatives in successive opinion polls, while NDP support collapsed.

THE ULTIMATE GAME: CHANGING ATTITUDES?

Stephen Harper's attempts to change Canadians' thinking also initially appeared to have been more successful than many would have predicted, especially given the huge gap between his policy priorities and those of most Canadians. Opinion polls repeatedly showed that Canadians saw health care, the environment, and post-secondary education as top priorities, and believed the country should emphasize its role as peacekeeper, foreign-aid donor, and model international citizen. Still, Harper was long viewed as the most credible leader, despite his diametrically opposed policy agenda.

Interestingly, one area where the Conservatives failed to make any breakthrough was in the secular nature of Canadian political culture. Support for measures such as legislation supporting gay marriage, abortion, and the decriminalization of marijuana remained strong. If anything, Canadians appeared to be growing further apart from the evangelical base of the Harper Conservatives and the Republican Right. Indeed, as pollster Michael Adams wrote, "the myth of converging values" promoted by right-wing Canadian media and politicians [is] exactly that.[45]

One example of successful attitudinal change initially appeared to be the Conservatives' law-and-order agenda. Countless experts and practitioners repeatedly demonstrated that the incidence of criminal activity, and violent crime especially, had been decreasing for decades. Yet public opinion was at odds with reality for some time. Lack of data, and a persistent disinformation campaign by several Harper ministers, appeared to have played a major role in promoting public fear. However, by 2012 several polls demonstrated public perception was shifting and falling into line with the facts.[46]

Undoubtedly the most far-reaching and potentially long-lasting impact of the Conservatives' efforts to alter the political culture is their promotion of small government and lower taxation. The Harper government's string of tax-reduction measures seem to have convinced many voters that tax increases – once taken for granted, because the cost of living and demand for government services inevitably increase – are no longer inevitable or even acceptable. Similarly, the Conservatives appear to have made considerable inroads with their argument that deficits must be avoided if at all possible, and eliminated quickly when inevitable, even at the expense of government programs and services. This new normal was responsible for Liberal platforms in the 2008 and 2011 elections which attempted to square the circle by simultaneously promising action on important policy fronts without increasing taxes or incurring new debt, something the public found unconvincing.[47] The electoral future of the Conservatives, therefore, may depend more on this issue than on any other, and on the ability of the Liberals to create a successful alternative narrative.

Conclusion

I believe the long Liberal era has truly ended. As with disco-balls and bell-bottoms, Canadians have moved on ... We are moving Canada in a Conservative direction, and Canadians are moving in that direction with us.

Rt Hon. Stephen Harper, 15 July 2011

Stephen Harper came to power in 2006, promising to change Canada. His Canada would be one that saw citizens rely more on themselves and less on government, a country of free enterprise, where anyone could become wealthy. It would be a country with a strong moral compass, embracing a deep-seated commitment to family values, an appreciation of the importance of tradition, and a renewed respect for law and order. Internationally, it would be known for taking a "principled" stand on difficult issues, regardless of the potential cost, and for pulling its weight in defending freedom and democracy – by force if necessary. In short, Canada would become a beacon of hope for conservatives in the increasingly dark liberal world of "moral nihilism." In the process, Canadians would come to see Harper's Conservative Party as the natural governing party, replacing the Liberals, who were the authors of this moral ambivalence.

Harper believed all his objectives could be obtained without recourse to constitutional change, given sufficient political will, and he was convinced he could achieve many of his short-term goals through simple policy reforms. But he also recognized that lasting change would require a major restructuring of Canada's political culture, and the destruction of his principal opponent, the Liberal Party of Canada. This would all take time, and time was something he might not have. To that end, he immediately took control of the levers of power. He launched an unprecedented assault on parliamentary convention, legislative oversight, ministerial responsibility, and judicial review in his rush to achieve as much as possible, as quickly as possible. Given his uncompromising mindset, and the perceived urgency of his mission, his government pursued the new Conservative agenda with a ruthless determination, shutting down potential dissent, marginalizing civil society, neutralizing the national media, and crippling opposition parties.

As the 2015 federal election approaches, and after more than eight years in power, the obvious question is "How much progress has he made?" The answer is not so obvious. On the one hand, as this book has demonstrated, he has made considerable inroads on some areas of his policy agenda. On the other hand, despite intensive efforts, his progress is not nearly as substantial as he had once hoped, or as some of his critics feared. Certainly his bravado in announcing the end of a long liberal era in Canada was misplaced. Interestingly, while most of his critics have focused on the potential for his government to inflict irreversible damage, it seems that Harper, like Ronald Reagan, is also increasingly the subject of criticism from some of his fellow conservatives for his failure to go further. Other unabashed conservatives have been appalled by the way he has gone about implementing his agenda, and have not hesitated to say so.

Still, the more important question – as noted in the introduction – is whether any of the changes he has made are likely to be permanent. Here again, however, the answer is not clear. An examination of his initiatives suggests that many could be temporary, as long as future governments choose to reverse them. Others may be far more difficult to undo.

THE CONSERVATIVES' SHORT-TERM POLICY AGENDA

Stephen Harper has undoubtedly introduced many radical policy reforms. His lack of progress on some others is partly due to his inability to push the envelope too far. Small incremental steps were indeed the only safe way to proceed politically, but the very pragmatism that allowed him to recognize this, and stay in power, is also a key reason why he has not made more of an impact. In addition, despite his willingness to ignore parliamentary procedures and conventions, there were also constitutional and legal limitations on his ability to impose his agenda, as the Supreme Court repeatedly reminded him. Finally, some failures were due to the unexpected events that confront any government, events that the Conservatives often seemed singularly unprepared or unequipped to handle.

In terms of the economy, for example, Harper's original determination to scale back federal intervention quickly came face to face with political reality after the 2008 global recession. As a result, for years the Conservative government's budgets – the renamed Economic Action Plans – delivered substantial federal investment in stimulus projects, something which would have been anathema to the early Stephen Harper. Similarly his finance minister, Jim Flaherty, actively intervened in the private sector on numerous occasions. Meanwhile Harper's signature plan to create a national securities regulator fell afoul of provincial opposition and the constitution, as did his efforts to promote the Northern Gateway pipeline to the West Coast over the concerns of British Columbia's government, environmental groups, and the many aboriginal communities affected.

Perhaps most humiliating of all, his early determination to cut government expenditures and slash the bureaucracy proved unequal to the task. Like Thatcher, Reagan, and Mulroney, Harper saw federal spending rise on his watch and the public service grow dramatically. Worse still, his plan to follow Grover Norquist's dictum and "starve the beast" by cutting taxes led to an unexpected and philosophically unacceptable deficit, when the $13-billion surplus inherited from the Liberals melted away after the 2008 recession. By 2011, he was forced to abandon stealth tactics and introduce draconian, politically unpopular, measures in order to balance the books before 2015.

This is not to suggest that Harper accomplished very little of his economic agenda. On the contrary, his determination to cut taxes was steadfast, and his various measures to reduce personal, corporate, and consumption taxes deprived the federal government of major sources of badly needed revenue. He also eliminated the Wheat Board, deregulated many industries, and eliminated much of the environmental-protection legislation put in place by successive Liberal and Progressive Conservative governments, as he had promised.

His aggressive response to the self-induced federal deficit, meanwhile, led to the recent massive cutbacks to the public service, with all their implications for reduced service and program delivery, as well as loss of institutional memory, just as his deep-seated hostility towards labour unions led to a severe loss of protection for many working Canadians. At the same time, several of his actions have had unanticipated, and undesirable, consequences. The belated and deep cuts to the public service, for example, could no longer be dismissed as mere administrative streamlining, which would have no impact on ordinary Canadians. The widely reported closures of regional offices, delays in the processing of applications, and embarrassing revelations about cutbacks to military spending (at one point forcing technicians to scavenge parts for search-and-rescue planes in a museum and reducing the navy to one supply ship for the entire fleet), began to take their toll on the credibility of the government's claims. So, too, did the reports that the Canada Revenue Agency was eliminating more than fifty senior administrative auditors in response to the 2014 budget cuts, thereby undermining the government's claim to be cracking down on international tax cheats. In fact, numerous reports concluded that the fired auditors – considered the most highly skilled members of the offshore tax-evasion team – would soon be working for "the other side" at higher salaries, confounding the government's crackdown efforts.[1]

As someone whose primary economic objective was for government to do less, not more, Harper's inaction on a number of files has also had a significant impact, for example with respect to municipal infrastructure renewal, the creation of a national broadband network, or other measures to enhance productivity and competitiveness. Likewise, his preference for resource-based western industries over central-Canadian manufacturing has arguably cost the economy billions of dollars in lost productivity and job creation.

Still, the lack of action on so many fronts, while damaging in the short-term, need not be permanent. It can be corrected by a future government committed to proactive measures, just as the lack of revenue for programs and services can be corrected by a progressive government willing to challenge the conservative mantra on taxation and deficits. Probably the most serious challenge facing future governments will flow from the Harper Conservatives' wholesale deregulation of environmental-protection measures. On paper this, too, can be reversed by a future government, but any damage already inflicted may not be easily contained or rectified.

Similarly Harper's domestic agenda, with its heavy emphasis on law and order, has undoubtedly made an impact on the criminal-justice system, which is leaner and meaner. Very possibly it has also made Canadian communities less safe. Yet these changes, too, are vulnerable to reversal by a future government. Since much of this tough-on-crime agenda was accomplished through regulation, cutbacks, and appointments to various boards and agencies, it can be reversed in the same way. His lack of support for social-action programs and elimination of funding for various NGOs under his family-values initiative can also be redressed relatively easily by a future government.

On the other hand, the gun registry has been eliminated and, like Brian Mulroney's privatization of Crown corporations, this cannot be undone, due to the massive financial and political costs involved. But Harper's record number of appointments to the bench have proved a disappointment to him. The string of unfavourable Supreme Court decisions in 2013 and 2014 repeatedly thwarted his agenda, despite the presence on the court of several of his own appointees, suggesting that judicial independence is alive and well in Canada.

Meanwhile Harper's patriotic militarism and promise of beefed-up military expenditures soon bogged down under the weight of massive costs, apparent incompetence, and scandal. At the same time, evidence was mounting of a disconnect between his government's commitment to hardware purchases and its seeming lack of concern for military personnel, epitomized by a number of unflattering revelations about the treatment of veterans. Moreover, Harper's enthusiasm for military adventures and his desire to impress his allies, so evident in the early engagements in Afghanistan and Libya, quickly faded. The 2012 Mali crisis saw Harper refuse to intervene, despite considerable international pressure to do so, and his efforts to reposition Canada as a player in the international defence community appear to have been greatly scaled back.

Conversely, Harper's determination to pursue "principled" foreign-policy positions did indeed result in a change in Canada's image abroad, but not in the way he hoped. His relentless criticism of the UN, repudiation of international treaties, unqualified support for Israel, and major cuts to foreign aid led to a dramatic decline in Canada's international reputation.[2] It cost the country a seat on the Security Council and made it an international pariah on the global-warming file. Even in Canada–US relations, where Harper's priorities allegedly lay, his criticism of the Obama administration and his naive demands for US approval of the Keystone XL pipeline actually caused a chill in the relationship.

Yet here, too, the damage is hardly permanent. A return to a more traditional Canadian role is easily possible. A future government's emphasis on peacekeeping and a renewed commitment to foreign aid, and proactive participation in the United Nations and the Commonwealth, would undoubtedly be welcomed by our allies, consigning the Harper era to posterity as an aberration. A far more serious and potentially lasting challenge will no doubt be the task of rebuilding Canadian credibility in the Middle East.

Unquestionably, the Harper Conservatives' most significant impact has been on the welfare state. Reductions in federal funding, and an abdication of responsibility on national standards, combined with a total lack of interest in providing leadership on new and emerging issues, have undoubtedly had a negative impact on social cohesion and damaged the fabric of the social union. As numerous studies have demonstrated, the gap between rich and poor has widened dramatically in the past decade,[3] as has the gap between have and have-not provinces. Still, the Harper Conservatives' determination to abandon the social union to the provinces, in the hope that this would lead to the unravelling of the welfare state, appears to have run into unexpected opposition. First, it has led premiers to recognize, and publicly acknowledge, the important role played by the federal government. It has also caused the premiers to come together to provide creative alternatives, such as their collective response on improvements to the health-care system and their opposition to his government's regressive jobs-strategy proposal. Similarly, by late 2013 a frustrated Ontario premier Kathleen Wynne and PEI premier Robert Ghiz declared they would establish their own parallel pension plans if the federal government failed to act in a timely manner.

Meanwhile, the provincial Conservative Party's selection of Jim Prentice as premier of Alberta, and the re-election of Christy Clark's Liberal government in BC, may signal a trend towards the emergence of more liberal regimes in western Canada in response to the extreme conservative agenda being promoted in Ottawa. As a result, with another federal election approaching, the political constraints on Harper's policy agenda have increased significantly.

Interestingly, it was the Conservatives' long-term objective of moving the political culture to the right, and destroying the federal Liberal Party, that initially appeared to have been among their most successful efforts. Indeed, even before their 2011 majority victory, this favourable assessment of their progress had become conventional wisdom. Yet the facts do not bear this out. As columnist Jeffrey Simpson concluded, the idea that Canadians are moving further to the right "is an assertion based sometimes on hope, often on conjecture, occasionally on fragmentary evidence, but never on serious facts and deep analysis."[4] Similarly, as public-opinion polling and several 2013 and 2014 by-elections indicated, the Liberal brand has remained credible, and the Liberal Party under Justin Trudeau appears to be resurgent.

THE LONG GAME: CHANGING THE POLITICAL CULTURE

Countless opinion polls since 2006 have demonstrated that liberal values continue to underpin Canadians' policy priorities and views on the state. In 2011, pollster Frank Graves of EKOS found that Canadians' opposition to the decriminalization of marijuana had actually declined from 2006, when the Harper government was first elected. Similarly, in 2006 some 39 per cent of Canadians felt the government should spend more on the justice system (but on preventive measures, not prisons). In 2010, after four years of Harper's law-and-order agenda, the number had declined to 24 per cent. Also in 2011, Michael Adams of Environics reported that a "huge jump" in support for gay marriage and legal abortions had taken place in the previous four years. As for the evangelical Christian influence on Harper's government, in 2011 nearly half of all Canadians agreed with the statement that religion "does more harm than good." Meanwhile, fully 84 per cent of Canadians agreed that governments, not families or voluntary groups, "should reduce the gap between rich and poor."

Despite Harper's declaration that there is no such thing as a good tax, in 2005 an impressive 72 per cent of Canadians agreed that taxes are "mostly good," and that number had not changed by 2010.[5] Even in Alberta, polls demonstrated that residents were willing to pay more in taxes to improve services and reduce poverty. Moreover Canadians' top spending priorities for government were antithetical to the Harper government's agenda. Instead of the military and prisons, Canadians ranked health care, programs for the elderly, child poverty, and the environment as their most pressing policy concerns. By May 2012, several additional polls demonstrated that income inequality had actually risen to the top of their list, displacing health care for the first time. Some 88 per cent of Canadians said they believed the gap between rich and poor had risen on the Conservatives' watch.[6] By 2013, another EKOS poll found more than twice as many Canadians self-identified as liberals than conservatives. By 2013 this was at its highest level in nearly twenty years.

In addition to polling data, the results of the May 2011 election, when more than 60 per cent of Canadians voted against the Harper Conservatives' agenda, speak for themselves. Indeed, in the absence of a credible Liberal alternative, many turned to a more left-wing option, the federal New Democrats. Subsequent polls throughout 2013 and 2014 have demonstrated a steady decline in support for the Conservatives and a rise in Liberal Party fortunes, placing Harper's long-term goal even further out of reach.

UNANTICIPATED CONSEQUENCES?

If the extent of the Harper Conservatives' failure to introduce lasting policy change or modify the political culture have proven surprising, the unanticipated consequences of their actions may be equally significant. Perhaps the first and most obvious victim of the Conservatives' time in office has been the deteriorating level of political discourse and behaviour. The new low in politicians' conduct in parliament and during elections has raised concerns even among Conservatives, and casts doubt on the ability of any future government to restore the credibility of the democratic system.[7]

Another striking development has been the dramatic deterioration in federal-provincial relations. Given the Harper government's longstanding emphasis on "open federalism" and pledge to promote intergovernmental harmony, the spectre of provincial premiers closing ranks and presenting a united front against the federal government is not only unexpected but hugely revealing. Despite the creation of the Council of the Federation in 2003, with its express mandate to "provide a united front amongst the provincial and territorial governments when interacting with the federal government," at no point in its history had the council managed to achieve anything like a consensus until the advent of the Harper government.

Another unexpected development is the growing alienation of Ontario, a province the Conservatives depended on for their 2011 majority and will need again if they are to have any hope of repeating that feat. Yet several of Harper's ministers have treated the province with contempt. In addition to frequent and overtly partisan criticism of the provincial Liberal government, the Conservatives have taken policy decisions that run directly counter to the interests of the province, over the vociferous objections of the premier. They have also formed highly public alliances with their provincial Conservative counterparts and, indeed, with like-minded politicians at the municipal level. From the personal friendship of Jim Flaherty and Toronto mayor Rob Ford, to the prime minister's personal visits to Toronto to announce federal funding for projects requested by the city, but rejected by the province, it would appear the Harper government either has few qualms about the political fallout from such antagonistic behaviour, or is convinced the benefits will more than compensate. Yet Liberal premier Kathleen Wynne's convincing win in the June 2014 provincial election suggests otherwise, particularly since her campaign was deliberately fought against the Harper Conservatives rather than her provincial party opponents.

Another key element of growing intergovernmental angst has been the alienation of Quebec. The Harper government's right-wing agenda, and its many direct confrontations with premier Jean Charest, followed by its outright feud with the subsequent PQ government of Pauline Marois, left Quebecers feeling alienated and resentful. It remains to be seen whether the election of a new Liberal government under the staunchly federalist Philippe Couillard will prove an antidote.

Certainly Harper's disregard for many Quebec concerns has led to a dramatic decline in support for his party in that province. Although his 2011 electoral majority was achieved without Quebec, that majority was made possible by the collapse of the Liberal Party and the Bloc Québécois and the unexpected surge in support for the NDP. But the so-called Orange Wave that carried the NDP to Official Opposition status has crashed on shore and dissipated. Increasingly it is the Liberals who appear to have benefited most from the Conservatives' single-digit support in Quebec, bolstered by the strong performance of leader Justin Trudeau in taking on the PQ's Charter of Values.

In addition, Harper's vaunted political machine has increasingly appeared to be in disarray. His attempt to restore order to the party by appointing his former director of communications and personal friend, Dimitri Soudas, as the party's National Director, failed dramatically when Soudas was accused of using his office to aid his girlfriend, MP Eve Adams, in her bid to leave her existing base and become the party's candidate in a new riding. Soudas's resignation led to a period of unusual public criticism of the prime minister and his office by rank-and-file party members, as did the ongoing problems related to the upcoming criminal trial of former senator Mike Duffy, Harper's personal pick. Within the PMO, Harper's decision to replace the disgraced chief of staff Nigel Wright with long-time aide and ally Ray Novak, a dyed-in-the-wool Reformer, suggested to many observers that the prime minister felt the need to circle the wagons.

These developments could lead to serious problems for the Conservatives in the next election, particularly since they have been accompanied by an apparent resurgence of Liberal support in Ontario. Several polls in late 2013 actually found the Liberals had taken the lead in the 905 region around Toronto and in the province,[8] a trend confirmed by two decisive by-election wins in the region in June 2014. Indeed, the consensus of five polling experts in the late summer of 2014 suggested the Harper government could not hope for more than a minority in the next (October 2015) election, and could well find itself relegated to the position of Official Opposition.[9]

A number of experts have outlined the difficulties Stephen Harper faces in maintaining his support beyond his narrow base. One problem is the political fallout from scandals involving the Senate and the PMO. Another is the fact that the party has defined itself by its enemies, now too numerous to name, rather than by its positive achievements. In addition, after nine years in power, it will be impossible for the Conservatives to present themselves as outsiders, or to run against their record.

Another problem the party faces with all voters is that it has so little to offer in 2015, apart from more potential tax cuts, a scenario Jim Flaherty actually discouraged. Inevitably, any party whose primary ambition is to shrink the size of government and withdraw from policy areas faces a serious problem when voters expect positive proposals, and Canadians are no exception. Yet this is a government that has staked its claim on what it will not do, or will undo. As a result, since the list of negative promises made earlier has been addressed, the slim docket of legislative initiatives in recent parliaments speaks volumes about the Conservatives' lack of future direction. This policy vacuum inadvertently was confirmed by the prime minister in a campaign-style speech to Tory faithful in Ottawa in September 2014, where he made two specific promises. First, he pledged that his government would introduce even more tax cuts in the next budget, and, second, he pledged that – having earlier abolished the faint-hope clause – he would now table legislation to eliminate the one remaining chance of parole for those serving life sentences. While both subjects may be of intense interest to the party's narrow base, observers concluded that neither commitment would be likely to influence the majority of Canadians, and certainly would do nothing to improve the Conservatives' chances in the next election.[10]

There is therefore reason to conclude that a return to liberal-minded government could well be the result of the next election. This possibility becomes even more likely with the passage of time. In the past, nine years in power has marked the end of the road for federal governments of all political stripes. This held true for the Liberals, and more significantly for Brian Mulroney, a man whose original personal popularity and the size of his majorities dwarfed Harper's. Mulroney himself made this point in a devastating series of interviews to mark the thirtieth anniversary of his 1984 election victory. When told the Harperites were frustrated by Justin Trudeau's growing popularity, because he had no policies, Mulroney replied that Trudeau did have a policy. "His policy is that he's not Stephen Harper."[11]

Although Stephen Harper has benefited from considerable public tolerance or ignorance of his government's many gaffes and scandals, the public perception of its aggressive style and tone, and of his own hyperpartisan behaviour, has become well-entrenched. Taken together, the ongoing accumulation of baggage could well result in a wholesale rejection of his party and its leader. In that event, the legacy of the Harper Conservatives will likely be much less significant than originally expected or feared.

In the end, it would seem that Harper's new conservative agenda was doomed to failure from the beginning. His major policy initiatives could always be reversed by a future progressive government, unless he was successful in changing the political culture as well. But this second objective was evidently a bridge too far for any conservative politician in Canada, however determined.

Notes

INTRODUCTION

1 Bruce Doern, "The Chrétien Liberals' Third Mandate" in *How Ottawa Spends, 2002–2003*, ed. Bruce Doern (Don Mills: Oxford, 2003), 3.
2 Tom Flanagan, *Winning Power: Canadian Campaigning in the Twenty-First Century* (Montreal: McGill-Queen's University Press, 2014); Bob Plamondon, *Full Circle: Death and Resurrection in Canadian Politics* (Toronto: Key Porter, 2006).
3 In his June 2003 speech in Toronto to the ultraconservative Civitas Society, Harper specifically referred to Hobbes and Burke as philosophical inspirations.
4 Ibid.
5 John Pammett, Lawrence LeDuc, et al., *Dynasties and Interlude: Past and Present in Canadian Electoral Politics* (Toronto: Dundurn, 2010).
6 For detailed explanations, see Brooke Jeffrey, "Missed Opportunity: The Invisible Liberals," in *The Canadian Federal Election of 2008*, edited by Jon H. Pammett and Christopher Dornan (Toronto: Dundurn, 2009), 63–97, and Brooke Jeffrey, "The Disappearing Liberals: Caught in the Crossfire," in *The Canadian Federal Election of 2011*, edited by Jon H. Pammett and Christopher Dornan (Toronto: Dundurn, 2012), 45–76.
7 See, for example, the excellent opinion piece by John Meisel, "Harperizing Our Minds," *Toronto Star* (19 April 2011).
8 For more detail, see Jeremy van Loon, "Canadians Overestimate Contribution of Oilsands to Economy," *Bloomberg News* (4 July 2014).

CHAPTER ONE

1 Leslie MacKinnon, "Harper Slams Trudeau for Comments on Boston Bombings," *CBC News*, 17 April 2013, http://www.cbc.ca/news/politics/harper-slams-trudeau-for-comments-on-boston-bombings-1.1394586.

2 In 2006 at his swearing-in ceremony, Harper told a reporter, "I don't think my fundamental beliefs have changed in a decade" (cited in "Harper, the Cerebral," cbc.ca, 16 March 2006).

3 For a detailed discussion of this philosophical framework, see the excellent H.B. McCullough, *Political Ideologies* (Toronto: Oxford, 2010), 8–29.

4 See, for example, Louis Hartz, *The Liberal Tradition in America* (New York: Harcourt Brace, 1953) and Kenneth McRae, "Louis Hartz's Concept of the Fragment Society and Its Application to Canada," *Études canadiennes* 5 (1978), 17–30.

5 Robert Jackson, Doreen Jackson, and Nick Baxter-Moore, *Politics in Canada: Culture, Institutions, Behaviour* (Scarborough: Prentice-Hall, 1986), 83–6. For more detail see Gad Horowitz, "Conservatism, Liberalism, and Socialism in Canada: An Interpretation," *Canadian Journal of Political Science* 32, no. 2 (1966), 143–71.

6 David Bell and Lorne Tepperman, *The Roots of Disunity: A Look at Canadian Political Culture* (Toronto: McClelland and Stewart, 1979), 232.

7 Rodney Lowe, "Torn Between Europe and America: The British Welfare State from Beveridge to Blair" in *The Great, the New, and the British: Essays on Post-war Britain*, ed. Anneke Ribberink and Hans Righart (Cambridge: Cambridge University Press, 2000).

8 See for example Richard J. Terrill, "Margaret Thatcher's Law and Order Agenda," *The American Journal of Comparative Law* 37, no. 3 (Summer, 1989): 429–56.

9 Brooke Jeffrey, *Hard Right Turn: The New Face of Neoconservatism in Canada* (Toronto: HarperCollins, 1999), 11.

10 Sunder Katwala, "Ideology in Politics: Reflections on Lady Thatcher's Legacy," *Juncture* (April 2013): http://www.ippr.org/juncture/ideology-in-politics-reflections-on-lady-thatchers-legacy.

11 Hugo Young and Anne Sloman, *The Thatcher Phenomenon* (London: BBC, 1986), 33.

12 Peter Hennessy, *Cabinet* (Oxford: Basil Blackwell, 1986), 122.

13 Ibid.

14 *Right Thinking*, Conservative Party Manifesto (1979).

15 Alan Travis, "Margaret Thatcher's Role in Plan to Dismantle Welfare State Revealed," *The Guardian* (28 December 2012), 1.

16 Steven Chase and Campbell Clark, "For Canadian Conservatives, a Saviour," *Globe and Mail* (9 April 2013).

17 Jeffrey Simpson, "Thatcher's Children Have Their Hands Full," *Globe and Mail* (1 March 2014).

18 Geoffrey Hodgson, *The World Turned Upside Right* (New York: Houghton Mifflin, 1996), 261.

19 Milton Friedman, "The Real Free Lunch: Markets and Private Property," *The CATO Policy Report* XV, no. 4 (August 1983): 1.
20 See Kevin Phillips, *The Politics of Rich and Poor: Wealth and the American Electorate in the Reagan Aftermath* (New York: Harper Collins, 1991) for a detailed criticism of Reagan's policies by a former senior adviser and well-known Republican.
21 See for example B. Harrison and B. Bluestone, *The Great U Turn* (New York: Basic Books, 1990) for an in-depth examination of the problems deregulation produced in the transportation sector.
22 For more detail, see J. Krieger, "Social Policy in the Age of Reagan and Thatcher," *Socialist Register* 23 (1987).
23 John Palmer, ed., *Perspectives on the Reagan Years* (Washington, DC: Urban Institute Press, 1986).
24 Elizabeth Drew, "The Real Struggle for Political Power in America" (Stanford: Knight Fellowship Lecture, 1997).
25 Jonathan Haidt, *The Righteous Mind* (New York: Pantheon Books, 2012), 297–306.
26 "Candidate: Rondo Thomas," *GlobeandMail.com*, access date 13 January 2006, http://www.theglobeandmail.com/elections/fed2005/candidates/generated/35001_CON.html.
27 See for example Jeffrey, *Hard Right Turn*, 148–279.
28 Joseph Heath, "In Defence of Sociology," *Ottawa Citizen* (1 May 2013), A13.
29 See for example Marci McDonald, "The Man Behind Stephen Harper," *The Walrus* (12 September 2012), and D. Gutstein, "Harper, Bush Share Roots in Controversial Philosophy," *The Tyee* (25 November 2005).
30 Bill Curry and Tavia Grant, "Ottawa Asks Business to Help Fund Social Programs," *Globe and Mail* (8 November 2012).
31 Christian Nadeau, *Rogue in Power* (Toronto: Lorimer, 2010), 37.
32 See for example Gad Horowitz, "Conservatism, Liberalism, and Socialism in Canada," *Canadian Journal of Economics and Political Science* 32 (1966), 143–71, and Kenneth McRae, "Louis Hartz's Concept of the Fragment Society and Its Application to Canada," Études canadiennes 5: 17–30.
33 Tom Flanagan and Stephen Harper, "Our Benign Dictatorship," *Next City* (Winter 1996–97).
34 Stephen Harper, "Speech to the National Policy Council," Montreal, QC (June 1997).
35 CTV.ca, "Question Period," 26 April 2004. ctestp.ctv.ca/servlet/an/local/CTVNews/20040426/qp-clark040425?hub... (archived). The CTV

interview was reported by the CBC on 27 April at http://www.cbc.ca/news/canada/clark-says-harper-would-be-dangerous-leader-1.502393, but the specific reference to the Harper Conservatives not being the Tories is not included.

36 Hugh Segal, *No Surrender* (New York: Harper Perennial Canada, 1996), 225.
37 Stephen Harper, *The New Canada Plan* (Ottawa: Reform Party of Canada, 1995).
38 James Farney, *Social Conservatives in Canada and the United States* (Toronto: University of Toronto Press, 2012).
39 William Christian and Colin Campbell, *Political Parties and Ideologies in Canada: Liberals, Conservatives, Socialists, Nationalists* (Toronto: McGraw-Hill Ryerson, 1974), 76.
40 Farney, *Social Conservatives in Canada and the United States*, 84.
41 Brooke Jeffrey, *Hard Right Turn*, 331–7.
42 Ibid., 347
43 Stephen Harper, "Speech delivered to the Civitas Society" (Toronto, June 2003).
44 Stephen Harper, "Speech delivered to the American Council for National Policy," Montreal, QC (June 1997).
45 Stephen Harper et al., "An Open Letter to Ralph Klein," *National Post* (24 January 2001).
46 Tom Flanagan, *Harper's Team* (Montreal: McGill-Queen's University Press, 2009), 369.
47 The speech, once readily available, has now been expunged from most websites. It can be reliably accessed in its entirety at present only on the following site: http://www.cannabisculture.com/articles/4629.html. However segments of the speech are widely reproduced in Nadeau (*Rogue in Power*), Lawrence Martin, *Haperland: The Politics of Control* (Toronto: Viking Canada, 2010), and articles by Paul Wells in *Maclean's*.
48 Christian Nadeau, *Rogue in Power*, 35–6.
49 John Ibbitson, "Harper Cuts Loose on Air Strip ATV Joyride," *Globe and Mail* (26 August 2010), A8.

CHAPTER TWO

1 G. Bruce Doern, "The Chrétien Liberals' Third Mandate" in *How Ottawa Spends, 2002–2003* (Don Mills: Oxford University Press, 2003) 3.
2 Joseph Crespino, *In Search of Another Country: Mississippi and the Conservative Counterrevolution* (Princeton: Princeton University Press, 2007), 1.

3 For more detail, see Brooke Jeffrey, *Hard Right Turn: The New Face of Neoconservatism in Canada* (Toronto: HarperCollins, 1999), 404–25.
4 Kenneth Carty, William Cross, and Lisa Young, *Rebuilding Canadian Party Politics* (Vancouver: UBC Press, 2000).
5 Tom Flanagan, "Though Shalt Not Lean Too Far to the Right," *Globe and Mail* (22 September 2007), F6.
6 Tom Flanagan and Stephen Harper, "Our Benign Dictatorship," *Next City* (Winter 1997).
7 Ibid.
8 Susan Delacourt, "Seeds Planted for Opposition to Unity Plan," *Globe and Mail* (18 September 1997).
9 Stephen Harper, "Speech to the Colin Brown Memorial Dinner" (National Citizens Coalition, 1994).
10 For a detailed analysis of the Conservative campaign and the election results, see Faron Ellis and Peter Woolstencroft, "New Conservatives, Old Realities: The 2004 Election Campaign," in *The Canadian General Election of 2004*, edited by Jon Pammett and Christopher Dornan (Toronto: Dundurn, 2005), 66–107.
11 For more detail, see the analysis of the election in Faron Ellis and Peter Woolstencroft, "A Change of Government Not a Change of Country," in *The Canadian General Election of 2006*, edited by Jon Pammett and Christopher Dornan (Toronto: Dundurn, 2007), 58–92.
12 Tom Flanagan, *Harper's Team: Behind the Scenes in the Conservatives' Rise to Power* (Montreal: McGill-Queen's University Press, 2007), 275.
13 L. Ian MacDonald, "Tax Cut Already Cost Charest," *Montreal Gazette* (25 May 2007).
14 See, for example, Reginald Bibby, *Beyond the Gods and Back* (Lethbridge: Project Canada Books, 2011) and Michael Adams, *Fire and Ice* (Toronto: Penguin Books, 2009).
15 Patrick Fournier et al., *The 2011 Canadian Election Study* [dataset]. This conclusion was also supported by Ipsos Reid's 2 May 2011 exit poll, which found the Conservatives received the support of 50 per cent of voters who said they attended a church or temple every week and 42 per cent of those who said they had "some religious identity." This was compared with only 16 per cent for the Liberals. The numbers are even more significant considering that one-quarter of Canadians indicate they have "no religion."
16 Dennis Gruending, *Pulpit and Politics* (Ottawa: Kingsley, 2011), 16–17; Marci McDonald, *The Armageddon Factor* (Toronto: Random House, 2010), 37.

17 Although many westerners are convinced that they are "underrepresented" in Parliament, in reality the constraints of geography and uneven demographic distribution in Canada have meant that western and/or rural votes are "worth more" in an effort to provide a reasonable accommodation with the principle of one person, one vote. (As of 1993, one expert estimated that a vote in a rural BC riding was equivalent to the votes of 2 ½ individuals in downtown Toronto.)
18 As cited in Gruending, *Pulpit and Politics*, 19.
19 Robert Dreyfuss, "Reverend Doomsday," *Rolling Stone* (28 January 2004).
20 McDonald, *The Armageddon Factor*, see especially 50–141.
21 Life Training Institute, "Endorsements." Accessed at http:/ www.prolifetraining.com (April 2006) archived. Kenney also referred to his meeting with and support for Klusendorf when he raised the issue of the "rights of the unborn" in the House of Commons. *Hansard* no. 34, 37th Parliament, 1st Session (22 March 2001).
22 Pauline Tam, "Onward Christian Soldiers," *Ottawa Citizen* (15 January 2006).
23 Flanagan, *Harper's Team*, 280.
24 Alec Castonguay, "The Inside Story of Jason Kenney's Campaign to Win Over Ethnic Votes," *Maclean*'s, trans. from *L'actualité* (2 February 2013).
25 The author has a copy of Kenney's memo and plan.
26 Tobi Cohen, "Kenney Defends $750K Tab for Monitoring Ethnic Media," *Ottawa Citizen* (5 November 2012).
27 Carty, Cross, and Young, *Rebuilding Canadian Political Parties*.
28 For more detail, see Jon Pammett and Lawrence LeDuc, Chap. 14 in *Dynasties and Interludes: Past and Present in Canadian Electoral Politics* (Toronto: Dundurn, 2010).
29 Lawrence LeDuc and Jon Pammett, "The Evolution of the Harper Dynasty," *The Canadian General Election of 2011*, edited by Jon Pammett and Christopher Dornan (Toronto: Dundurn, 2012), 329.
30 Chris Plecash, "Tories Focus on Ethnic Outreach with Multiple Multiculturalism Ministers," *Hill Times* (26 August 2013).
31 James Moore and Wayne Slater, *The Architect: Karl Rove and the Master Plan for Absolute Power* (New York: Crown, 2006), 4.
32 See, for example, Norman Ornstein and Thomas Mann (eds.), *The Permanent Campaign and Its Future* (Washington: Brookings Institute, 2000) and Cory Cook, "The Permanence of the Permanent Campaign: George W. Bush's Public Presidency," *Presidential Studies Quarterly* 32, no. 4 (2002), 753–64.

33 Despite his large client base among Republicans, Luntz has been censored by almost every professional polling organization at one time or another, primarily for refusing to release data on which his polling results are based.
34 Canwest News, "American Strategist Teaches Tories Tips on Keeping Power" (7 May 2006).
35 Tom Flanagan, *Winning Power* (Montreal: McGill-Queen's University Press, 2014), 125–63.
36 For a detailed account see Faron Ellis, "The More Things Change: The Alliance Campaign," in *The Canadian General Election of 2000*, edited by Jon Pammett and Christopher Dornan (Toronto: Dundurn, 2001).
37 Tom Flanagan and Harold Jensen, "Election Campaigns Under Canada's Party Finance Laws," in *The Canadian General Election of 2008*, edited by Jon Pammett and Christopher Dornan (Toronto: Dundurn, 2009), 210.
38 See, for example, the analysis by Flanagan and Jensen, in *The Canadian General Election of 2008*, 212.
39 Brooke Jeffrey, "Missed Opportunity: The Invisible Liberals," in *The Canadian General Election of 2008*, 90.
40 Flanagan and Jensen, "Election Campaigns under Canada's Party Finance Laws," 210.
41 Brooke Jeffrey, "Caught in the Crossfire: The Disappearing Liberals," in *The Canadian General Election of 2011*, edited by Jon Pammett and Christopher Dornan (Toronto: Dundurn, 2012), 55.
42 Bea Vongdouangchanh, "Liberals Want to Limit Pre-Writ Political Advertising," *Hill Times* (1 June 2009), 32.
43 Lawrence Martin, "Harper's Attacks on Trudeau Will Be Vicious," *Globe and Mail* (27 November 2012).
44 John Ibbitson, "Tory Attack Ads Pack a Punch that Leaves Liberals Reeling," *Globe and Mail* (21 February 2011).
45 Christopher Dornan, "The Outcome in Retrospect," in *The Canadian General Election of 2008*, 8.
46 Flanagan and Jensen, "Election Campaigns under Canada's Party Finance Laws," 207.
47 "Tories Cross the Line," *Ottawa Citizen* (27 April 2013).
48 Lawrence Martin, "Harper's Attacks on Trudeau Will Be Vicious," *Globe and Mail* (27 November 2012).
49 Michael Woods, "Conservatives Take an Early Jab at Justin Trudeau," *Postmedia News* (15 April 2013).
50 Ibid.

51 Mark Kennedy, "Attack Ads on Trudeau Not Working, Says Former Harper Adviser," *Postmedia News* (25 February 2014).

CHAPTER THREE

1 Tom Flanagan, *Harper's Team* (Montreal: McGill-Queen's University Press, 2007), 60.
2 Donald Savoie, *Power: Where Is It?* (Montreal: McGill-Queen's University Press, 2010).
3 Jim Bronskill and Mike Blanchfield, "Harper's Message Tool Reveals 'Hyper-Extreme' Control," *Globe and Mail* (7 June 2010).
4 David Pugliese, "Fed Up Media Officers Desert DND," *Ottawa Citizen* (25 September 2011).
5 Jeffrey Simpson, "Canada's 'No Comment' Conservative Government," *Globe and Mail* (24 November 2012), F9.
6 Laura Ryckewaert, "Harper Takes Communications Strategy to New Level," *Hill Times* (21 November 2011).
7 Jim Bronskill and Mike Blanchfield, "Harper's Message Tool Reveals 'Hyper-Extreme' Control."
8 "PMO wanted Gainey Death Report Held until Campaign Over: Emails," *Canadian Press* (3 April 2009).
9 Simpson, "Canada's No Comment Conservative Government," F9.
10 Lawrence Martin, *Harperland* (Toronto: Viking Canada, 2010), 58–63
11 Hon. David Emerson, as quoted in Lawrence Martin, *Harperland*, 55.
12 Jessica Bruno and Michael Lapointe, "PMO's Enemies List Reveals Tight Management of Cabinet Say Former Conservative Staffers," *Hill Times* (23 July 2013).
13 Lee Berthiaume, "Anger Erupts over PMO's Enemies List," *Ottawa Citizen* (17 July 2013).
14 Martin, *Harperland*, 56.
15 Ibid., 55.
16 Charles Smith, "Women Kick Harper's Ass," *Georgia Straight* (13 December 2006).
17 Bruce Cheadle, "Tories Re-Brand Government in Harper's Name," *Canadian Press* (3 March 2011).
18 Sylvia Stead, "Ottawa Versus the Harper Government," *Globe and Mail* (15 June 2013).
19 Cheadle, "Tories Re-Brand Government in Harper's Name."
20 Errol Mendes, "The Party Is Not the Government," *Ottawa Citizen* (28 October 2009).

21 Cheadle, "Tories Re-Brand Government in Harper's Name."
22 Jane Taber, "Meet the Oilsands Muse," *Globe and Mail* (19 January 2011).
23 Brooke Jeffrey, *Divided Loyalties* (Toronto: University of Toronto Press, 2010), 517.
24 Dean Beeby, "Language Czar Urges Baird to Trash Unilingual Business Cards," *Ottawa Citizen* (3 August 2013).
25 Mark Kennedy, "PMO Breaking Bank for Propaganda," *Ottawa Citizen* (30 October 2010).
26 Economic Action Plan Inefficient, Survey Finds," *Canadian Press* (21 July 2013).
27 Tobi Cohen, "Kenney Defends $750,000 Tab for Monitoring Ethnic Media," *Ottawa Citizen* (17 November 2012).
28 "Probe into Liberal Polling Practices Dings Tories Instead," *Canadian Press* (13 December 2007).
29 Jeffrey Simpson, "The Conservatives' Very Own Oscar Selfie," *Globe and Mail* (8 March 2014).
30 Jane Taber, "Hates the Media, Loves Sandra Buckler," *Globe and Mail* (4 August 2007).
31 Bea Vongdouangchanh, "PMO Picks Fight, Media Push Back," *Hill Times* (21 October 2013).
32 Alex Marland, "Political Photography, Journalism and Framing in the Digital Age: The Management of the Visual Media by the Prime Minister of Canada," *International Journal of Press/Politics* (2 February 2012). http:/hij.sagepub.com/content/17/2/214.
33 Ralph Surette, "Why Harper Must Not Have His Majority," *The Chronicle Herald* (2 April 2011).
34 Simpson,"Canada's No Comment Conservative Government," F9.
35 Andrew Mayeda, "CRTC Offers to Review Internet Billing Decision," *Postmedia News* (3 February 2011).
36 "Commissioner Slams Harper for About-Face on Info Access Reform," *Canadian Press* (28 April 2006).
37 Gloria Galloway and Bill Curry, "Five Years Later, Information Access Is Still Stalled" *Globe and Mail* (8 October 2010).
38 As reported in the CAUT/ACPPU *Bulletin* (February 2011), A5.
39 Steven Chase, "Five Ways Ottawa Stymies Access to Information," *Globe and Mail* (15 January 2011).
40 Kristen Douglas et al., *The* Access to Information Act *and Proposals for Reform* (Ottawa: Library of Parliament, 2005), updated 6 June 2012.
41 Carol Goar, "Harper Is Cutting Off 'Lifeblood of Democracy,'" *Toronto Star* (23 February 2011).

42 Penni Stewart, "Harper Government Puts Library and Archives Canada at Risk," CAUT/ACPPU *Bulletin* 58, no. 4 (April 2011).
43 Margaret Munro, "Muzzling of Federal Scientists Called a Threat to Democracy," *Postmedia News* (20 February 2013).
44 Laura Ryckewaert, "Voluntary Census Already Damaging Reliability of Statistics," *Hill Times* (26 August 2013).
45 Editorial, *Globe and Mail* (26 June 2013).
46 Bill Curry, "Internal Memo Reveals Ottawa Cut Labour Market Data Spending," *Globe and Mail* (11 June 2014).
47 Thomas Homer-Dixon, Heather Douglas, and Lucie Edwards, "Fix the Link Where Science and Policy Meet," *Globe and Mail* (23 June 2014).
48 Harris MaCleod, "Census Controversy Affecting StatsCan Morale in Major Way," *Hill Times* (2 August 2010).
49 Scott Taylor, "The Black and White Vision of John Baird," *Halifax Herald* (18 May 2014).
50 Gary Corbett, "The Harper Government's Disdain for Science," *Ottawa Life* (September 2012).
51 Kathryn May, "Harper's Suspicions of PS Hint at Rocky Relations to Come," *Ottawa Citizen* (18 January 2006).
52 Ibid.
53 Ish Theilheimer, "Work Grinds to a Halt in Harper's Civil Service," *Straight Goods News* (25 November 2010).
54 Sharon Sutherland, "The Unaccountable *Federal Accountability Act*: Goodbye to Responsible Government?" *Revue Gouvernance* 3, no. 2 (December 2006): 30–42.
55 Mike De Souza, "Climate Change Scientists Feel 'Muzzled': Survey," *Ottawa Citizen* (15 March 2010).
56 Tom Spears, "Scientists Unite to Protest Death of Research," *Ottawa Citizen* (9 July 2012); Margaret Munro, "Feds Silence Scientist over Salmon Study," *Postmedia News* (27 July 2011).
57 Editorial, "Harper Conservatives Aim to Guarantee Public Ignorance," *New York Times* (22 September 2013).
58 Stephen Chase and Campbell Clark, "Diplomats Condemn Harper Government's Treatment of Colvin," *Toronto Star* (8 December 2009).
59 Martin, *Harperland*, 128.
60 Michael Ivanco, "Safety Before Expediency: Harper Government Must Reconsider AECL Sale," *Press Release* (21 March 2011).
61 For more detail see Brooke Jeffrey, "Strained Relations: The Harper Government and the Federal Bureaucracy," Paper presented to the annual

Canadian Political Science Association meeting, Kitchener, Ontario (22 May 2011).

62 Sylvia Bashevkin, *Women, Power, Politics: The Hidden Story of Canada's Unfinished Democracy* (Toronto: Oxford University Press, 2009).

63 Cynthia Munster, "Harper Government More Connected to Organized Anti-feminism," *Hill Times* (10 August 2009).

64 National Union of Public and General Employees, "NUPGE Condemns Ideological Attack by Harper Conservatives on Civil Society Organizations," Press Release, Vancouver (19 June 2010).

65 Susan Riley, "Gloves Are Off in War on Greens," *Ottawa Citizen* (16 March 2012).

66 CBC, "Power and Politics" (1 May 2012). Kent first made the accusation on "The House" on 28 April.

67 Shawn McCarthy and Oliver Moore, "Suzuki Laments Chill on Green Groups," *Globe and Mail* (13 April 2012).

68 Susan Delacourt and Bruce Campion-Smith, "Tories Accused of Digging Up Dirt on 'Liberal' Profs," *Toronto Star* (11 February 2011).

69 As quoted in Martin, *Harperland*, 6.

70 See "Federal Government Moves to Kill Per-Vote Subsidy," Canadian Press (5 October 2011). http://www.ctvnews.ca/federal-government-moves-to-kill-per-vote-party-subsidy-1.707244.

71 Jane Taber, "First He Routed Liberals, Now He Hopes to Bankrupt Them," *Globe and Mail* (17 April 2011).

72 "Harper, Quebec Differ on Per-Vote Subsidy," *Canadian Press* (1 April 2011).

73 Tom Flanagan and Harold J. Jansen, "Election Campaigns under Canada's Party Finance Laws," in *The Canadian Federal Election of 2008*, edited by Jon Pammett and Christopher Dornan (Toronto: Dundurn, 2009), 201

74 Murray Dobbin, "Harper's Hitlist: Thirteen Months, Two Prorogations of Parliament," *Rabble Rouser* (4 March 2010), http://rabble.ca/news/2010/03/thirteen-months-two-prorogations-parliament.

75 J.-P. Kingsley, Testimony before Standing Committee on Procedure and House Affairs, *Hansard* No. 021, 2nd Session, 41st Parliament, 25 March 2014.

76 Errol Mendes, "Harper Aims to Financially Suffocate Opposition Parties," *iPolitics* (12 October 2011), http://www.ipolitics.ca/2011/10/12/errol-mendes-limiting-canadian-democracy-by-stealth-and-suffocation/.

77 Andrew Cohen, "Harper Takes No Prisoners," *Ottawa Citizen* (29 March 2011).

78 Gerry Nicholls, "Kill the Subsidy, Not the Liberal Party," *Ottawa Citizen* (24 May 2011).

CHAPTER FOUR

1 Preston Manning, *Think Big: My Adventures in Life and Democracy* (Toronto: McClelland and Stewart, 2003).

2 See for example Donald Savoie, *Governing from the Centre: The Concentration of Power in Canadian Politics* (Toronto: University of Toronto Press, 1999).

3 P. Laundy and N. Wilding, *An Encyclopaedia of Parliament*, 4th ed. (London: Cassell & Company Ltd., 1972), 605.

4 Audrey O'Brien and Marc Bosc, *House of Commons Procedure and Practice*, 2nd ed., Chapter 5, "Parliamentary Procedure" (Ottawa: Éditions Yvon Blais, 2009). http://www.parl.gc.ca/procedure-book-livre/Document.aspx?sbdid=3F9BF9DA-8073-48FA-A8B9-651585F97654&sbpidx=1&Language=E&Mode=1.

5 Ibid.

6 Laura Stone, "Lunch with Tom Flanagan: Back in Favour but Not in Politics," *Global News* (3 March 2014), http://globalnews.ca/news/1182441/stephen-is-a-predator-lunch-with-tom-flanagan-back-in-action-but-not-in-politics/.

7 Andrew Coyne, "A Normal Government Wouldn't Ram Through This Election Bill," *Ottawa Citizen* (29 March 2014), B7.

8 Robert Hazell and Akash Paun (eds.), *Making Minority Governments Work: Hung Parliaments and the Challenges for Westminster and Whitehall* (London: Institute for Governance, 2010).

9 David E. Smith, *Across the Aisle: Opposition in Canadian Politics* (Toronto: University of Toronto Press, 2013).

10 Aaron Wherry, "The Commons in Review," *Maclean's* (23 June 2008), http://www.macleans.ca/authors/aaron-wherry/the-commons-in-review/.

11 Aaron Wherry, "The Man Who Ate Question Period," *Maclean's* (11 June 2008).

12 Don Newman, CBC Interview with John Baird, 4 December 2008. Available in full at https://www.youtube.com/watch?v=KL76A5jUq1k and quoted at http://unseatharper.ca/john-baird.php.

13 David Smith, *Across the Aisle*, 150.

14 Steven Chase, "Baird Becomes New Tory Point Man in Commons," *Globe and Mail* (6 August 2010), A7.

15 Ibid.

16 Christopher Curtis, "Written Questions to MPs Cost $1.2 Million," *Ottawa Citizen* (18 December 2012), A3.
17 Ibid.
18 As quoted in *Macleans.ca,* "Bilingualism Spat Gets Nasty," 16 May 2007.
19 Don Martin, "Harper Government Whips Tories in Line with Secret Handbook," *Calgary Herald* (18 May 2007).
20 Green Party of Canada, "Harper Conservatives Threaten to Make Committee Business Secret," *Press Release* (13 February 2012).
21 Tim Naumetz, "Sharp Decline in Parliamentary Reviews of AG's Scrutiny," *Hill Times* (7 November 2013).
22 "Conservative Demand for CBC Documents Unlawful," 14 November 2011, http://charlieangus.ndp.ca/conservative-demand-for-cbc-docs-unlawful.
23 Colin Horgan, "What in the World Is Happening at Finance Committee?" *iPolitics*, 23 November 2012, http://www.ipolitics.ca/2012/11/23/what-in-the-world-is-happening-at-finance-committee/.
24 Opposition Leader Stephen Harper. House of Commons. *Debates.* 25 March 1994, http://www.parl.gc.ca/HousePublications/Publication.aspx?DocId=2332300&Language=E&Mode=1.
25 See, for example, Jessica Murphy, "Harper Fends Off Omnibus Bill Attacks," *Chatham Daily News* (12 June 2012); "Harper's Omnibus Bill Has Too Much Baggage," *Globe and Mail,* Editorial (15 May 2012).
26 Carlito Pablo, "Stephen Harper's Political Tactics Are Nothing New," *Georgia Straight* (13 June 2012). (Interview with Lawrence Martin about *Harperland.*) http://www.straight.com/news/stephen-harpers-political-tactics-are-nothing-new.
27 John Ibbitson and Rhéal Séguin, "Sound and Fury as Tories Limit Debate," *Globe and Mail* (18 November 2011), A4.
28 Ibid.
29 François Plante, "The Curtailment of Debate in the House of Commons," *Canadian Parliamentary Review* (Spring 2013).
30 Konrad Yakabuski. "Bills Promote Backbenchers from Nobodies to Pawns," *Globe and Mail,* (8 September 2014). See also Sean Fine, "Major Tory Crime Bills Get Scant Scrutiny," *Globe and Mail* (29 August 2014).
31 Gerald Caplan, "How Can Conservative Senators Look at Themselves in the Mirror?" *Globe and Mail,* 1 April 2011, http://www.revparl.ca/english/issue.asp?param=214&art=1519.
32 Gloria Galloway, "Conservative MPs Chafe under Harper's Restraints," *Globe and Mail* (27 March 2013).

33 Steven Chase and Gloria Galloway, "MPs Plead for Greater Freedom," *Globe and Mail* (29 March 2013).
34 Mark Kennedy, "Ex Minister Decries Gagging of MPs," *Ottawa Citizen* (16 April 2013).
35 Brent Rathgeber, "I Stand Alone," 6 June 2013, http://brentrathgeber.ca/wordpress/i-stand-alone/.
36 Josh Wingrove, "For New Whip, Harper Turns to Reform Roots," *Globe and Mail* (19 July 2013).
37 Don Newman, CBC Interview with John Baird. 4 December 2008. Available in full at https://www.youtube.com/watch?v=KL76A5jUq1k and quoted at http://unseatharper.ca/john-baird.php
38 David E. Smith, Across the Aisle, 150.
39 Quoted in Tim Naumetz, "Tories Begin Battle Against Coalition," accessed at http:/www.cbc.ca/Canada/story/2008/12/02/harper-coalition.html.
40 Nelson Wiseman, "The Use, Misuse and Abuse of Prorogation," *Hill Times*, 3 January 2010, http://www.hilltimes.com/columns/2010/03/01/the-use-misuse-and-abuse-of-prorogation/23383.
41 "Harper Goes Prorogue," *The Economist* (7 January 2010), 14.
42 John Ibbitson, "Few Countries Can Claim Such a Pathetic Parliament," *Globe and Mail* (8 January, 2010), F1.
43 Susan Delacourt, "Parliament Wins in Showdown with Stephen Harper Government," Toronto Star, 27 April 2010. (A full copy of the Speaker's report can be found at House of Commons Debates, Vol. 145, No. 34. 3rd Session, 40th Parliament, 27 April 2010.)
44 Jonathan Malloy, "Why You Should Care How Parliament Operates," *Ottawa Citizen* (16 March 2011), A13.
45 W.T. Stanbury, "Broken Windows and the Undermining of Canadian Democracy," *Hill Times*, (14 March, 2011).
46 Lorraine Weinrib, "Prime Minister Harper's Parliamentary Time Out," in *Parliamentary Democracy in Crisis*, edited by Peter H. Russell and Lorne Sossin (Toronto: University of Toronto Press, 2009), 74.
47 James Travers, "Harper Is Changing the Country More than We Realize," *Toronto Star* (18 January 2011).
48 Paul Benoit and Gary Levy, "Viability of Our Political Institutions Being Questioned," *Hill Times* (25 April 2011).
49 Jonathan Malloy, "Why You Should Care How Parliament Operates," *Ottawa Citizen* (16 March 2011).
50 David Asper Centre for Constitutional Rights, "Adjusting to a New Era of Parliamentary Government," *Report of a Workshop on Constitutional Conventions* (Toronto: University of Toronto, 2011).

CHAPTER FIVE

1 Jeffrey Simpson, "Conservatives Sailing Close to the Wind," *Globe and Mail* (29 May 2013).
2 Rob Nicholson (30 May 2006), http://www.cbc.ca/canada/story/2007/05/02/fixed:elections.html.
3 Gary Levy, "Canada's Fixed Election Date Law Is a Serious Problem," *Hill Times* (11 October 2010).
4 See for example Glen McGregor, "Tories Plead Guilty in In-and-Out Scandal," *Ottawa Citizen* (10 November 2011).
5 Tim Naumetz, "MPs Can Vote to Suspend Tory MPs," *Hill Times* (12 June 2013).
6 Cited in Lawrence Martin, "Tory Tactics, GOP Precedents?" *Globe and Mail* (15 April 2014).
7 Tim Naumetz, "Ending Vouchers, Voter ID Cards Could Disenfranchise 520,000 Electors," *Hill Times* (27 March 2014).
8 Susan Delacourt, "Canadians Believe Tory Election Act Settling Scores," *Toronto Star* (23 March 2014).
9 Vic Toews, Radio Interview with Concerned Women for America (2003). Full broadcast available at http://gideon.cwfa.org/radioarch.asp?broadcastID=1945).
10 As cited in Dan Gardner, "Harper Could Shape the Judiciary for a Generation," *Ottawa Citizen* (6 May 2011).
11 Andrew Stobo Sniderman, "Harper vs. the Judges," *Maclean's* (21 August 2012).
12 Steven Chase and Paul Waldie, "Wheat Board Sues Ottawa Over Plan to End Monopoly," *Globe and Mail* (27 October 2011).
13 Paul Waldie, "Wheat Board Bill Is Illegal, Court Rules," *Globe and Mail* (8 December 2011).
14 Sniderman, "Harper vs. the Judges,"
15 Ibid.
16 Kirk Makin, "Supreme Court Backs Insite Drug Clinic," *Globe and Mail* (1 October 2011).
17 Kelly Duval, "Health Organizations Claim Bill C-2 Infringes on Rights," The Concordian (29 October 2013).
18 Dan Gardner, "It's Not Just About Khadr," *Ottawa Citizen* (18 July 2012).
19 Robert Reich, "The Republicans of the Supreme Court" (23 July 2013), robertreich.org/post/54383380713 5.
20 The social-psychology concept of "fundamental attribution error" downplays the importance of partisan bias, but the arguments remain

controversial. See, for example, Adam Benforado and Jon D. Hanson (Harvard Law School), "The Great Attributional Divide: How Divergent Views of Human Behavior Are Shaping Legal Policy," *Emory Law Journal* 57 (2008).

21 "Toews Sticks to Guns in Battle with Court," *Winnipeg Sun*, Editorial (11 November 2006).

22 Interview found in "Let No One Put Asunder," documentary by Alexis Mackintosh shown on CBC-TV (27 September 2004).

23 Sniderman, "Harper vs. the Judges."

24 Ibid.

25 Paul Wells, "Stephen Harper's Spite of Charter, 30th Anniversary Edition," *Maclean's* (16 April 2012).

26 Grant Buckler, "DoJ Lawyer Suspended for Whistleblowing," Accessed on J-Source, 3 February 2013, http://j-source.ca/article/doj-lawyer-suspended-whistleblowing.

CHAPTER SIX

1 On a provincial level in Canada, the Lac Megantic train derailment or the Alberta floods of 2013 would be considered equivalent events.

2 See for example John Kingdon, *Agendas, Alternatives, and Public Policies* (New York: Longman, 2003); Thomas Birkland, *After Disaster: Agenda Setting, Public Policy, and Focusing Events* (Washington, DC: Georgetown University Press, 1997); and William Lowry, "Potential Focusing Projects and Policy Change,"*Policy Studies Journal* 34, no. 3 (August 2006): 313–45.

3 See Brooke Jeffrey, *Divided Loyalties* (Toronto: University of Toronto Press, 2010). Chaps. 10 and 11.

4 Ironically some of Harper's earlier associates, such as the National Citizens Coalition and the Canadian Taxpayers' Federation, took the lead in accusing his government of abandoning conservative economic principles, as did right-wing commentators such as Andrew Coyne and Terence Corcoran.

5 Conservative Party of Canada, Stand Up for Canada, Federal Election Program (2006), 16.

6 John Geddes, "Ian Brodie Offers a Candid View of Politics and Public Policy," *Maclean's* (27 March 2009).

7 Barrie McKenna, "Canada Lost When Ottawa Cut the GST," *Globe and Mail* (24 March 2013).

8 Armine Yalnizyan, "Stephen Harper's Record: Best in Show?" *Behind the Numbers*, Canadian Centre for Policy Alternatives (28 April 2011).

9 Kurt Badenhausen, "Best Countries for Business," *Forbes* (3 October 2011).
10 "Businesses Getting Billions in Tax Cuts Despite Rising Corporate Cash Reserves," *Canadian Press* (1 January 2012).
11 Two useful articles which summarize these developments are Eugene Lang, "Stephen Harper's Tax-cutting Legacy," *Toronto Star* (27 December 2013) and Armine Yalnizyan, "Stephen Harper's Economic Record: Best in Show?"
12 Murray Dobbin, "Why Canada's Housing Bubble Will Burst," *The Tyee* (October 22, 2010).
13 As cited in an interview with Peter Mansbridge on CBC-TV (7 October 2008), http://www.cbc.ca/news/canada/this-prime-minister-isn-t-going-to-panic-harper-to-mansbridge-1.740038.
14 See for example Brooke Jeffrey, "Missed Opportunity: The Invisible Liberals," in *The Canadian Federal Election of 2008*, edited by Jon H. Pammett and Christopher Dornan (Toronto: Dundurn Press, 2009).
15 Mark Milke, "Canada's Auto Bailout: Still Waiting for the Payback," *Financial Post* (31 May 2013).
16 It should be noted that the CBC was not immune from the deficit-reduction exercise of Jean Chrétien and Paul Martin either, but in the case of the Liberals the cuts were accompanied by a commitment to provide stable, long-term funding, and the overall amounts were increased when the deficit had been eliminated.
17 Jason Fekete, "Dumbest Sale in History of Canada," *Ottawa Citizen* (28 September 2011).
18 A detailed discussion of this situation can be found in Brooke Jeffrey, "From Collaborative Federalism to the New Unilateralism," in *Continuity and Change in Canadian Politics,* edited by Hans Michelmann and Christine de Clercy (Toronto: University of Toronto Press, 2006).
19 Steven Chase, "PM Insists Cuts, Not Stimulus, Best Policy," *Globe and Mail* (12 August 2011).
20 Bill Curry, "Ottawa Urged to Ease Fiscal Restraint after Dismal Job Report," *Globe and Mail* (11 January 2014).
21 Ultimately a commitment from the government of Ontario and the Winnipeg-based Institute for Sustainable Development to cover the costs saved this latter project at the eleventh hour.
22 See for example Patrik Marier, *Pension Politics: Consensus and Social Conflicts* (New York: Routledge, 2008).
23 Bill Curry, "There Is No Old Age Security Crisis, PBO Report Shows," *Globe and Mail* (8 February 2012).

24 Kathryn May, "$5.2 Billion Only Half of Coming Cuts: PBO Report," *Ottawa Citizen* (April 18, 2012).
25 Tim Naumetz, "Parliament Should Not Have to Pay for Information on Feds' Spending Cuts, Says Canada's PBO," *Hill Times* (17 January 2014).
26 David Pugliese, "Military Plans Sell-off to Save Cash," *Ottawa Citizen* (12 April 2012).
27 Dan Gardner, "Harper Still Believes in Homo Economicus," *Ottawa Citizen* (13 January 2006).
28 Mark Kennedy, "Harper to Summit: Capitalism Works Best," *Ottawa Citizen* (24 January 2012).
29 Sarah Schmidt, "Tories Ground Flight Poster Plan," *Ottawa Citizen* (6 September 2011).
30 41st Parliament, *Hansard Parliamentary Debates*, Session 1, no. 206 (7 February 2013).
31 Kennedy Stewart, "NRC Has Become a 1-800 Concierge Service," *Hill Times* (9 September 2013).
32 See CBC interview with Minister Goodyear: http://www.cbc.ca/news/technology/national-research-council-to-refocus-to-serve-business-1.1216848 and his statement before the Standing Committee on Industry, Science, and Technology: http://www.parl.gc.ca/HousePublications/ Publication.aspx?Language=E&DocId=5899675#Int-7824933.
33 Bill Curry, "Food Safety Workers Among Hardest Hit by Harper Budget Cuts," *Globe and Mail* (11 April 2012).
34 Josh Wingrove, "E. coli Outbreak at Alberta Beef Plant a Sign of System in Overhaul," *Globe and Mail* (28 September 2012).
35 Ibid.
36 André Picard, "Bad Meat Is Your Problem," *Globe and Mail* (22 October 2012).
37 Shawn McCarthy, "Budget Bill Gives Harper Cabinet Free Hand on Environmental Assessments," *Globe and Mail* (9 May 2012).
38 Sean Kilpatrick, "Four Former Fisheries Ministers Have Sent an Open Letter to Prime Minister Stephen Harper," *Canadian Press* (29 May 2012).
39 See for example Heather Scoffield, "Pipeline Industry Drove Changes to Navigable Waters Protection Act, Documents Show," *Toronto Star* (20 February 2013).
40 Robert Hiltz and Jordan Press, "Tories Will Prevent Potential Stoppages at Air Canada," *Ottawa Citizen* (13 March 2012).
41 Ian Lee, "Striking Out: The New Normal in Canadian Labour Relations?" *Journal of Parliament and Political Law* (June 2012), 219.

42 Anil Verma, CBC Interview (13 March 2012).
43 "CP Trains to Start Rolling Friday After Government Ends Strike," *Reuters Business and Financial News* (31 May 2012).
44 Gary Corbett, "Stephen Harper's Assault on Democracy," *Ottawa Life* (January 2013).
45 Kim Mackrael, "Ontario Warns Ottawa Over Union Bill," *Globe and Mail* (18 December 2013).
46 Dave Robinson, "Poll Results Show Majority of Canadians Hold Favourable Views of Unions," *CAUT Bulletin* (December 2013).
47 Mark Dunn. "Nobel Laureates to Harper: Stop Oilsands," *Ottawa Citizen* (28 September 2011).
48 Shawn McCarthy and Nathan VanderKlippe, "Feds Bow to Alberta on Carbon Rules," *Globe and Mail* (9 August 2012).
49 Jim Prentice, "Expanding Export Markets a 'Defining Opportunity' for Canada," *Vancouver Sun* (30 June 2012).
50 As cited in Justine Hunter, "Ottawa to Blame for First Nations' Pipeline Stand, PM Appointee Says," *Globe and Mail* (16 June 2014).

CHAPTER SEVEN

1 James Travers, "Changing Canada by Stealth," *Toronto Star* (21 October 2004).
2 See for example Michael Adams, *Fire and Ice: The United States, Canada and the Myth of Converging Values* (Toronto: Penguin Canada, 2003) and Reginald Bibby, *The Bibby Report: Social Trends in Style* (Toronto: Stoddart, 1995).
3 "MPs Reject Reopening Same-Sex Marriage Issue," *CTV News* (12 December 2006).
4 "Tories Cut Funding for Gay Festival," *Slap Upside the Head* (6 October 2008), www.slapupsidethehead.com/tag/canadian-heritage-department/.
5 Steven Chase, "Minister Punished for Funding Gay Pride Week," *Globe and Mail* (8 July 2009).
6 Brooke Jeffrey, *Hard Right Turn: The New Face of Conservatism* (Toronto: HarperCollins, 1995), 435.
7 Ibid., 312.
8 Susan Delacourt, "Aid Groups Advised to 'Shut the F…k Up," *Toronto Star* (3 May 2010).
9 Stephen Harper, *NCC Overview* (Fall 1998).
10 Murray Dobbin, "Harper's Attack on Women's Rights and Equality," *The Tyee* (8 February 2010).

11 National Union of Public and General Employees, "Equal Opportunity at Work Is the Latest Tory Target," *Press Release* (28 June 2010).
12 See for example, Jon Pammett and Christopher Dornan (eds.) *The Canadian General Election of 1997* (Toronto: Dundurn, 1998) and *The Canadian General Election of 2000* (Toronto: Dundurn, 2001).
13 Stephen Maher, "Tories Going Too Far in Push to Get Rid of Registry," *Ottawa Citizen* (15 December 2011).
14 Tonda MacCharles, "Tories Target Gun Crime," *Toronto Star* (5 May 2006).
15 Tom Flanagan, "It's No Time to Be Complacent about Doing Time," *Globe and Mail* (15 April 2010).
16 Kirk Makin, "Canadians Get It," *Globe and Mail* (26 January 2012).
17 Kathryn Blaze Carlson and Jill Mahoney, "PM Rejects Inquiry Calls after Girl's Death," *Ottawa Citizen* (22 August 2014).
18 "Corrections and Conditional Release Statistical Overview 2009," *Public Safety Canada*, http://www.publicsafety.gc.ca/cnt/rsrcs/pblctns/2009-ccrs/index-eng.aspx.
19 W.T. Stanbury, "Examining the Retribution or Just Desserts Rationale for Imprisonment and Other Forms of Punishment," *Hill Times* (19 September 2009).
20 "A Flawed Compass: A Human Rights Analysis of the Roadmap to Strengthening Public Safety" (24 September 2009), http://www.justice-behindthewalls.net/news.asp?nid=78.
21 Conrad Black, "Harper's Insane Prison Plan," *National Post* (29 May 2010).
22 Glen McGregor, "Parole Board Getting Tougher on Offenders," *Ottawa Citizen* (21 February 2011).
23 Margaret Somerville, "Pizza and Punishment," *Globe and Mail* (4 January 2013).
24 Carys Mills, "More Convicts Must Pay Their Own Way in Prison," *Globe and Mail* (9 May 2012).
25 Leah DeVellis, "Plan to Cut Pay Will Accomplish Nothing," *Toronto Star* (14 May 2012).
26 Douglas Quan, "Federal Crime Policy Is 'Nasty' Former Top Safety Official Says," *Postmedia News Vancouver* (3 October 2013).
27 Anna Mehler Paperny, "Watchdog Says Prison Violence on the Rise, Toews Says It Has Decreased," *Globe and Mail* (9 August 2011).
28 Kirk Makin, "Judge Blasts Conservatives Over Sentencing Reforms," *Globe and Mail* (3 May 2013).
29 Yves Faguy, "Reactions to Proposed Prostitution Laws," *The National*, Canadian Bar Association (9 June 2014).

30 Michael Den Tandt, "Tories Make Law a Mess," *Ottawa Citizen* (6 June 2014).
31 "Harper Set to Introduce Citizens' Arrest Bill," CBC *News* (10 September 2011).
32 Liam Casey, *Toronto Star* (30 September 2013).
33 Sean Fine, "MacKay Fights Revolt, Accuses Judges of Contempt of the Law," *Globe and Mail* (17 December 2013).
34 Andrew Seymour, "MacKay Displays Bully Mentality: Judge," *Ottawa Citizen* (18 December 2013).
35 Dan Gardner, "If a Drug Policy Works, Harper Wants Nothing to Do with It," *Ottawa Citizen* (18 May 2011)
36 Paul Wells, "Insite: the Harper Governemnt's Sweeping, Narrow Defeat," *Maclean's* (30 September 2011).
37 Eric E. Sterling, "Canada Is Repeating US Mistakes on Drug Sentencing," *Ottawa Citizen* (20 February 2012).
38 Paula Mallea, *Fearmonger: Harper's Tough on Crime Agenda* (Toronto: Lorimer, 2011).
39 "Mr. Daubney's Warning," *Globe and Mail,* Editorial (12 December 2011).
40 Jason Kenney, *Hansard Parliamentary Debates* (14 February 2011).
41 John Ibbitson and Joe Friesen, "Tories Tread Careful Line on Immigration Policy," *Globe and Mail* (15 February 2011).
42 Haroon Siddiqui, "Immigration Reform Not Working," *Toronto Star* (26 May 2013).
43 David Koch, "Once, We Welcomed Tamil Refugees," *The Dominion* 77 (24 June 2011), http://www.dominionpaper.ca/articles/4000# June 24, 2011.
44 Louisa Taylor, "The Human Smuggling Bill Is Back," *Ottawa Citizen* (18 June 2011).
45 Mennonite Coalition for Refugee Support, "Key Concerns and Improvements with Bill C-4," at https://www.mcrs.ca/getinvolved/advocate.
46 Gloria Galloway, "Doctors Plead for Cuts to Refugee Health Coverage to Be Reversed," *Globe and Mail* (17 June 2013).
47 Stephanie Levitz, "Citizenship Fraud Crackdown Nets 12 Bogus Citizens," *Huffington Post* (28 February 2013).
48 Deborah Summers, "George Galloway Banned from Canada," *The Guardian* (20 March 2009).
49 Paul Koring, "Canadian-born Man Seeks Answers from Federal Court," *Globe and Mail* (16 October 2013).
50 Andrew Griffith, *Policy Arrogance or Innocent Bias: Resetting Citizenship and Multiculturalism* (Ottawa: Anar Press, 2013), as cited in Nathalie

Brender, "Half a Cheer for Jason Kenney's Revolution in Immigration Policy," *Toronto Star* (19 September 2013).

51 Stephen Harper and Stockwell Day, "Conservative Canadians Speak Out!" *Wall Street Journal* (29 March 2003).

52 Hon. Peter MacKay, "Restore the Honour!" Department of National Defence Press Release (16 August 2011).

53 John Geddes, "Is the Government's Spending at Unprecedented Highs?" *Maclean's* (25 June 2012).

54 Aaron Mehta, "F-35 Report Warns of Visibility, Other Safety Issues," *Defence News* (6 March 2013).

55 Michael Den Tandt, "F-35 Reset Unmitigated Disaster for Tories," *Ottawa Citizen* (14 December 2012).

56 David Pugliese, "Military Caught in Staffing Dilemma," *Ottawa Citizen* (14 January 2013).

57 "Defence Policy in Canada: Strong, Proud, Ready?" *The Economist*, Report on Canada (3 August 2013).

58 Murray Brewster, "Canadian Firms Lose Millions in NATO Cancellation," *Ottawa Citizen* (6 August 2013).

59 David Pugliese, "MacKay Blames Brass for Pay Issue," *Ottawa Citizen* (24 April 2013).

60 David Pugliese and Chris Cobb, "Troops Left to Stand Alone, Critics Say," *Ottawa Citizen* (4 May 2012).

61 Murray Brewster, "Tory Stance on Veterans Reprehensible," *Ottawa Citizen* (8 October 2013).

62 Lee Berthiaume, "Closures Worried Veterans Affairs Staff," *Ottawa Citizen* (14 February 2014).

CHAPTER EIGHT

1 Stephen Harper, "Speech to the Civitas Club" (Toronto, June 2003) (now found only at www.cannabisculture.com/articles/4629.html).

2 See for example Marci McDonald, *The Armageddon Factor* (Toronto: Random House, 2010).

3 Patrick Martin, "Baird Sticks to Party Line – Israel's Likud Party," *Globe and Mail* (3 February 2012).

4 Ibid.

5 Mike De Souza, "Harper Wants 'Durable and Lasting Peace' in Middle East," *National Post* (5 August 2006).

6 "Neutral Stance Rejected: Opposition Criticizes Harper's Tough Talk," *National Post*, Editorial (19 July 2006).

7 In addition to various anonymous sources, see, for example, Jeffrey Simpson, "With Friends Like Harper, Bibi Can Do No Wrong," *Globe and Mail* (2 March 2012).
8 Murray Dobbin, "Time to Zip Baird's Loose Lips," *The Tyee* (13 February 2012).
9 Patrick Martin, "Canadians Bear a Blunt Message to Palestinians," *Globe and Mail* (31 January 2012).
10 Murray Dobbin, "Time to Zip Baird's Loose Lips."
11 Campbell Clark, "On the Middle East, Canadians Give Baird Room to Play his Hand," *Globe and Mail* (2 February 2012).
12 William Marsden, "After Receiving World Statesman Award, Harper Slams Evil-Dominated Iranian Regime," *Postmedia News* (27 September 2012). Interestingly, both Brian Mulroney and Jean Chrétien had also received the award, despite following the more traditional and balanced approach to the Middle East for which Canada had been known.
13 Hon. John Baird, "Canada Closes Embassy in Iran, Expels Iranian Diplomats from Canada," Press Release, Department of Foreign Affairs, Trade and Development Canada, 7 September 2012.
14 Robert Sibley and Lee Berthiaume, "Canada Stands by Israel," *Ottawa Citizen* (21 November 2012).
15 Ibid.
16 See for example Gar Pardy, "Canadian Cheerleaders on Sidelines in Middle East," *Ottawa Citizen* (22 November 2012) and Janice Kennedy, "Canada's Simplistic Middle East Policy," *Ottawa Citizen* (24 November 2012).
17 Campbell Clark and Patrick Martin, "Palestinians Paint Canada as Too Extreme," *Globe and Mail* (1 December 2012).
18 Murray Brewster, "Baird Criticized for Israel Meeting," *Ottawa Citizen* (13 April 2012).
19 Lee Berthiaume, "Tories Express Anger at Qatar Bid for ICAO," *Ottawa Citizen* (3 May 2013).
20 John Ivison, "Harper to Announce First Visit to Israel," *National Post* (30 November 2013).
21 Mark MacKinnon, "How Harper's Foreign Policy Evolved from Human Rights to the Almighty Dollar," *Globe and Mail* (27 November 2013).
22 "Ignatieff Blasts Harper's Megaphone Diplomacy with China," CBC News, 16 November 2006, www.cbc.ca/news/canada/ignatieff-balsts-harper-s-megaphone-dpilomacy-with-china-1.600562
23 Geoffrey Johnston, "Harper Understands Some Regimes Can't Be Changed," *Kingston Whig Standard* (21 November 2013).

24 Matthew Fisher, "Harper Snubs Commonwealth," *Ottawa Citizen* (8 October 2013). See also "Talking Point," *Globe and Mail* (12 October 2013).
25 Steven Chase and Bill Curry, "PM Uses Ailing Europe as a Backdrop," *Globe and Mail* (28 January 2012).
26 Bill Curry, "Harper's Refusal to Bail Out Europe Draws Germany's Ire," *Globe and Mail* (7 June 2012), http://www.theglobeandmail.com/news/politics/harpers-refusal-to-help-bail-out-europe-draws-germanys-ire/article4240996/.
27 Ibid.
28 Campbell Clark, "Crisis Is Over, French Minister Insists," *Globe and Mail* (2 October 2013).
29 Rt Hon. Stephen Harper, in interview by Peter Mansbridge, *One on One,* CBC News (5 June 2012).
30 Bill Curry, "Harper's Refusal to Bail Out Europe Draws Germany's Ire."
31 Jason Fekete, "Harper Meets Hollande on Friday in Paris," 13 June 2013, www.o.canada.com.
32 Paul Waldie, "Putin Sides with Thugs, PM Says, as G8 Splits Over Syrian Conflict," *Globe and Mail* (17 June 2013).
33 Lee Berthiaume, "Canada, NATO Allies to Consider Military Deployment Over Ukraine," *Ottawa Citizen* (14 April 2014).
34 Steven Chase, "Tories Preach Religious Freedom Abroad," *Globe and Mail* (2 January 2012).
35 Jonathan Malloy, "Hidden in Plain Sight," *Globe and Mail* (13 April 2011).
36 Rt Hon. Stephen Harper, "Address to the 61st Opening Session of the United Nations General Assembly" (speech, New York, 21 September 2006).
37 John Ibbitson, "Canada's Cold Shoulder to the UN," *Globe and Mail* (2 October 2012).
38 Ibid.
39 Mike Blanchford, "Canada's Move Regrettable, UN Says," *Ottawa Citizen* (30 March 2013).
40 Lee Berthiaume, "Firearms Advocate's Position under Fire," *Ottawa Citizen* (9 March 2013).
41 Ibid.
42 Sarah Schmidt, "Canada Fights Proposal to Cut Fats, Salt and Sugar in Foods," *Ottawa Citizen* (31 August 2011).
43 Rt Hon. Stephen Harper, "Address to the 65th Session of the General Assembly of the United Nations" (speech, New York, 23 September 2010).

44 David Akin, "Canada Loses Bid for UN Security Council Seat," *Toronto Sun* (12 October 2010).
45 Ibid.
46 "Harper Government Again at War with UN Envoy," *Canadian Press* (4 March 2013).
47 Stephanie Levitz, "Canada Won't Trade Foreign Policy for Security Council Seat," *Ottawa Citizen* (3 May 2013).
48 Stephen Brown, "CIDA Under the Gun," in *Canada Among Nations 2007: What Room for Manoeuvre?* edited by Jean Daudelin and Daniel Schwanen (Montreal: McGill-Queen's University Press, 2008), 91–107.
49 Stephen Brown, "Aid Effectiveness and the Framing of New Canadian Aid Initiatives," unpublished chapter in *Readings in Canadian Foreign Policy: Classic Debates and New Ideas*, 2nd ed., edited by Duane Bratt and Christopher J. Kukucha (Toronto: Oxford University Press, 2013).
50 Hon. Colin Kenny, "Canadian Foreign Aid: Clever Politics, Poor Statesmanship," *Toronto Star* (24 June 2013).
51 Kim Mackrael, "Ottawa Signals Radical Shift in Foreign Policy," *Globe and Mail* (23 November 2012).
52 Maurice Strong, "I Founded CIDA but Its Death Worries Me Less Than Harper's Foreign-Aid Agenda," *Globe and Mail* (2 April 2013).
53 Janet Davison, "Does Cutting Foreign Aid Threaten Canada's Reputation in the World?" CBC News (3 April 2012).
54 Steven Chase, "Harper Irked by Foreign Travel, Wikileaks Reveals," *Globe and Mail* (6 September 2011).
55 "Canada Committed to Afghan Mission, Harper Tells Troops" (13 March 2006), http://www.cbc.ca/news/world/canada-committed-to-afghan-mission-harper-tells-troops-1.573722.
56 John Ibbitson, "Baird's Surprise Visit Reinforces Canada's Support for Revolution," *Globe and Mail* (27 June 2011).
57 Dept. of National Defence, "Statement by the Hon. Peter MacKay" (4 November 2011).
58 David Chan, "Harper Hails Libya Mission as Great Success," *Reuters/Canadian Press* (24 November 2011).
59 Lee Berthiaume, "Think Peace, Not War, Say Young in Polls," *Ottawa Citizen* (10 November 2012).
60 See for example David Crane, "TPP Neither Free nor Fair Trade," *Toronto Star* (1 December 2012) and John Ibbitson, "Transpacific Trade at What Price?" *Globe and Mail* (6 February 2012).
61 Eric Reguly, "Business Took a Back Seat on Harper's Thailand Trip," *Globe and Mail* (31 March 2012).

62 Matthew Fisher, "Harper the Forgotten Man in Malaysia," *Ottawa Citizen* (4 October 2013).
63 Brian Milner, "Price to Pay for Snubbing China," *Globe and Mail* (3 December 2009).
64 "No Abortion in Canada's G8 Maternal Health Plan," CBC News, 26 April 2010, http://www.cbc.ca/news/politics/no-abortion-in-canada-s-g8-maternal-health-plan-1.877257.
65 Ibid.
66 Joanna Slater, "Harper Stands Firm on Keystone," *Globe and Mail* (27 September 2013).
67 Joe Clark, *How We Lead: Canada in a Century of Change* (Toronto: Random House, 2013), 100.
68 J.L. Granatstein, "A Very Albertan Foreign Policy," *Ottawa Citizen* (11 September 2011).

CHAPTER NINE

1 Rt Hon. P.E. Trudeau, *Federalism and the French Canadians* (Toronto: Macmillan, 1968). Trudeau also expressed his views clearly in several texts after his resignation, including *With a Bang, Not a Whimper* (Toronto: Stoddart, 1992) and *Memoirs* (Toronto: McClelland and Stewart, 1995).
2 An earlier version of this chapter first appeared in "The Harper Government's Open Federalism: A Hidden Agenda?" a paper presented to the Canadian Political Science Association annual meeting in Ottawa in 2010, portions of which also were included in "The Harper Government and Open Federalism," in *Modern Canada: 1945 to Present*, ed. C. Briggs (Toronto: Oxford University Press, 2014).
3 Hon. Michael Kirby, "Meech Lake Pact Reflects Traditional Tory Views," *Toronto Star* (4 June 1988).
4 Hon. Sinclair Stevens, "One Canada or Ten Canadas?" *Toronto Star* (25 April 2008), AA06.
5 Stephen Harper, "The New Canada Plan" (Ottawa: Reform Party of Canada, 1995).
6 Peter Leslie, "The Two Faces of Open Federalism," *Open Federalism: Interpretation, Significance* (Kingston: Institute of Intergovernmental Affairs at Queens University, 2006), 39–66.
7 Stevens, "One Canada or Ten Canadas?" AA06.
8 L. Ian MacDonald, "A Conversation with the Prime Minister," *Policy Options* (February 2007), 5–11.
9 John Ibbitson, "Judicial Reform: It's the Newest 'Liberal' Initiative," *Globe and Mail* (21 February 2007), A7.

10 Rt Hon. Stephen Harper, "Prime Minister Outlines His Government's Priorities and His Open Federalism Approach" (speech delivered to the Montreal Board of Trade, Montreal, QC, 20 April 2006).
11 Kenneth Wheare, *Federal Government*, 5th ed. (Oxford: Oxford University Press, 1967).
12 Rt Hon. Stephen Harper. Montreal, Campaign Speech, cited in Canadian Press, "Tories True Quebec Nationalists, Harper Says" (24 June 2008).
13 Michael Behiels, "Harper Finds a Use for the Premiers," *Ottawa Citizen* (17 November 2008), A11.
14 Stephen Harper, "Harper Announces Conservative Platform for Quebec" (speech delivered to the Quebec City Chamber of Commerce, 19 December 2005).
15 Tom Kent, "The Harper Peril for Canadian Federalism," *Policy Options* (February 2008), 12–15.
16 Stephen Harper, "My Plan for Open Federalism," *National Post* (27 October 2004), A19.
17 Stephen Harper, Speech delivered to the American Council for National Policy, Montreal, 1997.
18 Stephen Harper, et al., "An Open Letter to Ralph Klein," *National Post* (24 January 2001).
19 Edward Greenspon, "Stephen Harper: A Neocon in the Land of Liberals," *Globe and Mail* (23 March 2002).
20 Barry Weingast, "The Economic Role of Political Institutions: Market-Preserving Federalism and Economic Development," *Journal of Economics and Organization* 11, no. 1 (1995): 1–31.
21 Adam Harmes, "Neoliberalism and Multilevel Governance," *Review of International Political Economy*, vol. 13, no. 5 (December 2006).
22 John Ibbitson, "Judicial Reform: It's the Newest 'Liberal' Initiative," *Globe and Mail* (21 February 2006), A7.
23 Peter Leslie, "The Two Faces of Open Federalism," *Open Federalism: Interpretation, Significance* (Kingston: Institute of Intergovernmental Affairs at Queen's University, 2006), 39–66.
24 Paul Forsyth, "Harper Toes Conservative Party Line," *Niagara This Week – St Catharines* (27 October 2006).
25 Teresa Healy, *The Harper Record* (Ottawa: Canadian Centre for Policy Alternatives, 2010), 501.
26 Murray Dobbin, "Why Canada's Housing Bubble Will Burst," *The Tyee* (22 October 2010).
27 Healy, *The Harper Record*, 501.
28 Mark Kennedy, "Tories Foresee Tough Choices in Health Accord Talks: Files," *Ottawa Citizen* (10 November 2011), B8.

29 Ibid.
30 Don Drummond, *Toronto Star* (10 November 2011). Drummond's full report, "Therapy or Surgery: A Prescription for Canada's Health Care System" can be found at http://www.cdhowe.org/pdf/Benefactors_Lecture_2011.pdf.
31 Greg Marchildon and Haizhen Mou. "The Funding Formula for Health Care Is Broken. Alberta's Windfall Proves It," *Globe and Mail* (19 October 2013).
32 Frances Russell, "Harper Creating 13 Kinds of Citizens," *Winnipeg Free Press* (16 November 2013).
33 Mike McBane, "Harper's Plan Would Kill Medicare," *Hill Times* (January 2012).
34 David McGrane, "National Unity through Disengagement," in *How Ottawa Spends 2013–14*, edited by Christopher Stoney and G. Bruce Doern (Montreal: McGill-Queen's University Press, 2013).
35 See for example Michael Mendelson and Chris Atchison, "Time for Talk, Not Action," *Vancouver Sun* (6 November 2013).
36 Editorial, "Premiers Right to Oppose Harper Government's Plan," *Toronto Star* (24 July 2013).
37 Adrian Morrow, "Jobs Training Plan in Jeopardy as Provinces Threaten Boycott," *Globe and Mail* (3 October 2013).
38 Matthew Pearson, "Ontario Won't Back Federal Jobs Program," *Ottawa Citizen* (8 November 2013).
39 Susan Mas, "Kenney Has Frosty, Tense Meeting with Premiers," CBC *News* (15 November 2013).
40 Chris Hall, "Ottawa Digging in for Canada Job Grant Fight with Premiers," CBC *News* (15 November 2013).
41 Jonathan Malloy, "Hidden in Plain Sight: The Tory Evangelical Factor," *Ottawa Citizen* (13 April 2011).
42 Tobi Cohen, "Tories Use Majority to Pass Omnibus Crime Bill," *Postmedia News* (12 March 2012).
43 "Provinces Bear Rising Justice Costs, Budget Watchdog Finds," *Canadian Press* (20 March 2013).
44 Carey Anne Hill, Trevor Lynn, and Jonathan MacFarlane, "Dangling Participants: Is the Kelowna Accord Constitutionally Binding as a Federal-Provincial Agreement or Treaty?" (Paper presented to the annual meeting of the Canadian Political Science Association, 2007), http://www.cpsa-acsp.ca/papers-2007/HillLynnMacfarlane.pdf.
45 Canadian Intergovernmental Conference Secretariat, *Press Release* (December 2005).

46 As reported by CBC *News*, 11 January 2006.
47 Hansard, House of Commons Parliamentary Debates, 2 June 2006.
48 Hill, Lynn, and MacFarlane, "Dangling Participants."
49 Sean Gordon. "Revive Kelowna Accord, Leaders Urge," *Toronto Star* (17 July 2008).
50 André Picard, "Tories Want Out of Aboriginal Business," *Globe and Mail* (10 April 2012).

CHAPTER TEN

1 Tom Flanagan, *Harper's Team* (Montreal: McGill-Queen's University Press, 2007).
2 Ibid, 275.
3 Brooke Jeffrey, "Missed Opportunity: The Invisible Liberals," in *The Canadian General Election of 2008*, edited by Jon Pammett and Christopher Dornan (Toronto: Dundurn, 2009), 63–97.
4 Conservative Party of Canada, *Stand Up for Canada: Platform of the Conservative Party of Canada* (Ottawa: Conservative Party of Canada, 2005).
5 Peter Leslie, "The Two Faces of Open Federalism," in *Open Federalism: Interpretations, Significance* (Kingston: Institute of Intergovernmental Relations, 2006).
6 Rt Hon. Stephen Harper, "Prime Minister Harper Outlines his Government's Priorities and his Open Federalism Approach," *Press Release for a Speech at the Montreal Board of Trade* (April 20, 2006).
7 Conservative Party of Canada, *Here for Canada: Platform of the Conservative Party of Canada* (Ottawa: Conservative Party of Canada, 2008).
8 Norman Spector, "Harper the Pragmatist," *Ottawa Citizen* (17 March 2009).
9 Rt Hon. Stephen Harper, "Le premier ministre Harper et le premier ministre Charest signent un accord historique," PMO Press Release (5 May 2006), http://www.pm.gc.ca/fra/nouvelles/2006/05/05/premier-ministre-harper-et-premier-ministre-charest-signent-accord-historique.
10 "Tories Tout Open Federalism on Quebec–France Labour Deal," *Ottawa Citizen* (31 July 2006), A17.
11 "Tougher Justice, Patchwork Nation," Editorial, *Globe and Mail* (23 September 2008), A20.
12 Konrad Yakabuski, "Harper's Open Federalism Not Rich Enough for Charest," *Globe and Mail* (2 October 2008).
13 André Pratte, "Une vraie ouverture," *La Presse* (18 July 2009).

14 Rhéal Séguin and Ingrid Peritz, "Quebec MNAs Challenge PM's Abortion Stand," *Globe and Mail* (20 May 2010), A7.
15 "Budget: Ottawa Ignore les Demandes de Quebec," *Presse Canadienne* (4 March 2010).
16 Antoine Robitaille, "Du fédéralisme a l'unilatéralisme," *Le Devoir* (29 January 2009).
17 Konrad Yakabuski, "A Cold War That Refuses to Thaw," *Globe and Mail* (29 January 2009), B2.
18 John Ibbitson, "Climate Change Drives Rift in National Politics as Charest Takes on Ottawa," *Globe and Mail* (4 February 2010), A1.
19 Joël-Denis Bellavance, "Feux croisés contre Charest," *La Presse* (23 December 2009).
20 Daniel Leblanc and Rhéal Séguin, "Quebec, Ottawa in Long Gun Showdown," *Globe and Mail* (October 27, 2011).
21 Rhéal Séguin, "Defiant Quebec Digs in Against Ottawa's Gun Plan," *Globe and Mail* (11 December 2011).
22 Sophie Cousineau, "Marois Takes Aim at Harper Foreign Policy," *Globe and Mail* (17 October 2012).
23 Canadian Press, "Quebec Seeks Own Global Aid Agency," *Ottawa Citizen* (7 February 2013).
24 Michael Behiels, "Harper Finds a Use for the Premiers," *Ottawa Citizen* (17 November 2008), A11.
25 André Pratte, "Une vraie ouverture," *La Presse* (18 July 2009).
26 Chantal Hébert, "Ottawa et Québec s'en vont en guerre," *L'actualité* (17 October 2009).
27 Rhéal Séguin, "Harper Rejects Quebec's Demand for EI Rules Changes," *Globe and Mail* (1 February 2013).
28 Philippe Teisceira-Lessard, "Quebec Goes It Alone with Cap and Trade Plan," *Globe and Mail* (15 December 2011).
29 Chantal Hébert, "Ottawa et Québec s'en vont en guerre."
30 Sean Fine, "Quebec Fights Nadon Selection," *Globe and Mail* (18 October 2013).
31 Tom Flanagan, "The Emerging Conservative Coalition," *Policy Options* (June 2011).
32 Stephen Maher, "PM's Choice Points to Quebec's Waning Clout," *Ottawa Citizen* (3 September 2011).
33 Pierre Paquette, "Un fédéralisme de pacotille?" *Parti Québécois*, March 2010, http://www.pierrepaquette.qc.ca.
34 Mike De Souza, "Harper Policies Boosting PQ," *Ottawa Citizen* (7 April 2012).

35 Mike De Souza, "Harper Aims to Boost Image," *Ottawa Citizen* (22 June 2012).

36 See for example Darrell Bricker's poll for Postmedia News and Global TV, 29 June 2012, and Jeffrey Simpson, "To Quebec, Canada Barely Exists," *Globe and Mail* (12 August 2012).

37 Daniel Leblanc. "Harper to Honour Cartier at Quebec Conference Ceremony" *Globe and Mail* (6 September 2014).

CHAPTER ELEVEN

1 Stephen Harper, "Speech to Council for National Policy," Montreal (1997).

2 Stephen Harper and Stockwell Day, "Canadians Stand With You," *Washington Times* (28 March 2003).

3 Interview, *New Brunswick Telegraph Journal* (29 May 2002). See also Brian Laghi, "Motion by MLA's Condemns Harper," *Globe and Mail* (31 May 2002).

4 Sidney Verba and Gabriel Almond, *The Civic Culture: Political Attitudes in Five Democracies* (New York: Sage, 1963).

5 Gabriel Almond and G. Bingham Powell, *Comparative Politics: A Developmental Approach* (Boston: Little Brown, 1966), 50.

6 R. Jackson, D. Jackson, and N. Baxter-Moore, *Politics in Canada: Culture, Institutions, Behaviour* (Scarborough: Prentice-Hall, 1986), 81.

7 Seymour Martin Lipset, "Revolution and Counterrevolution: Canada and the United States" in *The Canadian Political Process*, edited by O. Kruhlak et al. (Toronto: Holt, Rinehart and Winston, 1970), 13–38.

8 Allan Gregg and Michael Posner, *The Big Picture* (Toronto: Walter and Ross, 1993), 14–59.

9 Ibid.

10 Richard Gwynn, *The Forty-ninth Paradox* (Toronto: McClelland and Stewart, 1985) (as cited in Gregg and Posner, *The Big Picture*, 18).

11 Robert Fulford, *Remember Expo: A Pictorial Record* (Toronto: McClelland and Stewart Limited, 1968).

12 John Meisel, *Working Papers on Canadian Politics* (Montreal: McGill-Queen's University Press, 1972).

13 Tim Naumetz, "Sharp Decline in Parliamentary Reviews of AG's Scrutiny," *Hill Times* (7 November 2013).

14 Philip Isard, "Northern Vision: Diefenbaker's Northern Promise" (Waterloo: University of Waterloo Master's Thesis, 2010).

15 "Tough Talk Taps into National Pride," *CanWest News Service* (16 August 2008).

16 Michael Den Tandt, "Harper's Arctic Promises," *National Post* (21 August 2013).
17 Carl Meyer, "Harper's New Militarism Seen as Nothing but Rhetoric," *Embassy* (13 July 2011).
18 Lawrence Martin, "A Hawkish Harper Tempers His Ways," *iPolitics* (24 May 2012).
19 Alan Taylor, *The Civil War of 1812* (New York: Alfred Knopf, 2010).
20 Steven Chase and Daniel Leblanc, "Little Known War of 1812 Big Deal for Ottawa," *Globe and Mail* (25 April 2013).
21 Lysiane Gagnon, "Flag and Queen in Moderation," *Globe and Mail* (3 October 2011).
22 Lee Berthiaume, "Queen's Portrait to Hang in all Canadian Embassies," *Ottawa Citizen* (8 September 2011).
23 Jeffrey Simpson, "Yes, the PM's Now Meddling with the Honours System," *Globe and Mail* (15 January 2011).
24 Randy Boswell, "Former PM Questions Snub of Charter," *Ottawa Citizen* (11 April 2012).
25 John Meisel, "Harperizing our Minds," *Toronto Star* (19 April 2011).
26 All cited in Bruce Cheadle, "Bureaucrats Obliged to Use 'Harper Government' Instead of 'Government of Canada,'" *Canadian Press* (12 November 2012).
27 Andrew Cohen, "The Politicization of Canada's History," *Ottawa Citizen* (21 August 2012).
28 David Brock and Ari Rabin-Havt, *The Fox Effect* (New York: Anchor Books, 2012).
29 Richard Viguerie and David Franke, *America's Right Turn* (Chicago: Bonus Books, 2004), 325
30 Don Hazen, "Progressive Media Suffer Losses in the Fight against the Right-Wing Media Machine," *Alternet* (21 April 2011).
31 See for example Heather Mallick, "Sun TV News, Alias Fox News North, Tells CRTC to Make Us Pay," *Toronto Star* (26 April 2013).
32 "Blogger Ezra Levant Ordered to Pay Additional $32,500 Libel Damages," *Canadian Journalism Project*, 28 January 2011, http://j-source.ca/article/blogger-ezra-levant-ordered-pay-additional-32500-libel; Christie Blatchford, "Right-wing Conservative Writer Ezra Levant Unrepentant in Libel Trial," *Ocanada.com* (7 March 2014), http://o.canada.com/news/right-wing-conservative-writer-ezra-levant-unrepentant-in-libel-trial.
33 Jean Stefancic and Richard Delgado, *No Mercy: How Conservative Think Tanks and Foundations Changed America's Social Agenda* (Philadelphia: Temple University Press, 1996).

34 See for example Christopher Lasch, *Revolt of the Elites and Betrayal of Democracy* (New York: W.W. Norton & Company, 1991) and John Kenneth Galbraith, *The Culture of Contentment* (Penguin, 1992).
35 Centre for Media and Democracy, "Reports Expose Extreme Pressure Groups Masquerading as Think Tanks," Press Release (13 November 2013).
36 Brent Stafford. "Think Tanks in the News," *Newswatch Monitor* (Vancouver, Simon Fraser University, April 1997).
37 Kathleen Cross, "How the Fraser Institute Distorts Its News Monitoring Studies," *NewsWatch* (17 March 1997).
38 See for example Brooke Jeffrey and Michael Behiels, "Creating a Right-wing Parallel Universe and Exploiting the Name of Wilfrid Laurier," *Hill Times* (7 May 2012), 18.
39 Donald Gutstein, "Harper's Crime Floggers: The Case of the Macdonald-Laurier Institute, Key Accomplice to Tories in Their Assaults on Truth," *TheTyee.ca* (21 March 2011).
40 Brooke Jeffrey and Michael Behiels, "Creating a Right-wing Parallel Universe," the Hill Times online, May 7, 2012. www.hilltimes.com
41 See for example Donald E. Abelson, *Do Think Tanks Matter?: Assessing the Impact of Public Policy Institutes* (Montreal: McGill-Queen's University Press, 2002).
42 In addition to numerous public-opinion polls showing the Liberals in the lead nationally, with the Conservatives second and the NDP badly behind, the results of two by-elections in Ontario in June 2014, where the Liberals won and the NDP trailed the pack, suggest a continuing positive trend for the Liberal Party of Canada.
43 Jane Taber, "First Harper Routed Liberals, Now He Hopes to Bankrupt Them," *Globe and Mail* (17 May 2011).
44 Daniel Leblanc, "Justin Trudeau Seen as Best National Unity Defender," *Globe and Mail* (15 March 2014).
45 Michael Adams, *Fire and Ice: The United States, Canada and the Myth of Converging Values* (Toronto: Penguin, 2012).
46 Kirk Makin, "Canadians Finally Getting It: Crime Is on the Decline," *Globe and Mail* (25 January 2012).
47 Brooke Jeffrey, "The Disappearing Liberals," in *The Canadian General Election of 2011*, edited by Jon Pammett and Christopher Dornan (Toronto: Dundurn, 2012), 45–77.

CONCLUSION

1 Bill Curry, "CRA Shakeup Raises Concerns Over Offshore Tax Crackdown," *Globe and Mail* (20 September 2014).

2 A 2013 survey by the Reputation Institute, which claims to examine "the world's 50 most reputable countries," placed Canada first, a point raised by several right-wing commentators who neglected to mention the sample base of "consumers" and heavy emphasis on business factors and tourism. Nevertheless, it may also suggest a knowledge gap between international political elites and a general public that is unaware of major policy changes in recent years.

3 David Crane, "National Household Survey Shows Society Becoming Too Polarized," *Hill Times* (16 September 2013).

4 Jeffrey Simpson, "Are Canadians More Conservative? No," *Globe and Mail* (4 February 2011).

5 Dan Gardner, "Harper's Supposed Evil Plan Isn't Panning Out," *Ottawa Citizen* (4 February 2011).

6 Murray Dobbin, "Inequality Now Canadians' Top Concern," *Hill Times* (7 May 2012).

7 See for example Tom Flanagan, *Persona Non Grata: The Death of Free Speech in the Internet Age* (Toronto: McClelland and Stewart, 2014) and Margaret Wente, "How Tom Flanagan Went from Respected Academic to Pariah," *Globe and Mail* (25 April 2014).

8 Tim Naumetz, "Senate Expense Scandal Eating into Conservative Support in Ontario: Forum Research Poll," *Hill Times* (29 October 2013). Polls by Nanos and EKOS in late 2013 showed similar developments.

9 Laura Ryckewaert, "Tory Majority in 2015 Unlikely as Downward Trend in Polls Continues: Experts," *Hill Times* (25 August 2014).

10 Michael Den Tandt, "Harper Needs a New Line," *Ottawa Citizen* (7 July 2014).

11 Stephen Maher, "Mulroney Sticks His Stiletto into Harper," *Ottawa Citizen* (6 September 2014).

Index